Symbol and Truth in Blake's Myth

Leopold Damrosch, Jr.

Symbol and Truth in Blake's Myth

PRINCETON UNIVERSITY PRESS

Princeton, New Jersey

FOR MY PARENTS

Leopold Damrosch
and
Elizabeth Hammond Damrosch

[CONTENTS]

[LIST OF ILLUSTRATIONS]

[ACKNOWLEDGMENTS]

My first debt of gratitude is to the John Simon Guggenheim Memorial Foundation, which supported a year's leave from teaching duties in 1975-1976 that made possible the preliminary research from which this book has developed. My second debt is to the many undergraduate and graduate students at the University of Virginia who have helped me, over the past decade, to wrestle with the problems in Blake's thought and art. Many of my interpretations, as they will recognize, arise from happy moments of mutual discovery. At each stage in the evolution of this book I have had, in addition, astute advice from colleagues, students, and other friends who gave generously of their time to help me improve a long and complicated manuscript. Various drafts were read by Marshall Brown, Paul Cantor, David Damrosch, Craig Davis, C. Stephen Finley, Stephen Greenblatt, E. D. Hirsch, William Kerrigan, James Nohrnberg, Anne West, and David Wyatt. I am deeply grateful to each of them, and also to the two anonymous readers who transmitted to me, through Princeton University Press, a valuable collection of suggestions. At the Press, Marjorie Sherwood presided over the process with her usual expertness, Donald K. Moore brought invaluable learning to the labor of copyediting, Bruce Campbell designed the book, and Tam Curry saw it through the press.

Some expenses connected with preparation of the manuscript and illustrations were assisted by the Committee on Research Grants of the University of Virginia.

A Note on References

I have tried to make my citations easily accessible to users of either of the two standard editions: *The Poetry and Prose of William Blake*, edited by David V. Erdman with commentary by Harold Bloom (New York, 1965, rev. 1970), and the Oxford Standard Authors *Complete Writings of William Blake*, edited by Geoffrey Keynes (London, 1966). In all cases I follow the Erdman text, occasionally altering punctuation to spare the reader confusion. In some instances (notably *The Four Zoas*) Erdman's plate and line numbers do not correspond to those in Keynes, but since page references are given for both editions, the passages in question may still be looked up in either. The letter "E" identifies page numbers in Erdman, "K" in Keynes.

Some of the most frequently cited works are abbreviated as follows:

DC	*A Descriptive Catalogue*
EG	*The Everlasting Gospel*
FZ	*The Four Zoas*
J	*Jerusalem*
M	*Milton*
MHH	*The Marriage of Heaven and Hell*
VLJ	*A Vision of the Last Judgment*

Several collections of essays are identified by the names of their editors:

Curran and Wittreich   *Blake's Sublime Allegory: Essays on The Four Zoas, Milton, Jerusalem*, ed. Stuart Curran and Joseph Anthony Wittreich, Jr. (Madison, 1973)

Erdman and Grant   *Blake's Visionary Forms Dramatic*, ed. David V. Erdman and John E. Grant (Princeton, 1970)

Essick   *The Visionary Hand: Essays for the Study of Blake's Art and Aesthetics*, ed. Robert N. Essick (Los Angeles, 1973)

Essick and Pearce   *Blake in His Time*, ed. Robert N. Essick and Donald Pearce (Bloomington, 1978)

Paley and Phillips   *William Blake: Essays in Honour of Sir Geoffrey Keynes*, ed. Morton D. Paley and Michael Phillips (Oxford, 1973)

Rosenfeld   *William Blake: Essays for S. Foster Damon*, ed. Alvin H. Rosenfeld (Providence, 1969)

Biographical material is cited whenever possible from Bentley's superb *Blake Records* even when it comes from Gilchrist or some other standard source, both for convenience and because Bentley corrects many errors and supplies valuable elucidation. This work is referred to by title only:

Blake Records   G. E. Bentley, Jr., *Blake Records* (Oxford, 1969)

Symbol and Truth in Blake's Myth

[INTRODUCTION]

Where shall we take our stand to view the infinite & unbounded?
Four Zoas IX, 122:24

This book attempts to elucidate some fundamental problems in Blake's myth and in the theory of imagination on which it is implicitly founded. Despite years of trying earnestly to see the myth as philosophically coherent, I have come to believe that it contains serious inconsistencies and owes its lines of development to Blake's unceasing effort to reconcile them. I am deeply indebted, as will be obvious, to the rich variety of insights available in Blake scholarship, but I shall argue against both prevailing views that assume coherence in Blake's myth: the orthodox claim that it never changed, and the revisionist claim that it changed but was coherent at each stage of its evolution. My argument will be that potent contradictions lie at the heart of Blake's system and that the never-ending struggle to reconcile them gives his work its peculiar energy and value. I hope thus to account for the revisions and shifts of meaning in a myth that underwent constant renovation, and to display Blake as engaged in lifelong "Mental Fight" (*M* 1, E95/K481), attempting to reconcile the irreconcilable, rather than as celebrating a continuous victory that takes new forms from time to time but is always perfected.

My subject will be Blake's ideas about God and man, the psychological theology with which he sought to solve the age-old dilemmas and to achieve the longed-for regeneration from division into unity. These are not ideas that lie behind, or comment upon, or are suggested by his poems; they are the poems. The poems fail to achieve coherence at just the points where the ideas refuse to be reconciled, above all in the tension between immanence and transcendence and in the dualism thereby implied. I shall pursue this theme in four interrelated areas:

(a) Epistemologically, the tension between (imaginative) sense perception, and intuitive or visionary experience that bypasses the senses and the phenomenal world or transforms them out of all recognition.

(b) Psychologically, the tension between the self as subjective, alienated, even solipsistic, and the self as integrated into a universal Humanity that gives it both status and meaning.

(c) Ontologically, the tension between the divine principle as immanent, available in and validating this world, and the divine principle

3

as transcendent, entering this world in order to abolish illusion and re-store a supramundane Edenic state.

(d) Aesthetically, the tension between art as imaginative salvation, and art as a fallen and reductive imposition of spurious form.

The requirements of exposition make it necessary to impose an arbi-trary sequence upon ideas which Blake entertained as a single whole. Like the hermeneutic circle, a discussion of any part of Blake's thought has to assume knowledge of the rest of it (and, incidentally, I have as-sumed a reader with some prior interest in Blake, and have not tried to explain every allusion). But one must begin somewhere, and after re-peated trials I have chosen what I hope will be an intelligible order of topics, alluding proleptically to those that follow and supplying fre-quent cross-references for the reader who wishes to pursue a particular point in some other part of the book.

In exploring the contradictions in Blake's thought, I do not wish to imply, as D. G. James once roundly asserted, that his mind was merely confused.[1] Blake was far less confused than most men. His difficulties arose from the heroic ambition with which he tackled unresolvable tensions at the heart of Western thought, exploring them more search-ingly than most philosophers, let alone most poets, have been willing to do. But we should not forget how great were the obstacles that he confronted. Blake scholarship has tended to organize dilemmas into diagrams and to celebrate "contraries" without examining them rigorously, but what A. C. Bradley said of Wordsworth is still more true of Blake: the way into his mind "must be through his strangeness and his paradoxes, and not round them."[2]

Although this book is not a work of criticism, neither is it commen-tary; it is offered as a study in philosophical interpretation. I believe, indeed, that such interpretation is logically prior to commentary, however the two may coincide in practice, and that much existing commentary on Blake is hampered by its tendency to take basic as-sumptions for granted while devoting anxious and scrupulous atten-tion to details. Northrop Frye has acutely said, "Whatever Blake's prophecies may be, they can hardly be code messages. They may need interpretation, but not deciphering: there can be no 'key' and no

---

[1] "I believe . . . that Blake's mind was extremely confused; and that the huge difficulty and obscurity of his work arises from an intellectual and imaginative disorder" (*The Romantic Comedy: An Essay on English Romanticism* [London, 1948], p. 1). James's attack on Blake is of interest, incidentally, as illustrating the dangers in reading all of Blake's works in the light of the early *Marriage of Heaven and Hell*. Every one of his objections could be answered by showing that Blake himself understood the issues and sought to develop a system that would take adequate account of them.

[2] *Oxford Lectures on Poetry* (London, 1909), p. 101.

4

open-sesame formula and no patented system of translation." Subsequent scholarship has not always heeded this warning, freezing many of Frye's own insights into a system of dogmatic cryptography, and continuing to wrap the poems, as was already the case three decades earlier, in "a Laocoön tangle of encyclopedias, concordances, indexes, charts and diagrams."[3]

The Blake industry, whose mills surpass those of God in grinding rapidly as well as exceeding small, ought to take seriously the skepticism with which its claims and counterclaims are regarded by most outsiders. To quote a sarcastic reviewer, "Blake exegesis . . . is like a wonderful crossword puzzle, set by a master of obfuscation, of which no spoilsport solution will be published next day."[4] The reason why such an aspersion (whether just or not) can be cast is that the contradictions in Blake's myth make it possible to quote passages on two or more sides of every important question. The attempt to reconcile the contradictions within a single dynamic system—often by recourse to the hypothesis that when Blake seems to contradict himself he must be speaking ironically—has led to just the proliferation of interpretations that the reviewer objects to. But I do not believe that Blake is therefore uninterpretable. What is needed is metacommentary that examines the conceptual bases of his system and seeks to explain the difficulties that underlie the specific points around which commentary ordinarily swirls.

Thus I hope to place the interpretation of Blake in perspective rather than to dispense with it. I shall explore some of its guiding assumptions while remaining grateful for its practical results. Any novelty in my approach resides in the attempt to place the issues of interpretation in a wide context, focusing not only on *what* Blake means but also on *how* and *why* he means what he does. The book began as a rather brief investigation of the anomalies in Blake's myth. I soon realized that fuller philosophical contexts were needed; the present large volume is the result. For any points at which these materials may seem excessive, I apologize, but I remain convinced that Blake is best understood by placing his thought in a wide perspective, and that the self-referential tendency of Blake studies has encouraged the evasion or misunderstanding of some fundamental problems. In the hope of establishing such a perspective, I quote extensively from a considerable range of writers—for example, Alleau, Cassirer, Eliade, Jonas, Koyré, Langer, Ricoeur, Scholem, Charles Taylor—who never mention Blake but who illuminate the issues that are raised in his poems.

[3] *Fearful Symmetry: A Study of William Blake* (Princeton, 1947), pp. 7, 9.
[4] Bevis Hillier, *TLS*, 17 Feb. 1978, p. 212.

Two of my special emphases probably call for explanation: the extensive use of what are commonly called "sources," and more generally the investigation of philosophical ideas in the work of a man who was a symbolic poet rather than an abstract thinker. As to the first point, I am concerned with contexts rather than sources. Eliot claimed long ago that Blake lacked "a framework of accepted and traditional ideas which would have prevented him from indulging in a philosophy of his own,"[5] and a host of scholars have labored to show that this criticism is the opposite of the truth. The students of Blake's relation to tradition have formed two groups: those like Raine and Harper, who perceive an internally consistent Everlasting Gospel or Neoplatonism or occult treasury of wisdom, and those from Damon onward, who see Blake as rising above his sources to form an original system of his own. I see the tradition rather differently, as a nest of problems rather than either a ready-made philosophy or a quarry for Blakean symbols. It is *conceptually* significant because Blake went to out-of-the-way writers in his attempt to bypass eighteenth-century philosophy, and he made a powerful attempt to rethink the issues they explored. Plotinus and Boehme are vitally important to Blake, but it is misleading to concentrate on those passages in which he seems to borrow from or agree with them; very often we learn more from the points at which he contradicts them. Since I am interested in contexts or analogues rather than sources, I deal at some length with figures like Augustine, Cusanus, and Hegel—hardly noticed in Blake scholarship because they did not "influence" him—who wrestled with the problems that troubled him and can shed light on his attempted solutions.

I believe, moreover, that Blake intends an important hermeneutic lesson in his use of esoteric "tradition," which is certainly not to be explained on the hypothesis that he belonged to an occultist underground or that his idiosyncratic reading prevented him from realizing that ordinary readers would be baffled by his symbols. He knew very well that they would be baffled. The well-known assertion that "what is not too Explicit [is] the fittest for Instruction because it rouzes the faculties to act" (E676/K793) presumes an experience that is unsettling and even bewildering, for Blake's emphasis is on the fundamental problem of interpretation, of meaning itself, rather than on a body of doctrine that his adepts can learn to interpret with complacent ease. "The hermeneutical problem," H.-G. Gadamer says, "only emerges clearly when there is no powerful tradition present to absorb one's own attitude into itself, and when one is aware of confronting an alien

---

[5] T. S. Eliot, "William Blake" (1920), *Selected Essays* (London, 1951), p. 322.

tradition to which he has never belonged or one he no longer unquestioningly accepts."[6] Blake means to challenge us. He is deeply suspicious of all orthodox traditions, and he knows that we in turn (whether orthodox in belief or not) are bound to be suspicious of his strange symbols. As I shall try to show in detail, one of his most brilliant achievements is his exposure of the problem of symbolism at its very roots.

The more general objection is harder to answer: that any philosophical account of Blake is misguided. Faced with the flood of exegesis, some of his most intelligent critics have taken the desperate step of claiming that symbolism is antithetical to ordinary "meaning" and that any discussion of Blake's ideas is therefore a philistine vulgarization.[7] In a similar vein one often hears appeals to have done with commentary, either because it is futile or because its task is now completed, and to get on with literary criticism. Yet apart from the lyrics, where it has long flourished, criticism obstinately refuses to appear. One reason is the peculiar nature of Blake's prophetic art, which is resistant to criticism as ordinarily practiced; another is the underlying set of conceptual problems, which no amount of criticism can dispel if the problems themselves are not faced. For this reason, incidentally, I reserve for the end the topic of Blake as artist and prophet, which is the ultimate problem in his work rather than its axiomatic starting point.

Now, it is certainly true that symbolic thinking differs in important ways from discursive reasoning, and that a symbol cannot be reduced to paraphrase (which is not to say that it cannot be discussed at all). But the only writers whose work resists conceptual interpretation are those who claim, however quixotically, to offer a purely mimetic representation of "reality." Blake, however, abhorred mimetic art and was deeply and voraciously involved in the world of thought. His letters, notes in books, and recorded conversations are filled with ideas. His favorite authors were (apart from the Bible) philosophical poets like Milton and poetic philosophers like Plato and Boehme. The rela-

---

[6] Hans-Georg Gadamer, "On the Problem of Self-Understanding," in *Philosophical Hermeneutics*, trans. David E. Linge (Berkeley, 1976), p. 46.

[7] Thus David Wagenknecht declares, "I have displayed a bias in favor of the language of feigning, the language of art, as against the language of Blake's supposed doctrines. In other words, confusion of fictions with theology has led, it seems to me, to persistent misrepresentations of Blake's poems" (*Blake's Night: William Blake and the Idea of Pastoral* [Cambridge, Mass., 1973], p. 77). Jerome J. McGann states still more bluntly, "His poetry issued a call to life not through visionary ideas, which are a contradiction in terms, but through visionary forms, poetic tales. In this sense his poetry must be said to have no meaning" ("The Aim of Blake's Prophecies and the Uses of Blake Criticism," Curran & Wittreich, p. 11). Such an ideal is unrealizable. McGann's own discussion of Enion's lament is a valuable analysis of meaning, even though he hastens to deny it.

tion between symbol and idea is tense and oblique in Blake's works, but the relation does exist. Symbols must be understood symbolically, but they cry out to be understood. In Paul Ricoeur's phrase, "The symbol gives rise to thought."[8]

The alternative to philosophical interpretation is not criticism but confusion, for it has been shown over and over again that no critical account of Blake is reliable unless it is founded on a broad knowledge of his ideas, which in turn presupposes an active attempt to get inside and interpret them. With Blake more than with most poets we are faced with an immense problem in hermeneutics, and it is not enough to assert as Frye does that the poems are their own meaning: "Blake forces the reader to concentrate on the meaning of his work, but not didactically in the ordinary sense, because his meaning is his theme, the total simultaneous shape of his poem."[9] This exciting declaration has two drawbacks, one practical and one theoretical. Practically, it permits the critic to select passages for discusson without having to show why they are the right ones to select; hence the exceptional extent of ill-humored controversy in Blake studies. Theoretically, it assumes that Blake's poems do in fact embody coherent meanings in their "simultaneous shape"; but this is precisely what nonspecialists in Blake wish to see demonstrated, not assumed a priori.

I therefore consider it justifiable to emphasize content rather than form, if that ancient distinction be allowed. The reason why formalist criticism has never had much luck with Blake's long poems, and only ambiguous success with the lyrics, is that his mode is prophetic. The New Critic subordinates content to form, claiming that the two are inseparable but concentrating on formal relations and denouncing the "heresy of paraphrase." Blake does just the opposite, believing that form and content are inseparable but that form is determined by visionary meaning: the meaning is primary, the form only a vehicle to carry it to the reader or beholder. Attempts to study the Bible "as literature" are always disappointing because finally it has to be studied as what it is—as a bible. So also with Blake's poems. Above all it is useless to claim that the poems function symbolically rather than doctrinally. The doctrines are symbols, the symbols doctrines.

For the most part I have avoided the problems surrounding the chronology of Blake's ideas, which are peculiarly thorny since he never repudiated any of his engraved works and constantly returned to old symbols even when reconceiving them. I differ both from those

---

[8] *The Symbolism of Evil*, trans. Emerson Buchanan (Boston, 1969), p. 348. Ricoeur has often invoked this principle: "Le symbole donne à penser."

[9] "The Road of Excess," in *The Stubborn Structure: Essays on Criticism and Society* (Ithaca, 1970), p. 172. Frye's own interpretations of Blake are, in the best sense, didactic.

who hold that Blake's myth never changed and from those who hold that it changed in distinct stages, although of course I recognize that certain ideas alter at particular times. I agree with the latter group that there is much rethinking and revision in Blake's work, but with the former that Blake saw his myth as a continuous whole and did everything he could to reintegrate old materials in each new formulation. According to his conception of prophetic truth this was in fact inevitable, since he must have believed not that the earlier symbols were mistaken, but that he had not at first properly understood them.

> Reengravd Time after Time
> Ever in their youthful prime
> My Designs unchangd remain
> Time may rage but rage in vain
> (E472/K558)

Published in conjunction with the *Songs of Experience*, the *Songs of Innocence* are subject to a revised interpretation but are not cancelled. Published later on, in 1800 or 1810, the combined *Songs of Innocence and of Experience* are likewise gathered into a more advanced and differently articulated myth. The labor of understanding the stages in Blake's development is well worthwhile, but I do not consider it essential for my own project, which addresses the perennial dilemmas in Blake's myth in all of its shifting forms. In addition I say very little about the historical contexts of the poems, which have been admirably discussed by Erdman and others. The poems are filled with historical allusions, but after the disillusionment of the French Revolution period Blake seems to have been more concerned to assimilate the idea of history into his symbolic categories than to respond directly to the fluctuations of historical experience.

As a prophet Blake claims to announce the truth, and I have entitled this study *Symbol and Truth* because I think it important to consider how his poems might be perceived as true by modern readers. Granted, his myth is myth and not dogma. But are we able to receive it with the same easy suspension of disbelief that we bring to more conventional literary modes, or must we accept its insistent challenge to take a stand morally, intellectually, and imaginatively? In either case it is hard to know how to use the strange symbols of this remarkable myth. This aspect of my study is necessarily tentative and is largely postponed until the end. But I would not wish to evade it. Blake's prodigious genius is evident in the daring with which he attacks the most fundamental problems, and we read him only half-heartedly if we do not respond as human beings to his prophetic demands. The contradictions I examine are ones of which Blake was very well aware, and he devoted his life as thinker and artist to the attempt to resolve them. I hope to have thrown some light on the shape and emphases of his myth, but I know that in many places I must have failed to see what he really meant. In such instances I can only offer the apology, as Coleridge did after struggling with difficulties in Plato, that I am "ignorant of his understanding."[10]

[10] Samuel Taylor Coleridge, *Biographia Literaria*, ed. J. Shawcross (London, 1907), I, 161.

[ONE]

Vision and Perception

They haven't got no noses,
The fallen sons of Eve;
Even the smell of roses
Is not what they supposes,
But more than mind discloses
And more than men believe.
  G. K. Chesterton, "The Song of Quoodle"

Conceptions are artificial. Perceptions are essential.
  Wallace Stevens, *Adagia*

UNIVERSALS

Any attempt to understand what Blake's poems mean must begin by considering how they mean, for he and his modern interpreters assert that his meanings are fundamentally symbolic and are to be understood in a special way. In the twentieth century symbolism has been intensively studied in a wide range of disciplines, including anthropology, depth psychology, linguistics, and philosophy, not to mention literary criticism (usually drawing on one or more of the above). Blake, by contrast, had no such developed body of theory to work with, although he was of course familiar with the speculations of mythographers and iconographers. In his practice he was chiefly influenced by traditional ways of interpreting the Bible and by allegorical writers like Spenser and Bunyan. But his ideas about symbolism derive not so much from literature as from his theory of the mind.

Every currently respectable theory of symbolism takes for granted that symbols are mental constructs which create, rather than mirror, the reality they claim to represent. Some investigators believe that it is possible to get behind the symbols and detect what they "really" mean (for instance, the psychoanalyst interpreting the unconscious meanings of a dream, or the functional anthropologist identifying social relationships and institutions). Other theorists, particularly in aesthetics, regard all such ambitions as delusory and maintain that reality, such as it is, can lie no deeper than the symbols themselves. "What, therefore, is truth?" demands Nietzsche, ironically echoing Pilate. "A mobile army of metaphors, metonymies, anthropomorphisms: in short a sum of human relations which became poetically and rhetorically intensified, metamorphosed, adorned, and after long usage seem to a nation fixed, canonic and binding; truths are illusions of which one has forgotten that they *are* illusions; worn-out metaphors which have become powerless to affect the senses; coins which have their obverse (*Bild*) effaced and are now no longer of account as coins but merely as metal."[1]

Blake's implicit theory of symbolism is complex because he recognizes the force of this claim and attempts to counter it. Symbols are seriously compromised by their status in a fallen world and in a sense are illusory, but at the same time they participate in a reality whose existence cannot be doubted except by corrupted minds. Blake wants to remythologize, not demythologize, in order to recover a truth that is not just a bag of debased coins. And his theory is founded on a conception of language as shaped and re-created by the prophetic imagination, not as used by the ordinary community. Since for Blake reality is mental in a religious sense, not merely in a psychological and sociological sense, he could well endorse another of Nietzsche's pronouncements while placing his own affirmative construction upon it: "It is *we* alone who have devised cause, sequence, reciprocity, relativity, constraint, number, law, freedom, motive, and purpose; and when we interpret and intermix this symbol-world, as 'being in itself,' with things, we act once more as we have always acted—*mythologically*."[2] Blake would certainly recognize the force of this critique but would assert—in his theory of Jesus as the divine body of imagination—a principle that can preserve us from a merely arbitrary subjectivity.

Thus we are confronted with a typical Blakean antinomy: symbols are vitiated by the fallen world from which they are drawn, but are nevertheless our window to the real. Two related antinomies make up the full complex of problems that will occupy us throughout this chapter: the conflict between individual perception and universal truth, and the analogous conflict between a world of particulars and an ultimate reality composed of universal forms. Since the forms are crucial to Blake's theory and are presupposed in his discussion of its other aspects, let us begin with those.

"Vision or Imagination," Blake declares in an extended commen-

---

[1] "On Truth and Falsity in their Ultramoral Sense," trans. M. A. Mügge, in *Complete Works*, ed. Oscar Levy (New York, 1924), II, 180. I owe this quotation to Jacques Derrida's essay "White Mythology: Metaphor in the Text of Philosophy," *New Literary History*, 6 (1974), 15. Derrida's meditations on the sun are relevant to Blake on the same theme: "It is the paradigm of what is sensible *and* of what is metaphorical" (p. 52).

[2] *Beyond Good and Evil*, trans. Helen Zimmern, in *The Philosophy of Nietzsche* (New York, 1954), p. 404 (sec. 22).

tary on his most ambitious (and now lost) painting, "is a Representation of what Eternally Exists, Really & Unchangeably." And again, "The Nature of Visionary Fancy or Imagination is very little Known & the Eternal nature & permanence of its ever Existent Images is considered as less permanent than the things of Vegetative & Generative Nature yet the Oak dies as well as the Lettuce but Its Eternal Image & Individuality never dies, but renews by its seed. Just so the Imaginative Image returns by the seed of Contemplative Thought" (*VLJ*, E544-45/K604-605). Two points are particularly important: the forms are unchanging and eternal, and they are perceived in this world as imaginative "images." That is to say, their reality transcends the realm of "Vegetative & Generative Nature," where we ordinarily suppose that the objects of our perceptions are located. Vegetative oaks sprout, grow old, and die, but their "Eternal Image & Individuality never dies." Individuality is paradoxically generic.

Furthermore, Blake is at pains to deny, at many places in his writings, that these universal "images" are merely deduced or abstracted from particular sense impressions. In order to avoid such a conclusion—the usual one of eighteenth-century empiricism—he affirms his belief in the existence of a realm, very like that of Plato's Ideas, of which the world of empirical perception is but a shadow. "There Exist in that Eternal World the Permanent Realities of Every Thing which we see reflected in this Vegetable Glass of Nature" (E545/K605). In the terms of Blake's theology, the visible forms that die are the illusory products of "creation" by a fallen demiurge, whereas the eternal forms are literally eternal:

> Whatever can be Created can be Annihilated. Forms cannot.
> The Oak is cut down by the Ax, the Lamb falls by the Knife
> But their Forms Eternal Exist, For-ever. Amen Hallelujah.
> <div align="right">(<i>M</i> 32:36-38, E131/K522)</div>

These passages are familiar to all Blake scholars, yet their plain meaning is often evaded, because Blake is famous as the poet of minute particulars and because he sometimes seems to assert that each person shapes his own reality through individual vision. I want therefore to emphasize as strongly as possible that they are the foundation upon which our investigation must be built. Whatever Blake may say about individual vision, it must finally be reconciled with the integrity of the eternal forms; and this is so because to allow a merely subjective construction of reality would be, for Blake, to compromise fatally with empiricism and be left with no reality at all.

It must be stressed that Blake claimed to describe not a hypothesis but a direct intuition of truth. The theory seeks to make intelligible to others what is already known, rather than to advance by deductive steps into the unknown. The central source of insight, "Vision or Imagination," is the very life of man. Other aspects of experience are temporary "states," but "The Imagination is not a State: it is the Human Existence itself" (*M* 32:32, E131/K522). This conception retains its connection with *seeing*, although in a spiritualized mode of perception very different from the passive sense impressions of empiricist psychology. As numerous witnesses confirmed, Blake had vivid personal experience of visions which could be called up at will.[3] These were not ordinary hallucinations, since Blake knew that they inhabited a different realm from ordinary sense perception. As a patient once told Karl Jaspers, distinguishing ordinary imaginings from visions like Blake's, "I feel the figures of my imagination are not in space at all, but remain faint pictures in my brain or behind my eyes, while with these phenomena I experienced *a world*, but one which had nothing to do with the world of the senses."[4] Blake would say that that "world" was Eternity, and he held that most people could learn to see it if they would only try; he taught the technique to his wife.[5]

The function of visionary imagination is thus to get beyond the images of the ordinary world to the true forms in which they participate. "He who does not imagine in stronger and better lineaments, and in stronger and better light than his perishing mortal eye can see, does not imagine at all" (*DC*, E532/K576). Yet we see images made up of

---

[3] On "hypnogogic states" and "eidetic imagery" see, respectively, Mona Wilson, *The Life of William Blake* (London, 1971), pp. 73-80, and Morton D. Paley, *Energy and the Imagination: A Study of the Development of Blake's Thought* (Oxford, 1970), pp. 201-206. Recent writers have emphasized the basis of Blake's visions in the visual arts. Joseph Burke points out that a number of the visions resembled works with which Blake was familiar ("The Eidetic and the Borrowed Image," in Essick, pp. 253-302), and Bo Lindberg suggests that the metaphor in *The Marriage of Heaven and Hell* of "melting apparent surfaces away, and displaying the infinite which was hid" (E38/K154) is analogous to Michelangelo's well-known ability to "see" a statue in the block of marble (*William Blake's Illustrations to the Book of Job* [Abo, Finland, 1973], p. 156*n*).

[4] *General Psychopathology* (1923), quoted by Mary Warnock, *Imagination* (Berkeley, 1976), p. 168. This distinction has long been familiar in Roman Catholic devotional theology. Saint Teresa stated clearly that she had imaginative visions but never corporeal ones—i.e., not hallucinations (see Karl Rahner, *Visions and Prophecies*, trans. Charles Henkey and Richard Strachan [London, 1963], pp. 32-33). While agnostic philosophers are carefully open-minded on the truth value (or "veridicality") of mystical visions, religious writers like Rahner tend to display a hard-headed skepticism.

[5] "She, too, learned to have visions;—to see processions of figures wending along the river, in broad daylight; and would give a start when they disappeared in the water. As Blake truly maintained, the faculty for seeing such airy phantoms can be cultivated" (Gilchrist, in *Blake Records*, p. 237).

particulars, and we know that individual human beings do not all see alike. What epistemology can account for our vision of the forms?

PERCEPTION AND PARTICULARS

"Mental Things," Blake declared, "are alone Real. What is Calld Corporeal Nobody Knows of its dwelling Place it is in Fallacy & its Existence an Imposture. Where is the Existence Out of Mind or Thought" (*VLJ*, E555/K617). Berkeley had similarly argued, "As to what is said of the absolute existence of unthinking things without any relation to their being perceived, that seems perfectly unintelligible. Their *esse* is *percipi*, nor is it possible they should have any existence out of the minds or thinking things which perceive them."[6] Mental things are alone real because real things are mental. All forms of idealism tend to hold, as Whitehead says, that "apart from the experiences of subjects there is nothing, nothing, bare nothingness."[7] According to idealists in the Kantian tradition, reality is perceived through mental categories, so that in Susanne Langer's words "Images have all the characteristics of symbols," but what the symbols represent is indeed reality: "To see in certain forms is not to create their contents."[8] Perception is thus intelligible only as a mental or spiritual act. The Bible and great poems, Blake wrote to a baffled would-be patron, "are addressed to the Imagination which is Spiritual Sensation."[9] Imagination is actively creative, which suggests the motto *esse est percipere* rather than the passive *esse est percipi*.[10]

What remains to be explained in such a theory is the relation between imaginative and physical perception, and here Blake parts company with Berkeley in a significant way. "I question not my Corporeal or Vegetative Eye any more than I would Question a Window concerning a Sight. I look thro it & not with it" (*VLJ*, E555/K617). Now, according to Berkeley there is in effect a dual or sequential activity in perception, first the reception of sense data and then the mental process that gives them meaning. "Natural phenomena are only natural appearances. They are, therefore, such as we see and perceive

---

[6] *Principles of Human Knowledge*, par. 3.

[7] Alfred North Whitehead, *Process and Reality: An Essay in Cosmology* (New York, 1930), p. 254.

[8] *Philosophy in a New Key: A Study in the Symbolism of Reason, Rite, and Art* (Cambridge, Mass., 1942, repr. 1976), pp. 144, 263n.

[9] Letter to Dr. Trusler, 23 Aug. 1799 (E677/K794). Blake was replying indignantly to Trusler's complaint that his pictures were not lifelike enough. See David Bindman, *Blake as an Artist* (Oxford, 1977), pp. 115-116, and one of the offending pictures reproduced as pl. 96.

[10] As Frye remarks (*Fearful Symmetry*, p. 18).

them." But perceiving is not knowing: "We know a thing when we understand it; and we understand it when we can interpret or tell what it signifies. Strictly, the sense knows nothing."[11]

It is a mistake, Berkeley warns elsewhere, to suppose that our minds lurk inside our heads and inspect a series of disembodied images. "When we think of the pictures in the fund of the eye, we imagine ourselves looking on the fund of another's eye, or another looking on the fund of our own eye, and beholding the pictures painted thereon. . . . Further, there lies a mistake in our imagining that the pictures of external objects are painted on the bottom of the eye."[12] But in spite of this important insight Berkeley tended to endorse a faculty psychology that described reason as acting upon the data of perception: "Reason considers and judges of the imaginations."[13] Reading these words, Blake objected in the margin, "Knowledge is not by deduction but Immediate by Perception or Sense at once. Christ addresses himself to the Man not to his Reason" (E653/K774). And a few pages later, "Forms must be apprehended by Sense or the Eye of Imagination. Man is All Imagination" (E654/K775).

For the sake of theoretical consistency, Blake probably needs a distinction between sense perception as the empiricists understood it and intuitive perception that joins a mental process to it, but without treating that process as separate or posterior as Berkeley does. Kant, for instance, distinguishes between *Wahrnehmung*, sense perception, and *Anschauung*, the "looking at" that is commonly translated as "intuition." "Perception" and "vision" might serve to express this distinction in Blake, the point being that perception is necessary and cannot be bypassed, but is blind and fallible unless informed by vision. It is in this sense that we look through the eye and not with it. "Isaiah answer'd, I saw no God, nor heard any, in a finite organical perception; but my senses discover'd the infinite in every thing" (*MHH*, E38/K153).

Since this theory of perception is more hostile to empiricism than Berkeley's was, we should not be surprised to find a closer analogue in Plato than in Berkeley: "It appears to me, Socrates, that it is more proper to consider the eyes and ears as things through which, rather than as things by which, we perceive."[14] Nevertheless, Blake was unwilling to break altogether with the empiricist account of perception, and for a very important reason. It seemed to him that Platonizing

---

[11] *Siris*, pars. 292, 253.

[12] *A New Theory of Vision*, pars. 116, 117.

[13] *Siris*, par. 140.

[14] *Theaetetus* 184c, quoted by Kathleen Raine, *Blake and Tradition* (Princeton, 1968), II, 120 (from the 1804 translation of Thomas Taylor).

aesthetics—for instance in the *Discourses* of Reynolds, which he covered with execrations—degraded reality into a murky realm of abstractions instead of locating it in the vivid perception of particulars. "To Generalize is to be an Idiot. To Particularize is the Alone Distinction of Merit" (E630/K451). What Blake wanted—like Coleridge and the other Romantics who sought to establish idealism without abandoning the real contributions of empiricism—was a theory of the universal in the particular, Coleridge's "multeity in unity." It is easy enough to assert that Blake achieved this, merely by quoting the many passages in which he said he did. But it is more interesting, and gets us further into the fundamental difficulties of his thought, to consider the conceptual obstacles that lie in the way.

Briefly stated, the problem depends upon the status of perception that goes beyond or is different from the ordinary data of the senses, and yet apprehends particulars rather than abstract universals. The problem is not solved, though in an early work Blake may have thought it was, by asserting the existence of a higher mode of perceiving than the familiar five senses. "The desires & perceptions of man untaught by any thing but organs of sense, must be limited to objects of sense"; but we perceive and desire higher objects; ergo, these are the business of "the Poetic or Prophetic character."[15]

Blake is sometimes described as being peculiarly shrewd here. In fact the distinction is a very ancient one, lucidly expressed for instance in Boethius' attack on the Stoics: "Long ago the philosophers of the Porch at Athens, old men who saw things dimly, believed that sense impressions and images were impressed on the mind by external objects, just as then they used to mark letters on a blank page of wax with their quick pens. But, if the active mind can discover nothing by its own powers, and merely remains passively subject to the impressions of external bodies, like a mirror reflecting the empty shapes of other things, where does that power come from which dwells in souls and sees all things?"[16] A Platonist like Boethius could have no difficulty in answering this question, since he knew that the mind was active and was furnished with innate ideas independent of the illusions of sense. Such a position was deeply attractive to Blake, but in his struggle against dualism—a problem to which we shall return repeatedly in this book—he wanted to deny the divorce implied here between soul and body, and in fact to resist the siren call of idealism.[17]

---

[15] *There is No Natural Religion* [a], E1/K97.

[16] *The Consolation of Philosophy*, trans. Richard Green (New York, 1962), Book V, Poem iv, p. 112.

[17] "Far from adopting speculative idealism, he endeavoured to bring back a concrete and embodied individuality into the vacuum created by idealistic concepts of 'self-

And he had another motive as well. As he saw clearly, idealism leads all too easily to abstraction, so that whatever the higher mode of perception may be ("the Poetic or Prophetic character") it must in Blake's view *remain* perception, must transform but not abolish the phenomena of experience.

The danger, then, is perceived as a tempting compromise with empiricism. Once again Berkeley is a suggestive guide: "That philosopher [Aristotle] held that the mind of man was a *tabula rasa*, and that there were no innate ideas. Plato, on the contrary, held original ideas in the mind, that is, notions which never were or can be in the sense, such as being, beauty, goodness, likeness, parity. Some, perhaps, may think the truth to be this—that there are properly no ideas, or passive objects, in the mind but what were derived from sense: but that there are also besides these her own acts or operations: such are notions."[18] Even if Blake thought Berkeley too much an empiricist, he himself was unwilling to be a thoroughgoing Platonist. "It is an universally received maxim," says Berkeley's Philonous, "that every thing which exists is particular."[19] So also Blake declares in his annotations to Reynolds, "All Knowledge is Particular" (E637/K459). Now, it is crucial from Berkeley's point of view that *everything* be identified as "ideas" in the mind, things themselves as well as the notions we hold about them. For if we once admit that there is a reality outside our minds, even though we may still claim that our ideas correspond to Platonic forms, the battle is lost: "If they are looked on as notes or images, referred to *things* or *archetypes* existing without the mind, then are we involved all in *scepticism*."[20] In precisely this way, Blake does not want to call the universal form of the oak a Platonic archetype. It exists only in real oaks. And yet real oaks are "vegetative" and transitory, while the form is universal and permanent. "General Forms have their vitality in Particulars" (*J* 91:29, E249/K738).

According to Berkeley, the fact that we perceive particulars means that we perceive *only* particulars. "The idea of man that I frame to myself, must be either of a white, or a black, or a tawny, a straight, or a crooked, a tall, or a low, or a middle-sized man. I cannot by any effort of thought conceive the abstract idea above described."[21] When we

---

consciousness' and 'spirit,' and to eliminate the religious error that 'spirit' was life and 'body' of no account" (Peter F. Fisher, *The Valley of Vision: Blake as Prophet and Revolutionary* [Toronto, 1961], p. 239).

[18] *Siris*, par. 308.

[19] *Three Dialogues between Hylas and Philonous*, First Dialogue, in *The Works of George Berkeley*, ed. A. A. Luce and T. E. Jessop (London, 1949), II, 192.

[20] *Principles of Human Knowledge*, par. 87.

[21] *Principles of Human Knowledge*, introduction, par. 10.

use general terms, according to the empiricists, we are using verbal counters or signs rather than referring to anything real. But Blake does not want to concede this. He agrees with Berkeley that whatever we perceive must be distinct and individual. But he maintains that each individual is not merely an example of a general type but an embodiment of it. The universal, that is, rather than being an artificial counter, is fully real in every one of its individual manifestations.

To explain this conception Blake must find a principle at once within and outside the mind, an organizing entity that subsumes all particulars in a living whole. In order to establish this he has to do more than assert that sense perception cannot furnish ideas and that reality is a mental construction, for such a claim—common enough in modern symbolic theory—cannot sufficiently guarantee the *validity* of universals and of spiritual intuition. Kant, for example, with whom Blake is sometimes compared, identified a set of categories by which the mind organizes experience; but he was careful to distinguish knowledge of this kind from the absolute belief in truth that Blake insists upon. Demanding absolute rather than qualified certitude, Blake must base his epistemology on a theology.

JESUS THE UNIVERSAL FORM

Whenever Blake comes directly to grips with the problem of particulars and universals, he asserts that the two are reconciled in and through Jesus. "General Forms have their vitality in Particulars: & every / Particular is a Man; a Divine Member of the Divine Jesus" (*J* 91:29-30, E249/K738). Plato was wrong both in considering the forms to be general and in assuming that they were multiple; on the contrary, all particulars are subsumed in a single, living, and loving Universal. As the imaginative Zoa Los says accusingly to his Spectre,

> Swelld & bloated General Forms, repugnant to the Divine-
> Humanity, who is the Only General and Universal Form
> To which all Lineaments tend & seek with love & sympathy
> All broad & general principles belong to benevolence
> Who protects minute particulars, every one in their own identity.
> (*J* 38:19-23, E183/K672)

We are presented here, clearly enough, with an act of faith, but it is a philosophically elaborated faith that deserves close examination. If we can understand the relation between universal and particular in Jesus, we will have advanced a long way toward understanding why Blake's system, for all its humanism, cannot get along without the divine.

As is well known, Berkeley grounded the mental existence of reality

19

in the omniscient mind of God. The tree remains in the quad when we
stop thinking about it because God always thinks about it. "Sensible
things cannot exist otherwise than in a mind or spirit. Whence I conclude, not that they have no real existence, but that seeing they depend
not upon my thought, and have an existence distinct from being perceived by me, *there must be some other mind wherein they exist.* As sure
therefore as the sensible world really exists, so sure is there an infinite
omnipresent Spirit who contains and supports it."[22] Berkeley goes on
to say that his main concern is not to prove the nature of perception
from God's existence, but exactly the reverse: we know that reality
exists, we know that our own minds do not sustain it, and we therefore know that God exists. But from Blake's point of view, this argument (with its irrelevant ambition, as Blake would regard it, of proving what we can only know by direct intuition) opens a dangerous
gulf between God and man.[23]

It is not enough, therefore, to say that God thinks the universe or
that he fills it, as even Bacon could hold, with his symbols.[24] It is
necessary for Blake that the symbols be directly apprehended as true
and that the universals which they express be fully inherent in them.
That is why Jesus is invoked as "the Only General and Universal
Form." This theology of perception has appeared repeatedly in Neoplatonic systems whenever the same problem has been confronted. A
particularly interesting version, which deserves extended notice because it treats Blake's problem with exceptional clarity, is that of the
fifteenth-century bishop Nicholas Cusanus ("of Cusa"), sometimes
described as the father of German idealism, who studied the same
Neoplatonic classics that Blake did and evolved a very Blakean theory
of knowledge.[25]

[22] *Three Dialogues,* Second Dialogue, p. 212.
[23] Berkeley's *Principles* conceals its basis in faith, its role as theodicy. Only at the end
does it put forward a defense of the Christian system, and then with the claim that a
purely rational argument has produced it. But in fact, as Blake clearly sees, the whole
argument is premised on faith in a God who not only "thinks" everything that exists
but also does so in a wise and benevolent manner. Having absorbed the lesson of post-
Berkeleyan skepticism, Blake insists on the primacy of intuition.
[24] "Let men learn . . . the difference that exists between the idols of the human mind
and the ideas of the divine mind. The former are mere arbitrary abstractions; the latter
the true marks of the Creator on his creatures, as they are imprinted on, and defined in
matter, by true and exquisite touches" (*Novum Organum,* ed. Joseph Devey [New York,
1902], I, cxxiv, p. 100).
[25] Blake never mentions Cusanus and was probably unaware of him. It has been
shown that Cusanus (like Blake) was strongly influenced by Proclus, notably in deriv-
ing the principle of the coincidence of opposites from Proclus' commentary on the *Parmenides* (see R. Klibansky, "Plato's *Parmenides* in the Middle Ages and Renaissance,"
Medieval and Renaissance Studies, 1 [1943], 281-333). Cusanus' rejection of universals in

Like Blake, Cusanus stresses the *coincidentia oppositorum* and the supra-rational vision or *Nous* that apprehends their harmonious union in the Infinite. Now, the reconciliation of opposites was commonplace in the eighteenth century; as E. R. Wasserman has shown, *concordia discors* is the fundamental principle of Denham's *Cooper's Hill* and Pope's *Windsor Forest*.[26] But these poets postulated a God above and beyond the sublunary realm who harmonized opposites by manipulating them in a larger whole, the lights and shadows of a grand design. Cusanus, like Blake in his "marriage" of heaven and hell, sought a vital *union* of opposites in the ultimate order of things, not a reconciliation controlled, as it were, from above. For Cusanus the ultimate order is God, "because He is Himself the Absolute Ground, in which all otherness [*alteritas*] is unity, and all diversity is identity."[27] By the time of the prophetic books, Blake too invested Jesus, in however heterodox a manner, with the same status of ultimate ground of diversity-in-identity.

Cusanus' account of individual perception is of the greatest relevance to Blakean symbolism. For as he explains in his most famous work, *Of Learned Ignorance*, the correspondence of microcosm and macrocosm is much more than metaphorical. "In each individual the universe is by contraction [cf. Blake's "limit of contraction"] what the particular individual is; and every individual in the universe is the universe, though the universe is in each individual in a different way and each thing is in the universe in a different way."[28] With this literal and complete interpenetration of microcosm and macrocosm, Cusanus seeks to reconcile Plato and Aristotle and to show that although universals exist only in particulars, the particulars in turn exist in an ultimate order that subsumes them and gives them life. "The Peripatetics were right in saying that outside of things, universals have no actual existence. Only the singular has actual existence, and in the singular the universal by contraction is the singular." But the intellect can reverse that "contraction," exactly as in Blake the imagination "expands" to apprehend infinity (II.vi, pp. 87–88).

In the world as we perceive it, Cusanus holds like Blake that indi-

---

the scholastic sense is directly indebted to nominalism, just as Blake's insistence on particulars derives from that aspect of empiricism (as in Berkeley) which he was unwilling to reject.

[26] *The Subtler Language: Critical Readings of Neoclassic and Romantic Poems* (Baltimore, 1959), chs. 3 and 4.

[27] *The Vision of God* [*De Visione Dei*], trans. Emma Gurney-Salter (London, 1928), ch. III, p. 13.

[28] *Of Learned Ignorance* [*De Docta Ignorantia*], trans. Germain Heron (New Haven, 1954), II.v, p. 84.

viduality is fundamental. "No two men are identical in anything; their sense perceptions differ, their imaginations differ, their intellects differ; and their activities, whether they take the form of writing, painting, or any other form of art, are all different" (II.i, p. 69). Nevertheless, this individuality is subsumed in just that universal "humanity" that Blake, in his later works, identifies with Jesus. "The relationship of the universe to all things is that of humanity to men: humanity is neither Socrates nor Plato, but in Socrates it is Socrates and in Plato it is Plato" (II.iv, p. 82). Moreover, if all forms are united in God, then it is wrong to suppose as Plato did that our situation in the sensory realm cuts us off from truth. "The Platonists' theory about the images of forms has to be completely discounted, for there is but one infinite form of forms, and of it all forms are images" (II.ix, p. 102).

Of Learned Ignorance thus endorses both halves of its oxymoronic title. We are learned because we see God in the diversity of things; we are ignorant because symbolism, being the very basis of thought itself, is qualitatively different from dogmatic reason. As Ernst Cassirer expounds Cusanus' meaning, "The symbol cannot be adequate for knowledge, for dogmatic 'precision'; it is confined within the limits of 'otherness' and 'conjecture.' But, in so far as absolute being and absolute unity are knowable at all, it is in just this way that they can be truly known."[29] To avoid relativism and skepticism, Cusanus relies on a mystical apprehension of the incarnate God-Man in whom our "humanity" is merged, described theoretically in *Of Learned Ignorance* and recommended as a spiritual ideal in *The Vision of God*. Exactly as in the later Blake, God (or Jesus) is the necessary meeting place of epistemology and ontology, the sole guarantor of our faith that the multiplicity of perception is subsumed in unity. "Each face, then, that can look upon Thy face beholdeth naught other or differing from itself, because it beholdeth its own true type."[30] With similar logic Blake declares,

> The Vision of Christ that thou dost see
> Is my Visions Greatest Enemy
> Thine has a great hook nose like thine
> Mine has a snub nose like to mine
> (*EG*, E516/K748)

And Cusanus goes on to say, "If a lion were to attribute a face unto Thee, he would think of it as a lion's; an ox, as an ox's, and an eagle, as an eagle's" (p. 25). This notion, which as early as the pre-Socratics had

---

[29] *The Platonic Renaissance in England*, trans. James P. Pettegrove (Austin, 1953), p. 14.
[30] *Vision of God*, vi, p. 24.

pointed toward relativism, is for Cusanus a simple recognition of the way in which the absolute expresses itself in individual perception. Nor can it be accidental that his examples allude to the traditional symbols for the Evangelists, themselves taken from Ezekiel's vision that gives Blake his Zoas.

Where Cusanus finally takes a different path from Blake is in his insistence on mystical passivity and on the negative theology (God defined by what he is not) implicit in the doctrine of learned ignorance. "In all faces is seen the Face of faces, veiled, and in a riddle [*in aenigmate*, 1 Cor. 13:12]; howbeit unveiled it is not seen, until above all faces a man enter into a certain secret and mystic silence where there is no knowledge or concept of a face" (p. 26). Blake will never surrender in this way the primacy of the image, and always maintains that fourfold vision, purged of "Single vision & Newtons sleep,"[31] can attain a direct apprehension of truth. Nonetheless, Cusanus' theory of symbolism remains strikingly relevant to Blake's attempt to realize the universal in the particular. In Cassirer's commentary, "The ideal toward which our knowledge must strive does not lie in denying and rejecting particularity, but in allowing it to unfold in all its richness. For only the *totality* of faces gives us the One view of the Divine. The world becomes the symbol of God, not in that we pick out one part of it and provide it with some singular mark of value, but rather in that we pass through it in all of its forms, freely submitting ourselves to its multiplicity, to its antitheses."[32]

For both Cusanus and Blake the eternal forms exist only in variety, but we cannot know that they are eternal, indeed we cannot perceive them as forms, unless we elevate and invigorate the power that Cusanus calls *Nous* and Blake vision. When we truly understand that God (or the infinite) is in every particular, then and only then can we grasp the full significance of its particularity. Meditating on a nut tree, Cusanus invokes the *logoi spermatikoi* of Neoplatonism and extols "the marvellous might of that seed, wherein the entire tree, and all its nuts, and all the generative power of the nuts, and all trees, existed in the generative power of the nuts."[33] Blake speaks very similarly of the "Eternal Image & Individuality" which the oak renews by its seed

[31] Letter to Butts, 22 Nov. 1802 (E693/K818).

[32] *The Individual and the Cosmos in Renaissance Philosophy*, trans. Mario Domandi (Oxford, 1963), p. 37.

[33] *Vision of God*, vii, p. 28. On the seminal reasons (*logoi spermatikoi*) see James Nohrnberg, *The Analogy of the Faerie Queene* (Princeton, 1976), pp. 537ff., esp. the passages from Augustine that closely parallel Cusanus. Blake's remarks in *VLJ* on the relation between the "seed" and "Contemplative Thought" (see above, p. 13) are directly related to Plotinus' discussion of seminal reasons and of Generation as a form of Contemplation (see Nohrnberg, p. 658).

(*VLJ*, E545/K605). Blake's theory may be paradoxical, but it is not peculiarly so. From the same Scotist tradition that influenced Cusanus, Gerard Manley Hopkins developed a theology of the unity of all things in Jesus that has much in common with Blake's.[34]

What has to be emphasized above all is the *immediate* and *personal* nature of an individual's perception in the universal Jesus. Many Neoplatonists and other idealists were loth to admit any direct identification of mortal man with the remote and perfect Godhead. As Berkeley put it, "Sense is a passion; and passions imply imperfection. God knoweth all things as pure mind or intellect; but nothing by sense, nor in nor through a sensory."[35] To admit that we know through the senses, as Blake certainly does, would on this view entail admitting that our knowledge is different from God's, even if sustained by God's. Annotating this passage in Berkeley, Blake meets the issue head-on: "Imagination or the Human Eternal Body in Every Man" (E652/K773). A little later Berkeley distinguishes body from spirit and declares that God cannot have a body; Blake retorts, "Imagination or the Divine Body in Every Man." How and why is Blake's Jesus a body as well as a mind?

At another place in *Siris*, Berkeley argues that the apparent pantheism of the Egyptians is not contrary to Christian faith since they "considered God and nature as making one whole, or all things together as making one universe. In doing which they did not exclude the intelligent mind, but considered it as containing all things" (par. 300). Blake goes further: he is interested in Jesus as Imagination, not in God as mind (though he sometimes uses the term "intellect" to include imagination). In other words, reality is not only the totality of the ideas in God's mind, but those ideas are images in exactly the way that our visual perceptions are images, so long as we see actively "through" the eye rather than passively "with" it. It is not that our finite minds dimly perceive the universe that God thinks, but that God-in-us both thinks and perceives the universe in a single imaginative act. In so far as we have bodies (which we obviously do) and in so far as we perceive through our bodies, then the Imagination must be body as well as mind.

---

[34] In J. Hillis Miller's exposition, "God's perfection lies in the fact that he is the origin of difference, the meeting place of opposites. . . . [Christ] is, to give the Scotist term for this concept, the *natura communis*, the common nature who contains in himself all natures" (*The Disappearance of God* [Cambridge, Mass., 1963], pp. 303, 313). But it is instructive to notice how radically different Hopkins is from Blake in his evocation of the multiplicity of natural appearances, in his reliance on the ritual incarnation of the eucharist, and in the terrible spiritual desolation that attended his failure to sustain this complex faith.

[35] *Siris*, par. 289.

Blake declared in *The Marriage of Heaven and Hell*, "Man has no Body distinct from his Soul for that calld Body is a portion of Soul discernd by the five Senses, the chief inlets of Soul in this age" (E34/K149). Such a formulation does not, however, as is often claimed, identify reality as anything like the experience of the body as we know it.[36] We have to take seriously the call for an apocalypse in consuming flames which will free man from seeing "all things thro' narrow chinks of his cavern" (E39/K154), the Platonic image of the imprisoning cave. Until then, the body as we know it is crippled and blind, and in effect is not the imaginative body at all. Here once again is the paradox in Blake's theory of vision: it is inseparable from the bodily senses, but these are not the senses with which we are familiar.

Ultimately, the apocalypse of imagination can only be achieved through a divine intervention, in fact through an incarnation by which God enters our bodies and makes them his. In an early tract Blake declares, "He who sees the Infinite in all things sees God. He who sees the Ratio only, sees himself only. Therefore God becomes as we are, that we may be as he is."[37] The role of God or Jesus is much more equivocal in *The Marriage of Heaven and Hell* and in the so-called Lambeth books of the 1790s, but by the end of the decade Jesus is once again at the center of Blake's theory of imagination. In one sense this was due to a religious conversion and to a wholesale renovation of his theology, which will be discussed in a later chapter. But in another sense it was a solution which was virtually forced upon Blake by his philosophy of perception and his assertion of imaginative powers higher than those ordinarily experienced in this life. If he had not returned to (or renewed his) Christianity, he might have called his imaginative principle by some other name than Jesus, but he could not have managed without it.

INDIVIDUAL PERCEPTION

It is a commonplace of Blake criticism that he celebrates the uniqueness of individual vision. Did he not write to Dr. Trusler, with insulting implications, "As a man is So he Sees" (E677/K793)? And did he not proclaim in *The Mental Traveller*, "The Eye altering alters all"(E476/K426)? Yet an altogether individual vision cannot possibly be what Blake has in mind. Each private perception participates in, and in a deep sense conforms to, the universal form in the Divine Imagination.

It is worth noting that the problem of differences in individual per-

---

[36] This issue will be dealt with more fully in Chapter 5.
[37] *No Natural Religion* [b], E2/K98.

ception was an awkward stumbling block for the empiricist philosophers, who certainly did not regard it as an exhilarating sign of human diversity. Locke blandly dismissed it as trivial, but Berkeley saw its importance and argued his way into a vexing dilemma, while Hume restated it in terms that have continued to provoke debate to this day.[38] Blake's theory, like that of Cusanus, gets round the problem by abolishing it, subsuming all individual perceptions in one universal humanity. Of course Blake continues to insist upon human individuality, just as he insists upon minute particulars of every kind. "All Genius varies," he says; "Thus Devils are various; Angels are all alike."[39] But he never abandons the principle stated emphatically in the early *All Religions Are One*: "As all men are alike (tho' infinitely various) So all Religions & as all similars have one source" (E3/K98). They differ in the symbols through which they interpret the truth, because symbolism is a mode of understanding adapted to fallen minds. "As all men are alike in outward form, So (and with the same infinite variety) all are alike in the Poetic Genius. . . . All sects of Philosophy are from the Poetic Genius adapted to the weaknesses of every individual" (E2/K98). The picture illustrating the likeness of "outward form" shows Eve emerging from Adam's side, an emblem at once of the primal oneness of man and of the fall into division that lies at the heart of Blake's myth.[40] Symbols are a universal grammar, not a list of private idioms, and the liberated vision sees God rather than self: "He who sees the Infinite in all things sees God. He who sees the Ratio only sees himself only" (E2/K98).

The reference to the "ratio," or fallen reason, identifies the essential cause of the chaotic diversity of perception in the world as we know it. Separate "classes" of men exist because Los, the creative power of the fallen imagination, has been obliged to create them, just as his emanation Enitharmon has had to weave them bodies as a response to the breakup of the Divine Body.

Three Classes are Created by the Hammer of Los, & Woven
By Enitharmons Looms when Albion was slain upon his Mountains

[38] Locke dismisses the problem as being of no practical importance in the *Essay Concerning Human Understanding*, II.xxxii.15. Jonathan Bennett comments, "The incoherence of this shows Locke's failure to see the depth of his difficulty" (*Locke, Berkeley, Hume: Central Themes* [Oxford, 1971], p. 6). On the problem in Berkeley, see G. J. Warnock, *Berkeley* (Harmondsworth, 1969), pp. 141-157; for Hume, see Antony Flew, *Hume's Philosophy of Belief* (New York, 1961), pp. 19-50.

[39] Note on a pencil drawing of grotesque heads (E667/K773). "Devils" and "angels" have here the inverted valuation that they carry in *The Marriage of Heaven and Hell*.

[40] Reproductions of all plates of the illuminated works can be seen in *The Illuminated Blake*, richly annotated by David V. Erdman (New York, 1974).

> And in his Tent, thro envy of Living Form, even of the Divine
>   Vision
> And of the sports of Wisdom in the Human Imagination
> Which is the Divine Body of the Lord Jesus, blessed for ever.
>   (*M* 2:26–3:4, E96/K482)

The diversity of fallen forms is incoherent because it resists assimilation into the single "Living Form" and is the product of malicious
"envy." The Spectre, another manifestation of this fragmentation of
the self, is the quintessential expression of fallen reason:

> The Spectre is the Reasoning Power in Man; & when separated
> From Imagination, and closing itself as in steel, in a Ratio
> Of the Things of Memory. It thence frames Laws & Moralities
> To destroy Imagination! the Divine Body, by Martyrdoms & Wars.
>   (*J* 74:10–13, E227/K714)

Memory, which the empiricists saw as defining the self, is in Blake's
view the symptom of a fragmented consciousness that interprets reality as a collection of discrete phenomena instead of as a single Form.
Imagination, the reintegrated Divine Body, has no need of memory
because it perceives everything as simultaneous unity.

Now, it is perfectly obvious that few people actually experience
such a vision, and Blake's great myth is an attempt to explain why
they do not. "The Eye altering alters all" occurs in a poem that describes the imprisoning natural cycle of the fallen world. The eye alters
because we see with it and not through it.

> If Perceptive Organs vary: Objects of Perception seem to vary:
> If the Perceptive Organs close: their Objects seem to close also:
> Consider this O mortal Man! O worm of sixty winters said Los
> Consider Sexual Organization & hide thee in the dust.
>   (*J* 30:55–58, E175/K661)

The context is the fall into "Sexual Organization" and the desperate
creation of the "Two Limits, Satan and Adam" to prevent an irreversible collapse into incoherent fragments.

Fallen reason, according to Blake, is inseparable from fallen perception. We see once again why he would not concede that the mind operates at a remove from the data of the senses; abstraction occurs at the
moment of (fallen) perception, not during a mental operation that follows it. Abstraction results from hostility to the unified perception of
the Divine Body, "Abstract Philosophy warring in enmity against
Imagination / (Which is the Divine Body of the Lord Jesus, blessed for
ever)" (*J* 5:58–59, E147/K624). Blake's system is often called dialecti-

27

cal, but it is so only in a special sense, envisioning truth as the *simultaneous* union of all particulars rather than as the sequential development that we ordinarily expect in dialectic.[41]

In contrast with this unity in diversity, Satan (or the Spectre, or fallen Reason) seeks to impose a spurious kind of individuality, proclaiming "Let all obey my principles of moral individuality" (*M* 9:26, E102/K490) and compelling men to serve this factitious "identity":

> Where Satan making to himself Laws from his own identity,
> Compell'd others to serve him in moral gratitude & submission
> Being call'd God: setting himself above all that is called God.
> And all the Spectres of the Dead calling themselves Sons of God
> In his Synagogues worship Satan under the Unutterable Name.
> (*M* 11:10-14, E104/K491)

The "synagogue of Satan" (mentioned in Revelation 2:9) is the false church of the fallen world. The "Spectres of the Dead" are the ghostlike, fragmented shapes of those who struggle in spiritual sleep. Satan is not a real being but a "state," a projection of the mind that has fallen from vision and sees particulars as discrete instead of as unified. In accepting his dominion the Spectres acquiesce in his imposition of separate identities upon other beings in their otherness, externalized and alienated instead of united in the Body of Jesus. As Blake labors to make us understand—in terms that suggest either the inadequacy of language to his vision, or a final lack of clarity in the vision itself—the apparent particulars of fallen vision are really generalizations, while the particulars that unite in Jesus are manifestations of a single Form.

> You accumulate Particulars, & murder by analyzing, that you
> May take the aggregate; & you call the aggregate Moral Law:
> And you call that Swelld & bloated Form, a Minute Particular.
> But General Forms have their vitality in Particulars: & every
> Particular is a Man; a Divine Member of the Divine Jesus.
> (*J* 91:26-30, E249/K738)

Memory and Reason, Blake says explicitly, are temporary "states," but the Imagination is not (*M* 32:32ff., E131/K522). As projected in Satan, memory and imagination assemble particulars into a spurious "aggregate." As embodied in Jesus, imagination is wholeness.

In the fallen world, the best we can hope for is a partial and hard-to-sustain vision of eternal truth. Blake's imagery of inner apocalypse

---

[41] It will be evident that I do not regard the famous declaration "Without Contraries is no progression" (*MHH*, E34/K149) as the key to Blake's thought, at least not as it is usually interpreted. This subject will be treated further in Chapter 5.

is well known, and a familiar passage seems to imply that it can occur with decisive finality: "Whenever any Individual Rejects Error & Embraces Truth a Last Judgment passes upon that Individual" (*VLJ*, E551/K613). But in the same work Black ruefully admits that his own vision of the Last Judgment must differ from that of others, not because each person's vision is unique but because fallen vision is fallen. "I have represented it as I saw it. To different People it appears differently as every thing else does for tho on Earth things seem Permanent they are less permanent than a Shadow as we all know too well" (E544/K605). Blake's apocalyptic imagery, indeed, suggests an ongoing series of temporary victories rather than a conversion after which vision is permanently unencumbered by error.[42]

Faced with the unreliability and subjectivity of sense perception, the Platonic tradition held out for a nonsensory intuition of the intelligible, taking mathematics as the model of thought freed from things. As Descartes put it in his meditation "Of the True and the False," "I have been well accustomed these past days to detach my mind from my senses, and I have accurately observed that there are very few things that one knows with certainty respecting corporeal objects, . . . so that I shall now without any difficulty abstract my thoughts from the consideration of sensible or imaginable objects, and carry them to those which, being withdrawn from all contact with matter, are purely intelligible."[43] Blake rejects as incredible—just as positivist science does, though from the opposite standpoint—the Cartesian belief that man is a union of material body and immaterial soul. To detach one's mind from the senses is to fall into hopeless delusion, surrendering to that false Reason that claims to know more than the senses but in fact merely blinds them. Illustrating Young's line, "*Sense* runs Savage, broke from *Reason*'s chain," Blake shows "sense" as a beautiful naked girl about to be smothered by the cloak of a Urizenic ancient.[44] If we see idiosyncratically and mistakenly, it is because our senses have been warped, not because we use them at all.

The notion that the millennium would be achieved by a renovation of the senses was a traditional theme in inner-light religion.[45] The gap

[42] See below, pp. 336 ff.

[43] *Meditation* IV, in *The Philosophical Works of Descartes*, trans. Elizabeth Haldane and G.R.T. Ross (Cambridge, 1931), I, 171.

[44] See Jean H. Hagstrum, *William Blake: Poet and Painter* (Chicago, 1964), p. 123 and pl. 67A.

[45] M. H. Abrams points to some striking parallels between Blake and the seventeenth-century "Digger" leader Gerrard Winstanley, in *Natural Supernaturalism: Tradition and Revolution in Romantic Literature* (New York, 1971), pp. 52-55. Mircea Eliade says that grandiose claims for the unfallen senses are common in mythical thought: "For primitive ideology present-day mystical experience is inferior to the sensory experience

between what is and what seems must be bridged, once again, by incarnation in the Divine Body:

> Then those in Great Eternity who contemplate on Death
> Said thus. What seems to Be: Is: To those to whom
> It seems to Be; & is productive of the most dreadful
> Consequences to those to whom it seems to Be: even of
> Torments, Despair, Eternal Death; but the Divine Mercy
> Steps beyond and Redeems Man in the Body of Jesus Amen
> And Length Bredth Highth again Obey the Divine Vision
>   Hallelujah.
>
> (J 32:50-56, E177/K663-64)

The fallen senses are symptoms of man's descent into "meer Nature or Hell,"[46] and the apparent foundations of perception—Kant's categories—are the mistaken inventions of the fallen mind. "Length Bredth Highth" resume their proper status when they reenter the Divine Vision and are no longer interpreted as the underlying structure of reality. In Eternity, according to the Immortals, "the Human Organs" can contract into worms or expand into gods "till we / Contract or Expand Space at Will," which is possible because "Every one knows, we are One Family: One Man blessed for ever" (*J* 55:43-46, E203/K686-687). The many are joined in the one, and perception is no longer subjective in the way that it was when the eye altering altered all.

Clearly this theory of perception merges into a religion of salvation. The Divine Vision is not easily achieved, and we require the intervention of "Divine Mercy" to set us free. In technical language, Blake's epistemology becomes a soteriology, and vision is conversion. Each individual is "a Divine Member of the Divine Jesus" (*J* 91:30, E249/ K738), a fundamentally Pauline conception: "Now ye are the body of Christ, and members in particular" (1 Cor. 12:27). In the fallen state individual perception is blind and helpless, and can only learn to see through the sacrifice of Jesus. In words associated with the raising of Lazarus (John 11:25), "Jesus replied, I am the Resurrection & the Life. / I Die & pass the limits of possibility, as it appears / To individual perception" (*J* 62:18-20, E211/K696). Only as his members can individuals "behold as one, /As One Man all the Universal Family" (*J* 34:18-19, E178/K664).

---

of primordial man" (*Myths, Dreams, and Mysteries*, trans. Philip Mairet [London, 1960], p. 97).

[46] Swedenborg annotations, E595/K93. See also the extended description of the fallen senses on plate 49 of *Jerusalem* (E196/K679-680).

In another New Testament metaphor, "All Things are comprehended in their Eternal Forms in the Divine body of the Saviour the True Vine of Eternity The Human Imagination" (*VLJ*, E545/ K605–606). In the words of Blake's favorite Gospel, "I am the vine, ye are the branches. He that abideth in me, and I in him, the same bringeth forth much fruit; for without me ye can do nothing" (John 15:5). That is to say, the images of the sensible world are "comprehended" in Jesus in both senses of the word: they are understood, and they are contained. Jesus is the imagination and the imagination is life itself. Because we are "members" of Jesus, branches of his lifegiving vine, we are able to bear fruit. In a fine visual expression of the idea, Blake illustrates the same text from John in *Night Thoughts* (see fig. 1) by placing the words within the form of Jesus, around whom curl fruitful branches, with a pair of lovers and a nursing mother at his feet (which are joined in allusion to the pose of crucifixion).

Clearly, this "comprehension" in Jesus is easier to proclaim than to communicate. The problem of self-consciousness and the threat of subjectivity are very real in Blake's poems, and will occupy us later. Here it is enough to stress that however much Blake may talk about the individuality of vision, he strives constantly to show that it is universal as well. Nothing could be further from his ideal than the declaration of Milton's Satan, "The mind is its own place," which many Romantic writers seized upon as an existential manifesto for the mind's power to create its own reality and values.[47] Blake would define the "mind" here as the fallen selfhood, and would respond more positively to that side of Romantic thought that saw self-consciousness as alienation and division.[48] The more one *is* anything distinct, the less one can be merged with everything and everyone else—an insight that is as old as the history of religion and implies, as Ricoeur observes, a wished-for hypothesis of prelapsarian unity which is defined by contrast with actual psychic experience.[49] Blake refuses to accept the distinction between unity and diversity, declaring over and over again that the many are one in Jesus, but admitting at the same time that this unity is hoped for more than experienced.

Hence the constant tension in Blake between the unity we ought to

[47] See Peter L. Thorslev, "The Romantic Mind Is Its Own Place," *Comparative Literature*, 15 (1963), 250–268. The quotation is from *Paradise Lost* I.253; Milton intended it to expose the emptiness of the Stoic ideal of self-sufficiency.

[48] For a lucid survey see Geoffrey Hartman, "Romanticism and Anti-Self-Consciousness," *Beyond Formalism* (New Haven, 1970), pp. 298–310.

[49] "It is only in intention that the myth restores some wholeness; it is because he himself has lost that wholeness that man re-enacts and imitates it in myth and rite. The primitive man is already a man of division" (*Symbolism of Evil*, p. 167).

1. *Christ the Vine*, illustration for Edward Young's *Night Thoughts*.

enjoy, in which subjectivity would disappear along with the gap between subject and object, and the individual perception that in fact
separates us from each other. If, as Frye says, "there are exactly as
many kinds of reality as there are men,"[50] that is true only in the fallen
world, where reality is smothered by the veil of illusion. In Eternity,
as we are repeatedly told, the variations of time and space "vary according as the Organs of Perception vary," but all perceive "as One
Man" (J 98:38-39, E255/K746), and whatever is implied by that, it is
not the kind of subjectivity we now know.

In our fallen world we inevitably locate ourselves as the focus of all
that we perceive. Lavater said, in an aphorism which Blake underlined, "As in looking upward each beholder thinks himself the centre
of the sky; so Nature formed her individuals, that each must see himself the centre of being" (E573/K65). Phenomenologically, we see the
world from the constantly changing standpoint that moves as we
move.[51] But in contrast with phenomenology, Blake rejects the primacy of the experiencing self, which he symbolizes as the "vortex" of
fallen perception. It is the fallen Urizen, not Los, who creates "many a
Vortex."[52] What Blake wants is a condition that will recover the primal unity by reversing the fall and transforming the *cogito* of
phenomenology, the individual center of consciousness, into a universal consciousness in Jesus. Mircea Eliade speaks of the widespread desire "to find oneself always and without effort in the Centre of the

---

[50] *Fearful Symmetry*, p. 19.

[51] As Stuart Hampshire says, "It is unavoidable that any speaker or thinker should
carry with him the idea of referring to at least one persisting object, namely, himself.
With this idea he carries the idea of himself as an object changing his standpoint and
changing his relation to constant objects around him, and to objects around him changing in relation to himself. He can therefore attach even his most impressionistic and subjective descriptions to a particular position in space and time, and because of this there
arises the possibility of incompatible statements referring to the same subject" (*Thought
and Action* [London, 1959], p. 30). What for Hampshire is an argument to establish the
possibility of knowledge would be, for Blake, a proof of the fallen limits of knowledge.

[52] *FZ* 72:13, E342/K316. The symbol of the vortex, which used to be interpreted in
positive terms, is clearly associated with the Fall; see the discussions by Thomas R.
Frosch, *The Awakening of Albion: The Renovation of the Body in the Poetry of William Blake*
(Ithaca, 1974), pp. 70-81; Susan Fox, *Poetic Form in Blake's Milton* (Princeton, 1976), pp.
71-72; and Donald Ault, *Visionary Physics: Blake's Response to Newton* (Chicago, 1974),
ch. 5. Frosch's book demonstrates that phenomenology can yield valuable insights in
the study of Blake, but a point must come at which the phenomenologist parts company
with Blake. As Frosch notes (p. 11), Blake refuses to accept the eye as the axis of the
world. And more generally, as Hazard Adams observes, phenomenology proposes to
get behind the symbolic construction of reality to the unmediated experience that lies
behind it, whereas Blake regards reality *as* symbolic and has no interest in the kind of
experience that phenomenologists discuss ("Blake and the Postmodern," in Rosenfeld,
p. 17).

World, at the heart of reality; and by a short cut and in a natural manner to transcend the human condition, and to recover the divine condition—as a Christian would say, the condition before the Fall."[53] That is precisely the colossal goal Blake sets for himself: in a natural manner to transcend the human condition. "The Nature of my Work is Visionary or Imaginative it is an Endeavour to Restore what the Ancients calld the Golden Age" (*VLJ*, E545/K605).

It is because truth is subsumed in Jesus that "Every thing.possible to be believ'd is an image of truth" (*MHH*, E36/K151); at least that aphorism requires some such conception to make it work. As often interpreted it makes no sense, since nothing is more obvious than the compatibility of fervent belief with error; a recent analyst states as self-evident, "Truth is independent of belief, since anything that is believed can be false."[54] Nor is it sufficient to defend Blake's position by arguing that all versions of "truth" are in fact beliefs, so that every mode of conceiving reality has its own phenomenological integrity.[55] What Blake actually means is explained by another proverb, the Socratic statement that "Truth can never be told so as to be understood, and not be believ'd" (E37/K152). In other words, he refuses to separate belief from knowledge, as Kant did and as most moderns do, and holds in effect that belief in falsehood is not belief at all. As Berkeley says in a narrower context, "Strictly speaking, to believe that which involves a contradiction, or has no meaning in it, is impossible."[56]

"Firmness of persuasion," Locke said, cannot be adequate grounds for belief. In contradiction to this, when the speaker in *The Marriage of Heaven and Hell* asks, "Does a firm persuasion that a thing is so, make it so?" Isaiah replies, "All poets believe that it does."[57] However, the basis of belief in Blake is the wholeness of the Divine Body, not the vehemence with which an individual may happen to entertain it. If in-

[53] *Images and Symbols: Studies in Religious Symbolism*, trans. Philip Mairet (New York, 1961), p. 55.

[54] Bernard Mayo, "Belief and Constraint," in *Knowledge and Belief*, ed. A. Phillips Griffiths (London, 1967). It is of course also the case that "what is believed, even if it happens to be false, is *believed to be true*." But Blake claims much more than that.

[55] Blake's phrase "an *image* of truth" might seem to imply a position like Susanne Langer's: "There is, in fact, no such thing as *the* form of the 'real' world; physics is one pattern which may be found in it, and 'appearance,' or the pattern of *things* with their qualities and characters, is another" (*Philosophy in a New Key*, p. 91). Blake did understand, very brilliantly, that Newton's physics was a mental construct rather than a direct representation of reality (see Ault, *Visionary Physics*, for a searching exploration of this subject). But Blake also held that Newton was *wrong*.

[56] *Principles of Human Knowledge*, par. 54.

[57] *MHH*, E38/K153. Raine notes the relation between this passage and Locke's (*Blake and Tradition*, II, 112). The reference is to the *Essay Concerning Human Understanding*, IV.xix.12.

dividals differ in intensity of belief, this is a consequence of the relative occlusion of their vision. As Cusanus says, "If the faith of one man does not attain the degree of another's because equality is impossible—just as a thing seen is not seen as exactly the same by several different people—this nevertheless is essential, that each one believe to the full power of belief that is in him."[58]

Cut off from this central ground of faith, we are lost in a wilderness of error and cannot properly be said to believe at all. Everything that exists is mental, but not everything that is mental exists:

> The Gods of the earth and sea,
> Sought thro' Nature to find this Tree
> But their search was all in vain:
> There grows one in the Human Brain.[59]

Similarly, everything that is believed exists, and whatever does not exist cannot be believed. If Blake violates the ordinary usage of words here, he does so deliberately, to emphasize as strongly as possible that belief is knowledge, not a Pascalian leap in the dark. The distinction between faith and reason is itself the fruit of the poison tree of good and evil, a symptom of fallen doubt rather than an insight into reality. As Blake objected to Bacon, "Self Evident Truth is one Thing and Truth the result of Reasoning is another Thing. Rational Truth is not the Truth of Christ but of Pilate. It is the Tree of the Knowledge of Good & Evil" (E610/K397).

Stated poetically, the same doctrine is expressed in *Auguries of Innocence*:

> He who Doubts from what he sees
> Will neer Believe do what you Please
> If the Sun & Moon should doubt
> Theyd immediately Go out.
>
> (E483/K433)

Bacon's first principle, Blake said, was "Unbelief" (E637/K459), and unbelief is sterile and destructive. The truth of "Virtue & Honesty i.e. Inspiration," Blake wrote in the margin of an *Apology for the Bible* by a rationalist bishop, "is Evident as the Sun & Moon" (E603/K386). The sun and moon do not go out, because they do not and cannot doubt.

Descartes, setting up his program of radical doubt, took it for granted that some principles at least were certain. "I did not for all that deny that we must first of all know *what is knowledge, what is existence,*

---

[58] *Of Learned Ignorance*, III.xi, p. 163.
[59] "The Human Abstract," E27/K217.

35

and what is certainty, and that *in order to think we must be*, and such like; but because these are notions of the simplest possible kind, which of themselves give us no knowledge of anything that exists, I did not think them worthy of being put on record."[60] The matter is far less simple than that, as Hume delighted to show. But from Blake's point of view, Descartes illustrates the futility of doubt rather than its philosophical uses, and Hume's skepticism is only a further adventure down the same blind alley. With profound insight he therefore makes doubt an affliction that besets Urthona, the Zoa of imagination: "Urizen, cold & scientific; . . . Urthona, doubting & despairing" (*J* 38:2-3, E182/K671). For doubt is *proper* to Urizen, as the tool of discursive investigation, and will lead him into error but never into despair. It is Urthona, rather, who can be poisoned by it, and if he were to be fully infected by this disease, the sun and moon would indeed go out.

Thus truth does not take infinite forms. It has but one form, the Form of Jesus, although our fallen vision may be too weak to see it clearly, and although in perceiving it through the symbols of the natural world—the theme of the next chapter—we distort it in many ways. Another Proverb of Hell should be quoted here: "If the fool would persist in his folly he would become wise" (E36/K151). This is often interpreted as a celebration of childlike seeing, as in the saintly fool of medieval tradition.[61] But in his later writings Blake has only contempt for fools. "A Last Judgment is Necessary because Fools flourish" (*VLJ*, E551/K612). "The Fool shall not enter into Heaven let him be ever so Holy" (E554/K615). So the meaning may be that the fool who sincerely persists in his folly has some chance of breaking *out* of folly, just as apocalypse follows the consolidation of Satan and Rahab. Moreover, Blake believes that folly is often nothing more than a cloak for knavery. Another proverb tells us, "The selfish smiling fool, & the sullen frowning fool, shall be both thought wise, that they may be a rod" (*MHH*, E36/K151). Their worldly wisdom-in-folly is a tactic for scourging and punishing; it is taking advantage of a pose of folly, not pressing beyond it in the earnest search for truth that must end in wisdom.[62]

[60] *The Principles of Philosophy*, no. 10, in *Philosophical Works*, I, 222.

[61] Quite possibly Blake is alluding to 1 Cor. 3:18, "If any man among you seemeth to be wise in this world, let him become a fool, that he may be wise."

[62] It needs to be noted, moreover, that the Proverbs of Hell are deliberately elliptical and tantalizing. "Listen to the fools reproach! it is a kingly title" (E36/K152) might mean any of three things: (1) If the fool reproaches you, you have in reality a kingly title, because fools reproach what is actually noble. (2) People often reproach fools (i.e., the reproach *of being* a fool), but what most people call folly is actually wisdom; so to be called a fool (as Blake the apparent *naif* sometimes was) is in reality to receive unintended praise. (3) Kings are fools; the proper evaluation of a king is to reproach him for folly.

Throughout this investigation we have been faced with Blake's difficulty in achieving his vision of unity in a fallen world of alienated subjectivity. As we have seen, he postulates a divine principle that can rescue us and make us whole again. But he also maintains that this must be a true and complete incarnation, resulting in an improvement rather than abolition of the body and its senses. And he also wants to hold that the appearances of this world, however defective, are the window through which we see the truth. In order to pursue this theme, we must examine the theory of symbolism on which his private myth is based.

[T W O]

The Truth of Symbols

> Things admit of being used as symbols because nature is a symbol,
> in the whole, and in every part. . . . We are symbols and inhabit
> symbols.
>
> Emerson, "The Poet"

SYMBOLIC SEEING

Even when we have understood that Blake's theory of perception is grounded in the Divine Body of Jesus, an unresolved
antinomy remains. Are symbols arbitrary and inadequate
images from the fallen world that will be superseded in Edenic perception, or are they the very basis of experience and the guarantee of
truth? Blake's answer, ultimately, is that symbols become true by
being organized into myth, where they take on conceptual form and
are available to imaginative interpretation. But before we consider
how his myth works, we need to examine closely the basis of its symbols in a theory of perception.

It was a commonplace of religious hermeneutics that the symbols of
art should, in Swedenborg's words, "call to mind the heavenly things
they signified."[1] But what exactly is the relation between signifier and
signified? Jacob Boehme, one of Blake's favorite authors, responded to
the hermeneutic problem—how do we understand what we read in
the Bible or see in the world?—with his doctrine of signatures. The
text or observed object arouses images and ideas in our minds, and
each individual mind gives the object a new and particular shade of
meaning, but all meanings participate in the archetype. As Alexandre
Koyré elaborates, "Boehme seeks to explicate the synthesis of the particular and the general, between the irreducible and necessary individuality of each man and the total, universal, complete and supra-
essential harmony of God."[2] This is the very synthesis that Blake
sought. At the same time, however, Boehme exhibits a strong distrust
of the images of the fallen world, and aspires to a vision that will
supersede them. "Thou must learn to distinguish well betwixt the
Thing, and that which only is an image thereof. . . . But if thou have

---

[1] *The True Christian Religion*, par. 205.

[2] *La Philosophie de Jacob Boehme* (Paris, 1929), p. 495, discussing *De Signatura Rerum*.
When not otherwise indicated, translations are my own.

left the *imaginary* Life, and quitted the low imaged condition of it; then art thou come into the super-imaginariness . . . which is a State of living *above Images*, Figures, and Shadows."[3]

As has often been remarked, Blake is hostile to disembodied mysticism of this kind. Yet he distrusts sensory images in just the way that Boehme does, and is therefore faced with a considerable problem not only in interpreting symbols, but also in establishing their validity in the first place. So he oscillates between a Platonic and a Berkeleyan pole. He is Platonic (or Neoplatonic) when he emphasizes the primacy of eternal forms that are superior to—even though seen in or through—the phenomena of the fallen world. He is Berkeleyan when he emphasizes the nonexistence of universals apart from particulars, and when, instead of dismissing the phenomena of this world as mere illusion, he claims that only in them do universals exist at all. But the crucial point is that these phenomena, and the vision that perceives them, are fallen. We need a transcendent or divine principle to enable us to see unity in them. For all his insistence on particulars, Blake is notably laconic in allusions to the familiar phenomena of our world; he customarily presents a series of bare nouns without many details from phenomenological experience. In fact he seems to believe, like other idealists, that when the phenomenon is given symbolic meaning in art it is more intelligible, and even more real, than in actual experience. As Hegel says, in a passage cited by W. K. Wimsatt in his famous essay "The Concrete Universal," "The hard rind of nature and the common world give the mind more trouble in breaking through to the idea than do the products of art."[4]

Modern theories like Wimsatt's assume that the universal is indefinitely multiplex, so that each poem and each symbol points to it in unique and unparaphrasable ways. As Philip Wheelwright expounds Goethe, the archetype (*Urphänomen*) exists only in the concrete event (*Phänomen*) "and hence can be known only by opening our eyes and ears and hearts to the sensuous living world."[5] Blake would regard this as misleading in several respects. First, it takes for granted the real existence of the universal in the particular, a relation which for Blake is the fundamental problem, not an obvious axiom from which to set

[3] "Of the Supersensual Life," *Works* (London, 1763-1781), IV, 75. The relevance of this passage to Blake is noted by John Howard, *Blake's Milton: A Study in the Selfhood* (Cranbury, N.J., 1976), p. 263.

[4] *The Introduction to Hegel's Philosophy of Fine Art*, trans. Bernard Bosanquet (London, 1886), p. 16; quoted by Wimsatt, *The Verbal Icon: Studies in the Meaning of Poetry* (New York, 1962), p. 72.

[5] *The Burning Fountain: A Study in the Language of Symbolism* (Bloomington, 1968), p. 53.

out. (If his treatment of it is finally an act of faith, it is openly so, unlike the confident but mysterious assertions of "multeity in unity" that the New Critics used to invoke so freely.) Moreover, if every symbol is unique, how confident can we be that there *is* a universal? Many moderns, of course, are not particularly anxious about this point, but Blake certainly was. And finally, is the "sensuous living world" of which Wheelwright speaks really a reliable source of insight into truth? Whenever he confronts this question, Blake tends to align himself with the Platonic rather than the particularist side of Romanticism.

Like all symbols, those of Romantic poetry are synecdochal, claiming to participate in the reality which they represent. But despite their emphasis on natural images, the Romantics frequently groped for language with which to express a deeper reality at which the images could only hint. Coleridge speaks of "modes of inmost being" to which "the attributes of time and space are inapplicable and alien, but which yet can not be conveyed save in symbols of time and space." Similarly Wordsworth describes symbols as necessary to sustain the mind when it is out of its depth: "The concerns of religion refer to indefinite objects, and are too weighty for the mind to support them without relieving itself by resting a great part of the burthen upon words and symbols."[6] Blake's most biting comment on Wordsworth was elicited by lines in the *Excursion* that describe the "individual Mind" and "the external World" as exquisitely fitted to each other; Blake retorted, "You shall not bring me down to believe such fitting & fitted I know better & Please your Lordship" (E656/K784). And if he ever read the discussion just quoted, he would certainly have despised its symbolism of the "indefinite" and of the "etherial and transcendent" as no symbolism at all.

But on the other hand, although reality must fully inhere in the symbol, it cannot be identical with it, for that would mean endorsing the adequacy of the fallen world. Wordsworth might celebrate the "influence of natural objects/In calling forth and strengthening the Imagination"; Blake retorts, "Natural Objects always did & now do Weaken deaden & obliterate Imagination in Me."[7] A compromise is possible, however. Natural beauty need not be rejected so long as its "vegetative" impermanence is clearly understood. "To walk with him in the country," Blake's disciple Palmer wrote, "was to perceive the

---

[6] Coleridge, *Biographia Literaria*, ch. 22, II, 120; Wordsworth, *Essay Supplementary to the Preface* (1815), in *Prose Works*, ed. W.J.B. Owen and Jane W. Smith (Oxford, 1974), III, 65.

[7] Annotations to Wordsworth's *Poems*, E655/K783.

soul of beauty through the forms of matter."[8] It would be more exact philosophically to say that he perceived the forms of beauty through the glass or shadows of matter. "This World of Imagination is Infinite & Eternal whereas the world of Generation or Vegetation is Finite & Temporal. There Exist in that Eternal World the Permanent Realities of Every Thing which we see reflected in this Vegetable Glass of Nature" (*VLJ*, E545/K605). As has been said of the Kabbalah, "the whole outward world was omen and metaphrasis."[9] And much the same doctrine can be found in the eighteenth-century Platonism of the far from hermetic Shaftesbury: " 'Tis not the form rejoices, but that which is beneath the form. . . . For whatever is void of mind, is void and darkness to the mind's eye."[10]

Platonists like Shaftesbury rejoiced in the visible world as a reflection of the goodness of God, just as Berkeley extolled the beauty of nature that expresses its unseen Author.[11] But Berkeley was concerned to combat skepticism, not to justify natural symbols, and Shaftesbury was not a very deep aesthetician. Within the Platonic tradition, even the classic expressions of the beauty of nature are compromised by a recognition that appearances are illusions. Thus Plotinus, arguing against the Gnostic rejection of this world, held that it is beautiful because it reflects the intelligible realm, but he held also that the sensible world would be a "lie" if mistaken for the intelligible instead of being perceived as an imitation of it.[12] And Plotinus' disciple Proclus, in his commentaries on myths in Plato, distinguished expressly between allegorical likeness (*eikon*) and symbol (*symbolon*). The comparison of the structure of the universe to that of a political state is iconic: the congruence of the two conceptions is readily apparent. But the story of Atlantis is symbolic, because it does *not* admit of easy application. In the words of a modern expositor, "It is a prime characteristic of the symbol that it seems quite 'unlike' what it represents, so

---

[8] Letter to Alexander Gilchrist, 23 Aug. 1855, in *William Blake: The Critical Heritage*, ed. G. E. Bentley, Jr. (London, 1975), p. 31.

[9] A. E. Waite, *The Holy Kabbalah* (New York, 1960), p. 186.

[10] Anthony Ashley Cooper, Third Earl of Shaftesbury, *The Moralists*, III.ii, in *Characteristics of Men, Manners, Opinions, Times* (1711), ed. J. M. Robertson (New York, 1964), pp. 142, 144.

[11] See the famous apostrophe that begins, "Look! are not the fields covered with a delightful verdure? Is there not something in the woods and groves, in the rivers and clear springs that soothes, that delights, that transports the soul?" (*Three Dialogues*, Second Dialogue, p. 210).

[12] See John N. Deck, *Nature, Contemplation, and the One: A Study in the Philosophy of Plotinus* (Toronto, 1967), pp. 76-77.

much so, in fact, that Proclus is compelled to speak of it as only 'hinting secretly' at what it ultimately represents."[13]

In Blake the matter is still more complicated, for however much he might insist on the primacy of images, he also tended to regard the world of experience as a ghastly swindle unless transformed by vision, much as did the Gnostics whom Plotinus opposed.[14] Accordingly, he can be found at one time or another taking all sorts of positions, sometimes proclaiming the validity of symbolic images and sometimes dismissing it. Always, of course, he insists on the requirement of seeing *through* the images. He once told a young follower, "I can look at a knot in a piece of wood till I am frightened at it" (*Blake Records*, p. 294), implying a fixity of gaze that would compel the object to yield up its hidden meaning.

In his positive vein, Blake describes art as organized vision that transforms appearances.

> Thou seest the gorgeous clothed Flies that dance & sport in summer
> Upon the sunny brooks & meadows: every one the dance
> Knows in its intricate mazes of delight artful to weave:
> Each one to sound his instruments of music in the dance,
> To touch each other & recede; to cross & change & return
> These are the Children of Los; thou seest the Trees on mountains
> The wind blows heavy, loud they thunder thro' the darksom sky
> Uttering prophecies & speaking instructive words to the sons
> Of men: These are the Sons of Los! These the Visions of Eternity
> But we see only as it were the hem of their garments
> When with our vegetable eyes we view these wond'rous Visions.
>
> (*M* 26:2-12, E122/K512)

The hum of the flies, which in everyday life one might dismiss as insignificant or annoying, becomes a rich music, and their random swarming an intricate dance. They are the children of Los the imagination, as the thunder is the prophetic voice of his sons. But this superb vision can only give us a glimpse of the Eternity that lies behind it, "the hem of their garments" which "our vegetable eyes" are too weak to see plainly. Los is after all the fallen form of Urthona, and the "vegetable world" is but a means to a higher end:

> And all this Vegetable World appeard on my left Foot,
> As a bright sandal formd immortal of precious stones & gold:

---

[13] James A. Coulter, *The Literary Microcosm: Theories of Interpretation of the Later Neoplatonists* (Leiden, 1976), pp. 42-43.

[14] Blake's dualism and his affinities with Gnosticism will be discussed in detail in Chapters 5 and 6.

I stooped down & bound it on to walk forward thro' Eternity.

(M 21:12-14, E114/K503)

"Sounds solid," Stephen Dedalus reflects as he walks with eyes closed, "made by the mallet of Los Demiurgos. Am I walking into eternity along Sandymount strand?" For Stephen this is only a passing conceit, as is the notion that visible phenomena are intelligible signatures of truth. "Signatures of all things I am here to read, seaspawn and seawrack, the nearing tide, that rusty boot."[15]

At bottom, Blake's conception is likewise a conceit. For hammer though he may at the materials of this world, Los finds them ultimately intractable. Although Los is a demiurge, as Stephen notes, he is not the only one: God as Jehovah Elohim is creator and prison-warden of the world we live in.[16] That God is Urizen, the human reason, which is to say that he and his world are but a lunatic projection of the brain. Accordingly the created world—as contrasted with the uncreated realm of Eternity—can be seen as mere dirt rather than as a sandal of imagination: "I assert for My self that I do not behold the Outward Creation & that to me it is hindrance & not Action it is as the Dirt upon my feet No part of Me."[17]

Thus the vision of the dancing flies is Los's conceit, a work of imagination which is only a temporary transformation of the fallen world. More often nature is described as the veil of Vala, all the more dangerous for its seductiveness.

> As a beautiful Veil so these Females shall fold & unfold
> According to their will the outside surface of the Earth
> An outside shadowy Surface superadded to the real Surface;
> Which is unchangeable for ever & ever Amen: so be it!

(J 83:45-48, E239/K728)

Appearances are only appearances. "Sometimes the Earth shall roll in the Abyss & sometimes / Stand in the Center & sometimes stretch flat in the Expanse." As W. H. Stevenson notes, we have here the Copernican, the Ptolemaic, and the biblical (flat-earth) systems.[18] The fallen mind creates alternative models of reality, but they are only models; under the surface is another surface, "the real Surface" which the imagination aspires to see. And if it could really do so, would it not be able to dispense with symbols and with art?

---

[15] James Joyce, Ulysses (New York, 1961), p. 37.

[16] See below, Chapter 6.

[17] VLJ, E555/K617. On the meaning of "hindrance" and "action" see below, p. 249.

[18] The Poems of William Blake, ed. W. H. Stevenson (London, 1971), p. 810n. These lines occur shortly before the passage just quoted.

Blake's treatment of the visible world could be further documented in scores of passages, and always with the same equivocal results. The world is comprehended in the Divine Body and we can only attain transcendence in and through it, but as Wagenknecht acutely comments, "The closer Blake comes to the achievement of imaginative transcendence, the more man comes to seem immersed in a satanic immanence. . . . The closer one came to achieving a total metaphorical form, the more heightened one's awareness of the tainted source of the imagery."[19] For this reason one must reject Frye's suggestion that the key to Blake's thought is the synonymity of "form" and "image."[20] On the contrary, form belongs to the eternal realm and image to the sensory. The image is supposed to embody the form, but in our experience it often (perhaps always) falls short of doing so. "Eternal Identity is one thing & Corporeal Vegetation is another thing" (*VLJ*, E546/K607). We see how profoundly Blake needed a religious assurance of union with the one central Form, and how important it must be, in his developed myth, for Jesus to descend into what St. Paul called "the body of this death" (Rom. 7:24) in order to save it from itself.

THE HUMANIZED UNIVERSE

Blake repeatedly asserts that the forms united in Jesus are "human." In attempting to understand what this might mean, we must begin by recognizing the immediacy and psychological authenticity of the visionary episodes that are the ultimate context of his myth.

Everyone who knew Blake spoke of his visions. They were fundamental to his imaginative life. The poems probably contain many references to specific moments of inspiration that underlie apparently arbitrary details. The line "Primrose Hill is the mouth of the Furnace & the Iron Door," for example, is surely related to the experience which Blake happened to mention to Crabb Robinson: "I have conversed with the Spiritual Sun—I saw him on Primrose-hill" (*Blake Records*, pp. 313-314). But in one instance, when Blake had a more sympathetic audience than Robinson and an occasion to describe his vision in writing rather than conversation, we have an extended account of the greatest value. When Blake had been a few days at Felpham, the

[19] *Blake's Night*, p. 6. Of course from another point of view Los labors to redeem the fallen forms; see Ault, *Visionary Physics*, pp. 136-140. But as Ault also observes, "The central crisis of vision in Blake . . . is traceable to the capacity of the Vala-like component of fallen events and thoughts to approximate Blake's own deepest artistic impulses" (p. 173).

[20] *Fearful Symmetry*, p. 15.

rural retreat by the sea that he and his friends expected to mark a decisive epoch in his imaginative life, his generous patron Thomas Butts sent a poem imagining the Blakes "In morn, at noon, & thro' the Night/From Visions fair receiving light" (*Blake Records*, p. 76). Blake promptly replied, also in couplets, in the poem of nearly eighty lines that begins, "To my Friend Butts I write/My first Vision of Light" (E683/K804).

The poem opens by describing the sun pouring out "His Glorious beams," and goes on to say that the poet was thereby inspired to rise above the mortal realm of anxiety and desire.

> My Eyes did Expand
> Into regions of air
> Away from all Care
> Into regions of fire
> Remote from Desire.

In *The Marriage of Heaven and Hell*, fire was symbolic of energy, particularly sexual energy; here it fills a region "Remote from Desire." Whatever this may mean, it certainly looks different from the celebration of desire that was there the key to fulfillment—"This will come to pass by an improvement of sensual enjoyment" (E38/K154).

Gazing upon a world lit up by "jewels of Light," the poet now has a vision of the world as literally human.

> I each particle gazed,
> Astonishd Amazed
> For each was a Man
> Human formd. Swift I ran
> For they beckond to me
> Remote by the Sea
> Saying, Each grain of Sand
> Every Stone on the Land
> Each rock & each hill
> Each fountain & rill
> Each herb & each tree
> Mountain hill Earth & Sea
> Cloud Meteor & Star
> Are Men Seen Afar. . . .

It is hard to know exactly what this vision could have been. Does Blake really mean that he saw the world as a swarm of tiny homunculi? It is reasonable to suppose that the poem dramatizes the symbolic nature of perception: Blake perceived the world as filled with life, and since the imagination is by definition human, he must see the world as filled with human forms (just as, to recall Cusanus' analogy, an eagle would perceive it as aquiliform). The vision of light is symbolic since—as will be emphasized shortly—we cannot *not* perceive symbolically. But these symbols are, to an exceptional degree, felt to be direct and unmediated.

Seeing the world as human, Blake recovers an innocence—in the sense of the *Songs of Innocence*—that allows him to understand how he and his wife have descended in their "Shadows" from a higher realm into the earth's bosom. He sees Felpham "In soft Female charms," and the Shadows descend "Like a weak mortal birth." Finally, there is an epiphany of Jesus, all the jewels of light organizing into "One Man" who frees the poet from his mortal body altogether (in Blakean terms, from the imagery of Beulah) and purges away the mortal clay on the analogy of alchemy.

> Till the Jewels of Light
> Heavenly Men beaming bright
> Appeard as One Man
> Who Complacent began
> My limbs to infold
> In his beams of bright gold
> Like dross purgd away
> All my mire & my clay.

The divine spirit then addresses the poet as a "Ram hornd with gold," which seems not to allude to any specific biblical passage, but to refer to the ram as the common beast of sacrifice and its consequent association with Christ.[21] As in the *Songs of Innocence*, the shepherd and his flock are as one. "And the voice faded mild / I remaind as a Child."

In interpreting this deceptively simple poem, I think we need to take what it says with the utmost seriousness. It is not merely an extended metaphor intended to suggest that Blake feels imaginatively free at Felpham, but rather the fervent testimony of a visionary experience. The simple syntax and diction mirror a childlike way of seeing to which the poet has returned. To put it another way, the experience has evidently challenged the limits of language, and although the poet must accept those limits in order to report it, the simple paratactic form indicates that complexity would be irrelevant. Nothing could be less Miltonic than Blake's style here. The prophetic books are Miltonic

---

[21] For instance, in the Abraham and Isaac story, the ram frequently being interpreted as a type of Christ. Stevenson proposes Dan. 8 as a source (*The Poems of Blake*, p. 472n), but the story there, an allegory of Greek victory over the twin horns of Media and Persia, has no apparent relevance, and the ram in Daniel is not horned with gold. At the end of the third book of the *Odyssey* there is a detailed account of a heifer's horns being sheathed in gold as a preliminary to sacrifice.

because they *are* prophecies, addressed to an audience—ourselves—that has not experienced the direct vision and will have to be teased toward it by rhetorical means. The poems to Butts are precious because in them, as in no other surviving record, we hear Blake describing the immediacy of vision itself. The symbols of the thyme and the lark in *Milton* may be founded upon visionary experience but are consciously shaped as symbols.[22] The symbols of the human forms and the golden-horned ram are *given* to the poet directly, the vision coming at once from within and without. As Blake expressed it in another poem to Butts,

> Now I a fourfold vision see
> And a fourfold vision is given to me.
> (E693/K818)

The apparent redundancy is anything but redundant; Blake testifies to the irrelevance of a distinction between the perceiving self and the informing vision that allows him to perceive.

I cannot emphasize too strongly, because I believe that this underlies Blake's lifelong vocation as artist and prophet, the immediacy with which he perceived his visions. By becoming as a child again he could return to the freshness of the visions in his childhood, a number of which were recorded by acquaintances. As a boy of eight or ten, for instance, he saw a tree on Peckham Rye filled with angels with bright wings, and at another time saw angels walking among the haymakers (*Blake Records*, p. 7). In more analytic terms, Blake returns in visions to the mythical mode of thinking which is often disparaged as "primitive" and associated with children because it is tolerated only in them. A modern writer on myth speaks of "an initial cognitive state of trustful receptivity to visions, sensory impressions, and authoritative statements," which changes with cultural evolution and growth to adulthood into "a state of constant distrust, with suspension of judgment, in the absence of indubitable proof."[23] One could not ask for a more concise account of what, in Blake's opinion, had gone wrong with civilization. Distrust and suspension of judgment are the doubt that makes the sun and moon go out.

It has been customary to deny that Blake was a mystic, and this is true enough if one has in mind the negative mysticism that suppresses sensory experience and seeks to lose the self in an undifferentiated Absolute. There is nothing in Blake of the *via negativa*, the detachment

---

[22] See below, pp. 85–86.

[23] Henry Murray, "The Possible Nature of a 'Mythology' to Come," in *Myth and Mythmaking*, ed. Murray (Boston, 1968), p. 314.

from all phenomena in search of an unnamable God of infinite negation.[24] But as a number of philosophers have recently shown, the search for a universal "core" of mystical experience has been a product of religious apologetics rather than of objective phenomenological inquiry.[25] "Mysticism" is an arbitrary descriptive term rather than the name of a specific thing, and to ask whether Blake was a mystic is to expect a different sort of answer than to ask whether he was a mammal.

After the appropriate distinctions have been made—in particular, between Western forms of mysticism and the very different forms in other cultures—we can say with confidence that Christianity has produced two major types. One is "introvertive" or negative mysticism; the other, the "extrovertive" type that glories in sensory images instead of seeking to bypass them. As W. T. Stace says, "The extrovertive mystic, using his physical senses, perceives the multiplicity of external material objects—the sea, the sky, the houses, the trees—mystically transfigured so that the One, or the Unity, shines through them."[26] This is precisely what is described in Blake's vision of light at Felpham. One specialist speaks of "a unitive experience with someone or something other than oneself," which is what Blake means by the One Man infolding him; another calls it "a species of divination, a grasping, by one stroke of imagination, the whole," an immediacy of perception that abolishes any distinction between subject and object and fills every sensory image with universal significance.[27]

Visions of light, in fact, are not uncommon in mystical experience, and Underhill identifies three characteristics that can easily be applied to Blake: joyous apprehension of the absolute, a new clarity of vision of the phenomenal world, and an enhanced sense of the intuitive or

[24] According to Albertus Magnus, who greatly influenced Eckhart and the German mystics, "When St. John says that God is a Spirit, and that He must be worshipped in spirit, he means that the mind must be cleared of all images. When thou prayest, shut thy door—that is, the doors of thy senses. Keep them barred and bolted against all phantasms and images" (De Adhaerendo Deo, quoted by Rufus M. Jones, Studies in Mystical Religion [London, 1919], p. 219). Blake never relinquished the conviction that the doors of perception must be cleansed (MHH, E39/K154), not closed. And he would certainly reject Eckhart's Abgeschiedenheit, the separation of the soul from all sensory images and even from all imaginable ones.

[25] See in particular the essays collected in Mysticism and Philosophical Analysis, ed. Steven T. Katz (New York, 1978).

[26] Mysticism and Philosophy (Philadelphia, 1960), p. 61. Stace has been criticized for a tendentious ranking of types of mysticism and for wrongly conflating Oriental with Western types; neither of these criticisms affects the validity of his description of extrovertive mysticism in the Western Christian tradition.

[27] R. C. Zaehner, Mysticism Sacred and Profane (Oxford, 1957), p. 32; David Baumgardt, The Great Western Mystics (New York, 1961), p. 7.

transcendental self.[28] The most striking feature of these experiences is the extreme clarity of insight that is felt to accompany a movement above, or outside of, one's usual self, as in the account quoted by William James: "Suddenly, without warning, I felt that I was in Heaven—an inward state of peace and joy and assurance indescribably intense, accompanied with a sense of being bathed in a warm glow of light, as though the external condition had brought about the internal effect—a feeling of having passed beyond the body, though the scene around me stood out more clearly and as if nearer to me than before, by reason of the illumination in the midst of which I seemed to be placed."[29]

What seems to be involved—although some religious writers resist the suggestion bitterly—is a physiological as well as spiritual phenomenon, which can be induced both by drugs and by ascetic discipline, and which some persons apparently experience spontaneously. A commentator on Plotinus notes that mysticism and psychedelic drugs both encourage "abolition of the subject–object distinction and of the restrictions of space and time, and awareness of an animation pervading even objects which common sense regards as lifeless." Huxley said that under the influence of mescalin "Visual impressions are greatly intensified and the eye recovers some of the perceptual innocence of childhood," and an informant told Stace that mescalin did not "produce" the sense that life shone through all things but only "inhibited the inhibitions which had previously prevented him from seeing things as they really are."[30] Each of these formulations could serve as a direct commentary on Blake's vision of light.

I have thought this documentation important—and it could be multiplied many times over—because it should compel a recognition that Blake's visions were actual experiences, not merely poetic metaphors, and were felt to be authentic and decisive. What makes Blake so extraordinarily interesting is his recognition of the difficulties not only in communicating such experiences to others, but also in interpreting their meaning for himself. The vision of light may have been felt as unmediated, but to think about it at all—even before trying to describe it in the poem to Butts—is to accept a hermeneutic task.

It is a commonplace that mystical experience is "ineffable." The mystics themselves have often said so. Wittgenstein declared in the

[28] Evelyn Underhill, *Mysticism* (New York, 1955), pp. 240–241; and see her extended account of "illuminations," pp. 249, 254–265.

[29] J. Trevor, *My Quest for God* (1897), quoted by James, *The Varieties of Religious Experience* (New York, 1958), p. 305.

[30] R. T. Wallis, *Neoplatonism* (London, 1972), p. 56n.; Aldous Huxley, *The Doors of Perception* (New York, 1963), p. 25; Stace, *Mysticism and Philosophy*, p. 71.

famous conclusion to the *Tractatus*, "There are, indeed, things that cannot be put into words. They *make themselves manifest (zeigt sich)*. They are what is mystical. . . . What we cannot speak about we must pass over in silence." Samuel Johnson, remarking on Boehme's claim to have seen "unutterable things" as St. Paul did, said that he "would have resembled St. Paul still more, by not attempting to utter them."[31] Yet mystics are notoriously garrulous, and with justification: many of them, and certainly the extrovertive mystics, want to report experiences that resist the categories of rational discourse but do not in the least resist the wider possibilities of language.[32] Hence the universality of symbolic imagery in mystical writing. Even Eckhart, who takes a strong theoretical line against images, is obliged to use them as soon as he attempts to express his "inexpressible" experiences. As Ernst Benz comments, in terms reminiscent of Wittgenstein's, "The only alternatives are to be silent or to speak in images."[33] The resolutely silent mystics are those whose names we have never heard.

Moreover, it is not just a question of using images in order to communicate a mystical experience to readers who have not themselves had it. In addition it seems clear that the experience itself has a symbolic component, which is to say that there is no such thing as a "pure" mystical experience which is subsequently translated into images. It sometimes used to be argued that all mystical experiences are identical but that they appear different when described in the language of different cultural groups. But it is surely more accurate to say that every mystic is guided by cultural assumptions, and often by specific programs of religious discipline, to anticipate what he will experience and to organize it *even as it occurs* in the categories of his tradition. And if this is so, then a philosophical explanation, however paradoxical its language may be, is not so much a translation after the fact as an interpretation of the experience within the categories that governed it. When one writer speaks of union with God, another of the Absolute Oneness, and a third of Nothingness, we cannot assume that they all "mean" the same thing. As Steven Katz says, " 'God' and *nirvana* or

---

[31] Ludwig Wittgenstein, *Tractatus Logico-Philosophicus*, ed. and trans. D. F. Pears and B. F. McGuinness (London, 1961), 6.522 and 7 (p. 151); James Boswell, *Life of Samuel Johnson*, ed. G. B. Hill, rev. L. F. Powell (Oxford, 1934), II, 123. The allusion is to 2 Cor. 12:2-4.

[32] Walter Kaufmann points out that claims of ineffability tend to occur in rationalist periods, in reaction to the prevailing intellectual mode (*Critique of Religion and Philosophy* [New York, 1961], p. 322). And the term "ineffable" is extremely loose; as William P. Alston argues, the assertion that God is ineffable may often mean something like "God cannot be positively characterized in literal terms" rather than that nothing whatever can be said about him ("Ineffability," *Philosophical Review*, 65 [1956], 506-522).

[33] *Die Vision: Erfahrungsformen und Bilderwelt* (Stuttgart, 1969), p. 318.

even 'Being' or *Urgrund* are not only or even primarily names but are, rather, descriptions, or at least disguised descriptions, and carry a meaning relative to some ontological structure."[34] Blake had a profound understanding of this truth, and his myth is a radical exploration of the symbolic meaning of human experience.

SYMBOLIC KNOWING: THE EXAMPLE OF THE SUN

In trying to understand the relationship between Blake's symbols and the humanized vision that inspires them, it will be helpful to concentrate on a simple and familiar example: the passage about the sun and the heavenly host at the end of *A Vision of the Last Judgment*. At this point in his fullest attempt to explain his ideas discursively, Blake announces a Berkeleyan theory of reality as mental, proclaims the Last Judgment as a burning up of error which is synonymous with the fallen or "created" world, and asserts that this apocalypse can occur within each person who learns to see imaginatively.

> It is Burnt up the Moment Men cease to behold it. I assert for My self that I do not behold the Outward Creation & that to me it is hindrance & not Action it is as the Dirt upon my feet No part of Me. What it will be Questiond When the Sun rises do you not see a round Disk of fire somewhat like a Guinea O no no I see an Innumerable company of the Heavenly host crying Holy Holy Holy is the Lord God Almighty I question not my Corporeal or Vegetative Eye any more than I would Question a Window concerning a Sight. I look thro it & not with it. (E555/K617)

What has to be emphasized at the outset is that the contrast is not between literal and symbolic seeing but between two *kinds* of symbolic seeing, one groveling and one spiritual. The ordinary observer knows as well as the scientist that the sun is not really a small disk. The scientist will proceed as Descartes does to define the sun by "astronomical reasonings" that replace the "adventitious ideas" derived from the senses.[35] Blake opposes here the sun of common sense, not the sun of science. His imaginary questioner sees a disk *somewhat like* a guinea; he knows it is not a guinea, but he must see it as something and he therefore sees it as what he loves. "To the Eyes of a Miser a Guinea is more beautiful than the Sun & a bag worn with the use of Money has more beautiful proportions than a Vine filled with Grapes."[36] Rather than

---

[34] "Language, Epistemology, and Mysticism," in *Mysticism and Philosophical Analysis*, ed. Katz, p. 56.

[35] Descartes, *Meditations*, No. III, in *Philosophical Works*, I, 161.

[36] Letter to Trusler, 23 Aug. 1799 (E677/K793).

humanizing the sun as Blake does, the miser dehumanizes it; both see it symbolically, but the miser's symbol is despicable.

In claiming that the sun is human, Blake goes well beyond the central Platonic tradition, which may be illustrated from John Dennis: "The Sun mention'd in ordinary Conversation, gives the Idea of a round flat shining Body, of about two foot diameter. But the Sun occurring to us in Meditation, gives the Idea of a vast and glorious Body, and the top of all the visible Creation, and the brightest material Image of the Divinity."[37] Dennis, although deeply religious and committed to an aesthetic of the sublime, translates the sun into abstract terms. His attitude is similar to Milton's in *Paradise Lost*: "God is light,/And never but in unapproachèd light/Dwelt from eternity" (III.3-6). We symbolize God by light not because we can see God but because he is the light, too blinding to look at directly, by which we see everything else. As Thomas Browne said, "The greatest mystery of Religion is expressed by adumbration, and in the noblest part of Jewish Types, we finde the Cherubims shadowing the Mercy-seat: Life it self is but the shadow of death, and souls departed but the shadows of the living: All things fall under this name. The Sunne it self is but the dark *simulachrum*, and light but the shadow of God."[38] Those shadowing cherubim appear often in Blake's poems, sometimes as the ambiguously protective Daughters of Beulah, sometimes as the Covering Cherub that excludes man from paradise.

For Dennis, Milton, and Browne, God is at once light and symbolized by light. Looking at the sun, Blake sees neither a guinea nor ineffable light. He sees a heavenly host. But he might have chosen some other symbol, provided always that the symbol was human.

> Thou seest the Sun in heavy clouds
> Struggling to rise above the Mountains, in his burning hand
> He takes his Bow, then chooses out his arrows of flaming gold....
> (J 95:11-13, E252/K742)

Hazard Adams comments finely on this passage, "Every morning *is* by the power of metaphor a vision of completed desire."[39] But it is

---

[37] *The Grounds of Criticism in Poetry* (1704) in *The Critical Works of John Dennis*, ed. Edward N. Hooker (Baltimore, 1939), I, 339.

[38] *The Garden of Cyrus*, ch. IV, in *The Prose of Sir Thomas Browne*, ed. Norman J. Endicott (New York, 1967), p. 335. The symbol of the sun goes back to the *Republic* of Plato (VI. 507-508).

[39] "Blake, *Jerusalem*, and Symbolic Form," *Blake Studies*, 7 (1975), p. 165. Compare Ernst Cassirer's description of Herder on Gen. 1: "For him the narrative of the creation is nothing other than the story of the birth of the light—as experienced by the mythical spirit in the rising of every new day, the coming of every new dawn. This dawning is for mythical vision no mere process; it is a true and original creation—not a periodically

more than metaphor. The universe is human, and the mind that so perceives it participates in, rather than merely invents, the humanized symbol. The human form is both tenor and vehicle; every morning *is* a completed desire.

Blake makes clear his contempt for the traditional symbolism of light:

> God appears & God is Light
> To those poor Souls who dwell in Night
> But does a Human Form Display
> To those who Dwell in Realms of day.[40]

Artists traditionally gave the sun a human face, and Blake evidently thought they understood the truth better than the theologians did. In pictures and text he consistently associates the sun with Los, who sometimes carries it as a lantern or globe (as on plate 97 of *Jerusalem*) and is sometimes a human form within it (as on plate 47 of *Milton*). At a crucial moment in *Milton*, Los appears to Blake as "a terrible flaming Sun," becomes "One Man" with him, and binds on his poetic sandals.[41] In elaborating this symbolism Blake may well be thinking of the "mighty angel" in Revelation whose face "was as it were the sun" (Rev. 10:1).[42] And in the passage in *A Vision of the Last Judgment* he has in mind an additional text from the same book: "The four beasts had each of them six wings about him; and they were full of eyes within: and they rest not day and night, saying, Holy, holy, holy, Lord God Almighty, which was, and is, and is to come" (Rev. 4:8; see Isa. 6:3). These are Blake's Zoas, the four living creatures who together make

---

recurring natural process following a determinate rule but something absolutely individual and unique. Heraclitus' saying, 'The sun is new each day,' is spoken in a truly mythical spirit" (*The Philosophy of Symbolic Forms*, vol. II, *Mythical Thought*, trans. Ralph Manheim [New Haven, 1955], p. 97).

[40] *Auguries of Innocence*, E487/K434.

[41] *M* 22:6-12, E116/K505; see the picture on pl. 47 of *Milton*. For a number of related passages, see Raine, *Blake and Tradition*, I, 222-230. As John Sutherland points out, the sun is also associated with Luvah/Orc and (especially) with Urizen ("Blake and Urizen," in Erdman and Grant, pp. 249-250). One might say that each Zoa has his solar aspect, but that as the symbol of imagination the sun is preeminently associated with Los. In Blake's pictorial symbolism it appears constantly as an emblem of imagination, sometimes rising, sometimes setting or occluded by clouds. See esp. the striking image of Hyperion as a powerful young man, firing shafts of light from a great bow while the Spectres of night scatter beneath him, in the sixth illustration to Gray's *Progress of Poesy* (reproduced in Irene Tayler, *Blake's Illustrations to the Poems of Gray* [Princeton, 1971]).

[42] For two very different pictorial treatments of this text, see pl. 62 of *Jerusalem* and the painting *The Angel of the Revelation*, reproduced in W.J.T. Mitchell, *Blake's Composite Art: A Study of the Illuminated Poetry* (Princeton, 1978), pl. 110 (and see Mitchell's commentary, p. 212).

up the human psyche and the imaginative universe. Blake can look at the sun and see Los as the mighty angel, or he can see the heavenly host singing the words of the Zoas. The sun thus symbolizes not the divine effluence that sustains life but the activity of life itself. As Frosch remarks, the synaesthesia is interesting: we look at a visual object and we hear singing.[43]

Just as the miser can see a guinea rather than a heavenly host, so even the humanized sun can be distorted and perverted. The fallen and Satanic Urizen is the Apollonian god of the fallen sun, as Blake explained to a bewildered Crabb Robinson in his remark about Primrose Hill: "I have conversed with the Spiritual Sun—I saw him on Primrose-hill. He said 'Do you take me for the Greek Apollo?' 'No,' I said, 'that (and Blake pointed to the sky) that is the Greek Apollo—He is Satan' " (Blake Records, pp. 313-314). The poet who lives in a fallen world, even if he sees the sun as human, may well mistake its meaning. The point is made obliquely in Blake's illustrations to L'Allegro. In the sixth picture the youthful poet dreams of "the more bright Sun of Imagination" (E665/K618) inhabited by human figures with ironically dark connotations. And although in another picture "the Great Sun" (see fig. 2) closely follows the Miltonic text, the heroic form in the sun dwarfing the human figures below, it betrays distinctly Satanic attributes and reminds us that Satan is Lucifer the son of the morning.[44]

The symbol gives rise to thought. However immediate the vision of a humanized sun may be, the symbol is not self-authenticating; it requires interpretation. Thus we have the "natural sun" of the fallen world and the humanized sun of the spiritual world, both of which sometimes appear in a single picture. On plate 18 of Blake's Job (see fig. 3) the spiritual sun bursts free of the frame of the page-within-the-page and fills the top margin, signifying its infinity, while the "natural sun" is just beginning to light up a localized region of the sky

[43] The Awakening of Albion, p. 106; Frosch discusses a number of striking examples of synaesthesia in Blake. Notice also "the sound of harps which I hear before the Sun's rising" mentioned in a letter to Hayley (K835; not in E).

[44] As John Grant observes, the figure has several Satanic characteristics, particularly his spiky crown ("Blake's Designs for L'Allegro and Il Penseroso," in Essick, pp. 429-430). I would add that the lily-tipped scepter resembles the demonic fleur-de-lys of numerous pictures (e.g., pl. 51 of Jerusalem and the ninety-ninth picture in the Dante series). On the picture of the youthful poet's dream, I am convinced by Grant's analysis in Erdman and Grant, pp. xi-xiv (see the color reproduction, pl. 1 in that volume). As so often, however, the images are open to a contrary interpretation; see Anne Kostelanetz Mellor, Blake's Human Form Divine (Berkeley, 1974), pp. 275-277. The problem of interpreting Blake's pictures will be taken up in the next chapter.

2. *The Great Sun*, illustration for Milton's *L'Allegro*.

behind the hill on the left.[45] On plate 17 God had appeared within the
sun and was at the same time at the level of Job and his wife, with the
text "I have heard thee with the hearing of the Ear but now my Eye
seeth thee" (see fig. 4). There are therefore three kinds of suns in two

[45] Wright makes the point about the spiritual sun, Lindberg about the spiritual versus
the natural sun (Andrew Wright, *Blake's Job: A Commentary* [Oxford, 1972], p. 45;
Lindberg, *William Blake's Illustrations . . .* , p. 328). A similar two-sun effect may be seen
in the crucifixion scene on pl. 76 of *Jerusalem*.

3. *The Book of Job*, plate 18.

consecutive pictures: the natural sun, the infinite spiritual sun, and the epiphanic vision of the humanized sun that inspires Job to go on giving thanks to the spiritual one even when it is again seen as a fiery form in the heavens. In each case what we *see* is the sun. However much Blake disliked the empiricist account of sense experience, he could hardly deny that certain images impress themselves on our eyes

4. *The Book of Job*, plate 17.

whenever we open them. The bodily eye sees a disk. The mental eye
sees a guinea—an uninspired metaphor, but a metaphor all the
same—or Apollo or Los or a heavenly host. As Frye reminds us, "The
'visionary' is the man who has passed through sight into vision, never
the man who has avoided seeing, who has not trained himself to see
clearly, or who generalizes among his stock of visual memories. . . . In

the world of sight we see what we have to see; in the world of vision we see what we want to see."[46]

While the empiricists looked down on imagination as "decaying sense," Blake stressed instead its superiority to decaying sense. "All that we See is VISION from Generated Organs gone as soon as come/ Permanent in The Imagination."[47] But whatever the imagination may see, that vision is only the starting point. It has then to organize perception into form and to make apparent the meaning that is latent in it. Both as celestial orb and as drop of blood, the sun is Los's handiwork: "The red Globule is the unwearied Sun by Los created/To measure Time and Space to mortal Men every morning" (M 29:23-24, E126/ K517). Newton would agree that the sun measures time and space, but not that the imagination empowers it to do so. If in some contexts the sun is Los, in others it is but a utensil for his use; plate 97 of *Jerusalem*, in which he holds it as a lamp, began as a sketch in which he held a traveler's staff.[48]

In a way, Blake is only literalizing the implications of Berkeley's theory that reality is mental. "It is indeed an opinion *strangely* prevailing amongst men," Berkeley says, "that houses, mountains, rivers, and in a word all sensible objects have an existence natural or real, distinct from their being perceived by the understanding."[49] But Berkeley would hold that what we perceive, though mental, has the form that our senses report. Blake takes the point further: if reality is mental, then it must correspond to the shape of our (human) minds. Berkeley's mountains and rivers become "Men seen Afar" in the "vision of light" poem (E683/K805), an identification repeated in *Jerusalem*, where "Cities/Are Men, fathers of multitudes, and Rivers & Mountains/Are also Men; every thing is Human, mighty! sublime!" (*J* 34:46-48, E178/K665). What this notion depends upon is an interpenetration of subject and object, a universe which is within rather than out there.

> For all are Men in Eternity. Rivers Mountains Cities Villages,
> All are Human & when you enter into their Bosoms you walk
> In Heavens & Earths; as in your own Bosom you bear your Heaven
> And Earth, & all you behold, tho it appears Without it is Within

[46] *Fearful Symmetry*, pp. 25, 26.

[47] *Laocoön* aphorisms, E271/K776.

[48] See the reproduction in Geoffrey Keynes, *Drawings of William Blake: 92 Pencil Studies* (New York, 1970), pl. 56. See also the frontispiece to *Jerusalem*, where Los, dressed as a pilgrim, carries the lamp-sun through a Gothic archway that Erdman identifies with the "wicket gate" in *Pilgrim's Progress* (*The Illuminated Blake*, p. 281).

[49] *Principles of Human Knowledge*, par. 4.

In your Imagination of which this World of Mortality is but a
    Shadow.

                             (*J* 71:15-19, E223/K709)

In such a vision nothing can be lifeless, "even Tree, Metal, Earth &
Stone: all/Human Forms identified" (*J* 99:1-2, E256/K747).

The vision of a humanized universe operates in two ways in Blake's
poems. It is first of all the way he sees, the lived basis of his art. But it
is also a problem to be explored in a fallen world where every image,
however humanized, is tainted by fallenness and cannot be trusted uncritically. If we read the imagery of mountains-as-men uncritically, we
may assume that it is casually celebratory; what we ought to see is that
it states the problem (our own relation to a universe which is both divine and fallen) rather than presenting the answer.

Another picture, *A Sunshine Holiday* in the *L'Allegro* series (see fig.
5), will drive home the point by returning us to the symbolism of the
vision of light. Blake conflates this passage in *L'Allegro* with the lines
"Mountains on whose barren breast/The Labring Clouds do often
rest," and literalizes the dead metaphor of the "breast": "Mountains
Clouds Rivers Trees appear Humanized on the Sunshine Holiday. The
Church Steeple with its merry bells The Clouds arise from the bosoms
of Mountains while Two Angels sound their Trumpets in the Heavens
to announce the Sunshine Holiday" (E664/K618). Young men and
women dance around a maypole, emblem of fertility, while the children who frolicked in "The Ecchoing Green" have here joined the old
folk in the shade. The river in the middle distance has a conventional
urn, while other humanized images in the trees and sky are superbly
realized, particularly the gloomy female mountain (suggested by the
"barren breast" in Milton) with her male consort, and the clouds as
angels soaring past a golden sun, blowing trumpets and bearing food
and drink. But the point is not merely that nature appears human.
Being human, it must have human *meaning*, and this remains to be deduced by the viewer, who may find that it contradicts surprisingly the
apparent jollity of the scene.[50] The symbolic interpretation is not self-

[50] There are many indications of a characteristic Blakean treatment of the fallen
world: the old man on his crutch, with a butterfly (emblem of escape into immortality)
in the tree beside him; the female mountain with a city in her loins, wearing what John
Grant calls "the battlemented crown of the Magna Mater" and with her hair forming a
waterfall—the water of materiality—that flows through the urn of the trite river goddess beneath (rivers as seen in conventional neoclassical imagery); the soaring angels in
the sun escaping this fallen world; and above all, the maypole dance symbolizing the
sexual cycle that traps man in mortality and links the children in the shade to the weary
oldsters. For valuable commentary see Mellor (who interprets the picture positively),
Blake's Human Form Divine, pp. 274-275, and Grant (negatively), "Blake's Designs for

5. *A Sunshine Holiday*, illustration for Milton's *L'Allegro*.

evident in the picture, but *an* interpretation is clearly called for. In this ambiguous landscape, at once merry and brooding, we have come a long way from the epiphanic immediacy of the vision of light, and we need a conceptual principle (specifically, the entrapment in "generation" that sexuality entails) in order to understand what we are seeing.

What is at issue is no simple reversal of apparent meaning, but a complex interpretation, on the part first of Blake and then of his viewer, of the implications of Milton's lines. Humanized nature is always better than unhumanized nature, as is indicated by the account of animist religion on plate 11 of *The Marriage of Heaven and Hell*, with its picture of a human face in a tree trunk very much as in *A Sunshine Holiday*. Milton has presented the imagery of what Blake calls Beulah, and the fact that Beulah is profoundly ambiguous (in ways that will be discussed in Chapter 5) does not cancel out its real attractiveness. A passage in the sixth Night of *The Four Zoas* provides a valuable gloss on *A Sunshine Holiday*: the fallen Urizen, appalled at the wreckage of his world and having cursed it vehemently, recalls with nostalgia an unfallen state "Where joy sang in the trees & pleasure sported on the rivers/And laughter sat beneath the Oaks & innocence sported round" (72:39–73:1, E343/K317). But the context shows that even the unfallen Beulah had in it the potential for fall, and Blake's picture may well illustrate its fallen condition:

> Beyond the bounds of their own self their senses cannot penetrate
> As the tree knows not what is outside of its leaves & bark
> And yet it drinks the summer joy & fears the winter sorrow. . . .
>   (FZ 70:12–14, E340/K314)

The tree spirits in *A Sunshine Holiday* are suggestive of the prison of the selfhood; as Wilkie and Johnson comment, the lines in *The Four Zoas* recall the passage in Dante's *Inferno* describing suicides who have been transformed into trees and cannot speak unless they are torn.[51] But Blake's picture also contains the solution to the problem: the sorrowful countenance among the leaves of the tree is surely that of Christ, whose incarnation—in the special Blakean sense to be discussed later—frees man from the prison of mortality.

As Blake clearly suggests by interpreting Milton's poem in this way, the poet who "has" the vision may not fully understand its significance. Similarly the hundred designs for the *Divine Comedy* are an

L'Allegro and *Il Penseroso*," in Essick, pp. 430–433. There is a color reproduction in Milton Klonsky, *William Blake: The Seer and His Visions* (New York, 1977), p. 84.

[51] Brian Wilkie and Mary Lynn Johnson, *Blake's Four Zoas: The Design of a Dream* (Cambridge, Mass., 1978), p. 271. Blake's illustration of this passage is reproduced in Klonsky, *William Blake*, p. 115.

extended critique of Dante's moral and spiritual understanding. The project would not have been worth undertaking if Dante were not indeed an inspired poet; Albert Roe aptly cites Blake's "vision of light" poem ("each was a Man/human-formd") in connection with the picture in which Dante drinks from a river of light that swirls with tiny human shapes.[52] But the vision of light is the beginning only. Even when it inspires a *Divine Comedy*, such a poem may nonetheless be filled with what Blake calls "error" and may require systematic reinterpretation by the meditative reader. Blake would agree wholeheartedly with Frye not only that the meaning of the *Divine Comedy* is not "a *simple* description of what 'really happened' to Dante," but also that when Dante comments on his work he is only another Dante critic—"What he says has a peculiar interest, but not a peculiar authority."[53] Every viewer or reader must interpret Blake's symbols anew, just as Blake has reinterpreted Dante's. And we must therefore turn from epistemology to hermeneutics, from the source of Blake's symbols to the theory of interpretation.

[52] Albert S. Roe, *Blake's Illustrations to the Divine Comedy* (Princeton, 1953), pp. 192-193 and pl. 98.

[53] *Anatomy of Criticism* (Princeton, 1957), pp. 77, 5.

[T H R E E]

Symbol, Myth, and Interpretation

And so, Glaucon, the tale was saved from perishing; and if we will
listen, it may save us, and all will be well when we cross the river
of Lethe.

Plato, *Republic* 621

THE MEANING OF SYMBOLS

Thus far we have concentrated on the epistemological and psychological basis of Blake's symbols. We shall now move toward an examination of the myth in which he organized them,
and raise more directly the problem of interpretation in its dual form:
Blake's understanding of his symbols' meaning, and the various kinds
of understanding that modern readers bring to them. I propose to
begin by considering some representative modern theories of symbolism, taking care at each point to note essential differences from
Blake's theory, but at the same time establishing perspectives that will
help to illuminate the peculiar difficulties of his theory.

It is far easier to say what symbols do than to explain how they do
it. In Wheelwright's fairly typical exposition, "A symbol cannot be
understood in itself, it must be taken correlatively with what it means.
A symbol owes its symbolic character to the fact that it stands for
something other than, or at least more than, what it immediately is."[1]
But how do we know what it means or "stands for"? Literary critics
often handle the question rather casually, having taken over from religion a set of assumptions that presuppose the validity of imaginative
truth and the superiority of multivalent symbols to other forms of discourse. But unless one is willing to assert a direct and completely intuitive response to the symbol—a response that seems inappropriate
for Blake at least, whose symbols are complex and endlessly de-
bated—then the problem of interpretation has still to be raised.

Consider Gadamer's observation that the symbol points beyond itself while yet containing meaning within itself, thus remaining in-
exhaustible to interpretation in contrast with the definiteness of allegory. Gadamer quotes Schelling's comment on the German word
Sinnbild (a "meaning image") that it is "concrete, resembling only itself, like an image, and yet as universal and full of meaning as a con-

[1] *The Burning Fountain*, p. 6.

63

cept." While the symbol coincides with that which is symbolized instead of merely pointing to it, obviously it cannot be identical with it. Accordingly, "The disproportion of form and essence is essential to the symbol inasmuch as the latter points by its meaning beyond its physical appearance."[2] As an instrument for literary commentary, this formulation can be readily applied to Blake. For example, the physical appearance of the sun is that of a disk. The metaphor of the guinea sticks close to appearances, since the sun and guinea are both round, golden, and invested (to use a "bivalent" word) with connotations of value. The heavenly-host metaphor is more obviously a mental construct, denying the Lockean sense impression of the sun and substituting another sense altogether (hearing, whereas nobody has actually *heard* the Lockean sun) and treating the connotations of value more generally within a (Christian) myth. But as an instrument of interpretation, Gadamer's formulation demands further exegesis, since it raises the crucial problem of the real existence (whether "out there" or in the mind) of the "essence" to which the form of the symbol "points."[3]

It is in fact quite remarkable, if the symbol is really multivalent and not reducible to paraphrase, that we are able to understand it at all. Theorists of symbolism commonly appeal to the Greek etymology in which the *symbolon* was a potsherd or other counter, broken in half to verify, once the halves were rejoined, that their bearers carried authorized information. But as Guy Rosolato sardonically remarks, to reconstruct the separated "symbols" in this way can be only a prelude to interpretation, and in fact the analogy reduces symbol to sign.[4] Rosolato's solution is the classic one of psychoanalysis: no symbol is arbitrary because every symbol proceeds from the unconscious, metaphor corresponding to Freudian condensation and metonymy to displace-

---

[2] Hans-Georg Gadamer, *Truth and Method*, trans. and ed. Garrett Barden and John Cumming (New York, 1975), pp. 69, 70. This account is notably congruent with the Neoplatonic theory of Proclus: see above, pp. 41-42.

[3] Gadamer's answer, like that of Cassirer to which we shall refer shortly, would doubtless be that the "essence" only exists *vis-à-vis* the "form"—that the symbol *generates* this structure, so that the essence cannot be separated from the symbol. Blake, as we shall see, would reject such an answer.

[4] "One must say that the sign is more clearly envisioned than the symbol in this relation, for if the two pieces of a stone carry an inscription, it then remains to decipher the sense; if the pieces exist only in their shapes which are sufficient in themselves, then fitting them together makes them disappear into a object that contains them. However, this object, once formed, may remain equivocal, at least as a stone; it has no place and belongs to no Parthenon whose columns need to be rediscovered; or, remaining a stone, it takes on meaning only when lost in the anonymity of a beach, among the pebbles" (*Essais sur le symbolique* [Paris, 1969], p. 115).

ment. In neurosis the symptom "is a sign of suffering, and mimics the symbol."[5]

The problem of meaning remains to be solved, since Freud held that all symbols are overdetermined, so that any simple translation of symbol into "meaning" merely reduces it once more to a sign. But here at any rate is a possible answer to the validation of symbols: they are rooted in the unconscious and are intelligible to those who have made a special study of psychology. But there is a further problem in that the Freudian symbol, since it proceeds from the unconscious, is by definition not chosen by the conscious intelligence and is usually opaque to it. Our treatment of the validity of symbols must take account of their deliberate and conscious use, whatever may be their ultimate source. A credible Freudian theory of art must allow at least that given the existence (or hypothesis) of unconscious "signifieds," the artist may choose the signifier in a conscious act of composition.

Another influential theory of symbolism has developed in the German idealist tradition, and can be summed up in Wilhelm Nestle's phrase "Vom Mythos zum Logos."[6] Ernst Cassirer, while emphasizing that all thought is symbolic and that what we regard as "reality" is in fact a Kantian construction, treats scientific thought as the highest stage because it goes beyond myth to recognize symbols for what they are: "What distinguishes science from other forms of cultural life is not that it requires no mediation of signs and symbols and confronts the unveiled truth of 'things in themselves,' but that, differently and more profoundly than is possible for other forms, it knows that the symbols it employs are *symbols* and comprehends them as such."[7]

There is much here that would appeal to Blake, since (as was argued in the last chapter) he was deeply conscious of the difference between the immediacy of experience and the symbols that interpret it. But the ultimate movement of Cassirer's thought would be repugnant to him, both because it approves of the increasing abstraction of scientific symbols and because it endorses the Kantian aesthetics of disinterested contemplation. "We cannot fail to recognize the specific difference between myth and art. A clue to this is to be found in Kant's statement that aesthetic contemplation is 'entirely indifferent to the existence or nonexistence of its object.' Precisely such an indifference, however, is

[5] Rosolato, *Essais sur le symbolique*, p. 116, with an anagrammatic pun: "Le symptôme, qui *signe* la souffrance, et *singe* le symbole." In the Freudian adaptation of metaphor and metonymy Rosolato follows Jacques Lacan.

[6] Quoted by R. M. Grant (who argues against this tendency) in *Gnosticism and Early Christianity* (New York, 1966), p. 120.

[7] *Mythical Thought*, p. 26.

entirely alien to the mythical imagination. In mythical imagination there is always implied an act of *belief*."[8] Kant's remarks on "existence or nonexistence" refer to mimetic fiction: we don't care whether a novel is about "real" people or invented ones. But Blake despised mimetic fiction *tout court* and insisted on the real existence of the truth symbolized by Odysseus or Bunyan's Christian (or, in negative terms, on the real nonexistence of Dante's Beatrice or Milton's God). Above all he abhorred aesthetic disinterestedness and regarded art as synonymous with myth. So far as he was concerned, the act of belief was fundamental to life itself ("If the sun and moon should doubt. . . .") not to mention to art. This is hardly the place to argue that Cassirer is wrong or that aesthetic disinterestedness is misconceived, but at any rate it is important to notice that his theory of symbolism, though attractive to many modern critics, is in systematic conflict with Blake's aesthetics.

For thinkers who remain skeptical of symbols in their neo-Kantian guise, another way of interpreting their mental origin is attractive. "Whoever says 'man' says 'language,' " Lévi-Strauss comments, "and whoever says 'language' says 'society.' "[9] According to structuralist anthropology, symbols arise from collective or social experience, and myths embody the unconscious needs and fears of a whole society. Myths and symbols are arbitrary in character; their users may ascribe "natural" qualities to them, but in fact they are infinitely malleable, and intelligible only as expressions of certain universal relationships (up/down, nature/culture, and so on) rather than as stable concepts.

Such a theory, though attractive to many literary critics because it furnishes a method for analysis, is destructive of Blakean myth for a number of reasons, above all the assumption that myth exists not to pose or answer questions but to "mediate" them. Even the classicist G. S. Kirk, who denies that myths are always modes of mediation between otherwise irreconcilable beliefs, describes the "speculative or explanatory" type as disposing of a problem "by simply obfuscating it, or making it appear abstract and unreal, or by stating in affective terms that it is insoluble or inevitable, part of the divine dispensation or natural order of things, or by offering some kind of palliation or apparent solution for it."[10] Blake's critique of the Christian myth de-

---

[8] Cassirer, *An Essay on Man: An Introduction to a Philosophy of Human Culture* (New Haven, 1944), p. 75.

[9] Claude Lévi-Strauss, *Tristes Tropiques* (Paris, 1955), p. 450. The standard English version, curiously, renders this as "Man is inseparable from language and language implies society" (*Tristes Tropiques*, trans. John and Doreen Weightman [New York, 1975], p. 390.) ("Qui dit homme dit langage, et qui dit langage dit société.")

[10] *Myth: Its Meaning and Functions in Ancient and Other Cultures* (Cambridge, 1970), p. 258.

tects and criticizes every one of these traditional evasions. Whatever his myth may be, it operates in a very different way from the collective myths examined by anthropology, particularly since it opposes rituals instead of reinforcing them.

What emerges most helpfully from the modern debate is a recognition that symbols are not simple signs, and furthermore that many myths operate against prevailing cultural assumptions instead of supporting them. In other words, it is a kind of intellectual hubris to presume to decode symbols as if the observer were sure of understanding them better than their inventors and users, and it is a mistake to assume the normal congruence of myth and symbol with social orthodoxy.

As to the first point, it has become increasingly apparent that Saussure, the father of semiotics, makes an unconvincing distinction between the arbitrariness of the sign (a stop light is red but might have been any other color) and the more intimate relation between signifier and signified in the symbol. "One characteristic of the symbol is that it is never wholly arbitrary; it is not empty, for there is the rudiment of a natural bond between the signifier and the signified. The symbol of justice, a pair of scales, could not be replaced by just any other symbol, such as a chariot."[11] This example of symbol is highly conventional and comes close to being a sign; it is the kind of symbol which, when we look at Blake's practice, we shall call iconic or emblematic. The example presumes that the symbol *signifies* just as the sign does. But most symbols—even emblematic symbols in law courts, perhaps—do not operate in that way. As René Alleau points out,

> Symbolism, that is to say the *usage* of symbols, is not a conceptual process. One cannot therefore apply our criteria of pertinence and rationality. A symbol *does not signify* a predetermined thing to anyone. It is at once a focus for the accumulation and concentration of images and their affective and emotional "charges," an analogical vector of orientation of intuition, and a magnetic field of the anthropological, cosmological and theological similitudes that are evoked. . . . The "signified," at each moment, may be considered as uncompleted [*inachevé*], as a simple element in an endless process of symbolization in which the "signifier" itself participates.[12]

Alleau urges in addition that Saussure's term "arbitrary" needs to be understood in two senses. In Saussure's usage it refers to the "unmotivated" character of the sign: there is nothing about an ox that requires

[11] Ferdinand de Saussure, *Course in General Linguistics*, ed. Charles Bally et al., trans. Wade Baskin (New York, 1966), p. 68.
[12] *La Science des Symboles* (Paris, 1976), p. 57.

the sign *boeuf* or *Ochs*. But the sign is also arbitrary in that it is freely agreed upon when some other sign might have been chosen in its stead; that is to say, its meaning depends on a convention that is so-cially accepted. And Piaget therefore observes that the sign requires social life for its establishment, while the symbol may be arbitrary in a quite different sense, being conceived by one individual alone (for in-stance by a small child; or, one might add, by William Blake). If a symbol is "socialized" it then becomes half sign, half symbol, whereas a pure sign is normally collective.[13]

Most anthropologists would agree with Victor Turner that the symbol is "dense with meaning" and that interpretation even of ap-parently simple symbols is an arduous intellectual task.[14] And some would go further and argue with Dan Sperber that semiotics is a blind alley and that symbols do not "mean" at all, but form a cognitive structure within which meanings can be organized rather than a code that transmits meanings themselves.[15] Without necessarily endorsing the extremity of this revolt against semiotics, we can be grateful for its emphasis on the origin of symbols not in codifying conventional meaning but in dealing with its limits. In Sperber's view, symbolism begins when the conceptual mechanism hits an impasse, so that "a representation is symbolic precisely to the extent that it is not entirely explicable, that is to say, expressible by semantic means. Semiological views are therefore not merely inadequate; they hide, from the outset, the defining features of symbolism."[16]

Blake might well find this formulation attractive, and could add that in his era the mind of an entire culture had broken down, needing a rediscovery of symbolism in order to fill the gap left by a bankrupt theory of cognition. And his reading of the Bible certainly convinced him that the symbolic artist operates in conflict with received values rather than codifying and confirming them. As Alleau says, "The lin-guistic and sociological approach to rites and symbols is insufficient to interpret them, since, far from constituting a means of organizing cul-tural and social 'discourse,' their express purpose is to disorganize and

[13] "Les symboles peuvent être socialisés, un symbole collectif étant alors en général mi-signe, mi-symbole; un pur signe est, par contre, toujours collectif" (Jean Piaget, *La Psychologie de l'intelligence*, quoted by Alleau, p. 50).

[14] Victor Turner, introduction to *Forms of Symbolic Action: Proceedings of the 1969 An-nual Spring Meeting of the American Ethnological Society*, ed. Robert F. Spencer (Seattle, 1969), p. 13.

[15] Dan Sperber, *Rethinking Symbolism*, trans. Alice Morton (Cambridge, 1975). Sperber offers his own subtle and witty attempts to penetrate the symbols used by the Dorze of Ethiopia.

[16] *Rethinking Symbolism*, p. 113.

destroy it."[17] The prophet is alienated because he withdraws from his culture in order to win through to truths which it cannot see.

At this point, however, Blake would part company with any objective or descriptive theory of symbolism, for he would hold not only that his symbols were a response to cultural crisis, but also that they carried authentic meaning and corresponded, however imperfectly at times, to ultimate truth. He would agree absolutely that they do not function as encoded signs, but would regard signs as trivial, not as typical of human discourse. The symbol for Blake is more than a magnetic field of emotional charges or a cognitive system within which experience can be organized. It is our best and subtlest means of insight into reality. The sun looks like a disk but is human.

Blake's symbols are religious symbols. They call for an act of faith—which the reader must postulate even if he does not share—in the validity of a way of knowing that sees *through* the phenomena of the world we live in. Attempts to make Blake a modern theorist of symbolism, though they clarify much that is important to him, must not be allowed to obscure this fundamental point. But if Blake's meaning is religious, it is essential to distinguish between two types of religious meaning. Augustine can revel in imaginative interpretation because every interpretation is finally authorized "by the standard of the harmonious unity of the Catholic faith."[18] Punning on the double meaning of the French word *spirituel*, a commentator on Augustine observes that interpretation is free to be inventively witty because it is secured by spiritual truth: "One does not outstrip the Holy Spirit, one does not go further than he. We are fortunate to go as far as he wants to lead us. . . . Strictly speaking these meanings are *spirituels*: they are echoes, reprises on a superior instrument, transpositions of the literal sense."[19] But this presumes that the meanings are mysterious because God, who knows them perfectly, has chosen not to let us see them plainly; it is the *in aenigmate* of Paul's "through a glass darkly." Meanwhile we are safe because we possess the literal sense.

Blake, however, has no use for symbols promulgated by a God of mystery and interpreted by the authority of the church. And his God is the fully immanent Jesus in whose imagination we imagine. Whatever is unclear is so because of the nature of things, not because God has set us a puzzle to solve. As we saw in the last chapter, Blake's mode of mystical experience is radically different from the kind described, for

[17] *La Science des Symboles*, p. 58.

[18] *The City of God*, trans. Henry Bettenson (Harmondsworth, 1972), XV.xxvi, p. 645. Augustine has been proposing various interpretations of the symbol of Christ as the ark.

[19] Maurice Pontet, *L'Exégèse de S. Augustin, prédicateur* (Paris, 1945), pp. 146, 147.

example, by Gershom Scholem: "A hidden and inexpressible reality finds its expression in the symbol. . . . The symbol 'signifies' nothing and communicates nothing, but makes something transparent which is beyond all expression."[20] In Blake's opinion mystery and hiddenness are abominable, and unless we see clearly we do not see at all.

Moreover, such a formulation is open to the charge of willful mystification and of evading the plain facts of human experience. It is for this reason that Paul De Man prefers allegory, which admits its artificiality, to symbol, which claims to hint at inexpressible mysteries.

> Whereas the symbol postulates the possibility of an identity or identification, allegory designates primarily a distance in relation to its own origin, and, renouncing the nostalgia and the desire to coincide, it establishes its language in the void of this temporal difference. In so doing, it prevents the self from an illusory identification with the non-self, which is now fully, though painfully, recognized as a non-self.

In De Man's terms, Blake's myth must be seen as a gigantic attempt to blur the distinction between self and nonself, a wish fulfillment on a cosmic scale that merges each individual in a single Divine Humanity which is identified with the entire universe. Baudelaire, as expounded by De Man, reminds man that "Nature can at all times treat him as if he were a thing and remind him of his factitiousness, whereas he is quite powerless to convert even the smallest particle of nature into something human."[21] Blake, on the contrary, claims that each particle of light and each grain of sand "Are Men Seen Afar" (E683/K805).

In an age when skeptics were demythologizing Christianity, Blake sought to remythologize it. There is no escaping the aptness of De Man's account of the Romantic symbol; the assertion of a humanized universe is central to Blake's vision, whatever the modern reader may choose to make of it.[22] But within the religious tradition, at least, Blake attempts a profound revaluation of symbolic meaning, which is neither a code as it was for Augustine nor an ineffable mystery as it was for many of the mystics. In interpreting symbols philosophically, in trying to compel them to yield up their meaning, he belongs with those religious believers who recognize the enormous conceptual problems in a truly critical religious hermeneutics.

[20] Gershom G. Scholem, *Major Trends in Jewish Mysticism* (New York, 1941), p. 27.

[21] "The Rhetoric of Temporality," in *Interpretation: Theory and Practice*, ed. Charles S. Singleton (Baltimore, 1969), pp. 191, 196.

[22] At the end of this book, with (I hope) due caution and respect, I shall reach a conclusion similar to De Man's, that Blake's myth chooses to deny essential facts of human experience.

Here, as throughout this book, I find Paul Ricoeur exceptionally helpful. In contrast with epistemological skeptics like Sperber, Ricoeur declares, "That symbols are signs is certain: they are expressions that communicate a meaning." And their signification depends upon an act of faith that intuits their relation to the divine. "Every symbol is finally a hierophany, a manifestation of the bond between man and the sacred."[23] Blake would agree wholeheartedly. Indeed his central image for the psyche and the universe, the Zoas, is directly inspired by the famous hierophany of Ezekiel. At the same time he resists the usual tendency to reduce hierophany to doctrine. And so does Ricoeur: "In poetry the symbol is caught at the moment when it is a welling up of language, 'when it puts language in a state of emergence' [Gaston Bachelard], instead of being regarded in its hieratic stability under the protection of rites and myths, as in the history of religions, or instead of being deciphered through the resurgences of a suppressed infancy" (p. 14). In other words, symbols are not the fossilized forms of orthodox religion or Freudian psychoanalysis, but rather the constantly developing significance of art. Blake hopes to persuade us to accept his myth, but not in the way that naïve believers accept the Fall and Crucifixion as presented in the Bible, which continues to be for him "the Great Code of Art."[24] "Perhaps there is a way," Ricoeur suggests, "of recovering the myth as myth, before it slipped into *gnosis*, in the nakedness and poverty of a symbol that is not an explanation but an opening up and a disclosure."[25] But if the symbol gives rise to thought, how can *gnosis* be avoided?

In systems like Blake's or Ricoeur's, symbols are at once primary, necessary, and maddeningly problematic. As Ricoeur elaborates the point in another work,

> There is something astonishing and even scandalous about the use of symbols.
>
> 1. The symbol remains opaque, not transparent, since it is given by means of an analogy based on a literal signification. The symbol is thus endowed with concrete roots and a certain material density and opacity.
>
> 2. The symbol is a prisoner of the diversity of languages and cultures and, for this reason, remains contingent: Why *these* symbols rather than any others?
>
> 3. The symbol is given to thought only by way of an interpreta-

---

[23] *Symbolism of Evil*, pp. 14, 356.
[24] *Laocoön* aphorisms, E271/K777.
[25] *Symbolism of Evil*, p. 165.

tion which remains inherently problematical. There is no myth
without exegesis, no exegesis without contestation.[26]

Each of these points is relevant to Blake. He chafes against the "material density and opacity" of symbols in their concrete (he would call it
"vegetative") basis; he ransacks various mythologies for symbols
while claiming that they all reflect a single unity; and he recognizes the
inevitable ambiguity of exegesis while insisting on the integrity of
truth.

In a much-quoted passage in *Jerusalem*, Blake introduces his terms
Bowlahoola and Allamanda, based apparently on "bowel" and "ali-
ment," and interrupts in a parenthesis,

(I call them by their English names: English, the rough basement.
Los built the stubborn structure of the Language, acting against
Albions melancholy, who must else have been a Dumb despair.)
                                              (*J* 36:58–60, E181/K668)

English is the rough basement not of languages but of thought; Italian
would be Dante's basement, Greek would be Plato's. The structure of
language is the necessary shield against inarticulate despair, but it is
stubborn and finally opaque. It is all we have with which to communicate the truth of epiphanic vision, but it is not enough. So the myth is
endlessly made and remade, the same symbols surviving through a
series of reinterpretations. The problematic status of symbolic meaning is not an occasion for celebrating the richness of human experience, but a demoralizing symptom of the Fall. In Eden, by contrast,
experience and art, vision and speech, unite in a single harmony:

And they conversed together in Visionary forms dramatic which
    bright
Redounded from their Tongues in thunderous majesty, in Visions
In new Expanses, creating exemplars of Memory and of Intellect
Creating Space, Creating Time according to the wonders Divine
Of Human Imagination. . . .
                                              (*J* 98:28–32, E255/K746)

But we do not live in Eden, and it would be wrong to suppose that
these lines describe experience as Blake actually knows it. They
prophesy what we can hope to know in a better state, after an
apocalypse of which our limited and temporary epiphanies are only
premonitions.[27] Symbols may lead us there, but Eden is greater than

---

[26] "The Hermeneutics of Symbols and Philosophical Reflection: II," in *The Conflict of
Interpretations: Essays in Hermeneutics*, ed. Don Ihde (Evanston, 1974), p. 317.

[27] These themes will be examined more fully in Chapters 5 and 7.

our symbols and can dispense with them. Hence the special urgency
and anguish of the role of the symbol-making artist in Blake's myth.

The Artist and His Myth

The symbolic ambiguity of vision accounts for much of the strangeness of Blake's myth. Imaginative experience is valid because it is
guaranteed by the Divine Imagination, but its expressive symbols are
contaminated by the fallen world from which they are drawn. The
languages in which symbols are represented—visual as well as
verbal—are "stubborn structures," barriers to vision as well as aids to
it. Drawing eclectically on many languages and mythologies, Blake
exhibits an almost Joycean awareness of the manipulability of words.
But behind the words he sees a divine vision to which they point, and
has little interest in words for their own sake.

Since the oddness of Blake's symbols derives from their complex
relation to "reality" rather than simply from the idiosyncrasy of his
imagination, it will be helpful to establish their conceptual context.
The best way of doing this is to see how symbols were used by writers
whom Blake admired; Koyré's summary of Boehme's practice can be
applied word for word to Blake:

> The great difficulty of Boehme's doctrine consists in its non-
> conceptual or, more exactly, semi-conceptual character. To tell the
> truth, it is not a "doctrine." It is a vision of the world which
> Boehme expresses through symbols, symbols that have all the "evi-
> dence" of sensory reality but at the same time all its obscurity.
> Boehme proceeds by means of images which give, if one may say
> so, a very clear *feeling* of his thought; which make, in their barba-
> rous freshness, an infinitely powerful impression. One grasps their
> "sense" immediately, one "comprehends" and "penetrates" them.
> But these symbols are in themselves as obscure and "mysterious" to
> reason as is the *mysterium* which they are charged with revealing. In-
> tuition (*Verstand*) grasps them in their symbolic import, but discur-
> sive reason (*Vernunft*) is incapable of fixing them. . . . But Boehme
> does not limit himself, unfortunately, to proposing symbols. He
> explains them, and his multiple and differing explications—for each
> actual symbol is charged with a multiple significance—diverge and
> introduce into his simple vision a conceptual confusion which is fur-
> ther aggravated by the confusion of his terminology.[28]

[28] *La Philosophie de Jacob Boehme*, p. 393. One could also apply to Blake the judgment
that "Each of his works is a complete exposition of the whole of his system, and the
repetitions are as frequent as the contradictions" (p. xi).

Koyré's term "semi-conceptual" is exactly right: this kind of symbolism embodies ideas, yet it resists as Urizenic our ordinary ways of handling them, even while it frustrates us by the facility with which it alters its apparent meanings.

Having had a look at Blake's *Songs*, Coleridge wrote wryly in a letter, "You perhaps smile at *my* calling another Poet, a *Mystic*; but verily I am in the very mire of commonplace common-sense compared with Mr. Blake, apo- or rather ana-calyptic Poet, and Painter." And in his notes on the poems, Coleridge mentioned as a fault "despotism in symbols."[29] These remarks are extremely acute. If *apocalyptic* means "taking off the veil," as in the removing of the seals in Revelation, then *anacalyptic* would mean "putting on the veil."[30] Blake is not, that is to say, the kind of visionary who penetrates the veils that shroud hermetic truth, but on the contrary *puts on* veils of his own, imposing symbols despotically rather than interpreting them piously. Although he draws upon traditional symbolism, he constantly reinvents it, and some of his most notable symbols are concoctions of his own. That is why the analogy with Boehme is so significant: both writers handle symbols in a most unusual way, inventing them as freely as modern poets do, yet proclaiming fervently that these dark and perplexing symbols afford knowledge of ultimate truth.

In contrast to the outstanding example of "apo-calyptic" symbolism, Renaissance hermeticism, Blake has no use for arcane secrets reserved for the adept. The material world is a Newtonian abstraction, not a mask concealing spiritual forces from all except occult perception and magical manipulation.

> The Spectre builded stupendous Works, taking the Starry Heavens
> Like to a curtain & folding them according to his will
> Repeating the Smaragdine Table of Hermes to draw Los down
> Into the Indefinite, refusing to believe without demonstration.
> (*J* 91:32-35, E249/K738)

Seeking to transmute the elements of the visible world, the followers of thrice-great Hermes were wasting their time. As with alchemy, so with astrology; although Blake drew upon the macrocosmic theories

---

[29] Letter to H. F. Cary, 6 Feb. 1818, and another shortly afterward to C. A. Tulk (*Blake Records*, pp. 251, 252).

[30] My colleague Gordon Braden, to whom I owe this elucidation, suggests as suitably Coleridgean translations "offmuffling" and "onmuffling." *Calyptic* is "hidden, veiled" (cf. Calypso, who "concealed" Ulysses). Given the ironic tone, this interpretation seems at least as probable as the alternative that would read "anacalyptic" as "unveiling" (see Michael Ferber, "Coleridge's 'Anacalyptic' Blake: An Exegesis," *Modern Philology*, 76 [1978], 189-93).

of both systems, he must have despised as grossly mechanist the attempt to reduce them to practical science. From his point of view the hermeticists used symbols without understanding their nature, and mistook them for reality. Blake would agree with Jung that alchemical symbolism is a projection on to matter of archetypes from the unconscious, and that it is of value as a means of insight into the psyche rather than as a tool for controlling the external world.[31] Albion *contains* the sun, moon, and stars rather than being subject to their influence.

At the same time, however, Blake resists the contrary tendency in the Platonic tradition, which was to seek intellectual insight in number rather than in myth and symbol. Kepler complained in a controversy with Robert Fludd, "He greatly delights in the dark riddles of things, while I try to bring into the light of the intellect things themselves involved in obscurity. The former is the familiar of chymists, Hermeticists, and Paracelsists; the latter is the possession of mathematicians." Similarly, the Cambridge Platonist Benjamin Whichcote asserted that "Christian Religion *is not* Mystical, Symbolical, Ænigmatical, Emblematical; but uncloathed, unbodied, intellectual, rational, spiritual."[32] There is plenty of numerology in Blake's prophecies, but it never seems structural; it is one mode of symbolism among many, not the bedrock of truth that symbols veil.[33] It would be surprising if Blake ignored number altogether, since it is inherent in reality as we perceive it and in the symbolic systems he admired. But his numbers carry symbolic weight in themselves—four Zoas, seven Eyes of God—rather than participating in mathematical relationships. "Satans Mathematic Holiness" (*M* 32:18, E131/K521) is a parody of "Los's Mathematic power" (*M* 29:38, E126/K517), and it is plausible to suggest that the power in each instance is a function of fallenness. Los uses it to form the "solid" called Adam which is the limit of contraction, as Satan is the limit of opacity; this is one of many ways of describing Jesus' merciful intervention in the fallen world. "The Divine Saviour/Formd it into a Solid by Los's Mathematic power" (29:37-38). Blake rejected Plato's mathematical philosophy because he believed

[31] See C. G. Jung, *Psychology and Alchemy*, trans. F. C. Hull (Princeton, 1968); and cf. Milton on the alchemists seeking the philosopher's stone "In vain, though by their powerful art they bind/Volatile Hermes" (*Paradise Lost* III.602-603).

[32] Kepler, *Harmonices Mundi*, quoted by J. H. Randall, Jr., *The Career of Philosophy* (New York, 1962), I, 322. Whichcote, *Moral and Religious Aphorisms* (1703), in *The Cambridge Platonists*, ed. C. A. Patrides (Cambridge, Mass., 1970), p. 334.

[33] George Mills Harper ("The Divine Tetrad in Blake's *Jerusalem*," in Rosenfeld, pp. 235-255) clarifies some of Blake's numerological passages without coming close to proving the claim that he was interested in Pythagorean or other philosophies of number as the constitutive structure of the universe.

that science, by abstracting and reifying the concept of number, attributes reality to abstractions rather than to living form. He could have found a very similar critique in Berkeley.[34] The world contains numbers, but Blake would never say as Plato does in the *Timaeus* that they are its soul. And he opposes the tendency of number-philosophy to honor stasis rather than activity; as has been said of Leibniz, "The world is a mathematical system, and in a mathematical system nothing ever happens: the same equations always hold."[35]

Above all, Blake rejected mathematics because it sought to bypass vision. As Coleridge remarks, both Plato and Pythagoras sought to liberate the mind from the "despotism of the eye," rebuking the "sensuous" tendency to complain that "invisible things are not the objects of vision."[36] Blake would consider that such an ambition, besides being futile, reflects an insultingly base notion of the possibilities of vision. Only the dupes of Satan and Urizen believe that anything real can be invisible.

Why, then, the notorious obscurity of Blake's symbolism? Blake's answer in effect is that poems and pictures mean nothing unless the reader and beholder can give them imaginative life, which involves participating in the symbol-making process and seeing through symbols to the reality they only partly express. Reality in itself is not mysterious, once vision has been cleansed—this at least is Blake's faith—but until we can participate directly in something like the "vision of light," we must grope toward it by means of symbols that share in the opacity of the fallen world. Blake writes in the *Descriptive Catalogue* that the poetic senses once knew "visions of the eternal attributes, or divine names" (E527/K571) but erected them into false gods and made them masters instead of servants. In other words, they reified symbols, which became mysterious because they were invested with a spurious autonomy and were no longer perceived with the imaginative eye of vision. Once symbols were cut off from the Divine Imagination, they became instruments of deception and oppression. In the fallen world no one can avoid some taint of fallen vision; Blake sadly admits that although Time should be seen as a vigorous youth and not as an old man, his own visions are "infected" by conventions and "I see Time Aged alas too much so" (*VLJ*, E553/K614).

The solution is to remythologize symbols, to understand that they

---

[34] See Warnock, *Berkeley*, ch. 11. Some of Blake's notes on *Siris* suggest that he suspected even Berkeley of mathematical Platonism. On his understanding of Plato on this point, see Peter F. Fisher, "Blake's Attacks on the Classical Tradition," *Philological Quarterly*, 40 (1961), 1-18.

[35] Randall, *The Career of Philosophy*, II, 32.

[36] *Biographia Literaria*, ch. 6, I, 74.

are symbols, and to learn again to see them in the universal imagination of Jesus. "They ought to be made to sacrifice to Man, and not man compelled to sacrifice to them; for when separated from man or humanity, who is Jesus the Saviour, the vine of eternity, they are thieves and rebels, they are destroyers" (*DC*, E527/K571). Elsewhere in the same work Blake speaks of visions of monumental works of art "containing mythological and recondite meaning, where more is meant than meets the eye" (E522/K566). The point is to urge the mind into thought. As Blake woundingly put it in a letter to a dissatisfied customer, "That which can be made Explicit to the Idiot is not worth my care. The wisest of the Ancients considered what is not too Explicit as the fittest for Instruction because it rouzes the faculties to act."[37]

Stated in more positive terms, this means that the reader will learn nothing unless he reimagines or re-creates the meaning for himself.

> If the Spectator could Enter into these Images in his Imagination approaching them on the Fiery Chariot of his Contemplative Thought if he could Enter into Noahs Rainbow or into his bosom or could make a Friend & Companion of one of these Images of wonder which always intreats him to leave mortal things as he must know then would he arise from his Grave then would he meet the Lord in the Air & then he would be happy. (*VLJ*, E550/K611)

Nothing esoteric need be implied here. As didactic writers from Augustine to Bunyan reiterate, we learn the most from "similitudes" that demand mental effort; and a quite similar case could be made in terms of a modern phenomenology of reading.[38] At the same time, Blake believed strongly that truth must remain hidden from "Single vision & Newtons sleep" (E693/K818), and for political as well as poetic reasons he generally expressed his ideas enigmatically. As John Linnell

---

[37] Letter to Trusler, 23 Aug. 1799 (E676/K793). George Mills Harper cites Thomas Taylor's commentary on Plotinus: "Oracles were often delivered in ambiguous terms, with a view to the advantage of those that heard them, viz. in order to exercise their cognitive powers" (*The Neoplatonism of William Blake* [Chapel Hill, 1961], p. 49).

[38] "No one doubts," Augustine says, "that things are perceived more readily through similitudes and that what is sought with difficulty is discovered with more pleasure" (*On Christian Doctrine*, trans. D. W. Robertson, Jr. [New York, 1958], II.vi, p. 38). Bunyan similarly argues that the godly mind responds best to "things that seem to be hid in words obscure" and expressed in "dark similitudes" (*The Pilgrim's Progress*, ed. Roger Sharrock [Harmondsworth, 1965], p. 215). A modern phenomenologist would add that even the most mimetic symbols call for a re-creative act on the part of the reader: "The iconic signs of literature constitute an organization of signifiers which do not serve to designate a signified object, but instead designate *instructions* for the *production* of the signified" (Wolfgang Iser, *The Act of Reading: A Theory of Aesthetic Response* [Baltimore, 1978], p. 65).

recalled, "He could always explain his paradoxes satisfactorily when he pleased but to many he spoke so that 'hearing they might not hear' " (*Blake Records*, p. 396). The allusion is to Isaiah 6:9, repeated in all four Gospels; in the synoptic Gospels it is spoken by Christ when his disciples question him about the parable of the sower: "Therefore I speak to them in parables: because they seeing see not; and hearing they hear not, neither do they understand" (Matt. 13:13). The context suggests that those who hear not are the worldly who are unworthy of the Kingdom of Heaven, and Paul applied the text to signify the separation of reprobate from elect.[39] Blake of course repudiated election in this sense, but he might well have applied the text to his own work, which is opaque to the worshippers of Antichrist and intelligible only to the spiritually awakened.

In organizing a poetic myth, Blake was thus guided by a subtle and even skeptical conception of the scope and value of symbolism. In contrast with modern mythmakers, he meant the myth to point to absolute truth, so that he did not see himself as manipulating symbols hypothetically or nostalgically. As Tillich trenchantly observes, "All the talk about the 'new myth' is an indication of how remote the new myth is in actuality. A myth that is sought for as myth is for that very reason repelled. Only when one's thinking has objective reference can a truly mythical element pulsate through it."[40] Yeats's spirit voices announced that they came to bring him metaphors for poetry; Blake's "friends in Eternity" brought him truth itself.[41] But unlike Augustine or Bunyan, Blake did not take it for granted that his symbols were reliable images of truth. Like Tillich, he understood the task of reconstruction that critical thought had imposed on religious symbols.

If we recall Piaget's distinction between collective signs and "socialized" symbols that are half sign and half symbol,[42] we can appreciate the special difficulties that Blake's mythmaking entailed. On the one hand, he needed to draw upon traditional symbols, so as not to be merely idiosyncratic, and for the sake of economy he wanted to establish some of them as readily recognizable signs. On the other hand, he needed to fight continually against the reader's tendency to turn them into signs of the most limiting kind. He therefore reshaped tradi-

[39] "Israel hath not obtained that which he seeketh for; but the election hath obtained it, and the rest were blinded. According as it is written . . . ," etc. (Rom. 11:7-8). See also Paul's final sermon in Acts 28:25-27, and Mark 4:12, Luke 8:10, John 12:40 (where the reference is to disbelief in miracles).

[40] Paul Tillich, "The Religious Symbol," in *Symbolism in Religion and Literature*, ed. Rollo May (New York, 1961), p. 88.

[41] Letter to Butts, 25 Apr. 1803 (E697/K822). Blake's concept of inspiration by friends in Eternity is discussed below, pp. 302 ff.

[42] See p. 68 above.

tional symbols so that they could, as it were, recover their symbolic value, and he also developed private symbols for which no collective understanding existed, forcing the reader to establish his own "community of understanding" by penetrating their meaning and endowing them with signification.

Another way of describing Blake's symbols is to say that they exhibit a constant interplay between the iconic and the dynamic. By an iconic symbol I mean, following Victor Turner, one which is perceived as having a natural or "real" relation to its associated meaning. This does not mean that all people in a given culture understand the symbol identically. But the iconic symbol is perceived as participating directly in the phenomenon or state of affairs to which it points.[43] For example, Blake adopts the Neoplatonic symbol of water as materiality. At the most general level, the reader must be willing to see a natural connection between water and the shifting, shapeless, potentially suffocating world of matter, or else Blake's symbol will seem merely arbitrary and his repeated use of water symbolism a private code rather than an apprehension of reality. This symbolism gains its special power by contradicting the positive connotations of the "water of life," and it therefore admits the force of the positive symbol while denying that water in the fallen world should be understood positively.[44] For example, at the beginning of the sixth Night of *The Four Zoas* Urizen wants to drink from a river, but his own "daughters" prevent him from doing so after the first and unsatisfying draught. Since the daughters are aspects of himself, this suggests that the fallen Urizen is incapable of being satisfied by water—he drinks from a warrior's helmet, like a figure in Homer or Ossian—and that fallen reason has cut itself off from the water of life. In thus thwarting itself, the reason *resymbolizes* water along Neoplatonic lines. We live in the fallen world; to restore the positive value of the river of life, we need a religious vision that will reverse Urizen's fall.[45]

The iconic symbol is essentially static, however richly it may de-

[43] For a concrete example, see Turner's discussion of "the basic color triad" white-red-black in *The Forest of Symbols: Aspects of Ndembu Ritual* (Ithaca, 1967), pp. 88-91. See also Mary Douglas' account of symbolism based on the human body in *Natural Symbols: Explorations in Cosmology* (London, 1973).

[44] Thus Jesus "is the Bread & the Wine he is the Water of Life" (*VLJ*, E551/K612). The water of the fallen world is a ghastly parody of water in its Edenic significance. Lifegiving water is perhaps not water as we know it but a transmutation of fire: "The Furnaces became/Fountains of Living Waters flowing from the Humanity Divine" (*J* 96:36-37, E253/K744).

[45] On Blake's painting "The River of Life," see below, p. 231. One might also instance the episode in *Milton* in which Satan strives to baptize Milton with the icy water of Jordan, while Milton shapes for him "a Human form" (19:14, E111/K500).

velop as we meet it in new contexts. Of quite a different order are those symbols which Blake invents as expressions of mental *activity*. The Zoas are his central achievement of this kind. Inspired by a passage in Ezekiel that celebrates the mysteriousness of God, they cry out for psychological interpretation. They must be understood not for what they are but for what they do. More than that, they are not referential in the way that water refers to materiality even as it "is" materiality. For Blake understands profoundly that the dynamics of the self can only be understood by entering into its activity, not by separating out discrete images of the iconic kind. Throughout his myth the two kinds of symbolism interpenetrate. For example, the realm of the fallen Tharmas, the "Parent power" (*FZ* 4:6, E297/K264), is water. As we think about Tharmas—always the most mysterious of the Zoas—we are helped by having a fairly clear idea of the symbolic significance of water. When Tharmas collapses into watery chaos we cannot easily say what he *is*, but we are assisted in perceiving what he *does*. The iconic symbol helps us to grasp the dynamic symbol.

Blake's symbols occupy a full range from the completely public to the completely private, requiring the reader at every point to revitalize the public symbol and to universalize the private. At the public extreme, the brief and splendid lyric "The Sick Rose" calls upon a very ancient set of associations concerning sexuality and impermanence, making a statement about corrupted sexuality that can be understood without reference to Blake's larger system.[46] Some of Blake's strangest symbols turn out to be no stranger than the sources in which he found them, for instance the "Odors" that sing above the wine-presses at the end of *The Four Zoas* (E389/K376), which Raine rather desperately identifies with the dismembered body of Dionysus as smelled by Zeus, but which are borrowed directly from the odors or "prayers of the saints" that sing a new song in Revelation 5:8-9.[47]

But many of Blake's symbols resist exegesis of this kind. Raine's researches, indeed, illustrate the limitations of source study: they often throw valuable light on Blake's meaning, but the assumption that his meaning is controlled by esoteric tradition can only lead to frustration,

---

[46] This being so, Michael Riffaterre should have chosen a more challenging text to support his argument that Blake's meanings need not be esoteric ("The Self-Sufficient Text," *Diacritics*, 3 [1973], 39-45). And even in this instance it is reductive to assume that the poem's meaning should be restricted to what can be deduced by a reader ignorant of Blake's ideas. The poem can be read in at least four ways—naturalistic (roses do decay), psychosexual, sociopolitical, and metaphysical—and while one is not *obliged* to read it in all of these ways, the poem is richer and more interesting (and certainly more Blakean) if one does so.

[47] See Raine, *Blake and Tradition*, I, 304-305. Paul Miner notes the allusion to Revelation in "Visions in the Darksome Air," in Rosenfeld, p. 270.

since his use of all traditions is highly independent. When the source helps us to understand a symbol it is usually because Blake thought the reference obvious (as in the text from Revelation), but sometimes it is due to his failure to supply adequate materials for interpretation to work upon. When Raine laments that "too often Blake's allusiveness defeats its own ends," she fails to consider that it is not intended as allusion. Her insight is shrewder when she remarks that "the symbols are used like words in a sentence of complex and ambiguous grammar."[48] In learning Blake's grammar we learn how to use his vocabulary; when we fail, it is either because we have not understood imaginatively enough or because he has not shown us what he means.

Whatever the source of a symbol—in "nature" or literary tradition or Blake's imagination—it takes on meaning from its context in Blake's myth. Ricoeur distinguishes helpfully between "primary symbols" that derive directly from the experience of nature, and "mythical symbols" that give order to that experience by articulating it in narrative structures.[49] Translated into the distinction between iconic and dynamic symbols, this means that in Blake the symbol only possesses meaning in active conjunction with other symbols. Myth is not an arbitrary way of manipulating symbols, but the conceptual framework in which they make sense. As Tzvetan Todorov says, "The symbol is not necessarily the essential notion of symbolism, any more than the word is of language."[50] If symbolism is indeed a grammar, it functions as a mode of organizing experience rather than as a code for describing it. As Sperber points out, we can be multilingual but not multisymbolic, so that Blake's tendency to assimilate symbols from diverse sources into a single system is in fact typical of the way everyone uses symbols.[51] Myths exist to explain the nature of things, and are necessarily related to each other insofar as human experience is universal. A story is complete in itself, a myth is part of mythology.

Where many students of Blake's myth go wrong is in assuming that because all myths are interrelated in conception, his work is intended to ratify some universal structure of human mythology. While Blake certainly believes in the unity of the imagination in Jesus, so that all religions "have one source" (E3/K98), he never suggests that all myths derive from a single Ur-myth, and his campaign against literalizing symbols implies a ruthlessly critical treatment of most existing symbols, embodied as they are in degraded mythologies. The classical

[48] Blake and Tradition, I, 233; II, 47.
[49] The Conflict of Interpretations, p. 289.
[50] "Introduction à la symbolique," Poétique, 11 (1972), 284.
[51] Rethinking Symbolism, pp. 87-88.

gods, so appealing to the Western poetic tradition, are fatally corrupted by the conception of reality that they symbolize, a point made
strikingly in the polemical design *Milton and the Spirit of Plato*, in
which several episodes in *Paradise Lost* are identified with visions projected by a Urizenic Plato: Venus presiding over the world of generation, Mars over a repressive state supported by Mosaic stone tablets,
and Jupiter over the fallen reason. The three Fates rule above, and the
whole is an expression of the thrice-great Hermes ("Trismegistus")
whose mystic cult was so repellent to Blake.[52]

If the classical gods are to regain imaginative validity, they must be
brought down from the skies and restored to their human meaning.
"The Plowman of Chaucer is Hercules in his supreme eternal state,
divested of his spectrous shadow; which is the Miller, a terrible fellow,
such as exists in all times and places, for the trial of men, to astonish
every neighbourhood, with brutal strength and courage, to get rich
and powerful to curb the pride of Man" (*DC*, E527/K571). The everyday English farmer and the (sometimes dishonest) miller to whom he
sells his grain are living embodiments of a universal truth, and
Chaucer has so depicted them. In mythological terms, they combine
to make up Hercules, whom the ancient mythographers failed to recognize as a divided being. In Blakean terms the apocalyptic plowman
(Urizen in *The Four Zoas*, Rintrah in *Milton*) is separated from the
spectral Satan, "the Miller of Eternity" (*M* 3:42, E97/K483). But the
myths are not interchangeable. Chaucer is unaware of the symbiotic
relation between his plowman and miller, and the Greeks and Romans
did not understand that their Hercules was a composite being. Blake's
myth exists not to confirm traditional intuitions but to make new
sense of them.

In building up his myth Blake thus means to use received materials
while compelling the reader to see them critically, and to force symbols to operate in a dynamic system instead of masquerading as static
images of truth. His procedure closely resembles that of the Gnostic
heresiarchs of the first Christian centuries, who sought to shock their
disciples into insight by subverting the orthodox myth. In his earlier
attempts, notably *The Marriage of Heaven and Hell*, Blake resembles the
Gnostics in the relative simplicity with which he simply inverts the
usual symbolic values.[53] By the time of the so-called Lambeth books

[52] See Mellor, *Blake's Human Form Divine*, pp. 280-282, and Grant, "Blake's Designs
for *L'Allegro* and *Il Penseroso*," pp. 438-442. There is a color reproduction in Morton
Paley, *William Blake* (London, 1978), pl. 57.

[53] Hans Jonas says of Gnostic allegory, "Instead of taking over the value-system of
the traditional myth, it proves the deeper 'knowledge' by reversing the roles of good
and evil, sublime and base, blest and accursed, found in the original" (*The Gnostic Religion* [Boston, 1963], p. 92).

he is reconstructing mythology in a way that also resembles the Gnostics, but in a strange mixture of image and concept—such as Koyré noted in Boehme—rather than in a routine inversion of values. As an expositor describes it, "For Gnostic thinking, concepts become ill-defined schemas, entities half abstract, half concrete, half personal, half impersonal; 'aeons,' *aion, 'olam*—fragments of time or spatialized and hypostatized periods of time—the elements or characters in a mythological drama; and for their part, historical individuals and facts are sublimated into something half way between the real and the symbolic."[54]

The symbols that result from this mode of thinking may sometimes be vague, but they are intended to force the reader (or believer) to be clear, to recognize the merely heuristic value of symbols and to penetrate beyond them. They are "half way between the real and the symbolic" because they deny the usual distinction between the two, claiming an immediacy of intuition in which symbols open directly into reality, but warning against the contrary errors of ordinary experience: taking symbols as if they were literally true, or taking them as wholly arbitrary signs pointing to a sensible realm that could be apprehended without any need of symbols. Like the Gnostics, Blake is thus committed to the peculiar richness but also the ambiguity of symbols *about* symbols, which can only be described in paradoxical terms, as for instance by Gilbert Durand: "They are symbols of the symbolic function itself, which is—like them!—mediatory between the transcendence of the signified and the manifested world of concrete, incarnated signs that become symbols through it."[55] Any such theory must presuppose the transcendent validity of whatever it is that symbols point to. But the Gnostic and Blakean systems, unlike the more familiar religious ones, regard the "naturalness" of symbols with extreme suspicion and concentrate on the conceptual role of the symbolizing function, rather than moving directly to a privileged realm "beyond" as well as "in" the symbols.

One of Blake's best-known pronouncements is "I must Create a System, or be enslav'd by another Mans" (*J* 10:20, E151/K629). The emphasis falls on "Create" rather than on "System." Los labors to make *us* creative, "Striving with Systems to deliver Individuals from those Systems" (11:5, E153/K630). The point is to use the system as a temporary structure that can be left behind, not to treat it as an end in itself. Thought is impossible without system; Blake creates his own because only in his own can he be imaginatively free. It follows that

[54] Henri-Charles Puech, "Gnosis and Time," in *Man and Time: Papers from the Eranos Yearbooks*, ed. Joseph Campbell, trans. Ralph Manheim (New York, 1957), p. 82.
[55] *L'Imagination Symbolique* (Paris, 1968), p. 25.

each reader must re-create Blake's system even as he studies it, approaching its symbols "on the Fiery Chariot of his Contemplative Thought" (E550/K611).

What matters finally is the truth of which the symbols are shadows. The more limited our vision, the more inert the images we see. The grim catalogue of the attributes of Ulro—cave, rock, tree, flaming darkness, "The land of snares & traps & wheels & pit-falls & dire mills"—takes the form of a static list because Ulro vision is static. But in a parenthesis Blake interrupts the list to say that "whatever is visible to the Generated Man, / Is a Creation of mercy & love, from the Satanic Void" (*J* 13:44–45, E156/K634). Even Ulro needs the Divine Vision in order to be conceived at all; even this list of archetypal horrors is intelligible because it is controlled by the imagination.

Seen imaginatively, the universe is human and the fall into Ulro is a vision of the anguish of dehumanization.

> The Sun forgets his course like a drunken man. . . .
> He bleeds in torrents of blood as he rolls thro heaven above
> He chokes up the paths of the sky; the Moon is leprous as snow:
> Trembling & descending down seeking to rest upon high Mona:
> Scattering her leprous snows in flakes of disease over Albion.
> The Stars flee remote: the heaven is iron, the earth is sulphur,
> And all the mountains & hills shrink up like a withering gourd,
> As the Senses of Men shrink together under the Knife of flint,
> In the hands of Albions Daughters, among the Druid Temples.
> (*J* 66:74–84, E217/K703)

Blake insists that the rationalistic, Newtonian world view is but a mask for "Druid" cruelty (Mona is the Druid center on the Isle of Man), and rather than translating reality into poetic anthropomorphism, he suggests by his imagery that our conventional idea of it is disastrously *de*-anthropomorphized. The heavens reel, bleed, and shrink (like Jonah's gourd) in withering sickness, and our perceiving senses shrink with them. Thereafter, instead of seeing the universe as human, we reject that vision as merely "poetic" and doggedly try to see it as inhuman.

In orthodox religious myth this dehumanization is reflected in a progression of fallen symbols:

> The Divine Vision became First a burning flame, then a column
> Of fire, then an awful fiery wheel surrounding earth & heaven:
> And then a globe of blood wandering distant in an unknown night.
> (*J* 66:41–43, E216/K702)

Here are Moses' burning bush, the pillar of fire of Exodus, the fiery wheel of Ezekiel's second vision,[56] and perhaps the moon that "became as blood" in Revelation 6:12 (also Acts 2:20). Each image is filled with the vitality of flame, unlike the dead objects of Ulro, but none is fully human. These are transformations of vision within the orthodox religious tradition, which venerates them as special divine visitations instead of recognizing that they are degradations of the Divine Vision. But the "globe of blood" indicates the potential of symbols for bursting into life again. If fallen vision sees it as a Newtonian sphere wandering in the void, imaginative vision knows it to be the measure of humanized existence as created by the imagination or Los:

> As to that false appearance which appears to the reasoner,
> As of a Globe rolling through Voidness, it is a delusion of Ulro. . . .
> The red Globule is the unwearied Sun by Los created
> To measure Time and Space to mortal Men, every morning.
> (M 29:15-24, E126/K516-517)

Here the symbol is alive, but *it remains a symbol.* Los is fallen, and so is the universe of time and space. The humanized globe is a richer and truer symbol than the burning bush or the pillar of fire, but it is not an unambiguous picture of reality.

The same is true of the lark in *Milton*, often mentioned by admirers of Blake who wish to refute the accusation that his poetry slights the natural world.

> The Lark sitting upon his earthy bed: just as the morn
> Appears; listens silent; then springing from the waving Corn-field! loud
> He leads the Choir of Day! trill, trill, trill, trill,
> Mounting upon the wings of light into the Great Expanse:
> Reecchoing against the lovely blue & shining heavenly Shell:
> His little throat labours with inspiration; every feather
> On throat & breast & wings vibrates with the effluence Divine. . . .
> (M 31:29-35, E129/K520)

Here is a real lark such as Blake no doubt heard at Felpham, but it precipitates an epiphany that immediately withdraws from the "natural" world into symbolic meaning, just as larks do in fact rise out of sight and furnish poets with imagery of song pouring from an unseen, aerial source. For Shelley, as for Blake, the vision is associated with light and fire, and implies a release from the familiar world:

> Higher still and higher
> From the earth thou springest

---

[56] As Stevenson notes (*The Poems of Blake*, p. 768n).

Like a cloud of fire;
   The blue deep thou wingest,
   And singing still dost soar, and soaring ever singest.[57]

The "inspiration" of Blake's lark is an overt reference to its metaphorical significance. Like the poet, it rises in a vision of light (though the "shining heavenly Shell" suggests that it remains imprisoned within the fallen universe, Blake's "mundane shell"). No sooner is the earthly image imagined than it becomes invisible to ordinary sight, and, like the heavenly host in the sun, combines form and color with song. The lark is not significant in itself, as an actual bird, but as a symbol of prophetic inspiration, which is made clear a little later in the image of a relay of larks as heavenly messengers. "To Immortals, the Lark is a mighty Angel" (*M* 36:12, E135/K527). The lark in *L'Allegro* sings from "his watch-tower in the skies," and Blake illustrates the line with a golden-winged angel soaring aloft.[58]

The phrase "effluence divine" is derived from the first lines of Book III of *Paradise Lost*, where Milton uses it in abstract theological terms: he fears to express his vision of God "unblam'd" and talks of him as too bright to look at. Since Blake humanizes light (the sun as singing angels rather than light inexpressible) he describes the inspired bird as participating in the effluence, not as blinded by it. Milton speaks a little later of the nightingale singing darkling (III. 38-40), an eloquent suggestion of himself as blind poet that evokes the traditional grief of the nightingale. Blake, on the contrary, introduces the passage about the lark with the line, "Thou hearest the Nightingale begin the Song of Spring" (*M* 31:28). It is wrong to ascribe pain to the nightingale, and wrong to see the lark as a symbol of song descending from blinding light. Milton uses visual images to suggest the superior status of an invisible God; Blake uses them to suggest the superior status of a humanized perception that knows images for what they are. The passage about the lark is "a Vision of the lamentation of Beulah" (*M* 31:63, E130/K521), the pastoral world that lacks the imaginative vitality of Eden. As Bloom comments, what to Generation looks like a song of spring seems to Eden an autumnal lament of Beulah (E838). And the reason is that the recurrence of spring, even in the gladness of its songs, is a symptom of the cyclical prison of the fallen world.

In thus transforming the images of experience, Blake's idealist aes-

[57] "To a Skylark." Is it possible that the last line is an ironic reply to Swift's vision in "The Progress of Poetry" of the poet as a goose that "singing flies, and flying sings/ While from below all Grub-street rings"?

[58] See the color reproduction in Raine, *Blake and Tradition*, II, 160, and Grant's commentary in Essick, pp. 426-429.

thetics goes far beyond the familiar Romantic reciprocity of subject and object that Wordsworth and Coleridge postulated. It is true that they, like Blake, appreciated the creative function of imagination. Whereas Pope or Thomson might use natural objects as an analogue for moral reflections, the Lake Poets understood that the mind endows what it sees with life.

> To every natural form, rock, fruit or flower,
> Even the loose stones that cover the highway,
> I gave a moral life: I saw them feel,
> Or linked them to some feeling. . . .[59]

But Wordsworth also held that nature has an existence in itself, of which man is but a part. He did not claim that it exists *because* man gives it a moral life.

When we notice, and rightly admire, Blake's use of natural images, we should remember as well what they are not.

> What want we? have we not perpetual streams,
> Warm woods, and sunny hills, and fresh green fields,
> And mountains not less green, and flocks and herds,
> And thickets full of songsters, and the voice
> Of lordly birds, an unexpected sound
> Heard now and then from morn to latest eve,
> Admonishing the man who walks below
> Of solitude and silence in the sky?[60]

Both the thought and the meditative music—filled with anticipatory echoes of Stevens' *Sunday Morning*—are radically un-Blakean. Blake's symbolism works at every point to liberate us from fallen existence, to reject its griefs and failures as mere illusion. Losing a loved brother, Wordsworth writes in the *Elegiac Stanzas*, "Not without hope we suffer and we mourn." Losing a loved brother, Blake pictures him in *Milton* as a mirror image of himself though inhabiting the realm of Eternity (plates 32 and 37) and writes to a patron that after thirteen years "with his spirit I converse daily & hourly in the Spirit" and "write from his Dictate" (E678/K797).

We shall return later to the ways in which Blake tries to overcome or deny suffering and mourning. What he most disliked in Wordsworth was the belief that the mind was "fitted" to the external world.[61] In Blake's terms Wordsworth is the poet of Vala, and after returning to the established church—which Blake must have regarded

[59] *The Prelude*, III.124-127 (1805 version), III.130-133 (1850).
[60] Wordsworth, *The Recluse: Home at Grasmere*, lines 126-133.
[61] See above, p. 40.

as entirely predictable—the poet of Rahab as well. Contrariwise, the Wordsworth whom Blake admired was the Platonizing poet of the *Intimations Ode*, which he praised when Robinson read it to him (*Blake Records*, p. 544). Natural appearances (songbirds, fields and sky) are never adequate in themselves. They do not even *exist* in themselves. They exist insofar as they are perceived imaginatively, which means that they receive both existence and significance from the Divine Imagination. Everything is subsumed in the myth because it only has value in dynamic relationship with the other elements of the myth.

The extended parallelism of Hebrew and English names in Blake's poems indicates their interchangeability: symbolic systems are mutually translatable since they receive their meaning from the unity of the Divine Imagination. The list of places on plate 16 of *Jerusalem*, for example, has caused irritation because it is only a list, but that is just Blake's point: for a believer the biblical names are resonant with meaning, and for an Englishman the English names are resonant too. A sunset "behind the Gardens of Kensington/On Tyburns River" is humanized by being perceived as "clouds of blood," and is then available as a symbol of Jesus: "in the Sun, a Human Form appeard/And thus the Voice Divine went forth upon the rocks of Albion" (*J* 43:2-5, E189/K653). The visible phenomena of Blake's England are but the tools of his art. In a daring metaphor, the Thames itself becomes the "black trough" in which he quenches the red-hot iron of his forge (*J* 16:14, E158/K636).

Blake struggles arduously to find appropriate symbols and to hammer them into shape, and is certain of what he has to tell if not of how best to tell it. Consider the example of the Mundane Shell. Schematic though it is in scholarly exposition, this symbol has its origin in an emotional response to the perception of the heavens as a prison, a palpable obstacle that presses in upon the beholder. When it is intellectualized as an infinite space in which the stars twinkle onward into infinity, then for Blake it becomes a vision of despair, the more horrible if people believe Newton's claim that it confirms divine benevolence.[62] The stars must not be perceived as dead matter suspended in emptiness; they must be human, which is to say that they must help us to see through the constricting shell to a living realm beyond. As has been excellently said of Gnostic speculation, "What seems to have struck men's gaze, during the long night of Egypt, was above all the element of obscurity in the heavens, of vastness, of omnipresence, the heavy opacity of this blackness that covered almost all of the sky. It

---

[62] As, for instance, in Addison's popular hymn that begins, "The spacious firmament on high."

hung like a veil, a wall of shadow encircling our earth, a murky circle through which, in places, the brilliant fires of another world escaped through crevices, faults, apertures. A gigantic black lid seals up our universe and grips us with its opacity."[63] To shatter this nightmare of imprisonment Blake reconceives the "shell" in various ways. It can be the egg from which the immortal soul breaks free, as in the sixth emblem in the series *For the Sexes* (E260/K765). And still more audaciously, it can be combined with the Polypus and the Zoas as an image of the human face.[64] Likewise, the stars are not fires that show through the shell but are singing angels. The visible world is made into a symbol and in that form can be transcended; Blake might say that the Gnostics knew the right questions but failed to understand that in Jesus they could have found the answer.

Blake's myth thus rests upon symbols in a peculiarly uneasy and equivocal way, as is apparent in his distrust of natural seeing coupled with his firm refusal to dispense with the metaphor of vision. The spectator on his fiery chariot of imagination is urged to "Enter into these *Images*" (E550/K611), and vision or imagination is "a *Representation* of what Eternally Exists" (E544/K604). Such a representation is the *Vorstellung* that Hegel criticizes as a limitation in art and religion, as contrasted with the pure concept (*Begriff*, a "grasping" of the truth) toward which the spirit advances.[65] Blake appreciates the limitations of symbols but believes that we must live in them. Accordingly, his attitude toward particular symbols is haunted by suspicion. As Alfred Kazin has said of his intellectual life, "It was the isolation of a mind that sought to make the best of heaven and earth, in the image of neither."[66] The status of natural images is vividly suggested in the tenth illustration to Gray's *Progress of Poesy*, in which Fancy pours out seductive but dangerous forms of the visible world for the poet Dryden, whom Blake undoubtedly regarded as hopelessly uninspired.[67]

Thus Blake recognizes the force of indictments of myth like that of Cassirer: "Myth rises spiritually above the world of things, but in the figures and images with which it replaces this world it merely substitutes for things another form of materiality and of bondage to

---

[63] Jacques Lacarrière, *Les Gnostiques* (Paris, 1973), pp. 16-17.

[64] In the picture on *Milton* 33 (E132/K523); this is discussed below, p. 128.

[65] The example of Hegel is relevant because he is just as critical as Blake is of deductive or positivist reasoning. "In Science we progress to ever more adequate modes of *conceiving*, not to new truths deductively entailed by previous truths" (J. N. Findlay, *Hegel: A Re-Examination* [London, 1958], p. 86).

[66] Introduction to *The Portable Blake* (New York, 1946, repr. 1968), pp. 2-3. Blake's symbols "stand apart from the natural world and defy it" (p. 19).

[67] See Irene Taylor's discussion, *Blake's Illustrations to the Poems of Gray*, pp. 91-92.

things.''[68] But there is no way out; symbols are all we have in the poverty of our world. I believe that a parable of this dilemma is embodied in the lovely tempera painting *Adam Naming the Beasts* (see fig. 6).[69] Adam stares straight at the viewer with an unwavering gaze, his lips slightly parted but not open, as if the naming were mental and need not be uttered. The beasts still inhabit a peaceable kingdom as they march to the left. Above Adam's head an oak bears fully grown acorns, suggesting perhaps the onset of winter (though seedtime and harvest were simultaneous in Paradise) since there are some bare trees in the right background. Elsewhere in Blake's myth the oak is the druidical tree and Christ is crucified upon it. Meanwhile, the serpent twines about Adam's left arm and he strokes its head with his left hand.

Clearly this is a vision of entrapment in the material world; and perhaps one can go further and propose that in the very act of *naming*, in choosing human symbols with which to represent experience, man has committed himself to the Fall.[70] But having said so much, one must recognize also that after the Fall, symbols are essential for spiritual life. In the watercolor of 1807 entitled *The Fall of Man* (see fig. 7), Christ leads Adam and Eve protectively out of Eden beneath "the Father indignant at the Fall," while below them "the Lion seizes the Bull, the Tiger the Horse, the Vulture and the Eagle contend for the Lamb" (E662/K441). Here are the contrary beasts of *The Marriage of Heaven and Hell* (e.g., tigers of wrath and horses of instruction), here are three of the four evangelist-Zoas (lion, bull, and eagle, the fourth having the face of a man), and here is the central symbol of the saving Lamb, persecuted by a Promethean vulture and defended by the eagle of inspiration. The serpent meanwhile continues to wreathe the fatal tree (hung with apples) while Michael seizes its neck and brandishes his fiery sword.[71] In short, the beasts not only have names but have become the active, competing symbols of the world of experience. And as Zoas they receive meaning from myth: Ezekiel's vision by the

[68] *Mythical Thought*, p. 24.

[69] There is a color reproduction in Paley, *William Blake*, pl. 77. This text (Gen. 2:19) was often invoked, both by Puritan writers and by theorists of scientific language, to prove that Adam enjoyed a perfect correspondence between words and things in a world as yet uncorrupted by the emotive imprecision of metaphor (see Stanley E. Fish, *Surprised by Sin: The Reader in Paradise Lost* [Berkeley, 1971], p. 113 ff.). Blake inverts this position: to name the beasts at all is to testify to the fact of the Fall. The fawn in *Alice* flees from her in terror when they emerge from the wood where things have no names.

[70] In *Paradise Lost* Adam says that in naming the beasts "I found not what methought I wanted still" (VIII.355)—that is, Eve. In Blake's terms this expresses very exactly the fall into sexual division, which will occupy us at length in Chapter 5.

[71] The theological implications of this picture are discussed below, pp. 277-278.

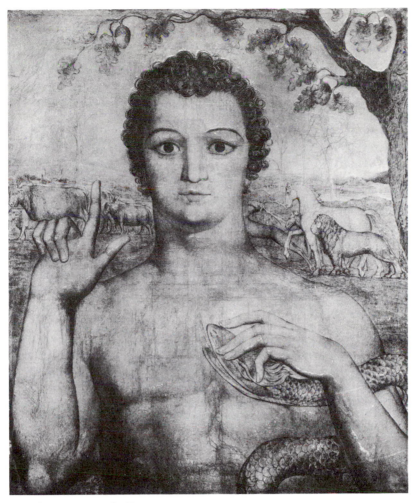

6. *Adam Naming the Beasts*.

river Chebar, John's re-creation of it in Patmos, and Blake's full-scale adaptation of it in his myth of the self. He has taken over the expulsion story from Genesis and remythologized it.

MYTH AND ALLEGORY

Given the equivocal status of symbols as images of the fallen world and windows into the unfallen world, the task of interpretation is peculiarly difficult. In one sense their meaning is fixed by their inventor, for Los (or Blake) hammers them out on the anvil and they mean

7. *The Fall of Man.*

what he wants them to mean. In another sense, however, they are "given" to him and their meaning is not immediately transparent.

> But Milton entering my Foot; I saw in the nether
> Regions of the Imagination; also all men on Earth,
> And all in Heaven, saw in the nether regions of the Imagination
> In Ulro beneath Beulah, the vast breach of Miltons descent.
> But I knew not that it was Milton, for man cannot know

What passes in his members till periods of Space & Time
Reveal the secrets of Eternity. . . .

(*M* 21:4-10, E114/K503)

In literal terms Blake is influenced by Milton but does not realize it; in
symbolic terms, his union with the spirit of prophecy, Milton/Los/
Jesus, has occurred without his at first understanding it.[72] He is a prisoner of space and time, below Beulah and (so he seems to say) below
even Generation, in the blindness of Ulro.

Blake forges his symbols but must also learn to interpret them. The
ongoing project of building and rebuilding the prophetic books is not
so much didactic as hermeneutic, a dramatization of the poet's own
struggle to understand. We, in turn, must interpret. Having considered the source and status of Blake's symbols, we must now try to
understand how they communicate their meaning to us.

Before examining some representative examples, it will be well to
look at the much-invoked distinction between allegory and myth or
symbol. It is usual in Blake studies to denounce offending interpretations as allegorical while presenting one's own as symbolic. To an out-
sider it may appear that all interpretations are in fact allegorical; as a
radical theologian protests, ''Even Blake's ablest interpreters again and
again fall back on a simple allegorical translation of Blake's symbols—despite the fact that Blake violently attacked such allegorical
thinking and insisted that it represents the antithesis of 'Vision.' ''[73]
Now, if even the ablest critics do this, it is easy to suspect that Blake's
practice encourages it, whatever his theory may say to the contrary.
And indeed, hostile discussions of Blake's poems constantly refer to
his symbols as murky allegorical abstractions.

Blake's own treatment of the issue is less dismissive of allegory than
is usually claimed. He attacked "Fable or Allegory" as an inferior kind
of poetry inspired by the Daughters of Memory, contrasting it with
inspired "Vision or Imagination" (*VLJ*, E544/K604). On this basis all
of the Greek myths are allegories, representing as they do a set of poetic fictions that ratify the fallen world. "Jupiter usurped the Throne of
his Father Saturn & brought on an Iron Age & Begat on Mnemosyne
or Memory The Greek Muses which are not Inspiration as the Bible is.
Reality was Forgot & the Vanities of Time & Space only Rememberd
& calld Reality. Such is the Mighty difference between Allegoric Fable

---

[72] On the complexity of Blake's sense of relationship with Milton, see Joseph Anthony Wittreich, Jr., *Angel of Apocalypse: Blake's Idea of Milton* (Madison, 1975).

[73] Thomas J. J. Altizer, *The New Apocalypse: The Radical Christian Vision of William
Blake* (East Lansing, 1967), p. xii.

& Spiritual Mystery" (E545/K605). One should notice, however, that this is a distinction between kinds of interpretation, not between interpretable allegories and uninterpretable symbols. The mistake of "Memory" lies in tying symbols down to the phenomena and events of the fallen world. Insofar as the literary genre known as allegory is open to imaginative rather than rationalist intepretation, it is *ipso facto* visionary: "Fable or Allegory is Seldom without some Vision. Pilgrims Progress is full of it the Greek Poets the same" (E544/K604). For this reason Blake can cheerfully tell Butts that his poems are a "Sublime Allegory" and go on to say, "Allegory address'd to the Intellectual powers, while it is altogether hidden from the Corporeal Understanding, is My Definition of the Most Sublime Poetry" (K825; not in E). Fallen reason is blind, but the imaginative "intellect" is not.

Blake's symbols call for interpretation just as much as do those of a groveling, "artificial" allegorist. The real question is the nature and scope of appropriate interpretation. If we leave aside Blake's theory and glance at modern accounts of allegory, it will be apparent that his poems are indeed allegorical in any useful sense of the term. But in a very interesting way he seeks to merge allegory with symbolic myth, compelling it to convey meaning while resisting its tendency to restrict itself to narrow didactic meaning. If allegory is ordinarily "a technique of controlled or stipulated meaning,"[74] then Blake's allegories are most unusual. But although he is not the kind of allegorist whose meanings are controlled by preexisting doctrine, neither is he the kind of symbolist whose images are infinitely open-ended and indefinitely suggestive.

Blake's position is closely bound up with his suspicion of the validation of symbols in sense experience. In Coleridge's definition of allegorical signification, "The difference is everywhere presented to the eye or imagination while the likeness is suggested to the mind." Or as Jonathan Culler elaborates the point, "Allegory . . . is the mode which recognizes the impossibility of fusing the empirical and the eternal and thus demystifies the symbolic relation by stressing the separateness of the two levels."[75] But this sounds very much like Blakean symbolism, which continually disturbs our imaginations with its aggressive strangeness. After Satan seizes the harrow of Palamabron and reduces his servants to drunken confusion, "Los took off his left sandal placing it on his head,/Signal of solemn mourning" (*M* 8:11-12, E101/K488). This is a symbolic action that demands a gloss, not a "natural" repre-

---

[74] Nohrnberg, *The Analogy of the Faerie Queene*, p. 93.

[75] Coleridge, *Miscellaneous Criticism*, ed. T. Raysor (London, 1936), p. 30. Culler, *Structuralist Poetics* (Ithaca, 1975), p. 230.

sentation. Would an exemplar of the poet in Wordsworth put a sandal on his head? Even in *The Marriage of Heaven and Hell,* for all its rhetoric of sensual enjoyment, the phenomena of this world are used to shock us into imaginative liberation. "I then asked Ezekiel, why he eat dung, & lay so long on his right & left side? he answerd, the desire of raising other men into a perception of the infinite" (E38/K154).

We begin to see that in Blake's poetry two aspects of the allegory/ symbol distinction are merged in a singular way. On the one hand, he denies any direct and unintellectualized relation between signifier and signified; as we have seen, he tends to suggest that the symbol requires the activity of the intellect to be understood, though of course he distinguishes imaginative intellect from Urizenic reason. In Coleridge's sense, therefore, he is certainly an allegorist. On the other hand, he is equally opposed to the tendency of allegory to use its symbols as simple, univalent counters chosen arbitrarily to illustrate predetermined truth. So in this sense he can only be described as a symbolist.

In religious terms (and Blake's terms are ultimately religious) he rejects dogmatic allegory while remaining deeply suspicious of sacramental symbol. M.-D. Chenu has shown that allegory in the Middle Ages was often a defense *against* symbolism, preferring the hard clarity of doctrinal verity to the openness of symbolic suggestion. In Chenu's terms Blake is heir to the symbolist Platonism of Dionysius, while allegory is influenced by the very different Platonism of Augustine and Boethius that emphasized sign instead of symbol.[76] The problem with any "anagogical" interpretation of Blake's symbols is that medieval anagogy aimed beyond symbols to an invisible reality. Thus Richard of St. Victor: "A symbol is a gathering [*collectio*] of visible forms for the demonstration of the invisible. Anagogy is the ascent or elevation of the mind for supernatural contemplation."[77] Blake claims to move within rather than above, and rejects the notion of invisible forms. Yet on the other hand he is unwilling, at least after the *Songs of Innocence,* to envision a genuinely sacramental relation between symbol and truth. If "the whole material world is held to be sacramental in the sense that material signs and channels of grace are everywhere, always available,"[78] then Blake can hardly be comfortable with a hermeneutic tradition that sees symbols as communicating the goodness of the

---

[76] *La Théologie au douzième siède* (Paris, 1957), p. 128.

[77] *In Apocalypsim,* quoted by Barbara Nolan, *The Gothic Visonary Perspective* (Princeton, 1977), p. 37.

[78] Mary Douglas, *Natural Symbols,* p. 27. E. D. Hirsch, Jr., gives a sensitive interpretation of the sacramental status of Innocence in *Innocence and Experience: An Introduction to Blake* (New Haven, 1964, 2nd ed. Chicago, 1975).

Creator of the material world. Blake's universe is the bungled product of a fallen demiurge, and symbols are dangerously misleading unless the Divine Imagination intervenes to control them.

This deep ambivalence toward symbols underlies many of the difficulties in Blake's myth. When it is most allegorical, he is trying to force it to do his bidding; when it is most symbolic, he hopes that by sharing in the Divine Vision we can see the truth without constant signposts to show us the way. It has been said that true myths "always strike us like the pronouncements of an anonymous voice, intimate and forceful," and that "we never acknowledge a myth as such unless it is a myth belonging to someone else."[79] In other words, our own mythic systems are so fully internalized that we regard them as simple reality. True though this may be for cultural myths, it does not work for Blake's, which is filled throughout with his individual voice even while he asserts that it describes what occurs within all men. By constantly altering his myth and by imploring us to make it our own, Blake hopes to stave off the inevitable decay of myth into allegory. Emerson says in his essay "The Poet" that "the history of hierarchies seems to show that all religious error consisted in making the symbol too stark and solid, and was at last nothing but an excess of the organ of language." And he objects elsewhere to Swedenborg, in terms that Blake would heartily approve, that his system "wants central spontaneity; it is dynamic, not vital, and lacks power to generate life."[80] It is both busy and dead; motion is not necessarily living activity.

Creating a system, Blake always runs the risk of becoming its prisoner instead of its master, and we would do well to admit that sometimes his symbols degenerate into hieroglyphs. Frye calls *Jerusalem* a "dehydrated epic";[81] at times it is positively anhydrous. The remedy, as Emerson says, is to keep symbols alive by resisting the systematic impulse, but that in turn implies an indefiniteness of meaning that appealed to the New England transcendentalist much more than to Blake. Even if all symbols are united in Jesus, fallen men should be wary of assuming that they understand them. Emerson can say breezily, "The central identity enables any one symbol to express successively all the qualities and shades of real being. In the transmission of the heavenly waters, every hose fits every hydrant."[82] From Blake's

---

[79] Pierre Smith, "The Nature of Myths," *Diogène*, 82 (1973), 71, 72.

[80] "Swedenborg; or, the Mystic." Later in the same essay Emerson adds, "The warm-many-weathered, passionate-peopled world is to him a grammar of hieroglyphs, or an emblematic freemason's procession. How different is Jacob Behmen!" Blake says, "Any man of mechanical talents may from the writings of Paracelsus or Jacob Behmen, produce ten thousand volumes of equal value with Swedenborg's" (*MHH*, E42/K158).

[81] *Fearful Symmetry*, p. 359.   [82] "Swedenborg; or, the Mystic."

point of view such a statement betrays an abject sell-out to the maimed and degraded symbols of this world, and is a facile evasion of the task of interpretation.

Blake is thus confronted with the fundamental problem of symbolism. In Ricoeur's terms, when we "live in" symbols they are vital but incoherent; when we "think from" them they collapse into allegorical *gnosis*.[83] The solution, if it exists, is to resist the reification of symbols and to hold them suspended in living interaction, as in Blake's symbol of the interpenetrating life of the Zoas. But this ensures that the symbols will often be in conflict. As Ricoeur says elsewhere, "The world of symbols is not a tranquil and reconciled world; every symbol is iconoclastic in comparison with some other symbol, just as every symbol, left to itself, tends to thicken, to become solidified in an idolatry."[84]

It is odd that so many Blakeans insist on the seamless unity of his myth when they themselves celebrate the conflict of contraries and recognize that Blake's symbol for life in Eden is mental warfare. If we are content to read the poems passively, letting the symbols reverberate without examining them closely, we may be able to ignore the antinomies that are built into the myth. But as soon as we try to understand the myth—as at every point we are urged to do—the old tension between symbol and allegory reasserts itself. It has been said that "There are universal symbols, like the sun for God, water for purity, or blood for life, but there are no universal allegories."[85] Not only is this true of Blake's symbolic allegory, which is mute until it is interpreted, but it is true as well of his allegorical symbols. He revalues every one of these examples—the humanized sun, the water of materiality, the blood of the fallen body—and we understand them only after an arduous process of exegesis and reflection.

"MOCK ON" AND INTERPRETATION

As Blake understands his symbols their interpretation is a complex process, calling for the simultaneous presence of two kinds of insight. We must appreciate the importance of, and aspire to share in, an immediacy of vision that apprehends the oneness of truth in Jesus; and we must recognize the limitations of the symbols that attempt to convey that vision. Seeing the sun symbolically, we learn to weigh and judge the various possible symbols that the sun may evoke. To a mode of vision we must thus join an art of interpretation. My purpose here

[83] *The Conflict of Interpretations*, pp. 297-299.
[84] *The Symbolism of Evil*, p. 354.
[85] Peter Fingesten, *The Eclipse of Symbolism* (Columbia, S.C., 1970), p. 126.

is to discuss the kind of interpretation that Blake demands, and then to point to some of the more prosaic considerations that an interpreter needs to bear in mind.

Every one of Blake's symbols has the dual quality of pointing to the infinite and yet falling short of it, and every symbol has to be interpreted in itself and in context. To see how Blake thinks this ought to be done, let us consider a short poem that is expressly concerned with contrary modes of vision:

> Mock on Mock on Voltaire Rousseau
> Mock on Mock on tis all in vain
> You throw the sand against the wind
> And the wind blows it back again
>
> And every sand becomes a Gem
> Reflected in the beams divine
> Blown back they blind the mocking Eye
> But still in Israels paths they shine
>
> The Atoms of Democritus
> And Newtons Particles of light
> Are sands upon the Red sea shore
> Where Israels tents do shine so bright
>
> (E468/K418)

To the fallen eye the sands are like the atoms or light corpuscles of physics; individuality is sameness, since in Newton's own words the rays of light differ from each other "like as the sands on the shore."[86] Blake hates Democritean atomism both for its reductiveness and for its determinism—the ceaseless, meaningless, irreversible rain of atoms through the void. In a bitter attack on the "Rational Power," Blake makes the Spectre speak of "fortuitous concourse of memorys accumulated & lost" (J 29:8, E173/K659). The phrase can be traced to Cicero's account of the *concursus fortuitus* of atoms in Democritus.[87] Not only is such a theory determinist; in its very conception it assumes the primacy of the *it* in scientific thought, in opposition to everything Blake believes about the human universe. As Bruno Snell comments, "Democritus knows only one voice of the verb, the passive, and only one person, the third."[88]

[86] Quoted by Charles C. Gillispie, *The Edge of Objectivity: An Essay in the History of Scientific Ideas* (Princeton, 1960), p. 132.

[87] See Stevenson, *The Poems of Blake*, p. 682n.

[88] *The Discovery of the Mind: The Greek Origins of European Thought*, trans. T. G. Rosenmeyer (Cambridge, Mass., 1953), p. 241.

We see symbolically. The fallen eye sees the sand as a symbol of Ulro deadness. To the imaginative eye it shines in the sunlight like jewels, an identification enhanced by the usage in which "atom" could mean—as it does in Shelley—"one of the particles of dust which are rendered visible by light; a mote in the sunbeam."[89] And the sands of the desert have their symbolic value as the setting for spiritual activity, the imaginative Exodus that will culminate in arrival at the Promised Land.

But this lyric is about more than the distinction between two kinds of vision, though that is certainly involved.[90] It is also a comment upon the positive value of the Enlightenment's critique of Christianity. Hume, just as much as Blake, showed that there could be no natural religion, and Blake freely asserts after reading Bishop Watson's attacks on Paine, "It appears to me Now that Tom Paine is a better Christian than the Bishop" (E609/K396). Hume called for a rejection of "celibacy, fasting, penance, mortification, self-denial, humility, silence, solitude, and the whole train of monkish virtues."[91] So did Blake. Peter Gay remarks that Christianity taught man to be a son dependent on a paternal God, while the Enlightenment taught him to be an adult dependent on himself.[92] Blake would approve. In his poem *The French Revolution*, the shivering "spectres of religious men" are driven out of their abbeys by "the fiery cloud of Voltaire, and thund'rous rocks of Rousseau" (14:274-76, E294-95/K146). But in purging Christianity of its errors the *philosophes* failed to appreciate its imaginative truth. When Paine in conversation called religion "a law & a tye to all able minds," Blake retorted that "the religion of Jesus was a perfect law of Liberty" (*Blake Records*, p. 531).

Thus the mockery of Voltaire and Rousseau (antagonists united by Blake as equally deistical) has positive effects even though they are too blinded to understand what they have done. Every sand *becomes*, not *is*, a gem, as the *philosophes* throw it into the wind and cause it to sparkle in the light.

> Rahab created Voltaire; Tirzah created Rousseau;
> Asserting the Self-righteousness against the Universal Saviour,
> Mocking the Confessors & Martyrs, claiming Self-righteousness.
> (*M* 22:41-43, E116/K506)

[89] OED definition, as noted by Wasserman, *The Subtler Language*, p. 334.

[90] As acutely analyzed by Ault, *Visionary Physics*, pp. 54-56, 145-147.

[91] David Hume, *An Inquiry Concerning the Principles of Morals*, ed. Charles W. Hendel (New York, 1957), IX.i, p. 91.

[92] *The Enlightenment: An Interpretation*, vol. II, *The Science of Freedom* (New York, 1969), p. 174.

Voltaire was educated by the Jesuits (Rahab, the Whore of Babylon, the fallen church), Rousseau claimed to be a child of nature (Tirzah, the fallen realm of the senses). Blake says elsewhere that Voltaire was "as intolerant as an Inquisitor" (*VLJ*, E553/K615), resembling the enemy he attacked; the context of the passage in *Milton* makes it clear that in assailing repressive religion the Enlightenment condemned itself to reaction instead of creative growth. Blake despises the *philosophes'* critique of religion not because it is radical but because it is not nearly radical enough. Like Carlyle he rebukes them for a merely destructive campaign that ignores the true value of myth. "Wilt thou help us to embody the divine Spirit of that Religion," Carlyle demands of Voltaire, "in a new Mythus, in a new vehicle and vesture, that our Souls, otherwise too like perishing, may live? What! thou has no faculty in that kind? Only a torch for burning, no hammer for building?"[93] Los is Blake's builder. Whereas the *philosophes* saw Christianity as merely symbolic, Blake sees it as supremely symbolic. Dogmatic doubt hid from their eyes the philosophical truth of the myth.

What Blake has to show, therefore, is that religion has perverted symbolism rather than inventing it, and that a symbolism cleansed of "mystery" is the necessary condition of a perception of truth. So in "Mock on" he deftly indicates first that the *philosophes* do in fact think in symbols even if they do not know it (the atoms of Democritus being precisely that) and then that the same symbols, understood imaginatively rather than positivistically, open the mind to truth. As Blake told Crabb Robinson, Voltaire was "commissioned by God" to expose the natural sense of the Bible so that it could be understood in its spiritual sense (*Blake Records*, p. 322).

By throwing symbolic explanations out with the bath water, the *philosophes* were left with the world of sense perception and nothing more, which is to say that despite their attacks on natural religion they were in the end its victims.

> Are those who contemn Religion & seek to annihilate it
> Become in their Feminine portions the causes & promoters
> Of these Religions, how is this thing? this Newtonian Phantasm
> This Voltaire & Rousseau: this Hume & Gibbon & Bolingbroke
> This Natural Religion!
>
> (*M* 40:9-13, E140/K532)

Similarly in the *Song of Los* Urizen gives the "Philosophy of Five Senses" to Newton and Locke, whereupon "Clouds roll heavy upon

---

[93] *Sartor Resartus*, II.ix.

the Alps round Rousseau & Voltaire" (4:16–18, E66–67/K246). And from this it is but a short step to a realization that the mocking philosophers, far from inspiring the French Revolution, were the servants of the Female Will and the cause of its failure.

> Her Two Covering Cherubs afterwards named Voltaire &
> Rousseau:
> Two frowning Rocks: on each side of the Cove & Stone of Torture:
> Frozen Sons of the feminine Tabernacle of Bacon, Newton &
> Locke.
> For Luvah is France: the Victim of the Spectres of Albion.
> (*J* 66:12–15, E216/K702)

Only the imaginative Los can free man from the skeptical blindness of this deist religion that sees "limits" as natural necessity instead of as temporary structures set up by the merciful Jesus to arrest man's fall.

> Voltaire insinuates that these Limits are the cruel work of God,
> Mocking the Remover of Limits & the Resurrection of the Dead,
> Setting up Kings in wrath: in holiness of Natural Religion
> Which Los with his mighty Hammer demolishes time on time. . . .
> (*J* 73:29–32, E226/K713)

In *Candide* Voltaire amuses himself by showing that the Manichaean myth, as espoused by the bleak valet Martin, is superior to the Christian one. Clearly Voltaire thinks that it is foolish to accept any myth, and hints at the need for demythologizing. Blake too goes back to the Gnostics, but neither uncritically like Martin nor skeptically like Voltaire. He shows that Voltaire has a myth of his own whether he knows it nor not ("Rahab created Voltaire") and that it would be better to face openly the complexity of mythical thinking instead of trying in vain to get rid of it.

"Mock on" is a lyric, not an argument, but it epitomizes the function of symbol in Blake's thought. "Israels tents" are evocative because Blake rejects the literal historicism of Christians like Bishop Watson and insists on the Bible as myth. The Promised Land is a condition of achieved vision, not a place (either in this world or the next) reserved for the elect. "To me who believe the Bible & profess myself a Christian a defence of the Wickedness of the Israelites in murdering so many thousands [of Canaanites] under pretence of a command from God is altogether Abominable & Blasphemous. Wherefore did Christ come was it not to abolish the Jewish Imposture. . . . Christ died as an Unbeliever, & if the Bishops had their will so would Paine" (E603–604/K387). The Bible does not make sense when it glorifies ancient battles in the Middle East; on this point Blake is in perfect

agreement with Gibbon.[94] The Bible makes sense when it expresses
the spiritual significance of tents or tabernacles that move from place
to place as their users move with them—"Where Israels tents do shine
so bright"—and are not rigidified, like the holy of holies of Solomon's
Temple, into a "feminine Tabernacle" closed off from man by covering cherubs. In the words of the author of the Epistle to the Hebrews,
Abraham sojourned by faith "in the land of promise, as in a strange
country, dwelling in tabernacles with Isaac and Jacob, the heirs with
him of the same promise: For he looked for a city which hath foundations, whose builder and maker is God. . . . Therefore sprang there
even of one, and him as good as dead, so many as the stars of the sky in
multitude, and as the sand which is by the seashore innumerable"
(Heb. 11:9-12). In his vision of light Blake saw "Each grain of Sand"
as a human form (E683/K804), and he uses the image of the tent to
symbolize imaginative vision.

> The Sky is an immortal Tent built by the Sons of Los
> And every Space that a Man views around his dwelling-place:
> Standing on his own roof, or in his garden on a mount
> Of twenty-five cubits in height, such space is his Universe. . . .
>
> (M 29:4-7, E126/K516)

Bloom comments, "The sky is a tent on the analogue of the tents of
Israel in the Wandering; like those tents it is moved each time the di-
vinely led imagination of man chooses to move it" (E836).

The same complications that surround the "Mock on" lyric are
evident in Blake's most famous use of the grain of sand:

> To see a World in a Grain of Sand
> And a Heaven in a Wild Flower
> Hold Infinity in the palm of your hand
> And Eternity in an hour[95]

The presiding assumption of empiricist philosophy, supported by
classical ethics, was the limitation of human understanding. In Pope's
words, " 'Tis but a part we see, and not a whole." In the vast universe
man is confined to an insignificant corner, "His knowledge measur'd
to his state and place,/His time a moment, and a point his space."[96]

---

[94] "The conquest of the land of Canaan was accompanied with so many wonderful
and with so many bloody circumstances, that the victorious Jews were left in a state of
irreconcilable hostility with all their neighbours. They had been commanded to extir-
pate some of the most idolatrous tribes, and the execution of the Divine will had seldom
been retarded by the weakness of humanity" (Edward Gibbon, *The Decline and Fall of
the Roman Empire* [New York: Modern Library, n.d.], ch. 15, I, 386).

[95] *Auguries of Innocence* (E481/K431).

[96] *Essay on Man*, I.60, 71-72.

Against this very reasonable position Blake proclaims the presence of
infinity in a moment and eternity in a point.[97] What does he mean?

It is easy to see what Blake is against: the "variable finite," infinity
defined as the finite that can always be pushed one step further. In this
he is directly following the Platonists, who despised the variable finite
as "the irrational, evil, essentially formless or flowing principle, which
has to be dominated by 'the One' or 'the Limit' in order to give rise to
everything intelligible or good."[98] What science regards as infinity,
Blake abhors as chaos, and his entire philosophy, like his aesthetics, is
founded on the idea of coherent form or limit, the "hard and wirey"
line that separates reality from chaos. The ordinary spatial metaphor is
mistaken, according to Blake: time is not a line stretching on for ever,
and space is not indefinite extension. "What is Above is Within"
(*J* 71:6, E222/K709), which means that eternity and infinity are comprehended within the human imagination. In the printing house in
Hell, the eagle of inspiration "caused the inside of the cave to be infinite" (*MHH*, E39/K154); the cave is Blake's perennial symbol of the
fallen world and fallen mind, but it can open out (or in) into infinity.
And therefore the tiniest particle, like the grain of sand of the atomists,
contains the universe within itself. In Boehme's words, "When I take
up a stone or clod of earth and look upon it, then I see that which is
above and that which is below, yea, I see the whole world therein."[99]

Living in a world of time and space, we cannot escape it outright,
but we can transform it imaginatively. To some extent this is because,
as Hazard Adams says, "All space is inner and contained by the perceiver just as the grain of sand contains the whole."[100] But it is essential to realize that the grain of sand, though symbolizing the infinite
world, cannot actually take us there.

> There is a Grain of Sand in Lambeth that Satan cannot find
> Nor can his Watch Fiends find it: tis translucent & has many Angles
> But he who finds it will find Oothoons palace, for within
> Opening to Beulah every angle is a lovely heaven. . . .
>
> (*J* 37:15-18, E181/K668)

[97] The four verbs in these lines are often read as infinitives, which would mean that
the sentence never reaches its completion. But John Grant suggests that the last two
lines complete the first two: "In order to see a World and a Heaven, you must hold
Infinity and Eternity" ("Apocalypse in Blake's 'Auguries of Innocence,' " *Texas Studies
in Literature and Language*, 5 [1964], 493).

[98] J. N. Findlay, "The Notion of Infinity," in *Language, Mind and Value* (London,
1963), p. 148.

[99] Jacob Boehme, *Mysterium Magnum, Or, An Exposition of the First Book of Moses called
Genesis*, in the 1654 translation of John Sparrow (London, 1965, 2 vols. paginated as
one), p. 4.

[100] *William Blake: A Reading of the Shorter Poems* (Seattle, 1963), p. 34. Adams rather

Beulah is intimately involved with the fallen world, though in its most paradisal form, and its comforting visions are temporary stays against disaster rather than images of Edenic freedom. The weeping female who unites all the Emanations takes "a Moment of Time" and draws it out into a rainbow, making of it "a door to Eden." Likewise she takes an "Atom of Space" and opens it as "a Center/Into Beulah" (*J* 48:30-39, E195/K678). Both the moment and the point or atom are symbolic of our fallen world of indefinite time and space; the idea is to pare them down to their smallest fraction and then to revitalize them in imagination. Much the same notion is employed in Jonas's account of the Gnostics, who see in time "what Heidegger calls the 'moment' (*Augenblick*): moment, not duration, is the temporal mode of *this* 'present,' " in a fallen world that is "a derivative and 'deficient' mode of existence."[101] To understand the moment for what it is must be the prelude to breaking through it.

Once again Stephen Dedalus sees what Blake is trying to do: to deny the reality of the "real" world and to escape from it through a grain of sand or a drop of blood. "Space: what you damn well have to see. Through spaces smaller than red globules of man's blood they creepycrawl after Blake's buttocks into eternity of which this vegetable world is but a shadow. Hold to the now, the here, through which all future plunges to the past."[102] And if the grain of sand can be the symbol of liberation, it is always threatened by the nihilistic atomism of the mocking philosophers, so that it is equally suited to symbolizing the hopeless separateness of the isolated selfhood. Searching through the interior of Albion's bosom with "globe of fire" in hand, Los sees men's souls being molded into the inert bricks of the pyramids of Egyptian tyranny. And if the bricks should disintegrate, individual souls would flow in the gutters like so much dirt:

[Los] saw every minute particular, the jewels of Albion, running
    down
The kennels of the streets & lanes as if they were abhorrd.

---

weakens his analysis, though, by saying later that "all things are mental projections" (p. 41). If reality is within, then the metaphor of "projection" is a false externalization.

[101] *The Gnostic Religion*, p. 336. Similar formulations are common in mystical tradition. Eckhart says that God creates all things *in eine gegenwurtigen Nun* (an ever-present Now), and speaks of everything being present in a single moment and point, *alle miteinander in eine Blicke und in eine Punte*, very much as in Blake's symbolism of the moment and the grain of sand (quoted by Rufus M. Jones, *Studies in Mystical Religion*, pp. 228, 230).

[102] Joyce, *Ulysses*, p. 186.

Every Universal Form, was become barren mountains of Moral
Virtue: and every Minute Particular hardend into grains of sand.
(*J* 45:17–20, E192/K657)

This is the false universal of abstract, Satanic generality; as we have
seen, the minute particulars can sustain their living identity (as opposed to their isolated selfhoods) only in Jesus "the Only General and
Universal Form" (*J* 38:20, E183/K672).

It is a truism that Blake's symbols are multivalent. So are all symbols except the barest signs. Interpretation has then to ask two questions: Are any limits placed on the range of possible meanings? and,
Are there any principles by which the interpreter can prefer one meaning to another? In practice, to be sure, Blake's critics argue with great
vehemence for particular meanings, but in theory they tend to make
much of the multivalence of his symbols. This is partly due to Blake's
own theory of the individuality of perception, but as I have tried to
show, the theory distinguishes between true and false perceptions
rather than encouraging idiosyncrasy. In addition this attitude derives
from widespread assumptions about the positive value of multivalent
symbolism, often extolled as our best line of defense against positivist
reductionism. So we hear pronouncements like this one: "Blake holds
up an exemplary art, an art of poetic tales, because such forms are neutral. They can mean anything."[103] I deny it; they can mean many
things, but not *anything*.

What is really at issue is the familiar modern claim that every poem
is unique (and irreplaceable) in its symbolic openness. In Wheelwright's formulation, "The semantic function of poetry consists
largely in this: that poetry quickens and guides men's associative faculty, keeps it in athletic trim, and thus actually generates new
meanings—meanings that would lose their identity outside the context of the individual poem, but which are authentically real within
that context."[104] It is quite true that each new context is important for
Blake's meanings, but whatever may be the case in some kinds of
poetry, his poems are not discrete universes of special meanings that
can be intuited only in their unique expressions. His myth is built up
as a whole, and each part of it helps to control our understanding of
the other parts. Blake wants to tell us the truth, and although one aspect of that truth is that symbols are treacherous guides, he does not
expect us to interpret them in any way that happens to please us, much

---

[103] Jerome J. McGann, "The Aim of Blake's Prophecies," in Curran and Wittreich, p.
14.
[104] *The Burning Fountain*, p. 101.

less to dismiss the whole issue of interpretation as irrelevant. Of course, Blake could be wrong, but I shall argue that he is not, and that we can properly seek, though we may often fail to achieve to everyone's satisfaction, a standard of interpretation of his poems. Blake's symbols are multivalent but not omnivalent.

Let us conclude with some examples. First, a symbol whose multiple meanings are fairly clearly defined: the serpent. Essentially it is the serpent of Eden and the phallus, but both of these associations are transvalued in Blake's special conception of the Fall and of sexuality. In addition the serpent represents the natural world, which for Blake is synonymous with the fallen body of man, an association that makes all sorts of connections possible. Laocoön can be seen as man trapped in fallen nature, and various biblical serpents, some traditionally interpreted as types of Christ, can be ironically conflated. Northrop Frye, the most brilliant guide to this aspect of Blake, expounds a few of these associations as follows:

> Orc, or human imagination trying to burst out of the body, is often described as a serpent bound on the tree of mystery, dependent upon it, yet struggling to get free. The erection of the brazen serpent in the wilderness therefore represents in disguised form the more clearly symbolic story of the earlier poem. The energy of Orc which broke away from Egypt was perverted into the Sinaitic moral code, and thus is symbolized by the nailing of Orc in the form of a serpent to a tree. This was a prototype of the crucifixion of Jesus, and the crucifixion, the image of divine visionary power bound to a natural world symbolized by a tree of mystery, is the central symbol of the fallen world.[105]

Since the serpent sheds its skin it is also symbolic of immortality, an idea which can be negative if it means endless cycles of death-in-life, positive if it suggests spiritual immortality. And a wide range of other suggestions are called upon whenever Blake finds them useful: the dragon of the Apocalypse, the Covering Cherub of Ezekiel, the serpent of matter upon which the alchemist works his transformations.[106]

The crucial point is that Blake's serpent, like the alchemists', undergoes transformations rather than random or inexplicable change. To say what a given symbol means in Blake's work is impossible except in an extended essay on its various specific meanings, but those mean-

[105] *Fearful Symmetry*, pp. 136-137. In this connection, see Blake's picture *Moses Erecting the Brazen Serpent* (pl. 73 in Paley, *William Blake*, with commentary on p. 56).

[106] On this last, see Milton O. Percival, *William Blake's Circle of Destiny* (New York, 1938), pp. 213-214.

ings exist, established by their contexts, even if Blake sometimes furnishes too few clues to let us be certain of them. The serpent symbol functions in two essential ways: as an increasingly conventional sign that we learn to recognize with confidence whenever we see it, and as an example, in the very process by which we learn to interpret it, of the factitious and limited nature of all symbolism. As a sign, it can be used in a kind of rapid shorthand: "When Luvah in Orc became a Serpent he descended into/That state calld Satan" (*FZ* 115:26-27, E366/K351). Orc is the fallen form of Luvah; the "Orc cycle" (as Frye has definitively named it) is a type of the Crucifixion; the Crucifixion implies a voluntary descent by Jesus into the "state" of Satan. All of this can be very elliptically expressed because the reader has learned to read the symbol confidently. The same thing is true, incidentally, when we "read" the symbol in a picture like the design for *Paradise Lost* in which Michael foretells the Crucifixion (see fig. 8), where the same nail that pins Christ's feet to the cross impales the head of the serpent that twines around it. Beneath the cross are the prostrate forms of Urizen/Satan and Vala/Rahab; Adam adores the crucified Christ while Eve sleeps below. A serpent wound round the cross is a traditional symbol of Christ crucified, with reference to Moses and the brazen serpent in Numbers 21: 8.[107] Blake conflates the two images to provoke the viewer into going beyond allegorical identification to ask what it *means* that Christ should be imaged as a serpent.

Even as we learn to understand Blake's symbols, we are made to see that they are only symbols. In a striking passage in *Europe*, the King of England seeks out his druidic "temple serpent-form'd," and Blake goes on to evoke the zodiac as a delusion of the fallen senses "Turn'd outward, barr'd and petrify'd against the infinite." Immediately afterwards he adds, "Thought chang'd the infinite to a serpent" (10:2-16, E62/K241). Since the mind has degraded the infinite into a serpent (and institutionalized it in serpent-temples), it must now break through the symbolic fiction to the truth that it partly expresses but partly obscures.

Just as Blake expects us to learn what his symbols mean, so he expects us to cast a critical eye on their status in various mythologies. Consider, for instance, the often-mentioned connection between Christ, Prometheus, and Luvah/Orc. The connection is important, but it is not presented (as is sometimes supposed) in a kind of pan-mythic eclecticism in which every symbol accumulates analogues like a snowball. On the contrary, one must be struck by significant differ-

[107] Gertrude Grace Sill, *A Handbook of Symbols in Christian Art* (New York, 1975), p. 26. As early as *America* Blake identified this image of Christ with the serpent of Genesis: "The terror answer'd: I am Orc, wreath'd round the accursed tree" (8:1, E52/K198).

8. *Michael Foretells the Crucifixion*, illustration for Milton's
Paradise Lost.

ences as well as similarities. The Prometheus story certainly admits of
analogy with Christ, since it tells of a god who suffers on behalf of
mankind; patristic writers like Tertullian interpreted it so. But Christian theology, not to mention Blake's, wholly repudiates the idea of
suffering as an unjust punishment inflicted by a cruel God or Fate. And
more than that, Christ is a very different figure from the thief of fire
who brings man an essential but forbidden gift (warmth, civilization,

even thought itself, since "Prometheus" means "the fore-thinker"). Moreover, the Greek Prometheus suffers in heroic resistance rather than redemptive love; he is far from the "suffering servant" in Isaiah who is the type of Christ.[108] In his *Marriage of Heaven and Hell* period Blake may have entertained a "Romantic" idea of Satan and Prometheus, but by the time he became seriously interested in Christ while revising *The Four Zoas*, the analogy with Prometheus was taken in just the spirit that Tertullian took it. All myths are a partial embodiment of truth, but they are not synonymous. The Prometheus unjustly tortured by a degraded God (the fallen Jehovah of Blake's myth) has different symbolic connotations from the Christ who voluntarily chooses to accept incarnation and consequent crucifixion.

Thus Blake transforms the myth of Prometheus instead of simply using it. In the classical story Prometheus occupies a kind of absolute space, his rock of agony filling our imaginative vision. In Blake he plays a symbolic role in a larger structure, and since the structure itself is constantly open to reinterpretation, so is the symbol. In the Preludium of *America* (see fig. 9), Orc is stretched like Prometheus on his rock, but above him is a tree bent into a hollow cavelike shape, with a man and a woman in the posture of Adam and Eve at the Expulsion—alluding to the very different myth of Genesis—and beneath him are the tree's humanized roots. The Prometheus symbol is undergirded here by other symbols, or is shown breaking down into them. The rock is not absolute; the viewer gazes down upon it, and it is really only the surface of the ground, with roots below instead of the empty wasteland of the Caucasus.

To understand what all of this means, we are compelled to invoke the larger contexts of Blake's myth. This Eve and Adam can easily be seen as Enitharmon and Los after their son is bound with the chain of jealousy:

> Lo! the young limbs had strucken root into the rock & strong
> Fibres had from the Chain of Jealousy inwove themselves
> In a swift vegetation round the rock & round the Cave
> And over the immortal limbs of the terrible fiery boy
> In vain they strove now to unchain.
>
> (*FZ* 62:22–26, E335/K309)

If indeed the Oedipal relation between Orc and Los is implied here,[109]

---

[108] I follow the admirable analysis of R.J.Z. Werblowsky, *Lucifer and Prometheus: A Study of Milton's Satan* (London, 1952), esp. pp. 60–64.

[109] See below, p. 215. One cannot be sure how much of this myth had been developed at the time of *America*, but the later Blake would certainly interpret the picture in terms like these.

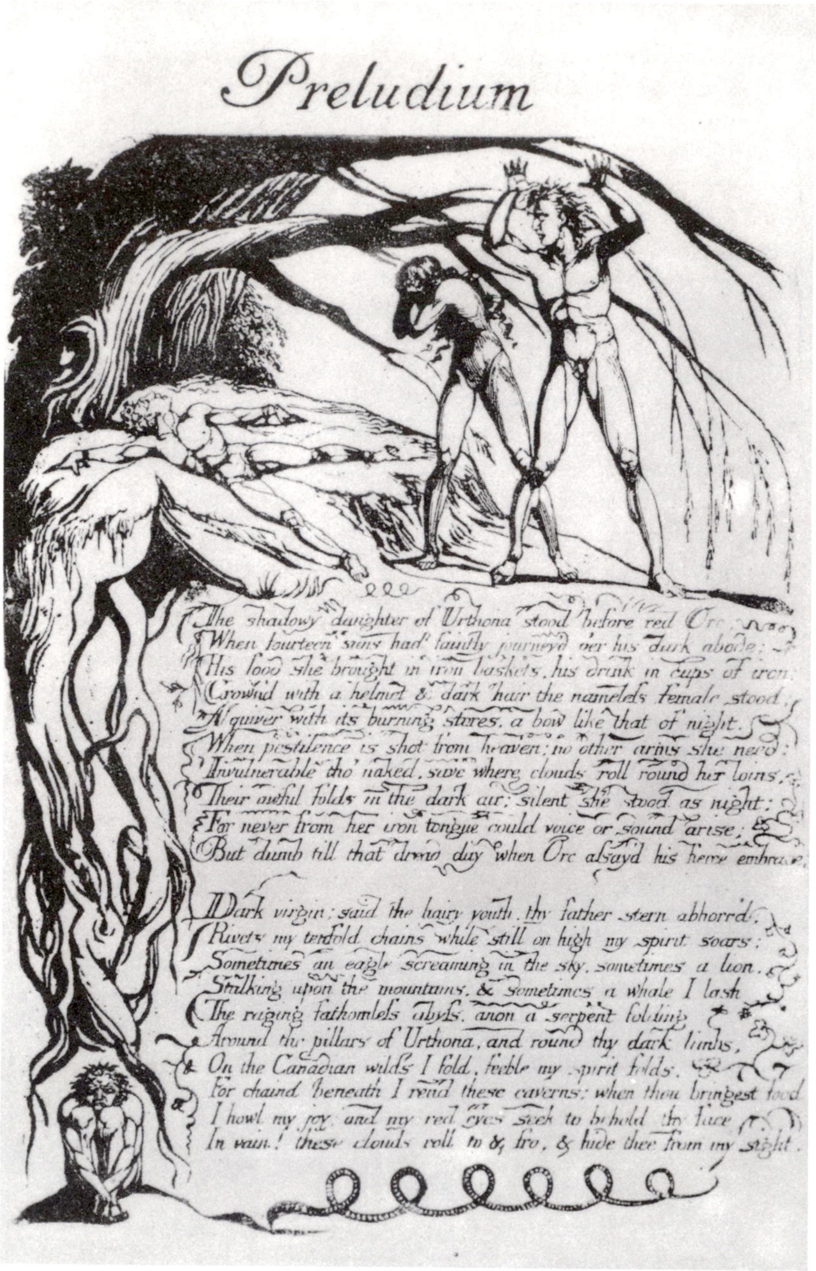

9. *America*, Preludium.

then Blake is giving us a complex conflation of the Prometheus myth with his own reinterpretation of the Fall of Man. Prometheus the Forethinker has brought a knowledge of good and evil which has precipitated the Fall, or more accurately is synonymous with the Fall. From this follows sexual division, with Orc the embodiment of libidinal energy in the fallen world, and his position on the rock is therefore the crucifixion of sexuality. The female figure (Enitharmon or Eve) is reminiscent of Mary Magdalen, whom Blake several times invokes in contexts of sexual guilt and penitence.

If we distinguish between iconic and dynamic symbols in Blake,[110] the serpent is an example of an iconic symbol which has more than one meaning, but whose meanings all conform to a single pattern. The relation between Prometheus and Christ is more equivocal, and calls for fresh reflection whenever it occurs. And most of Blake's symbols operate differently in different contexts. Consider the Mundane Shell. At one point it is described as a defense of Ulro against Los, who walks about outside it. At other points in the same poem it is built by Los himself.[111] There is no contradiction, because the shell is not made once and for all by a single agent, in the way that the Trojan Horse is constructed in the *Aeneid*. It is a symbolic representation of the starry heavens, with all that they imply. In one context the heavens are the Newtonian obstacle that excludes imagination and must be penetrated by it (as in the picture of "Milton's track" entering the Mundane Shell from outside, E132/K523). In another context they are the structure that Los builds, a bulwark against chaos. In both cases the shell is a symbol of fallenness; that never changes. But to say who *made* it or who *uses* it is very different from saying what it *is*.

At many points Blake's symbols are still more resistant to interpretation, either because he has not supplied adequate clues or because he wants to rouse the reader's faculties to act. But these instances do not reflect his typical practice; they are problems rather than triumphs. That is notoriously true of some of the gnomic lyrics. "The Blossom," for example, can be plausibly interpreted as symbolic of sexual experience, with the sobbing robin expressive of mother love; Hagstrum cites the proverb of Hell, "Joys impregnate. Sorrows bring forth." But it can also be interpreted Neoplatonically, as Hirsch does, as an account of the soul's demoralizing imprisonment in the body.[112]

---

[110] See above, p. 79.

[111] *J* 13:52-55, E156/K634; 42:78, E188/K671; 59:5-9, E206/K691.

[112] Hagstrum, *William Blake: Poet and Painter*, pp. 82-83; Hirsch, *Innocence and Experience*, pp. 181-184. In support of the idea that the poem deals with the suffering of generation and mortality, one might recall "Who killed Cock Robin?" with its confession, "I, said the sparrow, with my little bow and arrow. . . ." Writing for children in the *Songs of*

Both interpretations are plausible, but they are mutually contradictory: if the body is a prison, then it is not a source of joy. I do not believe that Blake intended both interpretations (or other possible ones) to be regarded as equally valid; I am sure he had a particular meaning in mind. In this case, however, he does not make it clear. Accordingly, one must be governed by a general sense of the meaning of "Innocence," which entails in turn a general theory of Blake's myth and of the place of "Innocence" in its development. Quite possibly Blake's own interpretation of "Innocence" and of "The Blossom" changed as his thought evolved. But at all events I would insist that there is potentially a right interpretation of a poem like "The Blossom," even if we cannot be sure what it is. And our interpretations should therefore be guided, as both Hagstrum's and Hirsch's are, by an attempt to present evidence that will enable a critical conclusion, not by claims that symbolism is so open-ended (either because all symbols are, or because Blake in particular sees a universe in each grain of sand) that every poem can mean anything at all.

The task of interpretation is implicit in the prophecies, and is epitomized in the questions in the Motto to the *Book of Thel*:

> Does the Eagle know what is in the pit?
> Or wilt thou go ask the Mole?
> Can Wisdom be put in a silver rod?
> Or Love in a golden bowl?
>
> (E3/K127)

In a fine piece of exegesis W.J.T. Mitchell traces a number of traditional connotations of eagles, moles, silver and gold, noting imagery of vision, authority, the brain, the nervous system, and the genitals. The lines demand to be unpacked in this way. But the real lesson, as Mitchell says, is that questioning and interpreting are obligatory. "It is precisely Thel's insistence on asking questions and striving for knowledge which identifies her as the only fully human character in the poem."[113] The questions posed in the Motto are meaningless until they are interpreted, which means finding the contexts in which they can make sense. The act of interpretation is the active questioning that characterizes the imagination.

We are called upon to realize Blake's meaning in both senses of the word: to recognize it and to make it real. Blake would say that we do

---

Innocence, Blake might well expect them to associate robins and sparrows with the familiar nursery rhyme.

[113] *Blake's Composite Art: A Study of the Illuminated Poetry* (Princeton, 1978), pp. 85-86, 88.

so by participating in the Divine Body of Jesus. More prosaically, we may say that in accordance with E. D. Hirsch's concept of "shared types," we learn to see implications that belong to Blake's meanings just as recognizable traits belong to types.[114] There are at least three possible answers to the question of how Blake expects us to share his types. (1) He draws on an unconscious reservoir of archetypes which we share without knowing it (as in the various Jungian readings of Blake). (2) He teaches us to share his types by repeating them in so many variations and contexts that we gradually learn them, as we would a language. (3) He frustrates our ordinary expectations by withholding the necessary validation, provoking us into an epiphanic experience that forces us to re-create the types for ourselves (as in the more apocalyptic theories of reading Blake) or impelling us to hurl his book away in disgust (as recommended by various readers hostile to Blake).

My view is that there is some validity in each of these positions. (1) Blake believed that he drew upon archetypes, and we understand him best if we know that he believed that, whether or not we believe in them ourselves. In more conventional terms, Blake appeals to our experience of religious and poetic tradition, and exploits symbolic associations with which we are or could be familiar even if we are not fully aware of them. (2) We have to learn to interpret Blake's symbols, to get inside them and make them our own, so that reading him is a long (potentially a lifelong) process of interpretation. This is of course true of any great writer, but it is true of Blake in an unusually demanding way. (3) At times and to some extent—the nature of the experience will vary from reader to reader—the symbols remain frustratingly opaque, by which I mean that we can surmise what he meant by them but cannot our selves enter into them; we behold them with puzzled detachment, the one attitude most destructive of a successful reading of Blake. "If the Spectator could Enter into these Images in his Imagination approaching them on the Fiery Chariot of his Contemplative Thought . . . then would he arise from his Grave then would he meet the Lord in the Air & then he would be happy" (*VLJ*, E550/K611). Everyone who loves Blake has had personal experience of something like this, of a breakthrough into sudden understanding. But sometimes, unhappily, our chariot remains grounded.

The remainder of this book will explore some philosophical reasons for the knottiest problems in Blake's myth, the problematic meanings and shifts in meaning that often baffle interpretation. My thesis will be

---

[114] *Validity in Interpretation* (New Haven, 1967), pp. 64–66. Hirsch postulates a connection between the "willed type" of the author and the "shared type" that is common to author and reader.

that they give trouble because they cannot be coherently reconciled, not because they depend upon a mode of symbolism that transcends ordinary understanding and reconciles apparent antinomies with suprarational ease. My guiding assumption is that Blake's difficulties are evidence of his immense genius. Rather than accepting one or another of the compromise solutions that have been developed over the centuries, he aspired to put the entire structure of Western thought back together again. If he failed, it was where none have succeeded and where only the greatest have ventured at all.

I must emphasize, finally, that in drawing attention to Blake's conceptual dilemmas I do not regard him as incoherent. Insoluble philosophical problems need not , and usually do not, give rise to uninterpretable poetry. The problem in *Paradise Lost* is logically insoluble: why should an omnipotent and benevolent God permit the existence of evil? The orthodox answer was that we cannot tell; faith and our emotions assure us that there is no problem, even as reason confesses its impotence to resolve it. *O altitudo*! exclaims St. Paul—"O the depth of the riches both of the wisdom and knowledge of God! how unsearchable are his judgments, and his ways past finding out!" (Rom. 11:33). *Paradise Lost* fails to resolve the problem, but the poem is fully interpretable. Blake responded with exceptional insight to Milton's poem; it claims to justify the ways of God to men, and Blake saw that it had not done so. It is in fact one of a series of ever less convincing theodicies, from Leibniz through Bishop King and Pope's *Essay on Man*, that made theodicy itself a laughingstock in the intellectual world of the Enlightenment. When Blake places as epigraph to his *Milton* the line "To Justify the Ways of God to Men" (E94/K480) he is being at once deeply ironic and heroically daring. His aspiration is no less than to succeed where Milton had failed.

WORDS AND PICTURES

There is no doubt whatever that Blake, for whom "vision" was the model of imaginative activity, had a powerful visual imagination, and that his conceptions must often have begun in pictorial rather than verbal form. No doubt too these images were rendered vivid and memorable by the "distinct, sharp, and wirey . . . bounding line" (*DC*, E540/K585) that was always Blake's pictorial ideal. In committing these images to paper, however, Blake gave them symbolic form exactly as he did when he sought verbal equivalents for imaginative experience; the living form is perceived by intellectual vision rather than by the bodily eye, and requires interpretation just as poetry does. This is not to say that each art does not have its proper media and

methods, though Blake seldom deals directly with the differences between the arts; one wishes he had commented on Lessing's *Laokoön*.[115]
But all of the arts are committed, in Blake's opinion, to expressing the
same visionary truths, and those truths are so clearly symbolic and intellectual that he constantly reiterates his hatred of chiaroscuro, naturalistic coloring, and anything else that might seduce the viewer into
accepting the images of Vala's world.[116]

Blake's doctrine of the wiry outline thus postulates an art that
means but does not imitate, as in his praise of Dürer's woodcuts for
being "everything and yet nothing" (*Blake Records*, p. 315). Outline is
meaning in art just as melody is in music: "Nature has no Outline: but
Imagination has. Nature has no Tune: but Imagination has!"[117] To
copy nature is therefore to attempt a pointless "deception" and to betray the function of art: "A Man sets himself down with Colours &
with all the Articles of Painting he puts a Model before him & he
copies that so neat as to make it a Deception. Now let any Man of
Sense ask himself one Question: Is this Art. can it be worthy of admiration to any body of Understanding."[118] As Malkin wrote in 1806,
"He professes drawing from life always to have been hateful to him;
and speaks of it as looking more like death, or smelling of mortality"
(*Blake Records*, p. 423). When very rarely Blake uses naturalistic perspective, it is to drive home a moral point about the destructive illusions of Experience.[119]

---

[115] David Bindman thinks that Blake did not know of Lessing (*Blake as an Artist* [Ox-
ford, 1977], p. 106) and Mitchell remarks that in any case Lessing would have offended
Blake by accepting nature as the source of art and by emphasizing the differences between the arts (*Blake's Composite Art*, p. 34).

[116] Blake used color as well as line, and his theory seems to have held that the two are
complementary as female and male, Enitharmon and Los: see Edward J. Rose, "The
Spirit of the Bounding Line: Blake's Los," *Criticism*, 13 (1971), 54-76. But Blake's attitude toward color is clearly expressed in the *Descriptive Catalogue* when he denounces
the "light and shadow" of the Flemish and Venetian painters and adds, "Mr. B's practice is unbroken lines, unbroken masses, and unbroken colours. Their art is to lose form,
his art is to find form, and to keep it" (E529/K573). Even the gorgeous colors in the late
copies of the *Songs of Innocence* obey this principle. Alan Cunningham observed as long
ago as 1830 that Blake "was a most splendid tinter, but not colourist" (*Blake Records*, p.
503). An interest in naturalistic coloring is a symptom of fallen vision: "That God is
colouring Newton does shew" ("To Venetian Artists," E507/K554).

[117] *The Ghost of Abel*, E268/K779.

[118] *Public Address*, E566/K597.

[119] See the city scene for "The Chimney Sweeper" in the *Songs of Experience*: there is
no room for visionary symbols here, only a bitter depiction of what the fallen mind sees
as real. Note also the absence of color: since the fallen world is illusory, it is blank in
contrast with the brilliant reds and golds of Innocence or the rainbow in the title page of
Visions of the Daughters of Albion. Solid tints are visionary; bleached colorlessness and
illusionistic "Venetian" coloring are both Satanic. It is worth remarking that in Blake's

Blake's insistence on copying works of art is part of the same set of ideas. It is a means by which to "copy Imagination."[120] The fact (a commonplace nowadays) that artists see in conventional images was for Blake a welcome escape from the trap of nature. Blake's characteristic mode is therefore hieratic and iconic, and is accurately described by an art historian as "a heraldic style that evokes the symbolic language of the Middle Ages."[121] A symbolic language has to be interpreted, and whatever its pictorial values may be, no competent art historian would claim that it can be adequately understood in purely visual terms. Some of Blake's images are conventional emblems, and he was of course familiar with the traditional emblematic code: "the tender maggot emblem of Immortality" (*FZ* 136:32, E389/K377). But it is worth remarking that the traditional meanings had often been lost by the end of the eighteenth century, depending as they did on a system of natural correspondences that no one believed in any more.[122] Blake as a professional artist had a remarkable command of the subject, but he was far from wedded to the handed-down exegesis of even the most familiar emblems, and to detect their presence in his pictures is never a sure guide to his meaning.

Even an apparently literal representation of a text or idea is seldom as simple as it seems. Consider the illustration (see fig. 10) of the lines in *Macbeth*,

> And Pity, like a naked new-born babe,
> Striding the blast, or heaven's Cherubins, hors'd
> Upon the sightless couriers of the air,
> Shall blow the horrid deed in every eye,
> That tears shall drown the wind.[123]

In their original context these lines have excited considerable critical debate, one result of which must be the recognition that they do not

---

practice the artist first conceives a design, then engraves it on metal, then prints it on a press, and only afterwards applies colors. To *begin* with a sensuous apprehension of coloration is disastrous. The imaginative eye perceives form above all.

[120] *Public Address*, E563/K594.

[121] Robert Rosenblum, *Transformations in Late Eighteenth Century Art* (Princeton, 1969), p. 158.

[122] As Alleau points out, both Jean-Baptiste Boudard in *L'Iconologie* (1759) and the great Winckelmann in his *Essai sur l'allégorie* (1766) grapple in vain with possible reasons for illustrating Fever by a woman on a lion, not realizing that fevers are associated with the sun's position in August in the zodiac. "The simplest and most evident cosmological interpretation seems no longer understood by Boudard or Winckelmann in the eighteenth century" (Alleau, *La Science des Symboles*, p. 173).

[123] *Macbeth* I.vii.21-25. The picture is reproduced in color in Raine, *William Blake*, p. 88, and in Klonsky, *William Blake*, p. 61.

10. *Pity*.

lend themselves readily to visualization.[124] The literalness of Blake's picture has often been remarked, each word or image receiving a pictorial equivalent (the horses have closed eyes to illustrate "sightless couriers"). It was usual in eighteenth-century verse to expect the reader to visualize personifications, and we know that Blake's friend Fuseli depicted literary similes in the same way that Blake does here.[125] Nevertheless, the full meaning of the *Pity* picture is unavailable to a viewer who knows nothing of Blake's thought. Who is the recumbent woman in the foreground? Mellor suggests persuasively that she is a mother dying in childbirth, symbolizing the division of the self upon entering mortal life, with a more immediate reference to

[124] In a famous essay in *The Well Wrought Urn* (New York, 1947), Cleanth Brooks argued that imagery of babes pervades the play and that the naked babe in this passage is at once helpless and avenging. Helen Gardner retorted in *The Business of Criticism* (Oxford, 1959) that this was to overinterpret and that the point of the lines is simply the human feelings they arouse, and the "world of appalling loneliness" that Macbeth fears having to enter (p. 61). Whatever the merits of their respective arguments, Brooks and Gardner both assume that the proper effect of the passage is emotive or symbolic rather than literal, and they show no interest in working out the images in a point-for-point visualization. Brooks, indeed, argues implicitly that the tendency of the images is contradictory (babe and avenging angel) so that it would be impossible to visualize them.

[125] See Bindman, *Blake as an Artist*, p. 106.

Macbeth's murderous breaking of human bonds.[126] This interpretation explains the strangeness of the tiny baby, in its characteristically Blakean pose of leaping with arms outstretched. But who is the woman on horseback who receives it so deliberately into her hands? Evidently one of the "cherubin," either mighty angels or baby cherubs (the point of disagreement between Brooks and Gardner); in Blake's picture they are neither. Mellor proposes that this is Enitharmon, whose "pity" is consistently described as possessive and destructive in Blake's poems, and the identification is at least plausible.

Thus Blake's art is fundamentally conceptual, and even an apparently literal visualization of a text by another poet is filled with philosophical ideas that can only be deduced through knowledge of the myth. Enitharmon cannot be detected by the uninstructed viewer. This is not to say that the picture cannot in some sense stand alone. And it is not to say that pity is inevitably bad; Blake refers at one point to the Divine Vision as "the ever pitying one" (*FZ* 71:25, E341/K316), and pity has a wide range of connotations in different contexts.[127] But this is as much as to say that it is not self-explanatory either in iconographic or in formal terms. If Rosenblum is right in claiming that "few of the countless studies of Blake are very revealing for the art historian,"[128] he betrays a serious defect in the intellectual curiosity of art historians, who would certainly not condone the ignorance of implication in Michelangelo or Raphael that is apparently acceptable for Blake.

Even within the circle of Blake studies, the pictures depend so intimately on verbal exegesis that glaring errors can easily persist in the

---

[126] *Blake's Human Form Divine*, p. 163.

[127] Thus in *The Four Zoas* pity is a positive force when it impels Los to reunite with his Spectre "first as a brother/Then as another Self" (85:28-30, E353/K328). More grimly, it is implicated in the separation of Enitharmon from the loins of Los or the Spectre of Urthona (50:14-17, E327/K300, recalling the *Book of Urizen* 13:51 ff.). When the Spectres of the dead descend into Ulro's night they pass through Enitharmon's "Gate of Pity" (99:23, E358/K341), so that it is involved with female sexuality and the realm of generation. And at times it has the wholly pejorative connotations of Experience, as when Urizen reads from his book of brass: "Flatter his wife pity his children till we can/Reduce all to our will as spaniels are taught with art" (80:20-21, E348/K323). That pity is limited even at its best is suggested by its complete absence in the ninth Night, after some two dozen references previously. After the Crucifixion, evidently, it no longer characterizes the Divine Vision.

[128] *Transformations . . .* , p. 155n. Rosenblum involuntarily illustrates the point by asserting that Blake's imaginary architecture "conforms closely" to the primitivist ideal of Boullée and Gilly, "including even representations of Stonehenge and dolmens (as in plates from *Jerusalem* and *Milton*)." An interest in dolmens may have been widespread, but Rosenblum evidently has no inkling of their profoundly negative place in Blake's symbolism.

absence of decisive extra-pictorial clues. *God Judging Adam* was known for years as *Elijah*, which is to say that its actual meaning is almost the opposite of what was long believed, and the identification of *Glad Day* has similarly had to give way to the very different implications of *Albion Rose*.[129] When the necessary clues are missing, controversy may well be interminable, as looks like being the case with the so-called *Arlington Court Picture*, a major painting that is named after its place of discovery for lack of certainty about its meaning.[130] Contrariwise, when we are certain of the subject and the broad outline of the meaning, we should not imagine that we have achieved our knowledge through unaided inspection of pictorial forms.

In short, Blake "painted ideas," as Kazin says, and the ideas cry out to be understood, even if they begin by being seen. When Arthur Symons told Rodin that Blake actually saw his visions, Rodin replied, "Yes, he saw them once; he should have seen them three or four times." Blunt comments, "Blake saw vividly, but he saw schematically. To express what he wanted to convey, a series of symbols was often enough, with the result that his works are sometimes *thought* rather than *seen*."[131] Apart from technical limitations that may have struck Rodin, it does not follow that this is a weakness. As Socrates told Phaedrus, "The productions of painting look like living beings, but if you ask them a question they maintain a solemn silence. The same holds true of written words; you might suppose that they understand what they are saying, but if you ask them what they mean by anything they simply return the same answer over and over again."[132] Socrates goes on to say that the spoken word is written on the soul and the understanding. Blake holds that the symbol, when fully received into the imagination, comes alive in the same way.

It is quite possible that Blake expected the reader or viewer to achieve a direct intuition of meaning, to understand *Pity* or the *Arlington Court Picture* without external aids. But if so, he presumed a commitment to visionary knowing which the modern viewer does

[129] See Martin Butlin, "Blake's 'God Judging Adam' Rediscovered," *The Burlington Magazine*, 107 (1965), 88-89, and Erdman's trenchant critique of the mislabelling of *Albion Rose* (*Blake: Prophet Against Empire* [Princeton, 1954, rev. 1977], pp. 7-11).

[130] Reproduced in color in Klonsky, *William Blake*, p. 105, and in Raine, *Blake and Tradition*, I, 74. Some sort of Neoplatonic symbolism is clearly involved, but the details remain obscure and have occasioned a debate too long and inconclusive to summarize here. As so often, the participants have been more interested in asserting definitive interpretations than in using the occasion to consider the nature and limits of reliable interpretation of Blake.

[131] Kazin, *Portable Blake*, p. 5; Anthony Blunt, *The Art of William Blake* (New York, 1959), p. 94.

[132] Plato, *Phaedrus*, trans. Walter Hamilton (Harmondsworth, 1973), p. 97.

not share and ordinarily does not believe possible, so that we are obliged to interpret as best we can. Yet I would not suggest that our interpretations should directly contradict the apparent pictorial meanings. A Blakean reading of *Pity* deepens an ordinary intelligent appreciation rather than wholly overturning it; Enitharmon's pity may be finally destructive but it is not despicable. And this is true even of works in which the Blakean meaning seems to fly in the face of customary associations. The painter Tom Phillips, reviewing a Blake exhibition, rightly reminds us that the frontispiece to *Europe*, called *The Ancient of Days* (see fig. 26, p. 265) and the *Newton* mean almost exactly the opposite to an unguided viewer from what Blake intended. This is not, however, due to a simple failure on Blake's part to anticipate the spectator's confusion, and it is wrong to call him "the evangelist who has seen something clearly, who utters it, and is mystified at any resistance to a transparent truth that he thought he had merely to pass on."[133] In these pictures Blake deliberately exploits the usual associations of the bearded God of Genesis and the classically beautiful human body, as well as of compasses as instruments of order and design. The symbolic meaning of the pictures is an interpretation that we bring to them by criticizing these associations, not an intuition that arises from the visual forms themselves. The majesty of God and the heroic beauty of Newton are really "there"; what is at issue is the attitude we are to take toward these feelings.

Just as his poetic symbols do, Blake's pictorial ones give rise to thought. When he told Robinson that the diagrams in Law's edition of Boehme were very beautiful and that Michelangelo could not have done better (*Blake Records*, p. 313), he meant what he said; he appears to have been increasingly concerned with conceptual rather than formal response, as is suggested by the surprising crudity of many of the plates in *Milton* and *Jerusalem*. Indeed the pictures in the late prophecies often seem incommensurate with the poetry, as Bloom has observed: "I read one of the most eloquent descriptive passages in the language, I stare, disbelievingly, at an inadequate engraved illumination and then try, too strenuously, to isolate an image that Blake, as a poet, knew better than to isolate."[134] As recent scholarship has made clear, the pictures are as likely to play off against the poetic image as to translate it directly, and they are often mysterious—even bizarre—in ways that the texts are not. It has been shrewdly said that "the thousand words that a picture is worth are mostly nouns and adjectives, whereas a

---

[133] "The Heraldry of Heaven and Hell," *TLS*, 24 Mar. 1978, p. 349.
[134] "Visionary Cinema of Romantic Poetry," *The Ringers in the Tower: Studies in Romantic Tradition* (Chicago, 1971), pp. 37-38.

story needs verbs."[135] Blake makes a virtue of this distinction, freezing his pictures into static shapes that require interpretation to be released into living movement again. Hegel observed after gazing at a waterfall, "The sensuous presence of the painting does not permit the imagination to expand the object that is represented. . . . Moreover, even in the best painting the most attractive and essential feature of such a spectacle would be missing: eternal life, the tremendous motion in it."[136] From a Blakean point of view this insight testifies to the necessity of visionary rather than mimetic art, dispensing with "sensuous presence" and aspiring to break through the iconic image to the "eternal life" in all things.

[135] John Szarkowski, *Looking at Photographs* (New York, 1973), p. 154.
[136] Diary of a journey in the Alps in 1796, in Walter Kaufmann, *Hegel: A Reinterpretation* (New York, 1966), p. 308.

[F O U R]

The Zoas and the Self

> The subject does not belong to the world; rather, it is a limit of
> the world.
>
> Wittgenstein, *Tractatus* 5.632

> No one who, like me, conjures up the most evil of those half-
> tamed demons that inhabit the human breast, and seeks to wrestle
> with them, can expect to come through the struggle unscathed.
>
> Freud, "Fragment of an Analysis of a Case of Hysteria"
> (*Works* VII, 109)

THE WARRING ZOAS

Blake's myth is above all else psychological. His cosmology,
theology, and even epistemology are all transpositions of the
central inquiry into the self. This is no disinterested quest.
Like many in his age Blake was haunted, if not obsessed, by dividedness within the self and between self and world. As Hegel said in his
first published work, division or discord (*Entzweiung*) "is the source of
the need for philosophy." And both Hegel and Blake were convinced
that harmony must be achieved by restoring the fruitful interaction of
opposites, not by abolishing them. "When the power of unification
disappears from the life of men and opposites have lost their living
relation and reciprocity and gain independence, then the need for philosophy originates."[1] The problem was to understand why the opposites should ever have gained independence, and to find a way of putting them together again.

The myth Blake developed was that of the four Zoas, actively
cooperative in Eternity, locked in civil war in the fallen state. But this
in itself cannot exhaust Blake's psychology, for it leaves unexamined
the status of the self of which the Zoas are the members, a self that is
extremely hard to deduce from the myth but is clearly greater than the
sum of its parts. After discussing the strife of the Zoas we shall
broaden the investigation by taking up two special topics, desire and
the will, as a prelude to attempting a comprehensive account of the self
in Blake.

[1] *Difference of the Fichtean and Schellingean System of Philosophy* (1801), quoted by
Kaufmann, *Hegel*, pp. 49-50.

It is tempting, and certainly not irrelevant, to draw parallels between Blake's myth and modern clinical experience:

> The term *schizoid* refers to an individual the totality of whose experience is split in two main ways: in the first place, there is a rent in his relation with his world and, in the second, there is a disruption of his relation with himself. Such a person is not able to experience himself "together with" others or "at home in" the world, but, on the contrary, he experiences himself in despairing aloneness and isolation; moreover, he does not experience himself as a complete person but rather as "split" in various ways, perhaps as a mind more or less tenuously linked to a body, as two or more selves, and so on.[2]

In the terms of Blake's myth these experiences are far from being illusions: it is precisely the case that the self falls into division when its elements cease to work in harmony, and it is literally not "at home" in the world since the world of fallen perception is a horrible swindle concocted by the mind.

In developing a system of symbols of psychic life, Blake's thinking was guided by a resolute rejection of hierarchy, which had been the basis of faculty psychology since the time of the Greeks. In his view, reason was that part of the self which enslaves, not that which orders the rest. In opposition to traditional psychic schemes, whether Christian or pagan, he therefore proposed a myth of dynamic vitality rather than of hierarchical order. The fall will be reversed when the warring elements learn to live in harmony again, not when any one of them attains mastery over the others. This myth exactly inverts the traditional psychology, since the supremacy of reason which Milton's Jesus promotes as the antidote to "anarchy within"[3] is, according to Blake, the very recipe for the anarchy that is provoked by reaction to tyranny.

Now, this rejection of hierarchy entails serious difficulties for Blake's model of the self, since if no faculty or element is predominant, it is hard to locate the "I" or to understand how it can will or act.

---

[2] R. D. Laing, *The Divided Self* (Harmondsworth, 1969), p. 17. Laing recommends study of Blake's prophetic books "not to elucidate Blake's psychopathology, but in order to learn from him what, somehow, he knew about it in a most intimate fashion, while remaining sane" (p. 162). Laing would undoubtedly appreciate Blake's opinion, as reported by the painter James Ward, that "there are probably men shut up as mad in Bedlam, who are not so: that possibly the madmen outside have shut up the sane people" (*Blake Records*, p. 268). In this chapter I shall treat Blake's myth of the self as an intellectual structure, reserving speculations on his personal experience for Chapter 7.

[3] *Paradise Regained*, II.471. See the description in *Paradise Lost* of appetite usurping sway over "sovereign reason" (IX.1125-31).

These matters will occupy us presently. Here we must make as much sense as we can of the Zoas themselves, and the first thing to notice is that they exist as such only in the fallen state:

And the Four Zoas who are the Four Eternal Senses of Man
Became Four Elements separating from the Limbs of Albion
These are their names in the Vegetative Generation
And Accident & Chance were found hidden in Length Bredth &
　　Highth
And they divided into Four ravening deathlike Forms.
(J 32:31-36, E177/K663)

This is the fallen world of Experience with its spurious categories that can only be dispelled when Jesus redeems man "And Length Bredth Highth again Obey the Divine Vision Hallelujah" (32:56).

Something very like this collapse of a fourfold self can be found in Boehme, who associates the parts with the four elements and cardinal points just as Blake does.[4] What no source would lead one to expect is the astonishing complexity and unpredictable shifts in implications of Blake's ever-growing cast of psychic characters.[5] And this is the essential point of adopting the vision of Ezekiel 1, the chariot of the Lord supported by four living creatures (the zōa of Revelation 4:6). It symbolizes a complex interaction that cannot be reduced to diagrammatic form.

The tradition of interpreting Ezekiel's vision as a Christophany derives from Irenaeus, who described the four living creatures as "images of the activity of the sons of God." Correspondences were soon worked out with the four evangelists, whose iconographic emblems were taken from the living creatures, as well as with the four cardinal points. As a recent survey of Christian symbolism reminds us, the "tetramorph" is hard if not impossible to visualize and must be handled symbolically rather than representationally.[6] The present form of

[4] "For he [Adam before the fall] stood in equal essence; but now, every astrum of every essence of all the creatures in man do depart from their mutual accord, and each steps into its selfhood; whence the strife, contrariety and enmity arose in the essence, that one property doth oppose itself against the other. Thus likewise the outward spirit of the outward astrum and four elements did presently domineer in them [Adam and Eve], and heat and cold were also manifest in their body; moreover, the property of all evil and good beasts: all which properties, before, did lie hidden" (<i>Mysterium Magnum</i>, ch. 20, p. 123).

[5] As G. E. Bentley, Jr., notes, the original version of <i>The Four Zoas</i> (entitled <i>Vala</i>) began with a relatively simple cast of characters, vastly enlarged in later additions (<i>Vala or the Four Zoas</i> [Oxford, 1963], pp. 171-175).

[6] "Following a habitual procedure of Semitic thought, which was to become generalized in the style of the apocalypses, the prophet accumulates, without care for picto-

Blake's Zoas is a symptom of fallenness, and the very conception of four creatures supporting a "higher" divinity is grievously misguided. This is surely the conclusion we are to draw from Blake's painting of *Ezekiel's Vision* (see fig. 11), in which only three of the "creatures" are visible in the triple-headed figure below whom a rapt Ezekiel reclines. Of course the fourth face might be looking away from us; but it is equally possible that it has been displaced to the top of the composition in the form of Urizen, who usurps supremacy: "Am I not God said Urizen. Who is Equal to me" (*FZ* 42:19, E322/K294). If the winged shapes recall the cherubim in the Temple of Solomon,[7] that fact is profoundly equivocal, for they are then associated with the Covering Cherub of the blocking selfhood and repressive law. Ezekiel has seen a theophany, not a Christophany; the figure with hand raised in benediction is Urizen/Jehovah, not Jesus. And true fourfold Zoas are displaced to the margins, the four faces gazing outward from behind the swirling whirlwind.[8]

By contrast, the unfallen Zoas are suggested on the fourteenth plate of the *Job* series, "When the morning Stars sang together" (see fig. 12). At the middle of the picture, a somber Urizen presides over the fallen world, with his solar aspect beneath his right arm and his lunar beneath his left—Satan/Apollo with the horses of the sun and Rahab/Diana with a pair of sexual dragons. Beneath them, in a cave formed by thick cloud, Job broods with his wife and misguided comforters. But this vision is not definitive. At the top of the picture, four angels sing with arms and hands alternating in a pattern of mutual concord (the left hand of the first figure meeting the right hand of the third, and so onward). In a watercolor version Blake made the sky a gorgeous blue, contrasted with isolated patches of color in the darkness below.[9]

---

rial effect, the most heteroclite symbolic features. It is these symbols and not their vehicular images that are juxtaposed to recreate the mental picture which the author wants to suggest" (Gérard de Champeaux and Dom Sébastien Sterckx, *Introduction au Monde des Symboles* [Saint-Leger-Vauban, Yonne, 1972], p. 433. Irenaeus is quoted at p. 430).

[7] As Bindman suggests (*Blake as an Artist*, p. 142).

[8] Directly above Ezekiel is a cycle of eyes which are presumably the Seven Eyes of God, the progressive revelation in Blake's system of the meaning of the divine (see below, pp. 255 ff.).

[9] There is a color reproduction in Raine, *William Blake*, p. 165. I am aware that S. Foster Damon interprets Urizen here as the Divine Imagination and that he sees the whole picture as symbolic of the Zoas, rather than of the fallen and unfallen states (*William Blake's Illustrations of the Book of Job* [New York, 1969], p. 38). My point is that to ignore the *fallenness* of the Zoas is to underestimate the seriousness of their errors, and to fail to appreciate how different their condition would be in a renewed Eden. My interpretation is close to that of Frye: "There are three levels in this plate: Job and his

11. *Ezekiel's Vision.*

In the uncolored engraving he had the inspiration of adding another
interlocking arm at each end of the series. The four angels in their interconnection represent the perfect equality of the unfallen Zoas, and
the figures at the margins suggest that the whole symbolism of the

friends are on earth; above them is a Demiurge or creator-God controlling the order of
nature, and above that is the infinite human universe, in which the morning stars and the
sons of God are the same thing" ("Blake's Reading of the Book of Job," in Rosenfeld, p.
233).

12. *The Book of Job*, plate 14.

tetramorph loses its significance in Eden, where hierarchical roles are irrelevant and the chain of singing figures can be imagined as infinite.

But the unfallen Zoas are remote from human experience, and Blake states flatly at the beginning of *The Four Zoas*, "What are the Natures of those Living Creatures the Heavenly Father only/Knoweth no Individual Knoweth nor Can know in all Eternity" (3:7-8, E297/K264). Likewise at the end of *Jerusalem* we are told that "The Four Living Creatures Chariots of Humanity Divine Incomprehensible/In beautiful Paradises expand" (98:24-25, E255/K745). Blake does not use

127

a word like "incomprehensible" loosely. In the fallen state we can know what the Zoas are because they are in us; Ezekiel saw them, though he partly misunderstood what he saw. In Eden, however, they "expand" into something very different. They no longer support the throne of divinity, but are all of them "Chariots of Humanity Divine." Blake does not say that this state is incomprehensible because God is ineffable; it is so because our fallen vision is not yet strong enough to see it clearly. The whole subject of Eden or Eternity remains deeply problematic in Blake's myth, but for the present it is enough to recognize that the Zoas as we know them are a condition of fallen existence.

In Blake's one schematic diagram of the Zoas (*M* 33, E132/K523), the four circles are tangential in such a way that at any point each Zoa interpenetrates with the two with which it has the greatest affinity (e.g., Urthona with Tharmas and Luvah) and touches its antitype at a single point only (Urthona and Urizen). John Howard suggests that if the picture is viewed upside down, the flamelike shapes within the mundane egg resemble the Polypus, Blake's symbol for vegetated life.[10] Moreover, the egg then becomes a human head, with Urizen at the top (the fallen brain) rather than in the south where he belongs, as in the right-side-up version. And when the picture is inverted Milton's track becomes a descent, just as it is in the falling star of plate 2. The warring Zoas, with Urizen claiming supremacy, belong to an inverted world. The power that rescues them must come from outside: Milton's descent is analogous to—and in some sense identical with—that of Jesus, and in fact the idea of "Milton's track" may have been suggested to Blake by a diagram of Jesus entering the created universe in Law's edition of Boehme.[11]

In the first extended version of Blake's myth, the warfare of the Zoas is a nightmare in nine nights.

> The Fallen Man stretchd like a Corse upon the oozy Rock
> Washd with the tides Pale overgrown with weeds
> That movd with horrible dreams hovring high over his head.
> (*FZ* 99:4-6, E357/K341)

The Zoas are not faculties, and certainly not discrete beings; they are an ever-shifting system of relationships within the self. Each has an Emanation, and (in theory at least) a Spectre, which would make twelve "characters" in all if Blake cared to deploy them. The very complexity of this psychic myth should warn us not to reduce it to

---

[10] *Blake's Milton*, pp. 40-41.
[11] See the illustration in Raine, *Blake and Tradition*, II, 24.

tabular form. The Zoas are significant for what they do, not for what they are. To drive home the point, Blake constantly varies the relationships among them. Los, the fallen Urthona, is the "son" of Tharmas and Enion, while Orc, the fallen Luvah, is the "son" of Los and Enitharmon (herself, as Los's Emanation, the daughter of Tharmas and Enion and thus Los's "sister"). If this were construed as a literal or even allegorical relationship, Orc would be Tharmas's grandson, while remaining the fallen form of Luvah who is coequal with Tharmas. Or again, Satan is a spectral form of Urizen, but at one point we are told that "Satan is the Spectre of Orc" (M 29:34, E126/K517). And at another point the Spectre of Urthona claims, rather mysteriously, that at the moment of separation from Enitharmon he was born from the "breathing nostrils" of Enion (FZ 50:22, E327/K300). This constant permutation of mythic origins indicates the irrelevance of ordinary causal and genetic assumptions. Relations among the Zoas are thematic and symbolic, continually reshaped and recommenced, like clouds merging and separating in a windy sky.

DESIRE

In Blake as in many thinkers, desire is the fundamental activity of the psyche. Now, the essence of desire is widely thought to reside in its insatiability, for it is in the very failure to be satisfied that it expresses the self. In recurring to the theme of desire Blake consciously addressed a classic problem of psychology, but he was unwilling to accept insatiableness as a definition of the human, and developed instead an argument that exploited, while subverting, a traditional argument of moral theology.

We read in the second *No Natural Religion* tractate,

V If the many become the same as the few when possess'd, More! More! is the cry of a mistaken soul, less than All cannot satisfy Man.

VI If any could desire what he is incapable of possessing, despair must be his eternal lot.

VII The desire of Man being Infinite the possession is Infinite & himself Infinite

Application. He who sees the Infinite in all things sees God. He who sees the Ratio only sees himself only.

Therefore God becomes as we are, that we may be as he is

(E2/K97-98)

How does Blake get from proposition VI to VII?

In a different form these principles were familiar in religious apologetics. As Young put it in the seventh Night of *Night Thoughts*, "To *love,* and *know*, in man/Is boundless appetite, and boundless pow'r,/And these demónstrate boundless objects too." But Blake's argument is founded on a radical naturalization of the infinite that would have scandalized Young, and invokes traditional Christian psychology while denying its conclusions.

The traditional psychology is summarized by Blake's enemy Locke: "The uneasiness a man finds in himself upon the absence of anything whose present enjoyment carries the idea of delight with it, is that we call *desire*; which is greater or less, as that uneasiness is more or less vehement. . . . *Despair* is the thought of the unattainableness of any good."[12] If our desires are unfulfilled but we do not despair, it must be that God uses this mechanism as a way of forcing us to aspire to another world in which satisfaction will be complete. Even on earth uneasiness is "the chief, if not only spur to human industry and action," for if the absence of something does not make us uneasy, "there is no desire of it, nor endeavour after it" (II.xx.6). We know that a benevolent God does not permit despair. He therefore intends that "we, finding imperfection, dissatisfaction, and want of complete happiness, in all the enjoyments which the creatures [i.e., created things] can afford us, might be led to seek it in the enjoyment of Him with whom there is fullness of joy, and at whose right hand are pleasures for evermore" (II.vii.5).

Christian moralists like Samuel Johnson concluded similarly that since God is good, he must have provided a nobler world for man than the one in which "many of his faculties can serve only for his torment, in which he is to be importuned by desires that never can be satisfied."[13] "More! More! is the cry of a mistaken soul," Blake tells us, and religious writers would agree. Anne Bradstreet says, "The eyes and the ears are the inlets or doors of the soul, through which innumerable objects enter; yet is not that spacious room filled, neither doth it ever say it is enough, but like the daughters of the horseleach, cries, 'Give, give'; and which is most strange, the more it receives, the more empty it finds itself, and sees an impossibility ever to be filled but by Him in whom all fullness dwells."[14]

Whether the infinitude of desire was perceived as agonizing or encouraging depended on temperament. Looking forward to eternity, one might well say with a visionary like Traherne, "It is of the Nobil-

---

[12] *Essay Concerning Human Understanding*, II.xx.6, 11.

[13] *Adventurer* 120. See also the conclusion of *The Vanity of Human Wishes*.

[14] *Meditations Divine and Moral*, no. 51, in *The Works of Anne Bradstreet*, ed. Jeannine Hensley (Cambridge, Mass., 1967), p. 282. The allusion is to Proverbs 30:15.

ity of Man's Soul that He is Insatiable."[15] Blake's solution, however, differs fundamentally from the classic Christian one. When he says that God becomes as we are so that we may be as he is, he means that this can and should occur here and now, not in another world at the end of life's trials, and that by becoming godlike we fully participate in an infinity that contains and gratifies desire. As Northrop Frye describes religious symbolism, "The apocalyptic world, the heaven of religion, presents, in the first place, the categories of reality in the forms of human desire."[16] The orthodox believe that God has shaped human desire to correspond to the structure of salvation; Blake believes that salvation is achieved by an inner apocalypse that gratifies desire through a transformation of vision.

Locke maintained that "eternity" and "infinity" have no meaning for the human mind, being "obscure and undetermined" hypotheses of time and space without end.[17] Blake on the other hand always held that spiritual vision apprehends infinity as organized form. "The Infinite alone resides in Definite & Determinate Identity" (*J* 55:64, E203/K687). It is surely this principle and not just the failure of political revolution that impelled Blake to abandon the ideal of unrestricted "energy" and to accept something like the Greek ideal of limit, which has been described as "that without which progress would be a meaningless process *ad infinitum*."[18] "Truth has bounds, Error none" (*Book of Los* 4:30, E91/K258). But unlike the Greeks, Blake endorsed the Pauline diagnosis of man's alienation: the fallen or "corporeal" world is everything that pessimistic moralists describe. As Frye says, "Man derives the knowledge that he is living in a fallen world from the contrast between his desire and his power, between what he would like to do and what he can do."[19] The Greek solution is to teach man to want to do what he can do; Christianity bids him aspire to a transcendent realm in which wanting and doing can merge; Blake undertakes to show that there need be no gap at all between the two. Such a claim demands the reintegration rather than repudiation of reason, a reconciliation of Apollo with Dionysus. And the rehabilitation of Urizen is therefore a decisive stage in the reconstruction of the self in *The Four Zoas*.

[15] Thomas Traherne, *Centuries, Poems, and Thanksgivings*, ed. H. M. Margoliouth (Oxford, 1958), I, 11.

[16] *Anatomy of Criticism*, p. 141.

[17] *Essay*, II.xxix.15, 16.

[18] Richard L. Nettleship, *Lectures on the Republic of Plato* (London, 1901), p. 39.

[19] *Fearful Symmetry*, p. 201. Pascal makes the same distinction between *vouloir* and *pouvoir*: *Pensées*, no. 123 (Lafuma numeration), 389 (Brunschvicg).

The discussion thus far has been intended to describe the existential crisis that Blake framed his myth to solve. He accepted the diagnosis of Christian theology but not its answers; he accepted the answers (roughly speaking) of the Greek philosophers but not their diagnosis. As we ponder his position we should recognize that his conception of the infinite differs in two important respects from that of Romanticism in general, the tradition in which he is ordinarily placed. Blake's infinite is neither limitless nor unattainable. Wordsworth typically writes,

> Our destiny, our being's heart and home,
> Is with infinitude, and only there;
> With hope it is, hope that can never die,
> Effort, and expectation, and desire,
> And something ever more about to be.

This realization is the fruit of reflection on the meaning of the exceptional moment, the epiphany in which "the light of sense/Goes out, but with a flash that has revealed/The invisible world."[20] For Blake, vision does not depend upon the rare moment of preternatural insight—although one might argue that in his experience, as opposed to his theory, it was in fact very similar to what Wordsworth describes—and there is no question of "something ever more about to be." Wordsworth speaks of desire, just as Locke did, as defined by the absence of the thing desired, and he may well fear its consummation as an end to further desiring. In such a conception infinity is by definition unattainable, though it can inspire hope and effort. Blake insists that in and through Jesus ("God becomes as we are") we experience infinite gratification of infinite desire.

What this means, ultimately, is that the distinction between subject and object is abolished, so that we are at one with a universal order in which we possess everything that we desire, and desire nothing that we cannot possess. According to Husserl, desire is always intentional, a desire *to*. In Blake's opinion that is due to the fall, in which desire (preeminently in its sexual form) is productive of disaster:

> Raging furious the flames of desire
> Ran thro' heaven & earth, living flames
> Intelligent, organiz'd: arm'd
> With destruction & plagues.[21]

Or as Blake says in the early Lavater annotations, "Hell is the being

---

[20] *The Prelude*, VI.538-542, 534-536 (1805), VI.604-608, 600-602 (1850).
[21] *Book of Los* 3:27-30, E90/K256.

shut up in the possession of corporeal desires which shortly weary the man, for *all life is holy*" (E579/K74). By abolishing finite objects ("More! More!") Blake can escape intentionality, merging all desire in the life of the Divine Humanity. Traherne says, "Having met with an infinite Benefactor, [man] would not be fit for his bounty, could any finite Object satisfie his Desire."[22] Blake maintains further that all men are fully united with Jesus, who is no longer an external benefactor but rather their truest self.

Such a position is, to say the least, highly paradoxical. Something like it can be found in Cusanus, who holds that to desire the infinite is to feel an ultimate yearning that somehow achieves the satisfaction which finite desires cannot. In Jaspers' exposition, "By its power of attraction the infinite engenders longing. When we accede to this longing, we are brought into the presence of the infinite. Longing and repose coincide."[23] In Cusanus' thought, this is so because God is the infinite, and when we truly desire God we desire all that we could possibly want. Blake never puts it like that, but the increasing importance of Jesus in his system serves an analogous function. At all events, his account of desire is put forward as a drastic revaluation of traditional psychology. Existence, Ricoeur says, "is desire and effort. We term it effort in order to stress its positive energy and its dynamism; we term it desire in order to designate its lack and its poverty."[24] Blake redefines desire so as to merge it with effort: instead of betraying a lack, it enjoys perfect completion.

But in proposing this solution Blake implies a condition very different from any that we now understand, and in retaining the principle of desire while abolishing the subject/object distinction he makes the status of the self extremely mysterious. One way of putting this would be to say that he preserves the motivating power of desire at the cost of eliminating the desiring self. Another, to which we now turn, would be to say that he postulates a willing self without conceding the existence, in any ultimate sense, of the will.

WILL

In the orthodox Christian myth we are told not only why the fall occurred, but also what faculty brought it about. Reason and the passions contributed, but nothing would have happened if the will had

[22] *Christian Ethicks* (1675), p. 93.

[23] Karl Jaspers, *The Great Philosophers*, ed. Hannah Arendt, trans. Ralph Manheim (New York, 1966), II, 127.

[24] "Existence and Hermeneutics," *The Conflict of Interpretations*, p. 21. See also p. 329 on the union of Platonic *eros* and Spinozan *conatus*.

not betrayed its trust. In Bunyan's psychomachia *The Holy War* the city of Mansoul sells out to the enemy Diabolus through the corruption of its governor Willbewill. Following St. Paul—"For the good that I would, I do not: but the evil which I would not, that I do" (Rom. 7:19)—it was customary to speak of man's bondage to sin, in contrast to Christian liberty in which the human will is merged in God's. As Augustine testifies, "The enemy had control of my will, and out of it he fashioned a chain and fettered me with it. For in truth lust is made out of a perverse will, and when lust is served, it becomes habit, and when habit is not resisted, it becomes necessity. By such links, joined one to another, as it were—for this reason I have called it a chain—a harsh bondage held me fast."[25] The emotions themselves, Augustine says elsewhere, must finally be understood as acts of will, since they only express themselves at its instigation: "If the will is wrongly directed, the emotions will be wrong; if the will is right, the emotions will be not only blameless, but praiseworthy. The will is engaged in all of them; in fact they are all essentially acts of will. For what is desire or joy but an act of will in agreement with what we wish for?"[26]

It has not been sufficiently noticed that this central function of will—in strong contrast to most Romantic thought—virtually disappears in Blakean psychology. The explanation cannot be simply that Blake followed different sources. Boehme, for example, is perfectly orthodox in describing the manifestation of God's being through his will: "The will is father; the mind is the conceived of the will, viz. the seat or habitation of the will, or the centre to something; and it is the will's heart; and the egress of the will and mind is the power and spirit." Boehme's God, like Luther's and Calvin's, is conceived in voluntarist terms with the will primary (not coordinated with reason as in Aquinas): "We acknowledge that God in his own essence is no essence, but only the alone power or the understanding to the essence, viz. an unsearchable eternal will, wherein all thing are couched."[27]

It was not through carelessness or indifference that Blake neglected to give the will this kind of primacy in his system. Instead, he undertook an implicit criticism of the psychology that sees the will as the master faculty that executes the decisions of reason. Just as he admits no inscrutable God whose disobeyed commands precipitate the fall, so also he will not allow that the human psyche is organized in a hierarchy of authority. A translator of the Lord's Prayer commented on the clause "Thy will be done" that "we are ordered to obey . . . the WILL of

[25] *Confessions*, trans. John K. Ryan (New York, 1960), VIII.v.10, p. 188.
[26] *City of God*, XIV.6, p. 555.
[27] *Mysterium Magnum*, chs. 1, 6, pp. 1-2, 23.

HIM, who is *uncontrolably powerful"*; Blake retorts, "So you See That God is just such a Tyrant as Augustus Caesar" (E658/K788). The tyrannical God is Blake's Nobodaddy. And in early annotations to Swedenborg Blake declares roundly, "There can be no Good-Will. Will is always Evil. It is pernicious to others or selfish. If God is anything he is Understanding. He is the Influx from that into the Will" (E591/K89). Blake's later formulations no longer countenance even a will that receives an "influx" of divine understanding. What takes its place?

As usual in Blake, there are at least two answers, one negative and one positive. The negative answer follows logically from the claim that "Will is always Evil." Will (whether called by that name or not) is the expression of the insane desires of the fallen selfhood, and must cease to be an issue when the self is renewed. In the fallen world it is manifested as the Female Will, that elaborate complex of evil impulses which, since it can only appear when the "female" has separated itself from the One Man, is in a real sense not part of himself at all. In Paracelsus and Swedenborg the mind was male, the will female.[28] What is implied by this conception of the female must be postponed until the next chapter. Meanwhile we observe that the will is objectified only in the *fallen* form of Albion's Emanation, Rahab or Vala. In the myth of the Zoas Vala is the Emanation of the passionate Luvah, and we thus find that Blake's "infinite desire" is indeed anterior to the will that carries it out in perverted form.

What would the will be in positive terms? Does it exist at all? Morton Paley glosses the action of *The Four Zoas* by saying that "Luvah, passion, rises into the brain and drives the chariot of slumbering reason, the will."[29] This is plausible, but it assumes just the kind of hierarchy that I do not find in Blake. Luvah's mistake in seizing Urizen's chariot (an adaptation of the myth of Phaëthon) is to suppose that Urizen *is* supreme. Blake imagines unfallen Man as literalizing the conception of Christian liberty, in which man's will is merged with God's and only desires what is right.

In thus limiting the will to its fallen or "female" manifestation, Blake offers a searching critique of the psychology which, ever since Paul's Epistles, had stressed obedience to an all-powerful God and had always run the risk of determinism.[30] We should never forget how strongly Blake feared the loss of freedom. As Percival rightly

---

[28] See Percival, *William Blake's Circle of Destiny*, p. 91.

[29] *Energy and the Imagination*, p. 94.

[30] Luther and Calvin declared unequivocally that man's will is not free. It has only the choice of bondage to Satan or to God, and even that choice is not its own except as enabled by unmerited grace.

observes, "No other poet has given us so profound a sense of the helplessness of man before the primal forces of life; and no other poet, so passionate a denial of that helplessness. He fears these forces, because he sees them as demonic, with power over him; but he takes hope from the fact that these forces are in him—that they are himself."[31] As the long torment of *The Four Zoas* shows, spiritual regeneration is something to be won by desperate effort, not a state of grace to be entered with habitual ease.

Blake therefore places the fallen will in the determinist world in which we find ourselves, whose apparently irresistible power is a projection of the fallen mind (or imposition of the fallen will) rather than the shape of reality itself. The connection between Newton and repressive religion is not factitious: both systems of thought take a determinist order for granted, and Newtonian physics helps to shore up Urizenic religion.[32]

> I turn my eyes to the Schools & Universities of Europe
> And there behold the Loom of Locke whose Woof rages dire
> Washd by the Water-wheels of Newton. black the cloth
> In heavy wreathes folds over every Nation; cruel Works
> Of many Wheels I view, wheel without wheel, with cogs tyrannic
> Moving by compulsion each other: not as those in Eden: which
> Wheel within Wheel in freedom revolve in harmony & peace.
>   (*J* 15:14-20, E157/K636)

Escape from these "dark Satanic Mills," as Blake calls them in the famous lyric in *Milton* (E95/K481) is achieved not by redirecting the will, as in Augustine or Luther, but by repudiating the fallen will and asserting the creative power of imagination. The spectral selfhood "must be put off & annihilated alway";

> I come in Self-annihilation & the grandeur of Inspiration
> To cast off Rational Demonstration by Faith in the Saviour
> To cast off the rotten rags of Memory by Inspiration
> To cast off Bacon, Locke & Newton from Albions covering
> To take off his filthy garments, & clothe him with Imagination. . . .
>   (*M* 40:36–41:6, E141/K533)

The faculties of the false selfhood are described in the language of the prophets, the "filthy rags" of man's righteousness (Isa. 64:6) and the "filthy garments" that Joshua exchanges for heavenly raiment (Zech. 3:3-4).

[31] *William Blake's Circle of Destiny*, p. 20.
[32] On Newtonian determinism, see Ault, *Visionary Physics*, pp. 91-95. It is always Urizen who feels himself "urg'd by necessity" (*FZ* 25:42, E310/K282).

Boehme, once again, can help us to understand what Blake has in mind. In its negative sense will is an expression of the fragmented self, Blake's Zoas: "Where there are many wills in a thing, they become contending, for each would go its own conceived way. . . . And thus we give you to understand life's contrariety, for life consists of many wills. . . . So likewise the life of man is at enmity with itself."[33] Similarly when Enitharmon has split off from Los "Two Wills they had; Two Intellects: & not as in times of old" (*J* 86:61, E243/K732). It is futile to expect any one Zoa to represent the will, because *each* has a will, which is precisely what has gone wrong.[34] In Boehme's thought the healthy will is not a master faculty that issues commands, like a ship's captain on the engine room telegraph, but a principle of unity that is best understood on the analogy of spiritual vision. "For Boehme," Koyré says, "the will is essentially spiritual; spirit is essentially vision."[35]

Now, Boehme expressly contrasts will with desire. Will is generous and "giving" (*gebende*) and seeks to incarnate itself in others; desire is tormented by emptiness and seeks forever to incorporate others in itself. If will is vision, desire is hunger. But ultimately they must cooperate in a dialectical process, the will desiring and the desire willing.[36] Like Boehme, Blake regards the strife of contraries as built into the nature of things, but aspires to a state in which will and desire are no longer opposed as giving and taking (the polarity of Experience, symbolically represented in "The Clod and the Pebble"). They are to merge in such a way that neither will survive as we now know it. "Less than All cannot satisfy Man" (E2/K97); regenerated man will possess All, neither desiring nor willing as those terms are ordinarily understood.[37] What is implied is something like the central role of will in existentialism, which rejects faculty psychology just as Blake does, but retains and indeed glorifies the existential act of willing. "Christianity in the New Testament," Kierkegaard says, "has to do with

---

[33] *Six Theosophic Points*, trans. John Rolleston Earle (Ann Arbor, Mich., 1968), IV.i–iii, p. 45.

[34] At one point Blake seems to say that in the fallen state each Zoa's will must be preserved in its separateness, as Urizen's is by "Providence divine" at the end of *FZ* VI (74:30-32, E344/K319). Elsewhere Los threatens the Spectre with the strength of "my great will" (*J* 10:36, E152/K629).

[35] *La Philosophie de Jacob Boehme*, p. 336.

[36] "En fait, la volonté est désirante et le désir lui-même est volontaire" (Koyré, p. 371; see p. 364 ff.).

[37] Michael G. Cooke comments that in *Dejection: An Ode* Coleridge "undergoes a lapse, or relapse, from an integrated being informed with will to a divided being, possessed of will" (*The Romantic Will* [New Haven, 1976], p. 16). In the ideal unfallen state, the will would be at one with the whole being and would have no separate existence.

man's will, everything turns upon changing the will."[38] But Blake insists beyond this that what is really involved is a change in perception. "Error or Creation" is burned up not when you change your will but simply when you "cease to behold it" (*VLJ*, E555/K617).

Such is the theory. Can Blake sustain it in practice? Everything depends on the ultimate truth of the symbols evoked by the inspired imagination, and the status of the "Saviour" in whom the rational and the not-human are washed off by the waters of life (E141/K533). Only in a theological context can these ideas be more than merely metaphorical and guarantee the regeneration which, as Percival says, Blake so desperately needs. At times Blake speaks of Albion or Man as if he had a will that controls the Zoas:

> They must renew their brightness & their disorganized functions
> Again reorganize till they resume the image of the human
> Cooperating in the bliss of Man obeying his Will
> Servants to the infinite & Eternal of the Human form.
> (*FZ* 126:14-17, E380/K366)

Meanwhile the human will is separate from the divine, and must remain in chains until the appointed apocalypse:

> But as the Will must not be bended but in the day of Divine
> Power: silent calm & motionless, in the mid-air sublime,
> The Family Divine hover around the darkend Albion.
> (*J* 39:18-20, E184/K674)

What is that day (*dies illa*)? What is that power, and who are the family divine? Before confronting these questions directly, we must return to the problem of the self in which the Zoas struggle and into which the saving Jesus descends.

SELF AND SELFHOOD

An analysis of the self in Blake is complicated by the fact that Albion, the Universal Man in whom the Zoas live, is represented as sunk in nightmare, an adaptation of the Neoplatonic and Gnostic idea of the sleep that follows the fall into matter. In the words of an imaginative expositor of the Gnostics, "Slumber is to consciousness what heaviness is to the body: a state of death, inertia, petrifaction of psychic life. We sleep. We pass our lives asleep. And only those who *know* can hope to break through the walls of mental inertia."[39] In contrast with the

---

[38] Søren Kierkegaard, *The Last Years: Journals 1853-55*, ed. and trans. Ronald Gregor Smith (New York, 1965), p. 226.

[39] Lacarrière, *Les Gnostiques*, p. 25.

Gnostics Blake represents this drugged condition as accompanied by tormented mental struggle; it is at once inertia and frantic activity. Moreover Man himself is asleep, not just individual men. The Gnostics taught that exceptional individuals might free themselves through *gnosis*, while Blake expects the Universal Man to awaken through the inspiration and incarnation of Jesus. Rather than seeing history (or the cosmos) as a nightmare from which we are trying to awake, Blake sees *ourselves* as the nightmare. The total self, Albion, groans and tosses in sleep upon the Rock of Ages while the giants within are locked in hopeless combat, a war none can win because each is inseparable from his foes.

For all its imaginative power, this myth entails immense conceptual difficulties. What is the status of the self that is symbolized by the dreaming Albion? By its very nature such an account of psychic life must be strange and dislocating—"As when a man dreams, he reflects not that his body sleeps,/Else he would wake" (*M* 15:1-2, E108/K496). One reason why it is hard to talk about motivation and the will is that Blake never represents them directly. Stuart Hampshire observes that "the sleeping and unconscious man is not an agent, and the effects of any movements that he may make cannot be related to his intentions. It is a necessary truth that he has no intentions under these conditions. Anything that can be said about him in a narrative covering the period of his unconsciousness—that he dreamt of so-and-so, that he called out a certain name, that he tried to raise himself and to walk—is so interpreted as not to attribute to him an action performed intentionally and at will."[40] At times Blake suggests that human beings are motivated—as it were, lived—by universal beings or agencies. "We who dwell on Earth can do nothing of ourselves, every thing is conducted by Spirits, no less than Digestion or Sleeping" (*J* 3, E144/K621). But let us postpone the problem of the individual, and postulate that the sleeping Albion is somehow conscious in his unconsciousness. What is his relation to the Zoas? And how is it that when they reorganize into "the human" they are described as "obeying his Will"? (*FZ* 126:15-16, E380/K366).

The answer must be that Albion "is" the Zoas in a symbolic mode of peculiar subtlety, so subtle in fact that Blake some of the time, and most readers most of the time, cannot help reifying him/it into a picture of the parts of the self instead of a dramatization of its activity.[41] Jonas comments on Gnosticism that the cosmos is represented within man, and that "man's inwardness is the natural scene for demonic ac-

---

[40] *Thought and Action*, p. 94.

[41] At many points in this book I myself am guilty of this offense. I believe that it is encouraged by Blake's practice, though condemned by his theory.

tivity, and his self is exposed to the play of forces which it does not control."[42] Just so in Blake's myth; but whereas the Gnostics regarded these forces as invaders from without—as demonic "possession"— Blake insists that the only demons are projections of the self. He aims, therefore, to symbolize at once the feeling of helplessness before inner chaos and the remedy by which the self can regain control. When Albion arises in anger at the end of *Jerusalem*, he *compels* the three errant Zoas back to their proper places while the inspired fourth is praised for its saving work:

> Compelling Urizen to his Furrow; & Tharmas to his Sheepfold;
> And Luvah to his Loom: Urthona he beheld mighty labouring at
> His Anvil, in the Great Spectre Los unwearied labouring & weeping
> Therefore the Sons of Eden praise Urthonas Spectre in songs
> Because he kept the Divine Vision in time of trouble.
>
> (*J* 95:16–20, E252/K742)

But if the Zoas have roles and places, if they dwell "in the Brain of Man" as Los declares (*FZ* 11:15, E302/K272), how can we avoid the metaphor of a container and the things contained?

The short answer is that we cannot. The long answer is that the same criticism can be lodged against any psychology whatever, for it is impossible to analyze the self without imposing a structural or topological myth. Some myths are more rigid than others—the classical theory of faculty psychology was especially rigid—but all must accept rigidity as the price of conceptual existence. A critical examination of any such myth, Freud's for example, may well conclude that the myth gets literalized and tends to obscure "the unity of the self."[43] But unless the postulated unity is to remain empty and unexplored, there is no avoiding the impulse to differentiate it into parts.

As against the notion of discrete faculties, Blake endorsed Berkeley's position: "A spirit is one simple, undivided, active being: as it perceives ideas, it is called the *understanding*, and as it produces or otherwise operates about them, it is called the *will*." Or again, "How often must I repeat, that I know or am conscious of my own being; and that I my self am not my ideas, but somewhat else, a thinking active principle that perceives, knows, wills, and operates about

---

[42] *The Gnostic Religion*, pp. 281–282.

[43] "Whatever anatomy of the self you propose, I believe you will be saddled with doctrines which are either not germane to the psychological phenomena, or else not cogent. Those in search of edification might conclude that we seem to have no alternative but to assume the unity of the self" (Irving Thalberg, "Freud's Anatomies of the Self," in *Freud: A Collection of Critical Essays*, ed. Richard Wollheim [New York, 1974], p. 171).

ideas."[44] In Blake's opinion Berkeley himself tended to lose sight of this principle, falling into conventional talk about the sequential operation of sense, imagination and understanding: "Knowledge is not by deduction but Immediate by Perception or Sense at once. Christ addresses himself to the Man not to his Reason. Plato did not bring Life & Immortality to Light Jesus only did this" (E653/K774). Plato is mentioned both because he exalted reason and also because he divided up the soul into distinct parts. In a way the Zoas correspond to Plato's model—Urizen as intellect, Urthona as the "spirited" *thymos*, Luvah as appetite—but Blake's myth is crucially completed by the addition of Tharmas, the "Parent power" (*FZ* 4:6, E297/K264) who underlies the activity of the rest. It is hard to say what Tharmas "is" because he is conceived as an alternative to personified faculties (and is the most shadowy in pictorial representation). His function closely resembles that of the Father in Boehme's system, "the vital and psychic force of the living body, or, if one prefers, the organic and psychic life of living matter."[45] He is, in some mysterious sense, the organizing principle of the self.

What we are repeatedly shown, therefore, is a dynamic of psychic parts that are not really parts at all, but aspects of a single whole. The three characters in *Visions of the Daughters of Albion*, for instance, represent conflicting modes of "seeing" that persist within the individual self.[46] More generally, the intermittent actions of Albion are intended to remind us that, asleep or not, he is fully implicated in the actions of his Zoas. Urizen can call himself God only because Albion is prepared to worship an externalized image of this part of himself:

Then Man ascended mourning into the splendors of his palace
Above him rose a Shadow from his wearied intellect
Of living gold, pure, perfect, holy; in white linen pure he hover'd
A sweet entrancing self delusion, a watry vision of Man
Soft exulting in existence all the Man absorbing
Man fell upon his face prostrate before the watry shadow
Saying O Lord whence is this change thou knowest I am nothing. . .
(*FZ* 40:2-8, E320/K293)

The irony is that it is the narcissistic Urizenic ideal and not Albion that is "nothing." Guilt has projected an idol of impossible purity, in the self-torture of conscience that invents an avenging deity by placating

[44] *Principles of Human Knowledge*, par. 27; *Three Dialogues*, Third Dialogue, p. 233.

[45] Koyré, *La Philosophie de Jacob Boehme*, p. 108.

[46] In schematic terms, Bromion might be described as Theotormon's Spectre and Oothoon as his Emanation (see Wagenknecht, *Blake's Night*, p. 207).

whom it can hope to win peace. But this tactic only produces further fragmentation and deeper anguish.

Yet it is impossible when actually reading the poems to remember that the Zoas are not distinct beings. Albion can address them— "Albion spoke in his dismal dreams: O thou deceitful friend" (*J* 42:9, E187/K669)—and can even fall in love with them as he does with Vala. And I would insist that this is as it should be, that if we read the myth *as* a myth and not as a mimetic narrative, we must accept the Zoas as independent agents. Urizen is no longer dominant as he was for Plato or Milton, but he is still Urizen, even if we *interpret* his function as the Urizenic aspect of Albion. And this permits Blake to express some of his most telling insights.

A historian of theories of the will states as self-evident, "We say that a man is overcome with grief, is overpowered by anger, or is under the dominion of appetite; we do not say that he is a victim to reason, or a slave to any cognitive process."[47] We may not, but Blake does. His psychology seeks to be at once active and passive. It confirms the sense of spiritual bondage of Paul and Augustine, but interprets bondage as "mind-forg'd manacles" ("London," E27/K216), which implies that the mind actively chooses to render itself passive, or that its passivity is a function of the wrong kind of activity. The fall can occur in any of a number of ways, depending upon which Zoa one listens to. It is futile, incidentally, to assume that one or another account is "wrong," as if there were a factual event behind the different reports; each is imaginatively true. And the fall is ultimately precipitated by Albion himself, in a flight from activity that displaces action into his warring members while the self falls into confusion.

But Albion fled from the Divine Vision, with the Plow of Nations
    enflaming
The Living Creatures maddend and Albion fell into the Furrow, and
The Plow went over him & the Living was Plowed in among the
    Dead
But his Spectre rose over the starry Plow. Albion fled beneath the
    Plow
Till he came to the Rock of Ages. & he took his Seat upon the Rock.
                      (*J* 57:12-16, E205/K689)

The proliferation of characters in Blake's myth is an essential means of making us recognize their symbolic role. The four Zoas by themselves may tend to become schematic, but the turbulent drama of their

---

[47] Archibald Alexander, *Theories of the Will in the History of Philosophy* (New York, 1898), p. 22.

Spectres and Emanations—and later developments like the invention of Jerusalem as the Emanation of Albion himself—oblige us to attend to what these figures do. The tendency of every quality or principle to generate its opposite is a fundamental symbolic mode of representing experience. As Terence Turner says, the bifurcation of characters is virtually universal in symbolic narrative: "According to this principle, the generation of complementary oppositions between a pair of general structural categories tends to be expressed in terms of the creation of *dramatis personae* who represent opposite aspects of the same essential characteristic."[48] Urthona breaks down into Los, Los separates from his Emanation Enitharmon, they produce complementary pairs of "sons" like Rintrah and Palamabron, and the "spectral" aspects of Los can be expressed as Satan (another "son") or as the Spectre of Urthona. These are not characters in an Olympian genealogy but symbolic expressions of cognate yet opposing aspects of the human imagination. Each Zoa must have both Emanation and Spectre—a trifurcation, really—because Blake increasingly perceives not only that contraries are integral to the self, but also that they exist within every subcategory of every category. The dialectical process is potentially endless because the active dialectic of human experience is endless.

Thus far, I hope to have shown that the relation between Albion and the Zoas is symbolically coherent despite its conceptual ambiguity. We must now confront the deeper and more intractable problem of the status of the self. Granted that Albion is his Zoas, who is Albion?

In the Cartesian tradition, the self is that which thinks, the *cogito* which has been described as elevating itself into the sole symbol of being and thereby subverting the possibility of symbolism.[49] Blake has no trouble in disposing of this, Urizen being a sinister union of the Mosaic Jehovah with the Cartesian *cogito*. What Blake has to explain instead is a self that is something more than the knowing "I" which, as Rodney Needham observes, is built into the very structure of language.[50]

<hr>

[48] "Oedipus: Time and Structure in Narrative Form," in *Forms of Symbolic Action*, ed. Spencer, p. 62.

[49] Gilbert Durand, *L'Imagination Symbolique*, p. 20. Durand sees this tendency as responsible for the collapse of symbol into sign in so many modern theories: "The symbol—of which the signifier is but the translucence of the sign—blurs little by little into pure semiology, and evaporates, so to speak, methodically into the sign." Here is a crucial point of disagreement between Blake and the Cartesian tradition, for if the *cogito* is fundamental to the idea of consciousness, the *méthode* is methodically destructive of symbolism. "Descartes cut the throat of poetry," Boileau said.

[50] "Language itself, by its indiscriminate employment of the first person singular pronoun, creates an impression which we are then disconcerted to find is not wholly or always correct. . . . Instead of saying that we change our minds, we can say that our

Locke located personal identity in consciousness and held that it was defined by memory. If memory fails, we cease to be the same self.[51] When Albion turns his back on the Divine Vision, "his Spectrous/ Chaos before his face appeard: an Unformed Memory" (*J* 29:1-2, E173/K659). Hume too saw the weakness of Locke's position, and mounted a critique in which the self finally collapses into an empty fiction embracing the "perpetual flux and movement" of mental events that are stimulated by external impressions.[52] By dismissing the role of memory Blake is safe from the particular thrust of Hume's attack, but his myth of the fragmented self in its larger dimensions may seem to play directly into Hume's hands.

To state the problem in this way is to give it a clarity and urgency that Blake himself did not. He was more concerned with the dynamics of the Zoas than with the status of Albion. But any attempt to understand the myth rather than simply to paraphrase it cannot avoid the problem. A helpful analogue is found in Hegel, who addressed the problem of the self from a conviction of dividedness very like Blake's, but strove as Blake did not to frame an answer in philosophical terms.[53] The self can only be perceived by itself; in Hegel's words, "Behind the so-called curtain, which is to hide the inner world, there is nothing to be seen unless we ourselves go behind there, as much in order that we may thereby see, as that there may be something behind there which can be seen."[54] We penetrate appearances to discover a realm in which subject and object are at one. But although complementary they are not identical. "Consciousness of an other, of an object in general, is indeed itself necessarily self-consciousness, reflectedness into self, consciousness of self in its otherness" (p. 211). It is just this principle of *otherness* that Blake balks at. What he seems to want—whether it is symbolized in Albion or in Jesus the divine body—is a whole whose parts are not parts, in which individuality can be preserved without concession to otherness.

---

ideas have changed or even that we have changed in our ideas" (*Belief, Language, and Experience* [Oxford, 1972], pp. 239, 241).

[51] *Essay*, II.xxvii.

[52] "Mankind . . . are nothing but a bundle or collection of different perceptions, which succeed each other with an inconceivable rapidity, and are in a perpetual flux and movement. . . . Thus we feign the continued existence of the perceptions of our senses, to remove the interruption; and run into the notion of a *soul*, and *self*, and *substance*, to disguise the variation" (*A Treatise of Human Nature*, ed. L. A. Selby-Bigge [Oxford, 1888, repr. New York, 1967], I.iv.6, pp. 252, 254).

[53] See Altizer on the "unhappy consciousness" in Hegel and Blake (*The New Apocalypse*, pp. 43-47).

[54] *The Phenomenology of Mind*, trans. J. B. Baillie (London, 1931, repr. New York, 1967), pp. 212-213.

Here is a central antinomy in Blake's thought, the wish to be at once individual and universal, self and not-self, human and divine. And his myth aspires to something very similar to Hegel's *Geist*. "Consciousness first finds in self-consciousness—the notion of mind—its turning-point, where it leaves the parti-coloured show of the sensuous immediate, passes from the dark void of the transcendent and remote super-sensuous, and steps into the spiritual daylight of the present."[55] Seeing through and not with the eye, we escape both the delusory appearances of Vala and the false transcendent of Urizen, and step into the eternal present.

But there is a further difficulty. In Hegel's thought, the interiorization of consciousness results, paradoxically, in an exteriorization, for whatever is manifested is necessarily perceived as exterior. To be aware of the parts of the self is to be aware of them as *parts*, and hence to see them in the competitive master-slave relationship that is explored both in the *Phenomenology* and in Blake's myth of the Zoas. "In so far as it is the other's action," Hegel says, "each aims at the destruction and death of the other. . . . The relation of both self-consciousnesses is in this way so constituted that they prove themselves and each other through a life-and-death struggle" (p. 232). Hegel sees this conflict as the necessary path of truth. Blake, despite his apparent celebration of contraries, sees it as spiritual death. So he resolutely maintains that exteriorization, far from being a necessary feature of consciousness, is a Satanic delusion.

> From every-one of the Four Regions of Human Majesty,
> There is an Outside spread Without, & an Outside spread Within
> Beyond the Outline of Identity both ways, which meet in One.
>
> (*J* 18:1-3, E161/K640)

By separating from each other the Zoas project a false "outside," which must be overcome by a journey within (which, in Blake's paradoxical language, is also an expansion). Los has just told his Spectre that man has become "a little grovelling Root, outside of Himself" (17:32, E160/K639). What is exterior can be recovered because the agent of exteriorization, the Spectre, is himself piteously anxious to restore the lost unity. As Blake's Milton exclaims,

> I have turned my back upon these Heavens builded on cruelty
> My Spectre still wandering thro' them follows my Emanation
> He hunts her footsteps thro' the snow & the wintry hail & rain.
>
> (*M* 32:3-5, E130/K521)

---

[55] *Phenomenology*, p. 227.

The baroque interplay between *an sich* and *für sich* in German idealist philosophy (or Sartre's *en-soi* and *pour-soi*) resists translation into Blakean terms because Blake is finally not interested in otherness except as an error to be dispelled. For this reason his dialectic is circular rather than progressive: it exhibits all the ways in which the self can go wrong, rather than postulating an upward movement to a new and higher unity. The Romantic philosophers, as M. H. Abrams has lucidly shown, tended to regard the lost primal unity as instinctual and the "Fall" as an inevitable consequence of man's discovery of freedom, of autonomous life. Such a lost unity is obviously irrecoverable and one would not want to recover it. But Blake would hold that this story is a Urizenic fiction, that the unfallen instincts are indistinguishable from imagination and intellect, not prior to them. And he would regard as positively Satanic Schiller's statement that "the fall of man from instinct—which to be sure brought moral evil into the creation, but only in order to make moral good therein possible—is, without any contradiction, the most fortunate and greatest event in the history of mankind."[56]

What Blake demands is an unmediated union with the absolute, of the kind described in his "vision of light" poem or by Traherne in "My Spirit":

> My Naked Simple Life was I.
>   That Act so Strongly Shind
> Upon the Earth, the Sea, the Skie,
>   It was the Substance of My Mind.
> The Sence it self was I. . . .
>
> It Acts not from a Centre to
>   Its Object as remote,
> But present is, when it doth view,
>   Being with the Being it doth note.

Sense and vision, Being and self are at one.

Stated in these terms, Blake's position sounds close to that of traditional religious mysticism. Yet as we have just observed, he has no use for self-abnegation, even while campaigning bitterly against the "selfhood." What is the distinction between self and selfhood, and how can one be rejected without the other? For if, as Rudolf Otto says, the mystic identifies "the personal self with the transcendent Reality," it is

---

[56] Essay on *The First Human Society* (1790), quoted by Abrams, *Natural Supernaturalism*, pp. 208-209. As Abrams remarks, "To Blake 'the lost Traveller's Dream under the Hill' is a wish-fulfilling fantasy" rather than a metaphor for the progress of the soul (p. 195).

also usual to conclude in "self-depreciation . . . the estimation of the self, of the personal 'I,' as something not perfectly or essentially real, or even as mere nullity."[57] And this is exactly how Blake describes the "selfhood": "In Selfhood we are nothing, but fade away in mornings breath" (*J* 40:13, E185/K675). Yet the self survives the extirpation of the selfhood, which is an ongoing process rather than a once-for-all event, and is expressly contrasted with the self-abnegation of conventional religion. As Milton tells his Spectre Satan in a powerful speech about "Self Annihilation,"

> Thy purpose & the purpose of thy Priests & of thy Churches
> Is to impress on men the fear of death; to teach
> Trembling & fear, terror, constriction; abject selfishness
> Mine is to teach Men to despise death & to go on
> In fearless majesty annihilating Self. . . .
>
> (*M* 38:37-40, E138/K530)

You can only remain *yourself* by not being attached to your *self*.[58]

Difficult though it is to make sense of this concept, Blake found ample precedent for it in the *Selbheit* and *Ichheit* of Boehme. As we have already noticed, the selfhood comes into existence, according to Boehme, as a consequence of the initial fragmentation. But unlike the German mystics who aspired to lose the self in God, Boehme insisted on the integrity of the personality, and maintained that Christ enters the soul without violating its individuality.[59] In a larger perspective it may be the case that any Christian mystic, in contrast with the Buddhist who seeks absolute escape from self, is committed to something like this position. For as Cassirer says,

> Christian mysticism, like other mysticisms, is threatened by the constant danger that this nothingness and meaninglessness will seize not only upon being but upon the I as well. And yet there remains a barrier beyond which, unlike Buddhist speculation, it does not go. For the problem of the individual I, of the individual soul, remains at the center of Christianity; and consequently liberation from the I can only be conceived as also signifying liberation *for* the I.[60]

---

[57] *The Idea of the Holy*, trans. John W. Harvey (London, 1950), pp. 22, 21.

[58] On the force of *go on* as "continuity, not finality," see Mitchell, *Blake's Composite Art*, p. 91n.

[59] See Koyré, *La Philosophie de Jacob Boehme*, pp. 482-487. John Joseph Stoudt comments that "Boehme, in distinction from Neoplatonic and oriental mystics, and in full accord with Western cherishing of personality, sought freedom *for* the self to become a perfect self. He was one mystic who did not want to get rid of his self, only of his sinful self" (*Sunrise to Eternity: A Study in Jacob Boehme's Life and Thought* [Philadelphia, 1957], pp. 231-232).

[60] *Mythical Thought*, p. 250.

Very much as Blake might, Hegel likewise criticizes the orthodox campaign against individuality and insists that self-realization is the true expression of the universal. The final page of Hegel's treatment of evil and forgiveness reads like a commentary on Blake, or rather like a transposition of Blake's terms into other but equally paradoxical ones. "The relinquishment of separate selfhood" is said to unite the "concrete actual Ego" with the universal. Clearly this is at bottom a religious conception, and requires a kind of theology, however humanized, for its basis. "It is God appearing in the midst of those who know themselves in the form of pure knowledge."[61]

As the parallels with Boehme and Hegel indicate, Blake's account of the union of the self with the divine is a defiantly paradoxical response to his deep sense of disunion. Eliade says, "The ideas of a *coincidentia oppositorum* always arouse ambivalent feelings; on the one side, man is haunted by the desire to escape from his particular situation and regain a transpersonal mode of life; on the other, he is paralysed by the fear of losing his 'identity' and 'forgetting' himself."[62] The antinomy is imaginatively fruitful just because it is conceptually intolerable. Boehme describes covetousness as a kind of parody of desire, which "causes war and strife, for it is never satisfied."[63] Likewise Blakean desire is deeply problematic, the Orcian energy that has to be tamed and yet ceases to be itself if tamed (Orc chained to his rock by his "father" Los). An interest in "energy" was not remarkable at the end of the eighteenth century; Lavater is fond of the word, and the Blakean phrase "prolific energy" appears—of all places!—in Burke's *Reflections on the Revolution in France*.[64] What is new in Blake, just as in Hegel, is the recognition that unity has no meaning if it does not admit the full significance of diversity, a coincidence of opposites that implies strife and exclusion as well as harmony and union.[65]

---

[61] *Phenomenology*, p. 679. William James remarks, "What reader of Hegel can doubt that that sense of a perfected Being with all its otherness soaked up into itself, which dominates his whole philosophy, must have come from the prominence in his consciousness of mystical moods . . . in most persons kept subliminal? The notion is thoroughly characteristic of the mystical level, and the *Aufgabe* of making it articulate was surely set to Hegel's intellect by mystical feeling" (*Varieties of Religious Experience*, pp. 298-299n).

[62] *The Two and the One*, trans. J. M. Cohen (New York, 1965), p. 123n.

[63] *Six Theosophic Points*, X.xiv, p. 107.

[64] Lavater says, in an aphorism underlined by Blake, "He alone has energy that cannot be deprived of it" (E580/K75); Edmund Burke, *Reflections on the Revolution in France*, ed. Conor Cruise O'Brien (Harmondsworth, 1969), p. 282.

[65] Hegel's phenomenology of religion has three stages, adapted from Boehme: the Father as logical concept; the Son as symbol of exteriority, and hence of the self-consciousness of the finite spirit that is exteriorized; and the Holy Spirit as symbol of the return of nature to full self-consciousness and union. As Charles Taylor describes it,

A consequence of Blake's myth of the Universal Man is that it is hard to understand, within the symbolic structure of his myth, what the status of individual men and women might be. When Blake addresses the issue directly he seems to say in Platonic terms that individuality persists in a universal rather than a particular sense. Ovid's *Metamorphoses* are to be interpreted symbolically as expressing the impossibility of true metamorphosis: the outward form may change but not the eternal identity. Similarly "Lots Wife being Changed into Pillar of Salt alludes to the Mortal Body being renderd a Permanent Statue but not Changed or Transformed into Another Identity while it retains its own Individuality. A Man can never become Ass nor Horse. Some are born with shapes of Men who may be both but Eternal Identity is one thing & Corporeal Vegetation is another thing" (*VLJ*, E546/K607). Is Lot's wife a uniquely individual person, or is she an eternal type as distinguished from mortal variations on the theme? A man is different from an ass or horse, but in what respects is he different from other men? "The characters of Chaucer's Pilgrims are the characters which compose all ages and nations: as one age falls, another rises, different to mortal sight, but to immortals only the same; for we see the same characters repeated again and again, in animals, vegetables, minerals, and in men; nothing new occurs in identical existence; Accident ever varies, Substance can never suffer change nor decay" (*DC*, E523/K567).

To say that all men are one Man may look like a flimsy disguise for solipsism, and Blake has often been accused of that. But he certainly did not mean to deny the value of individual human lives. On the contrary, he always claimed that it was Newtonian single vision that reduced them to meaningless grains of sand, and at many points he refers to individuals as the "little ones" of Jerusalem who revive from spiritual death in the apocalyptic harvest.[66] If, nonetheless, it is hard to deduce the status of individuals in the myth, that is the price Blake pays for emphasizing as he does the longed-for union that can put an end to the torment of otherness, the being-for-others which Sartre

---

"The active consciousness incurs evil inevitably, this is the essence of the doctrine of original sin; but the universal which is sinned against cannot exist except at this price; it therefore must accept realization at the hands of the individual, and 'forgive' this individual his particularity, which the latter for his part repents. In this way the two extremes come to unity" (*Hegel* [Cambridge, 1975], p. 213).

[66] See the eloquent treatment of Jerusalem's "little ones" in the lyric on pl. 27 of *Jerusalem*, in which "every English Child is seen/Children of Jesus & his Bride" (E170/K650). When the individual dead revive in *FZ* IX, each "appears as he had livd before" (122:41, E377/K363), and Urizen then sows the souls as seeds for the apocalyptic harvest.

analyzes so minutely and which Pascal describes in theological terms as the tendency of the hateful *moi* to become "the enemy that wishes to be tyrant over all the others."[67] To escape this warfare of human beings in their otherness, Blake is driven upon his paradoxical distinction between self and selfhood. Albion falls in the act of "turning his Eyes outward to Self" (*FZ* 23:2, E309/K280), whereas ordinary usage would speak of the self within. And the proclamation of one of the Eternals that "Man liveth not by Self alone" (*FZ* 133:25, E387/K374)—with its echo of "Man shall not live by bread alone" in the Gospel accounts of Christ tempted by Satan—is followed by the baking of the human harvest into "the Bread of Ages" (138:17, E391/K379).

If in the end Blake's myth is, in some sense, solipsistic, it is also an act of faith that strives mightily to overcome the imputation of solipsism by rejecting the mode of thinking that accepts otherness as a fact of existence. As Sartre emphasizes, positivist "rational" thought casts us upon "the reef of solipsism." Similarly Kierkegaard rejects "objective" knowledge, which is always provisional and problematic, and declares that "the only reality to which an existing individual may have a relation that is more than cognitive is his own reality, the fact that he exists."[68] These themes are pursued not by harmonious, comfortable personalities but by those who know the full weight of alienation. "Strangely severed from other men," Swinburne says brilliantly of Blake, "he was, or he conceived himself, more strangely interwoven with them."[69] It is because Blake feels keenly both the value and the pain of individuality that he imagines universal forms which "when distant . . . appear as One Man but as you approach they appear Multitudes of Nations" (*VLJ*, E546/K607).

In a moving letter to Butts Blake applies to himself some lines that may have been first written for the heroic outcast Mary Wollstonecraft:

> O why was I born with a different face
> Why was I not born like the rest of my race
> When I look each one starts! when I speak I offend
> Then I'm silent & passive & lose every Friend.[70]

---

[67] Jean-Paul Sartre, *Being and Nothingness*, trans. Hazel E. Barnes (New York, 1966), Part III; Pascal, *Pensées*, no. 141 (Lafuma), 455 (Brunschvicg).

[68] Sartre, *Being and Nothingness*, III.i.2, pp. 303ff.; Kierkegaard, *Concluding Unscientific Postscript*, trans. Walter Lowrie (Princeton, 1941), p. 280.

[69] Algernon Charles Swinburne, *William Blake: A Critical Essay*, ed. Hugh J. Luke (Lincoln, Neb., 1970), p. 43.

[70] 16 Aug. 1803 (E700/K828), written at the height of the crisis with Hayley. See the sixth stanza of "Mary" (E479/K428). By changing "Envious Race" to "the rest of my

The myth of Albion might be seen as freeing Blake from this isolation by identifying him (and all of us) with the universal. Schofield and Hayley and George III and Catherine Blake are made real in Blake's imagination or, as he would put it, in the Divine Body of Jesus. But the extreme difficulty of such an achievement is poignantly apparent. As Hagstrum says of the pictures, "The stretching of arms that almost touch and that strive to end separation and restore harmony is a characteristic Blakean signature."[71]

Whatever one finally makes of this thorny problem, it is well to admit that for all his praise of particulars, Blake never shows much interest in human uniqueness. "It was one of the greatest experiences of my life," Jung records, "to discover how enormously different people's psyches are."[72] Can one seriously imagine Blake saying this? For him all psyches are versions of the universal psyche to an extent which Jung, despite his interest in universal symbols, would never claim. To find appropriate analogues to Blake's doctrine one must look at some of the darker sayings of Plotinus and later Neo-platonists,[73] or Hegel's proclamation of a self-realization that understands the unity of all becoming, a *Begriff* or Concept that perceives the activity of Spirit in every particular manifestation. But Blake maintains further, as Hegel would not, that the whole is *fully* present in each particular member, and is unwilling to hold as Hegel does that the particulars are necessarily finite and transitory.[74] Instead of inter-subjectivity, Blake apparently aspires to a kind of omnisubjectivity.

---

race" Blake places the blame for differentness upon himself rather than others. On Wollstonecraft, see also below, p. 197.

[71] J. H. Hagstrum, "Romney and Blake: Gifts of Grace and Terror," in Essick & Pearce, p. 206.

[72] *Collected Works*, vol. X, *Civilization in Transition*, trans. R.F.C. Hull (New York, 1964), p. 137.

[73] "On the one hand, the individual retains his own identity; on the other, his contemplation embraces the whole Intelligible world and everything within it. Hence, since on this level subject and object are identical, each member of the Intelligible order is identical with the whole of that order, and with every other member thereof. . . . More precisely, each intelligence expresses the whole Intelligible order from its own particular viewpoint" (R. T. Wallis, *Neoplatonism*, p. 54, citing *Enneads* IV.iv.2, VI.v.7, V.viii.4). This has obvious affinities with the position of Cusanus, discussed in Chapter 1 above.

[74] Charles Taylor comments that finite things "must come into existence, but at the same time they are victims of an internal contradiction which assures that they will also pass away. They are necessarily mortal. But at the same time, in going under they have to be replaced by other similar things" (*Hegel*, p. 107). At times, as in his remarks on the oak and lettuce (*VLJ*, E545/K605), Blake comes close to saying this. But in general he treats the survival of the individual quite differently: "The generations of men run on in the tide of Time/But leave their destind lineaments permanent for ever & ever" (*M* 22:24-25, E116/K505).

When he speaks of "Eternal Individuality" (*J* 48:3, E194/K677) he is speaking of Albion.

THE FUNCTION OF THE MYTH

The purpose of Blake's myth is far from being merely descriptive. It is prescriptive: it aims to teach us the truth about ourselves, to restore the unity of which we are or should be members. A full account of Blake's hopes for his myth must await an examination of the role of Los, the prophetic imagination and artistic creator.[75] But we must never lose sight of the living and indeed therapeutic function of the myth for Blake and, so he hopes, for us.

Our theme throughout has been the vigor and intractableness of the antinomies that Blake seeks to reconcile. It may well be the case that every significant myth is born in just such a troubled intelligence. In Henry Murray's words, "The creative imaginations which participate in the formation of a *vital* myth must be those people—often alienated and withdrawn people—who have *experienced*, in their 'depths' and on their own pulses, one or more of the unsolved critical situations with which humanity at large or members of their own society are confronted."[76] A sociologist might say that the crisis Blake confronts is a reflection of his society; a psychoanalyst would identify it as neurosis. To the former, Blake would reply that society is the reflection of its members, and that the disastrous failure of political radicalism proved the need for inner change to precede outer. To the latter, he might invoke the testimony of the many friends like John Linnell who "never saw anything the least like madness" (*Blake Records*, p. 257), and more tellingly could urge that the prophetic books, however much they may reflect unconscious motives, are a superbly conscious attempt to shape a myth out of symbols that are known to be symbols. Anthony Storr, noting that creative people are often distinguished by "an exceptional degreee of division between opposites," adds that they also possess "an exceptional awareness of this division." Artistic creation represents a successful way of dealing with the inner division that is found in all people, whereas neurotic symptoms are its unsuccessful expression, and the neurotic is often unaware of his dividedness.[77]

The peculiarly unformal form of Blake's poems will concern us later, but we cannot forget that the lyrics are superbly ordered and that the strangeness of the prophecies is deliberately intended, whether or

[75] See below, Chapter 7.
[76] "The Possible Nature of a 'Mythology' to Come," in *Myth and Mythmaking*, ed. Murray, pp. 344-345.
[77] *The Dynamics of Creation* (London, 1972), p. 196.

not it wholly succeeds in its purpose. As Langer reminds us, "One does not say of a sleeper that he dreams clumsily, nor of a neurotic that his symptoms are carelessly strung together."[78] The story of the Zoas is the dream of Albion, but it is not Blake's dream. He has very deliberately developed, in response to spiritual inspiration, a system of "Poetical Personifications & Acts"[79] as a structure of symbols that can give rise to thought.

The function of myth is to explain our divided state and to prescribe the means of healing it. Like the Gnostics, from whom he partly borrowed, Blake projected a myth of the cosmos in order to "express and illuminate his understanding of himself,"[80] and like them he developed a myth of salvation in order to put an end to the sense of crippling alienation. "Knowledge of oneself implies redemption from oneself, just as knowledge of the universe implies the means of freeing oneself from the world and of dominating it."[81]

In the fundamental action of *The Four Zoas*, the fallen Urizen must rise again to play his proper role in the apocalyptic harvest. In the *No Natural Religion* tractates Blake had declared, "Man by his reasoning power can only compare & judge of what he has already perceiv'd" (E1/K97). But if it be granted that we have other than natural perceptions, why might not reason be able to compare and judge these as well? Logically it can; it is perception that needs to be redirected rather than reason, although fallen reason naturally refuses to recognize any but natural perceptions. So it is quite right that Urizen should be rehabilitated at the end of *The Four Zoas*, rising "in naked majesty/In radiant Youth" (*FZ* 121:31-32, E376/K362). It is he who wields the flail that separates truth from error, even as it must be the parent power Tharmas, in imagery drawn from Isaiah, who blows the chaff of error away with his winnowing whirlwind.[82] Once again the Zoas are coequal.

Powerful though this myth is, it did not satisfy Blake for long. As Erdman observes, his system never really allowed a workable role for

---

[78] *Feeling and Form*, p. 245.

[79] Letter to Dawson Turner, 9 June 1818 (K867; not in E).

[80] Grant, *Gnosticism and Early Christianity*, p. 9.

[81] Puech, "Gnosis and Time," p. 75. It is notable that Jonas seems irritated with the Gnostics for the persistently symbolic quality of their thinking: "Now what can a reader . . . make of the information that 'Anguish' became dense like a fog, that 'Error' elaborated 'its matter' in the void, that 'it' fashioned a formation, produced works, became angry, etc.?" (*The Gnostic Religion*, p. 315). Jonas, who acknowledges his debt to Bultmann, tries to demythologize the Gnostics, but this is in direct conflict with their own conscious attempt to remythologize metaphysics.

[82] *FZ* 133:34-134:4, E387/K374. The source is Isa. 41:15-16, as noted by A. Grace Wegner in *The Explicator*, 27 (1969), item 53.

reason.[83] So the purpose of the myth alters in *Milton* and *Jerusalem:* instead of dramatizing the restoration of the four Zoas (though this is never expressly denied) it emphasizes instead the primary role of Los and transposes Urizen into Satan in the doctrine of "states."

> The Imagination is not a State: it is the Human Existence itself
> Affection or Love becomes a State, when divided from Imagination
> The Memory is a State always, & the Reason is a State
> Created to be Annihilated. . . .

(M 32:32-35, E131/K522)

Despite Blake's frequent attempts to explain what the states are, they remain obscure. Sometimes it appears that they change while individuals do not; at other times, that individuals change while the states do not.[84] At any rate, the invention of states represents a decisive change in Blake's myth, and I think an unfortunate one. Instead of showing that all parts of the self must be rehabilitated and harmonized, he now defines the qualities that he dislikes—specifically, those that had been associated with the fallen Urizen—as Satanic, that is, as illusory and external to the self. And instead of rejecting the traditional pattern of hierarchical psychology, he now proposes something very like a hierarchy with Urthona (imagination) at the top, Luvah (affection, love) in the middle, and Urizen (memory, reason) at the bottom.

The new myth comes uncomfortably close to the aspect of mythical thinking which Cassirer describes as projecting outside the self any impulses which are felt to be hostile or unworthy. "Just as very different 'souls' can live peacefully side by side in one and the same man, so the empirical sequence of the events of life can be distributed among wholly different 'subjects,' each of which is not only *thought* in the form of a separate being, but also *felt* and *intuited* as a living demonic power which takes possession of the man."[85] Blake denies the existence of demonic powers and defines Satan as our own Spectre, yet his account of states looks like an externalization all the same. When we behave Satanically it is not really *we* at all, but the state of Satan through which we are passing. Seen in this light, the myth relaxes from the painful tension of *The Four Zoas*—and even there we find an awkward attempt to interpolate passages about the states—so that

---

[83] *Prophet Against Empire*, pp. 178-179.

[84] See Fox, *Poetic form in Blake's Milton*, p. 23. Evidently the "state" is not a consistent concept, but a range of metaphors that allows Blake to vary the relationships in his myth with considerable freedom. See Edward J. Rose, "Blake's Metaphorical States," *Blake Studies*, 4 (1971), 9-31.

[85] *Mythical Thought*, p. 165.

imagination becomes dominant and the negative aspects of psychic life are relegated to an inferior or even "unreal" status.

Very similarly, the three classes of Elect, Redeemed, and Reprobate have the function of distributing the self among different levels of reality. Milton is represented as existing on four separate levels: his "Redeemed portion" shapes Urizen out of clay, his "Mortal part" is frozen in the rock of the fallen world, his "real Human" walks above in majesty, and his "elect" Spectre separates from Blake's left foot (*M* 20:7-21, E113/K502). It is tempting to see an analogy with the Gnostic division of man into separate souls, the hylic (Blake's ironically named Elect), the psychic (the Redeemed), and the pneumatic (the Reprobate).[86] Once again, there is a repudiation of certain aspects of the self, or at least a suggestion that some parts are truer and more permanent than others. This was not the case in the original myth of the Zoas. But it points toward the increasingly soteriological nature of Blake's myth: through Los, and ultimately through Jesus who works in Los, we are not so much regenerated as rescued from ourselves. Stated psychologically, Blake's problem is to escape selfhood, the prison of the ego, without disintegrating into chaos. Stated metaphysically, it is to identify the force that can restore unity without returning the self to selfhood. The rehabilitation of Urizen in *The Four Zoas*, Blake must have come to believe, was nothing more than a covert return of Satan. What he needs is a divine principle that can "descend" into the self in order to save it, literalizing Milton's metaphor of Christ who in solitary meditation "into himself descended" (*Paradise Regained* II. 111).

BLAKE AND FREUD

We have noted affinities between Blake's myth and those of the Gnostics, Plotinus, Boehme, and Hegel. To see it from a more detached perspective, it should be helpful to consider some of its more striking divergencies from the most influential psychic myth of our own time, that of Freud. The least fruitful approach would be to translate Blake's terms into Freudian ones. If a modern equivalent were all that was desired, Jung's model of the four mental functions would be more relevant.[87] Moreover, the mechanist aspects of Freud's model of the self

[86] See Jonas, *The Gnostic Religion*, pp. 122-124.

[87] Thinking, feeling, sensing and intuiting would correspond to Urizen, Luvah, Tharmas, and Urthona/Los. The various Jungian readings of Blake are, however, disappointing, both because they accept Jung's system as scientifically valid and because they tend to psychoanalyze Blake rather than exploring the actual operation of his symbols. The points of affinity between the two, incidentally, are not at all surprising, since Jung studied many of the same sources (notably the alchemical tradition) that Blake did.

have often been criticized, and one critique, by calling it Newtonian, reminds us of just how much Blake would have disliked its structural assumptions.[88] What is more significant is the larger attention in both thinkers to the dynamic economy of the self, and the mission in both of freeing man from the guilt generated by Urizen or the superego. More generally still, both examine the symbols of inner life with scrupulous care, recognizing as Ricoeur says that " 'consciousness' of the self must become 'knowledge' of the self, i.e., indirect, mediate, and suspicious knowledge of the self."[89]

For Freud, such a project means above all an investigation of the unconscious. It is a fundamental mistake, he says, to equate the mind with consciousness. "Turn your eyes inward, look into your own depths, learn first to know yourself! Then you will understand why you were bound to fall ill; and perhaps, you will avoid falling ill in future."[90] When Blake turns his eyes inward he finds the Zoas in all their complex life. Freud, on the contrary, holds that the unconscious is inaccessible to direct inspection and can only be detected as it is betrayed by neurotic symptoms, dreams, significant "slips," and so on. In Freudian terms Blake would recognize at most the existence of the preconscious.

The point is important because Freud did not invent the unconscious, however much he may have taught the world to pay attention to it. Wordsworth pays tribute to its mysterious impulses in general terms, and philosophers like Schelling hail it explicitly as the source of our best impulses, "a power by which we, even in our free activity, without our knowledge, and even against our wills, realize goals unawares."[91] Earlier treatments of the unconscious tended to regard it as a nighttime, nightmare world of illicit impulses.[92] Blake refuses to postulate a gulf between ego and id, either of hostile opposition or of beneficent but hidden connections.

In Jung's expressive phrase, thought that draws upon the uncon-

[88] "The psychic apparatus is a thoroughly Newtonian engine, and the supposed laws by which it is governed are markedly similar to Newton's laws of motion" (Daniel Yankelovich and William Barrett, *Ego and Instinct: The Psychoanalytic View of Human Nature—Revised* [New York, 1970], p. 56.

[89] *Conflict of Interpretations*, p. 331. This "hermeneutics of suspicion" is a presiding theme in Ricoeur's *Freud and Philosophy;* Blake aspires to the same union of suspicion with a religious "restoration of meaning" that Ricoeur hopes to achieve (*Freud and Philosophy: An Essay on Interpretation*, trans. Denis Savage [New Haven, 1970], p. 32).

[90] "A Difficulty in the Path of Psycho-Analysis," in *The Standard Edition of the Complete Psychological Works of Sigmund Freud*, ed. James Strachey (London, 1955), XVII, 143.

[91] *Sämtliche Werke*, III, 616, as quoted by E. D. Hirsch, Jr., *Wordsworth and Schelling: A Typological Study of Romanticism* (New Haven, 1960), p. 109.

[92] See Lancelot Law Whyte, *The Unconscious Before Freud* (New York, 1960), esp. p. 71.

scious emerges with what seems at first "slime from the depths."[93] In Blake's myth that is the submarine world of the fallen Tharmas:

> Tharmas reard up his hands & stood on the affrighted Ocean
> The dead reard up his Voice & stood on the resounding shore
> Crying. Fury in my limbs. destruction in my bones & marrow
> My skull riven into filaments. my eyes into sea jellies
> Floating upon the tide wander bubbling & bubbling
> Uttering my lamentations & begetting little monsters
> Who sit mocking upon the little pebbles of the tide. . . .
> (*FZ* 44:21-27, E323/K296)

Now, whatever Tharmas' function may be, he is not a separate "part" of Albion, and accordingly whatever happens to him happens to Man.

> Of Man who lays upon the shores leaning his faded head
> Upon the Oozy rock inwrapped with the weeds of death
> His eyes sink hollow in his head his flesh coverd with slime. . . .
> (*FZ* 108:29-31, E369/K354)

Very similar imagery can be found in Plato's account of Glaucus in the *Republic*, which is allegorized by Proclus, as Berkeley notes, into a type of the soul's descent into matter.[94] Blake's method is more like that of Proclus than of Freud. His imagery of Tharmas and Albion in the sea is notable for its clarity, and Tharmas himself has a vivid understanding of his disintegrated state. To put it simply, in Blake the imagery of the depths does not connote the unknown. On the contrary, it is the rational Urizen who promotes the idea of mystery, while nothing can be mysterious for the visionary imagination.

Moreover, even if Tharmas the "parent power" corresponds in some respects to the Freudian id, it is certainly not the case that the conscious mind attempts to channel the irresistible impulses of the unconscious. "In relation to the id," Freud says of the ego, "it is like a man on horseback, who has to hold in check the superior strength of the horse; with this difference, that the rider tries to do so with his own strength, while the ego uses borrowed forces."[95] Freud adapts the Platonic metaphor of rider and horse, stipulating that the essential

---

[93] *Collected Works*, III: *The Structure and Dynamics of the Psyche*, trans. R.F.C. Hull (New York, 1960), p. 34.

[94] See the *Republic* X.611d, and Berkeley's *Siris*, par. 313. Paul Miner observes ("Visions in the Darksome Air," Rosenfeld, p. 266) that Blake may also have thought of Jonah 2:5, "The waters compassed me about, even to the soul: the depth closed me round about, the weeds were wrapped about my head."

[95] *The Ego and the Id*, trans. Joan Riviere, rev. James Strachey (New York, 1962), p. 15.

power belongs to the horse rather than the rider. In Blake energy is distributed among all four Zoas, even the rational Urizen, although it may take a different form in each; in a nice distinction, "Tharmas gave his Power to Los Urthona gave his strength" (*FZ* 107:31, E368/K353). Luvah, the specifically sexual Zoa, has neither power nor strength on this occasion, since he has just sacrificed himself in the crucifixion, the traditional Christian symbol of paradoxical power in weakness. And not only is libidinal energy identified with Luvah rather than Tharmas, it in no way precedes or determines the imaginative energy of Urthona/Los. In fact Los is least imaginative when he is most sexual, in thrall to the Female Will of Enitharmon, and Luvah as Orc is the *son* of Los and Enitharmon, the desire that is born of the limits of time and space. And although Los chaining Orc might seem to correspond to Freud's theory of repression, it is crucial to that theory that the ego cannot admit the existence of that which is repressed, whereas Los knows very well indeed what Orc is and why he is binding him. Each Zoa, in fact, behaves like a complete person, and in this respect Blake's myth is more like the psychomachia of traditional allegory than like psychoanalytic explanation.

It is quite true that Blake deeply understood the force of sexual desire, and brilliantly described how it can be deflected into aggression. "War is energy Enslavd" (*FZ* 120:42, E375/K361); the reference to Luvah implies, as Frye says, that "war is a perversion of the sexual impulse."[96] Traditional faculty psychology could scarcely have imagined such a displacement, let alone have dramatized it. Nor could the "machinery" of the gods make much of it: Mars is war and Venus is sex. War can be seduced by sex (Cleopatra putting on Antony's armor in play) but how can sex motivate war instead of inhibiting it?[97] But to recognize this insight in Blake is not to concede that sexual energy has the all-controlling power that it does in Freud's writings, where it has been described as "a sort of unmoved mover of the whole system."[98] Only at a moment of gross confusion like that at the beginning of *The Four Zoas* can Luvah be predominant. Luvah as Orc is untamable, like the Freudian id, and Blake does not even consider it useful to try to sublimate his energies; "civilization" in its traditional form is much

[96] *Fearful Symmetry*, p. 262.

[97] See for instance Ronald Paulson's analysis of the mutual taming of sex and war in Veronese's *Mars and Venus* (*Emblem and Expression* [London, 1975], pp. 12-13). Blake's far more subtle treatment of the theme reminds us, once again, of the limitations of traditional iconography in comparison with his symbolic range.

[98] Durand, *L'Imagination Symbolique*, p. 44. At times, however, Freud describes a fundamental "displaceable energy" that is neutral rather than specifically sexual (*The Ego and the Id*, p. 34). Blake's Tharmas could perhaps be translated into these terms.

less attractive to him than it is to Freud. Instead, he pursues the dream of *transforming* Orc by turning him "back" into Luvah, recovering his true nature of which the Orc state is only a distorted parody. According to Freud's much quoted aphorism, "Where id is, there ego shall be." Blake would say, "Where Orc is, there Luvah was and shall be again." And since the restoration of Luvah requires the descent of Jesus in Luvah's robes of blood, one might also say "Where Orc is, there Jesus shall be," postulating just that escape or rescue *from the self* that Freud would regard as pietistic delusion.

Most significantly of all, the Zoas are represented as fully human, with ideas and passions. Ricoeur comments, "The expressive force of the word 'id'—even more than that of the term 'unconscious'—guards us from the naïve realism of giving the unconscious a consciousness. . . . The unconscious is id and nothing but id."[99] In these terms there is no place at all in Blake's myth for the id. One may consider that this is an unfortunate limitation, that Blake claims to throw light where there can only be darkness. In Charles Baudouin's attractive metaphor, the structure of the self has two facades, one facing the street and the other a mysterious inner garden or *non-moi intérieur*.[100] In Blake there is no unknowable unconscious. Much in the self is confused and chaotic, some of it may even be a not-I in the sense of Satanic delusion, but nothing is invisible. On the other hand, if one happens not to accept Freudian theory, one may regard Blake's position as deeply imaginative and admire his refusal to portray any part of the human mind as a nonhuman "it." Blake would certainly have approved of MacIntyre's criticism that Freud makes the unconscious self-explanatory even though it is not open to inspection, and that he treats the mind as a substantive place that exists apart and can contain objects: "The unconscious is the ghost of the Cartesian consciousness."[101] A fundamental feature of the Zoas is their *humanness*: by personifying them, Blake avoids the modern notion of the person or self as inhabited by impersonal "drives" or "forces." Similarly, the Greek gods, even at their most trivialized, expressed the humanness of human feeling. To say that someone is possessed by Aphrodite is very different from saying that he or she is dominated by libido, even if both formulations refer to identical behavior.

[99] *Freud and Philosophy*, p. 438.

[100] *Psychanalyse du Symbole Religieux* (Paris, 1957), p. 104. Wittgenstein remarks wryly, "Many of these explanations are adopted because they have a peculiar charm. The picture of people having subconscious thoughts has a charm. The idea of an underworld, a secret cellar. Something hidden, uncanny" (*Lectures and Conversations on Aesthetics, Psychology and Religious Belief*, ed. Cyril Barrett [Berkeley, 1966], p. 25).

[101] A. C. MacIntyre, *The Unconscious: A Conceptual Analysis* (London, 1958), p. 73.

Whether or not Freud's theory of the unconscious is adequate, it remains striking that Blake's myth has so little room for anything like it. Ricoeur speaks of the dreamer as imprisoned in a "forbidden and mutilated discourse";[102] Blake's symbols may well emerge from some such realm, but he subjects them to artistic shaping and intellectual interpretation, and refuses to concede that any part of the self can remain opaque to imaginative vision. The primary agent of suffering and guilt is Urizen (or his spectre Satan, or his female aspect Rahab). Goya's etching "The Sleep of Reason Produces Monsters" has been cited so often in accounts of Blake's era that it has become trite. But it is less often noticed that in Blake the *waking* activity of reason produces monsters. Albion may be asleep, but Urizen is not. Eliade has said that the monsters of the unconscious permit man "to liberate himself, to complete his initiation."[103] If anything like the unconscious exists in Blake's myth, it is not clearly demarcated from the conscious mind, and monsters are the joint production of both.

Furthermore, if Urizen is awake and rational, then he cannot correspond as closely as is usually assumed to the Freudian superego. For it is of the essence of the superego that its imposition of guilt through the tyranny of conscience is only partly intelligible to the ego. "The super-ego is always close to the id and can act as its representative *vis-à-vis* the ego. It reaches deep down into the id and for that reason is farther from consciousness than the ego is."[104] Urizen is ego as well as superego, which is as much as to say that the distinction does not really exist in Blake, since Urthona/Los (who has no counterpart in Freud) is equally important to the ego and, in addition, draws freely on instinctual sources of inspiration.

We have been concerned thus far with differences between two models of the self. Both, as models, are inevitably abstract, and some of Blake's symbolic abstractions have much to commend them. A still more fundamental difference between Blake and Freud relates not to the structure of the self but to its history. In the tradition of Rousseau, Freud sees childhood experience as crucially formative and as underlying all later experience. For Blake childhood or Innocence is a state to pass through, not a permanent foundation for all later behavior. And the very distinction between "earlier" and "later" is systematically subverted by his myth.

Blake's representation of the self directly contradicts the Freudian reading of human experience as shaped in time. In Ricoeur's phrase Freudian analysis is an archaeology, "a revelation of the archaic, a

[102] *Freud and Philosophy*, p. 16.
[103] *Images and Symbols*, p. 14.
[104] Freud, *The Ego and the Id*, pp. 38–39.

manifestation of the ever prior."[105] Blake's thought claims to be a perpetual synthesis rather than analysis, a revelation of the ever present, the "eternal Now."[106] To be sure, Freud's genetic explanation is in a sense structural and synchronic: the past persists in the timeless unconscious. But it is still the *past* that persists, a residue of attitudes formed and traumas suffered in the first years of life. There can be no archaeology in Blake; the self is divided because of a breakdown in the inner dynamic, not in reaction to a history of external impressions. We have already remarked that there is little place for the "other" in Blake's myth, and we must now add that the experience of time, although often alluded to and indeed identified with Los, is equally shadowy.

Here, more clearly than in the case of the unconscious, Blake defies the main stream of traditional thought (and, one is tempted to say, of human experience). Unlike Augustine or Bunyan or Rousseau, he insists that the self is atemporal, and will admit no accumulated weight of experience. By so doing, of course, he can give a very different answer to the problem of alienation and guilt from those given either by Christian moralists or by Freud. We are guilty because we are self-alienated, projecting a Urizenic law that imposes guilt, not because we have done things of which we are personally guilty (Rousseau) or because all men are by nature guilty (Augustine, Bunyan), or because our relations with our parents in infancy have caused us to internalize the paternal model as the superego (Freud). Guilt—or shame, the terms being fairly synonymous in Blake—is the expression of Albion's self-exteriorization as his Zoas run amok and forget their unity:

Shame divides Families. Shame hath divided Albion in sunder!
First fled my Sons, & then my Daughters, then my Wild
    Animations
My Cattle next, last ev'n the Dog of my Gate. the Forests fled
The Corn-fields, & the breathing Gardens outside separated
The Sea; the Stars: the Sun: the Moon: drivn forth by my disease.
                                        (*J* 21:6-10, E164/K643)

Not only guilt or shame, but externality itself, is an illusion of the fallen mind. Guilt is therefore negated by denying its very existence, not by coming to terms with its significance in the history of the self. In Augustine or Rousseau guilt cannot be abolished because it is an appropriate, if lacerating, response to what really happened; in Freud, it cannot be abolished because the superego is a permanent and neces-

---

[105] *Freud and Philosophy*, p. 440.
[106] Annotations to Lavater, E581/K77. Cf. Eckhart's use of a similar phrase, p. 104n above.

sary element of the self. In both cases we are taught to understand our guilt and make it productive. But Blake claims in effect that guilt *is not*, that a regenerated Urizen or an Albion freed from the state of Satan will know it no more.

It is necessary to emphasize this point because some of the deepest conceptual and aesthetic problems in Blake's myth stem from it. One more corollary needs to be noted: that despite its turbulent inner conflicts, the self remains the same throughout. There are few hints in Blake's myth of the development of the self in relation not to its inner warfare but to external events.[107] "I cannot paint/What then I was," Wordsworth writes in *Tintern Abbey*. Blake would not want to try. You were what you are. It may perhaps be true that when Wordsworth writes of "two consciousnesses" in his mental history, the earlier as well as the later is a construction of the remembering imagination.[108] But in simpler terms we can certainly say that Blake has nothing like Wordsworth's theme of personal development or, on a wider stage, like the irreversible changes in the lives of human beings that are explored in a poem like *Michael*. One of Arnold's touchstones was the line from *Michael*, "And never lifted up a single stone." It could not be a Blakean line, since its whole force derives from the irrevocability of the past.

In the largest perspective we may say that Blake agrees with both Augustine and Freud that man is alienated, but differs from them in his proposed solution. One of Hegel's most sympathetic expositors has criticized his concept of the freedom of desire as failing to take account of the ways in which it is thwarted by "our own compulsions, fears, obsessions."[109] We remember Blake's treatment of infinite desire; he wants to reconstruct the self so that compulsions and obsessions disappear from the human condition. Plato says that "the body-prison in its cunning works through desire, contriving to make the prisoner aid and abet his own imprisonment as much as possible."[110] Here are the mind-forged manacles. The answer is to awaken the mind so that it can simply cast them off.

[107] Of purely internal development there is plenty; Los and Enitharmon are very different in *FZ* IX from what they were in IV. But external or social reality is much more tenuously present. The quarrel with Hayley that lies behind *Milton*, and the sedition trial that produces so many echoes in *Jerusalem*, are presented as significant for what they reveal about the nature of things rather than for a decisive temporal influence on personality.
[108] *The Prelude*, II.36. On this point see Thomas Weiskel, *The Romantic Sublime: Studies in the Structure and Psychology of Transcendence* (Baltimore, 1976), p. 170, with an interesting adaptation of Freud on "screen memories."
[109] Taylor, *Hegel*, p. 561.
[110] *Phaedo*, trans. R. S. Bluck (New York, 1955), 82e, p. 82.

I have been considering Blake's myth as an analogue to Freud's theory, and have avoided treating it as a subject for that theory. If one were to do so, the fragmented Albion might be seen as a neurotic perception (however controlled and modified by art) of the divided self; the increasing emphasis on Los would be the compensatory narcissism that exaggerates self-worth; and the myth as a whole might be a form of repetition compulsion. I do not wish to pursue such a critique, which, whether valid or not, would lead far from our central concerns. But it is impossible to close this chapter without stating clearly what has been increasingly apparent, that Blake openly defies the reality principle. In *The Ego and the Id* Freud discusses the ego's subservience to three masters, "the external world, the libido of the id, and the severity of super-ego" (p. 46). As best it can, it struggles to placate all three and render them compatible with each other, but it must always fail to some extent, and neurosis is the result. All three "masters" are visible in Blake's myth, but he asserts that they are false and can be dispensed with. The external world is a Lockean-Newtonian fiction; the libido is a crazed Orc who can be healed—and reconciled with the abdicated Tharmas—by the sacrifice of Jesus in Luvah's robes of blood; and the superego is the brooding Urizen whose Satanic state can be abolished so that he may resume his role as prince of light and plowman of eternity. Freud would diagnose this as wish-fulfillment of a peculiarly comprehensive kind; Blake would diagnose Freud as a craven victim of the spurious realism of the fallen world.

Here again is the problem of solipsism, the deepest and most intractable threat in Blake's myth. Desire, Cassirer says, asserts a magical power to create the world in its own image, but "true freedom of action presupposes an inner limitation, a recognition of certain objective limits of action. The I comes to itself only by positing these limits, by successively restricting the unconditional causality with respect to the world of things, which it initially imputed to itself."[111] This Blake will not allow. Desire is infinite; objective limits are demonic fictions. It is not simply that Blake is religious and that Freud characterized religion as a mass obsessional neurosis. It is also that Blake denies that our lives are controlled by a world outside ourselves (asserting that all selves are one in the Divine Humanity) and by a temporal history in which we live.[112] Moreover, Freud's reality principle applies not only

[111] *Mythical Thought*, p. 158.

[112] Here again existentialist thought is relevant, in combining an acute sense of the obstacles to freedom with an extravagant assertion of its possibility and scope. In Mary Warnock's exposition, "Freedom cannot emerge except against a background of unchosen elements. But these elements do not *restrict* freedom; we are totally free in the manner in which we experience these elements. Our freedom to choose ourselves is limit-

to external limits but also to the inner facts that cannot change. To quote Ricoeur once more, "Resignation to the ineluctable is not reducible to a mere knowledge of necessity, i.e. to a purely intellectual extension of what we called perceptual reality-testing; resignation is an affective task, a work of correction applied to the very core of the libido, to the heart of narcissism. Consequently, the scientific world view must be incorporated into a history of desire."[113] Blake will not do it.

---

less. An Existentialist psychoanalysis would seek to explain what it was that a man had chosen for himself in the future, rather than to explain the present in terms of the past" (*Existentialism* [Oxford, 1970], p. 122).

[113] *Freud and Philosophy*, p. 332. If, as Frye suggests, Urizen is the Freudian reality principle (*The Stubborn Structure*, p. 181), then Blake may be attempting the incorporation of which Ricoeur speaks when he dramatizes the rehabilitation of Urizen in *FZ* IX. But Urizen is rehabilitated only by being radically transformed; and in *Milton* and *Jerusalem* even this much reconciliation drops out of the myth, Urizen's attributes being largely displaced onto Satan.

[F I V E]

The Problem of Dualism

A call on *Blake*—My 3d Interview. I read him Wordsworth's in-
comparable Ode which he heartily enjoyed—The same half crazy
crotchets about the two worlds—the eternal repetition of which
must in time become tiresome—Again he repeated today—"I fear
Wordsworth loves Nature.". . . It was remarkable that the parts of
Wordsworths ode which he most enjoyed were the most obscure
& those I the least like & comprehend.

Crabb Robinson's diary, 24 Dec. 1825

Love's methods are war; love's basis is the mortal hatred between
the sexes.

Nietzsche, Ecce Homo

I am the poet of the Body and I am the poet of the Soul,
The pleasures of heaven are with me and the pains of hell are with
    me,
The first I graft and increase upon myself, the latter I translate into
    a new tongue.

Whitman, "Song of Myself"

VEGETATED AND SPIRITUAL BODIES

Was Blake a dualist or a monist? If that question had a simple
answer this book would not have been written. The answer
is highly complex because in certain respects Blake was
both, and because neither term has much meaning until it is illuminated by a specific context. Throughout his career Blake firmly opposed at least one form of dualism, the Cartesian distinction between
mind (or soul) and body. "Man has no Body distinct from his Soul for
that calld Body is a portion of Soul discernd by the five Senses, the
chief inlets of Soul in this age" (*MHH*, E34/K149). Modern philosophers of every type also reject that kind of dualism, since as soon as
one postulates an ontological gap between two realms (e.g., between
mental and nonmental) it becomes impossible to understand how
there can be any interaction between them, while the attempt to define
a means of interaction always results in breaking down the distinction
between the two realms.[1] In this sense most philosophers have always
been monists. But that is not to say that there can be no valid distinc-

---

[1] See John Passmore, "The Two-Worlds Argument," *Philosophical Reasoning* (New
York, 1961), pp. 38-57.

165

tions *within* a monistic universe. Mind and body may not be ontologically distinct, but we continue to speak intelligibly about bodies and
minds. There is a difference between a headache and a broken heart.

By contrast with the widespread modern attacks on the Cartesian
"ghost in the machine,"[2] Blake seeks to establish what one might call
the mind in the ghost—the true self within the fallen selfhood which is
the illusory body woven by Vala. There is a consensus nowadays that
Blake has nothing to do with conventional distinctions between mind
and body, subjective and objective realms. Yet we constantly find him
saying "The Natural Body is an Obstruction to the Soul or Spiritual
Body,"[3] and that "Imagination [is] the real & eternal World of which
this Vegetable Universe is but a faint shadow & in which we shall live
in our Eternal or Imaginative Bodies, when these Vegetable Mortal
Bodies are no more" (*J* 77, E229/K717). These passages—and there
are scores of them—refuse to be rescued from the imputation of
dualism.

At the very least one must accept Paley's conclusion that "Blake
was a monist who found his mythology entrapping him in a dualistic
position."[4] Since my conviction is that the mythology rests on the philosophy, I would say rather that Blake is a dualist who wishes he were
a monist. For dualism, as opposed to pluralism, is not so much a tem-
peramental commitment to variety as it is a response to the inherent
difficulties in monism. As Roland Hall says, it is commonly "the expression of a failed monism."[5] Body and mind may be versions of the
same thing, but why then do they seem so different to us? Blake's answer is that the bodies we think we have (or are) differ radically from
the bodies we ought to have (or be), either in a transformed version of
this world or in a spiritual realm that we shall enter after death. His
dualism is not Cartesian but Pauline.

Commentators on Plato have long wrestled with the problem that
in some ways the soul is described as unitary and divine, in others as
multiplex. "Pure was that light and pure were we from the pollution
of the walking sepulchre which we call a body, to which we are bound
like an oyster to its shell."[6] The solution seems to be that Plato regards

[2] Gilbert Ryle's famous phrase, in *The Concept of Mind* (New York, 1949). Antony
Flew says, "People are what you meet. We do not meet only the sinewy containers in
which other people are kept, and they do not encounter only the fleshy houses that we
ourselves inhabit" (*Encyclopedia of Philosophy*, ed. Paul Edwards [New York, 1967], IV,
142, art. "Immortality").

[3] Annotations to Berkeley (E653/K775).

[4] "The Figure of the Garment in *The Four Zoas, Milton,* and *Jerusalem,*" in Curran and
Wittreich, p. 123.

[5] *Encyclopedia of Philosophy*, V, 364, art. "Monism."

[6] *Phaedrus* 250, trans. Walter Hamilton (Harmondsworth, 1973), p. 57.

the soul as tripartite insofar as it is contaminated by this world of change and reincarnation, but as unitary insofar as, by love of wisdom, it is able to free itself from the world.[7] The soul is most free and reasons best, he says elsewhere, when it leaves the senses behind and has "no more communication with the body nor contact with it than is absolutely necessary."[8] Blake, we know, would reject this position. The body is the portion of the soul discerned by the five senses. But what does he mean by calling the senses "the chief inlets of Soul in this age?" Raine shrewdly comments, "Not the only inlets even in the present age, and in other ages not even the chief inlets."[9] We remember also the injunction to look through the eye and not with it. A thorough-going monist would say "I see"; anyone who tells us to look *through* the eye implies the existence of a self that is distinct from its physical senses.

Both sides of Blake's dilemma were anticipated by Plotinus, who developed his theory of emanation from the One to explain how the world could be good (because reflecting the One) and yet inferior and corrupt (because removed from the One). We have already noticed that he argued against the Gnostics that our world is beautiful, being an image of the intelligible world.[10] When Blake says that body is a portion of soul, he means as Plotinus does that the soul is not lodged in a container but on the contrary "as the superior reality *contains* the sensible universe."[11] At the same time matter is described as "nonbeing" and as unable to unite with the soul that contains it. One has to recognize that "nonbeing"—Blake's "Non-Entity"—is a technical term and does not imply a distinction between existence and nonexistence. "Matter is non-being in the sense that it is not form, not order, not knowledge." It follows that the intelligible world is not, as in Plato, remote from the world we live in. "Plotinus does not have two worlds, but only one. His world of true being is not, except metaphorically, a world above the everyday world. It *is* the everyday world."[12]

Ah, but the strength of that metaphor! If the real world is the everyday world, why does the everyday world look so different from it? Very much like Plotinus, Blake insists that reality is "within" rather than "above," yet his entire myth is predicated on the fact that we do

[7] For a survey of the problem and a critique of various attempts to solve it, see W.K.C. Guthrie, "Plato's Views on the Nature of the Soul," in *Plato: A Collection of Critical Essays*, ed. Gregory Vlastos (New York, 1971), II, 230-243.

[8] *Phaedo*, trans. Bluck, 65c, p. 49.

[9] *Blake and Tradition*, II, 105.

[10] See above, p. 41.

[11] John N. Deck, *Nature, Contemplation, and the One: A Study in the Philosophy of Plotinus*, p. 32.

[12] Deck, pp. 89, 91. On "non-entity," see the *Enneads*, I.viii.3.

not know how to look within. As Plotinus expounds the myth of Prometheus, he is fettered to the rock of the material world instead of remaining as he should in the intellectual world; and in another passage, the fallen soul is chained to the body, buried in a cave.[13] So also Blake's Luvah says that after his rebellion he found himself with Los "in the Cavern dark enslavd to vegetative forms" (*FZ* 83:30, E351/K326).

The fact is that both Plotinus and Blake say different things at different times, depending on context. "When thinking of the return of the soul to its source . . . Plotinus thinks of a flight from the world; and of souls living in the world as fallen and being punished for their fall by bodily life; when opposing the extreme dualism of the Gnostics, for whom the creator of the material universe is evil and his productions monstrous, Plotinus takes the contrary position and is almost Franciscan in his praises of the excellence of the cosmos and his talk of the importance of the soul as its maker and organizer."[14] It is clear in both Plotinus and Blake that matter is a falling away from reality and receives such existence as it has from the informing soul. In the not dissimilar Gnostic philosophy of Valentinus, "matter would appear to be a function rather than a substance on its own, a state or 'affection' of the absolute being, and the solidified external expression of that state. . . . This substance, then, psychical as well as material, is nothing else than a self-estranged and sunken form of the Spirit solidified from acts into habitual conditions and from inner process to outer fact."[15] Every word of this description can be applied to Blake, not because he "was" a Gnostic but because the Gnostic form of Neoplatonism arrived at similar answers by an analogous route. This is true both of doctrines of which Blake may have read and of others which he did not know but which anticipate the logic of his thought. Gnostic thinkers, for example, distinguished between the soul as *pneuma*, "a kind of spiritual 'body' of the absolute spirit," and the fallen *psyche* in which it sinks into "a form of alienation from itself."[16] Blake does not use these terms and never states the distinction so clearly, but it would nevertheless be easy to illustrate something like it in his poems.

We are presented, then, with a dualism that denies itself to be such by constantly defining one half of the duality out of existence. "Every thing that lives is Holy," Blake declares at the end of *The Marriage of Heaven and Hell* (E44/K160), and Oothoon repeats the slogan at the

---

[13] *Enneads*, IV.iii.14, IV.viii.4.

[14] J. M. Rist, *Plotinus: The Road to Reality* (Cambridge, 1967), p. 112.

[15] Jonas, *The Gnostic Religion*, pp. 174, 187.

[16] Jonas, "Myth and Mysticism: A Study of Objectification and Interiorization in Religious Thought," *Philosophical Essays*, p. 295.

end of *Visions of the Daughters of Albion* (E50/K195). At face value, this statement contradicts the traditional idea of the holy as the *mysterium tremendum* and "wholly other."[17] And this is accurate, inasmuch as Blake never admits a remote and mysterious realm of transcendence. But it may not follow that the slogan celebrates the adequacy of the immediate, as in primitive "mythical feeling."[18] For it may mean instead that reaility is holy *insofar as* it is fully informed by the divine, after the manner of Cusanus' doctrine of Jesus, of which Jaspers has said, "His is an all-embracing thought, lovingly close to reality and yet transcending it. The world is not circumvented but itself shines in the light of transcendence."[19] Philosophically speaking, both Plotinus and Blake would object that "reality" is used very loosely here, but one sees what Jaspers means: what we normally regard as real would not *be* real if it did not contain, or embody, or "shine" with the transcendent. So transcendence is everywhere and immanent, yet it remains transcendent.

Berkeley, with his air of bland common sense, shows us where this kind of idealism can lead. "I do not argue against the existence of any one thing that we can apprehend, either by sense or reflection. That the things I see with mine eyes and touch with my hands do exist, really exist, I make not the least question. The only thing whose existence we deny, is that which philosophers call matter or corporeal substance."[20] Everything is mind and form, and matter is only the visible manifestation of it. According to Spenser's Platonic *Hymne in Honour of Beautie*,

> For of the soule the bodie forme doth take:
> For soule is forme, and doth the bodie make.
> (132–133)

But it is very nearly impossible for the imagination to sustain this conviction, and only a few lines later Spenser says,

> Yet oft it falles, that many a gentle mynd
> Dwels in deformèd tabernacles drownd,
> Either by chaunce, against the course of kynd,
> Or through unaptnesse in the substance fownd.
> (141–144)

---

[17] Otto's terms in *The Idea of the Holy*.

[18] "For original mythical feeling the meaning and power of the sacred are limited to no particular sphere of reality or value. This meaning is rather imprinted upon the immediate concrete totality of existence and events" (Cassirer, *Mythical Thought*, p. 75).

[19] Karl Jaspers, *Way to Wisdom: An Introduction to Philosophy*, trans. Ralph Manheim (New Haven, 1951), p. 182.

[20] *Principles of Human Knowledge*, par. 35.

Despite all the warnings that Plotinus or Berkeley can issue, the distinction between soul and substance, the notion of mind lodged or trapped in matter, continues to obtrude. Like most Neoplatonists Blake wants to deny the distinction, but it is not clear that they or he can do so.

"Every thing that lives is Holy" cannot, as Blake's myth amply shows, imply a Wordsworthian natural piety. Very likely the stress ought to fall on the word *lives*: the point is not that *everything* is holy, but rather that everything is holy if it participates in imaginative life rather than Satanic deadness and "Non-Entity." In the midst of what Bloom calls a "hymn of the triumphant Female Will" (E871), Enitharmon proclaims her supremacy over Los and adds, "For every thing that lives is holy for the source of life/Descends to be a weeping babe" (*FZ* 34:80-81, E317/K289). Her use of the slogan is not a simple perversion of the ideal; it exposes the dilemma rooted in the concept itself, which is that "life" as we know it is inseparable from the world of Generation, of mothers and weeping babes, of the matter and substance which are supposed to be nonentity but in fact seem all too real. Everything that lives is holy because everything that is not holy— Satan, Rahab, and their works—does not exist. But the nonexistent, impertinently enough, keeps on asserting its reality.

Blake's dualism is an inevitable consequence of his philosophical position, but it is a consequence that he does his best to avoid. The many passages in which he denies it are far from irrelevant; they show us what he wanted to believe. But it is simply not true that his myth dramatizes the inseparability of body and soul in the manner of the Old Testament, of which it has been said that "the mind is not a member apart, but is itself transformed into passion."[21] In Blake's myth, on the contrary, "Vala produc'd the Bodies. Jerusalem gave the Souls" (*J* 18:7, E161/K640). Body and soul are imaginatively distinct, after all the efforts to make them identical. The natural world, whether illusory or real, remains to be transcended. The scarlet woman must be found and burned "as it is written in Revelations," an act which represents "the Eternal Consummation of Vegetable Life & Death with its Lusts" (*VLJ*, E548/K609).

In addition to Plotinus and Proclus, Blake had as his master St. Paul. He constantly uses the distinction between garment and self: Satan is a dunce because he does not know "the Garment from the Man."[22] But

[21] Abraham J. Heschel, *The Prophets: An Introduction* (New York, 1969), II, 37.

[22] *For the Sexes* (E266/K771). For a discussion of this topic see Paley, "The Figure of the Garment . . . ," in Curran and Wittreich, pp. 119-139. The metaphor of body as garment is common in Neoplatonism, and Raine quotes an apposite passage in Porphyry (*Blake and Tradition*, I, 88). But Blake's usage has at least as much in common

as Paul declares, the body-garment is not to be rejected altogether, only transformed. "For we that are in this tabernacle [cf. Spenser's "in deformèd tabernacle drownd"] do groan, being burdened: not for that we would be unclothed, but clothed upon, that mortality might be swallowed up of life" (2 Cor. 5:4). Or again, "It is sown a natural body; it is raised a spiritual body" (1 Cor. 15:44). By quoting this text in the illustration for "To Tirzah" (E30/K220) Blake evidently means to suggest that the resurrected body is transformed from, but still somehow continuous with, the mortal one.[23]

As Augustine expounds the same text, "Just as now the body is called *animate*, though it is a body and not a soul [*anima*], so then the body shall be called spiritual, though it shall be a body, not a spirit."[24] Yet it is hard to sustain a clear conception of this mysterious transformation that preserves identity. Augustine continues in the same passage, "So perfect shall then be the harmony between flesh and spirit, the spirit keeping alive the subjugated flesh without the need of any nourishment, that no part of our nature shall be in discord with another; but as we shall be free from enemies without, we shall not have ourselves for enemies within" (p. 106). The Neoplatonism that underlies Augustine's thought makes it tempting, if not irresistible, to conceive of "body" and "spirit" as separate modes of existence, especially since even in heaven one will remain "subjugated" to the other. And in the *Confessions* Augustine states plainly, exactly as Blake would, that the world perceived by the fallen senses is very different from the world occupied by the true self located in the mind.[25]

---

with the Pauline tradition, as seen for example in the ending of the first part of *Pilgrim's Progress*: "They had left their mortal garments behind them in the River" (John Bunyan, *The Pilgrim's Progress*, ed. Roger Sharrock [Harmondsworth, 1965], p. 200).

[23] "To Tirzah" was written a good deal later than the *Songs of Innocence and of Experience*, to which it was added (see Erdman's textual note, E722), but it only clarifies an idea which was already present, that Experience is a temporary state from which one can emerge by recognizing the delusive status of fallen existence: "The starry floor/The watry shore/Is giv'n thee till the break of day" (E18/K210). As elsewhere in his developing myth, Blake's reintroduction of Christian symbols refocuses but does not cancel out what had gone before.

[24] *The Enchiridion on Faith, Hope and Love*, trans. J. F. Shaw (New York, 1961), XCI, p. 105.

[25] "There is another power, by which I not only give life but sensation as well to my flesh, which the Lord has fashioned for me, commanding the eye that it should not hear, and the ear that it should not see, but giving to the first power so that I may see by it, and the other power so that I hear by it, and singly to each of the other senses powers proper to their organs and purposes. I, who am one single mind, perform these diverse things through the senses" (*Confessions*, X.vii, p. 235). It should be added that Augustine inverts the Neoplatonic position by attributing the Fall to the soul rather than the body:

Moreover, although Augustine sought to dispose of evil as mere privation by adapting the arguments of Plotinus, it is generally admitted that he never fully escaped the Manichaeism in which he had once believed, a dualism of good and evil principles that consigned the material world to evil and regarded the soul as imprisoned therein. Man is not only (in a central metaphor of the *Confessions*) an exile in a strange land, but he is trapped as well in a mortal body that labors in bondage to Satan. As Pascal tersely puts it, "Notre âme est jetée dans le corps, où elle trouve nombre, temps, dimensions."[26] Precisely so in Blake: number, time, and dimensions are consequences of the fall. Blake might reject the metaphor of those Gnostics who held that we are "intruders in a body that does not fit us."[27] But the body is nonetheless a garment, and we are to look forward to shedding the mortal garment for a better one.

The striking phrase "The Naked Human form divine" means exactly what it says: the *form* is divine and must be distinguished from "the Body of Clay/For dust & Clay is the Serpents meat" (*EG*, E514/ K755). In the apocalypse the "excrementitious/Husk & Covering" will be swept away, "evaporating revealing the lineaments of Man/Driving outward the Body of Death" (*J* 98:18-20, E255/K745). Meanwhile it is the reasoning Negation of the spectre, "a false Body: an Incrustation over my Immortal/Spirit" (*M* 40:35-36, E141/K533). The "Body of Death" derives from Paul: "O wretched man that I am! who shall deliver me from the body of this death?" (Rom. 7:24). In that crucial chapter of Romans, the body of death is a product of the implacable Law of the Old Testament, and so it is in Blake: Jehovah, the sixth of the "Eyes of God" who fail to save man, brings about the formation of "the Body of Death" (*M* 13:25, E106/K494), after which the seventh Eye, Jesus, descends to rescue man. Now, at last, everything that lives will indeed be holy:

> So Man looks out in tree & herb & fish & bird & beast
> Collecting up the scattered portions of his immortal body
> Into the Elemental forms of every thing that grows.
> (FZ 110:6-8, E370/K355)

Body and form are finally at one. But it is no longer body as we thought we knew it; that was the body of the "Creation that groans,

---

"It was not the corruptible flesh that made the soul sinful; it was the sinful soul that made the flesh corruptible" (*City of God*, XIV.iii, p. 551).

[26] *Pensées*, no. 343 (Lafuma), 233 (Brunschvicg). Pascal's term *jetée* is strikingly anticipatory of Heidegger's *geworfen*.

[27] Lacarrière, *Les Gnostiques*, p. 35.

living on Death" (*J* 50:5, E197/K681), a creation that is identified with the fallen Albion: "Throughout the whole Creation which groans to be deliverd/Albion groans in the deep slumbers of Death upon his Rock" (*J* 16:26-27, E158/K637). Once again the image is explicitly Pauline: "For we know that the whole creation groaneth and travaileth in pain together until now . . . waiting for the adoption, to wit, the redemption of our body" (Rom. 8:22-23).

Blake was preoccupied, even obsessed, with the horribleness of the fallen body. It may be unreal in the technical Neoplatonic sense, but it is far from being vague or shadowy, and the physicality of its organs is often dwelt upon, "my vegetating blood in veiny pipes" (*J* 34:36, E178/K665). In general these descriptions do not get into the designs, but the sketches for *Vala* (the *Four Zoas* manuscript) are filled with fascinated disgust, and on plate 23 of *Jerusalem* a hideous knot of intestines, symbolizing the veil of Vala, entangles Jerusalem.[28] If the generated body has spiritual significance, it can only be "in its inward form," as the Sons of Los labor to give imaginative life to forms "in Bowlahoola & Allamanda" (*M* 26:31-33). When it is raised a spiritual body it is no longer the body of this fallen life. Blake's picture for "To Tirzah" alludes to the raising of Lazarus, and elsewhere he says,

> When Jesus raisd Lazarus from the Grave I stood & saw
> Lazarus who is the Vehicular Body of Albion the Redeemd
> Arise into the Covering Cherub who is the Spectre of Albion. . . .
> (*M* 24:26-28, E119/K508)

The physical or "vehicular" body is assimilated to the Satanic "Covering Cherub," while the spirit rejoices in eternal life. "What is Mortality but the things relating to the Body, which Dies? What is Immortality but the things relating to the Spirit, which Lives Eternally?" (*J* 77, E229/K717).

Why, then, do Blake's symbolic forms have human bodies? It is possible to conclude that this is a paradox, that the artist glorifies forms which the poet condemns.[29] I propose on the contrary that

---

[28] Piloo Nanavutty suggests the relevance of the lines much later in the poem, "But in the midst of a devouring Stomach, Jerusalem/Hidden within the Covering Cherub as in a Tabernacle/Of threefold workmanship in allegoric delusion & woe" (*J* 89:43-45, E246/K735). See "A Title-Page in Blake's Illustrated Genesis Manuscript," in Essick, p. 133. And see also the design on *Jerusalem* 25, in which Rahab, Vala, and Tirzah play the three Fates as Tirzah draws Albion's intestines out of his navel.

[29] "Blake's philosophical condemnation of the human form . . . is presented in visual terms that glorify the human form" (Mellor, *Blake's Human Form Divine*, p. 103). Mellor argues that after the 1790s Blake returned to a belief in the holiness of the body, and that fourfold vision can transform anything "into a metaphor or image of potential infinity" (p. 198).

there is usually something ambiguous about beautiful bodies in Blake's designs, and moreover that his use of these images is controlled by the requirements of symbolic representation rather than by admiration for the body as such. We notice that Jerusalem is Michelangelesque on *Jerusalem* 46, at just the moment when she is being lured by Vala, and that on the very next plate her body and Vala's are contorted in mannerist extremity.[30] Roe observes that the most heroic male forms in the Dante series are reserved for Satan and other devils.[31] And two of the most beautiful bodies in all of the illuminated books, on the ninth plate of *Europe*, are those of a pair of spirits of plague and destruction.[32]

Nevertheless, Blake is committed to the human form, because the universe is human, and these are consequently the "forms and features that are capable of being the receptacles of intellect" (*DC*, E535/K579–580). In the light of Blake's theory a term like "receptacles" is incautious if not an outright blunder, but as we have seen, the metaphor of container and contents is nearly unavoidable. The body is in any case the form with which the artist has to deal. And for all his dislike of the Greek gods, Blake had little choice but to use traditional representations of them as his exemplars of "intellect."

It has been argued that religious symbols, referring to the "wholly other," must necessarily distort their phenomenal models in order to emphasize the inadequacy of the model to denote spiritual reality. Hegel was particularly interested in this way in the fantastic and zoomorphic gods of Asian religions.[33] Blake denied the existence of the wholly other, but he certainly held that the transformed body will

[30] I follow the sequence of plates as given in Erdman's *Illuminated Blake*.

[31] *Blake's Illustrations to the Divine Comedy*, p. 82. Critics who speak of Blake's debt to Michelangelo should consider how often his most Michelangelesque forms are fallen ones.

[32] There is a color reproduction in Raine, *William Blake*, p. 73. Paley mentions "the beauty of the ogee curve" as particularly seductive in this design (*William Blake*, p. 32). In general Blake tends to use the body iconically despite his reputation as the poet of sensual delight. His friend Fuseli, for example, illustrating the expulsion from Eden in *Paradise Lost*, portrayed a voluptuous Eve with an arm draped around Adam's neck and an ample hip pressed against his thigh. Blake's version of the same theme is hieratic and formal, with Michael separating Adam and Eve and holding each by the hand, and above them a stylized tongue of flame and the four bearded Zoas on their steeds like the horsemen of the apocalypse. See the reproductions and discussion in Kester Svendsen, "John Martin and the Expulsion Scene of Paradise Lost," *Studies in English Literature*, 1 (1961), 63–73.

[33] See Wilbur Marshall Urban, *Language and Reality* (London, 1939), pp. 582–585, on the "principle of distortion," combining Hegel's analysis with Otto's *mysterium tremendum*. As against myth, according to Urban, the religious symbol can never claim to be

be drastically different from the present body. The often weird combinations of animal with human forms in *Jerusalem* suggest that zoomorphic symbolism was of interest to Blake, though in general he associated it with the fallenness of nature religions. More significant is his insistence on forms as *forms*, so that "intellect" is not conveyed by facial expressions as one might expect.[34]

Blake's ambivalence toward the body, and more generally his tendency to dualism, are not incidental ambiguities. They are built into his philosophy just as they are in every form of Neoplatonism. Boehme, for example, "had no idealist antithesis between body and spirit; body was for him not flesh. It was rather form, definiteness, comprehensibility, that which can be known, willed, and loved, perhaps even personality."[35] Precisely so in Blake. But precisely what? This formulation is unintelligible except to mystical vision. And Boehme himself could not sustain it, for as Koyré says, "The human body is at once the effect of the fall and the token of the possibility of salvation. . . . The body is a screen and, at the same time, a life preserver."[36] Likewise in Blake the body is at once a merciful "limit of contraction" and a trap from which we must escape. But it is easier to say that it is both at once than to understand how it can be.

Blake's troubled dualism—his dualistic monism—is thus an inescapable feature of his thought. But it would be a grave mistake to conclude that he was merely confused. On the contrary, the lesson must be that he found simpler philosophies unacceptable and did his best to reconstruct the Western tradition, to add up the old questions and somehow get new answers. Perhaps he thought that he had succeeded, although the repeated rebuilding of the myth suggests that he was keenly aware of intractable difficulties. In the end he could not escape from the dualism that has haunted that tradition, so that Nietzsche's words can rightly be applied to him: "It was the body which despaired

---

that which it symbolizes, confined as it is to a sensible world distinct from the noumenal.

[34] Roe suggests that because "for many years Blake never worked from models, his faces tend to follow a number of set types, and attempts to show more intense emotion often . . . resulted in failure" (*Blake's Illustrations . . .* , p. 113). There is probably some truth to the suspicion that Blake had trouble drawing expressive faces. But it is also likely that he did not want them individualized like portraits, following instead stylized "pathos formulae," as Lindberg has shown (*William Blake's Illustrations . . .* , pp. 113-122, and many specific examples in commentary on the plates). As far as possible the bodily form must be transcended, must point to the universal form of which it is the vegetated shadow.

[35] Stoudt, *Sunrise to Eternity*, p. 263.

[36] *La Philosophie de Jacob Boehme*, p. 470.

of the body—it groped with the fingers of the infatuated spirit at the ultimate walls."[37]

CONTRARIES

No saying of Blake's is more famous than "Without Contraries is no progression" (*MHH*, E34/K149). Yet none is more problematic. It should be noted that he never repeated the statement in those terms, and found it far from easy to integrate a true dialectic of contraries in his later myth. To some extent, in fact, he tacitly repudiated the earlier doctrine, since he constantly strove to tame, limit, or expel some part of the contraries by reducing them to "negations," just as the unpleasant aspects of the fallen body were dismissed as "Non-Entity." But the ideal of the contraries remained very real to him, and the continuing publication of the *Songs of Innocence and of Experience* as "Shewing the Two Contrary States of the Human Soul" (E7/K210) indicates its importance. Once again, I propose to establish an intellectual context that will show not only what Blake seems to mean, but also why he finds it so hard to mean what he wants.

To judge from passing references to Blake's contraries, one would think they represented nothing more than a claim that the world is full of a number of things and that by opposing each other, as many of them do, they contribute to a larger harmony. In these terms we are presented with something like Heraclitus' tension between opposites, the bow and the lyre. And it would be easy to invoke modern theories that see in the bipolarity of symbolic structures an inherent tendency of the mind. Ideas like these do seem to have inspired Blake at the time of *The Marriage of Heaven and Hell*: "Attraction and Repulsion, Reason and Energy, Love and Hate, are necessary to Human existence" (E34/K149). But as I believe Blake saw with increasing clarity, such a statement, for all its fearlessness, is really no advance at all over the complacent Augustan notion of *concordia discors*.

> But ALL subsists by elemental strife;
> And Passions are the elements of Life.[38]

In the Augustan tradition the strife of opposites always implies a damping down of energy in mutual accommodation. As Denham sternly describes the struggle between kings and people in Norman times, "one excess/Made both, by striving to be greater, less."[39] In

[37] *Thus Spake Zarathustra*, trans. Thomas Common, in *The Philosophy of Nietzsche*, I.iii, p. 29.
[38] Pope, *Essay on Man*, I.169-170.
[39] Denham, *Cooper's Hill*, lines 347-348.

The Marriage of Heaven and Hell Blake confidently proclaimed the road of excess; in his later works the concept received a thorough reexamination. Surely, as Shelley said, the drama of contraries must not lead to "a catastrophe so feeble as that of reconciling the Champion with the Oppressor of mankind."[40] In the end Blake would hold that error precipitates the victory of truth by taking a visible and therefore vulnerable form, the temporary triumph of Satan and Rahab. It ceases to be a question, in any simple sense, of a marriage of heaven and hell. And it would be hard to prove that at any time Blake was really comfortable with a marriage of contraries in the Heraclitean or Augustan sense.

It was a commonplace of "optimistic" explanations of evil that a successful picture needs shade as well as light:

> Here in full Light the russet Plains extend;
> There wrapt in Clouds the blueish Hills ascend.

And the goal of such oppositions was harmony: "All Discord, Harmony not understood."[41] The later Blake explicitly rejects this aesthetic conception of opposition and harmony, just as he rejects the painterly aesthetics that it evokes as metaphor:

> The Sons of Albion are Twelve: The Sons of Jerusalem Sixteen
> I tell how Albions Sons by Harmonies of Concords & Discords
> Opposed to Melody, and by Lights & Shades, opposed to Outline
> And by Abstraction opposed to the Visions of Imagination
> By cruel Laws divided Sixteen into Twelve Divisions
> How Hyle roofd Los in Albions Cliffs. . . .

(*J* 74:23-28, E227/K715)

So much for *concordia discors* and lights and shades; they are instruments of "Hyle," matter and the fallen affections, and they imprison the visionary Los who sees outline and hears melody. When confronted with polarities Blake always tends to exalt one and repel or even exterminate the other.

Why, then, does Blake deal with contraries at all? The reason is not that reality presents itself as a harmony of opposites, but rather that an inescapable experience of pain and struggle is fundamental to any achievement. Blake's Eden, in contrast with conventional images of

---

[40] Preface to *Prometheus Unbound.*

[41] Pope, *Windsor Forest*, lines 23-24; *Essay on Man*, I.291. *Concordia discors* has its basis in an optimistic theology that celebrates the goodness of God's creation—a profoundly un-Blakean theme. See H.V.S. Ogden, "The Principle of Variety and Contrast in Seventeenth Century Aesthetics, and Milton's Poetry," *Journal of the History of Ideas*, 10 (1949), 159-182; and Leo Spitzer, *Classical and Christian Ideas of World Harmony* (Baltimore, 1963). The term also appears as *discordia concors*, e.g. in Johnson's *Life of Cowley*.

heaven, is founded on this fundamental insight.[42] So although Blake is constantly tempted to reject one half of any contrary pair, he is aware that to do so would be to falsify the truth as he perceives it. The contraries are a problem, not an answer. What has been said of Gnosticism could be applied word for word to Blake's myth:

> If the Gnostics propounded a dualist image of the world, it was not because their temperament predisposed them to see a contrary opposed to every entity, but because in the face of the omnipresent and tormenting evidence of evil, it was necessary to oppose something to it. But their goal was clearly to transcend this antinomy, which only reflects the division and ripping apart that are characteristic of this world.[43]

Blake's immediate master in this area was Jacob Boehme, who believed that his theology could answer the kinds of questions raised here. Rather than absolving the remote Unknown God, as the Gnostics did, of responsibility for the bungled universe of an inferior demiurge, Boehme sought to identify the contraries with the very nature of God in the symbolism of fire as heat and light, "wrath" and "meekness," which Blake echoes with the terms "wrath" and "pity": "To cast Luvah into the Wrath, and Albion into the Pity/In the Two Contraries of Humanity & in the Four Regions" (J 65:3-4, E214/ K699). At the time of *The Marriage of Heaven and Hell* Blake was clearly fascinated by Boehme's solution, which is closely reflected in his account of the Prolific and the Devouring (E39/K155), and in the statement that the Messiah "formed a heaven of what he stole from the Abyss" (E34/K150). The "Eternal Death, or Devouring" is another name in Boehme's writings for the *Ungrund* or *Nichts*, the abyss that is beyond being "on the other side of good and evil, of Yes and No, of freedom and desire."[44] But Boehme's doctrine requires that God be transcendent and unknowable, manifested only as his activity emerges into the world of active contraries from the mysterious abyss where desire is not. Moreover, the abyss is represented as a "dark world" of grief and horror, postulated as the necessary contrary of light and joy rather than as a positive value in itself.[45] As Raine remarks, Blake as-

---

[42] See below, pp. 233 ff.

[43] Lacarrière, *Les Gnostiques*, p. 143.

[44] Stoudt, *Sunrise to Eternity*, p. 199; see his quotation on p. 205. On the Devouring, see *Mysterium Magnum*, IV.xi-xiii.

[45] "That which in the dark world is a pang, is in the light world a pleasing delight; and what in the dark is a stinging and enmity, is in the light an uplifting joy. . . . The dark world is therefore the ground and origin of the light world; and the terrible evil

cribes "delight" to the devils in hell whom Boehme and Swedenborg saw as tormented and insane.[46] But in his later works he seems no longer satisfied with the idea of a dark "abyss" either as the source of energy and delight (as with the devils in *The Marriage*) or, in Boehme's terms, as the fixed *contrarium* against which life and light can define themselves. Boehme developed his doctrine to explain how a good God can permit evil, showing that evil is the wrath that is the other face of meekness. In developing the idea of Urizen as demiurge—a topic we shall explore in the next chapter—Blake abandons Boehme for something much closer to the Gnostic position.

"To grasp evil in the Divine Being itself as the wrath of God," Hegel writes, "that is the supreme effort, the severest strain, of which figurative thought, wrestling with its own limitations, is capable, an effort which, since it is devoid of the notion [*Begriff*], remains a fruitless struggle."[47] Hegel would say that Blake's myth is entrapped by its "figurative" conceptions, and would regret that Blake never elaborated the tantalizing suggestion of "progression" in "Without Contraries is no progression." It is tempting to understand Blake's aphorism as pointing to a Hegelian *Aufhebung*, the dialectic that simultaneously annuls each stage and raises it to a higher one. But the developed Blakean myth has no place for the upward spiral that absorbs each preceding stage, emphasizing instead that the spectral or Satanic must be expelled utterly. And in taking this position Blake tacitly recognizes the weakness of "progression," which is no easier to make sense of in Hegelian "concept" than it is in figurative form. As Taylor says, "The problem cannot be solved by a victory of one side over the other, by a simple undoing of separation in a spirit of unity; rather the two sides must be brought somehow to unity while each requirement is integrally satisfied. This is the task—perhaps an impossible one— which Hegel's mature system is meant to encompass."[48]

Another way of describing Blake's position is to say, drawing on our discussion in Chapter 4, that he will not admit the necessary role of the "other." He wants contraries but not otherness. Hence his account of the Negation is peculiarly tortuous and fraught with ambiguity. In Hegel it is axiomatic that "opposites negate each other, and since within everything that exists there is opposition, we can also say

---

must be a cause of the good, and all is God's. . . . The dark world is called death and hell, the abyss, a sting of death, despair, self-enmity and sorrowfulness" (Boehme, *Six Theosophic Points*, III.iii-vi, pp. 38-39).

[46] *Blake and Tradition*, I, 368.

[47] *Phenomenology*, p. 773.

[48] *Hegel*, p. 67.

that within everything there is negativity."[49] "Ich bin der Geist, der stets verneint!" says Goethe's Mephistopheles: "I am the spirit that continually negates."[50] But Blake comes to see negation not as the interplay of opposites, but rather as a principle that stands *outside of* the contraries and is the spectral "false Body" that must be "put off & annihilated alway":

> There is a Negation, & there is a Contrary
> The Negation must be destroyd to redeem the Contraries
> The Negation is the Spectre; the Reasoning Power in Man
> This is a false Body: an Incrustation over my Immortal
> Spirit; a Selfhood, which must be put off & annihilated alway.
> (*M* 40:32-36, E141/K533)

The force of "alway" is to suggest that annihilation must be ever renewed, so that in fact the negation cannot be decisively abolished. But we are also told that the productive interaction of the contraries is distinct from negation. Blake's meaning is that reason cannot tolerate contraries but always strives to negate them, whereas spiritual vision rejoices in them. It is therefore possible to assert that the entire structure of *Milton* is built upon contraries.[51] But I would argue that these interrelated pairs—time and space, male and female, time and eternity, lark and thyme—are not actually contraries at all, but opposed or reversed aspects of sameness.

In *Jerusalem* Blake states that contraries are made by the Sons of Albion, and that "From them they make an Abstract, which is a Negation" (*J* 10:10, E151/K629). Contraries and negations alike are expressions of fallen existence, and call for radical redefinition in Eden or Eternity. Meanwhile the Negation may have an ironically active role, as in *Milton* when Satan's mills are needed to grind the apocalyptic harvest. And Satan is a son of Los just as Rintrah and Palamabron are. But when Los is restored to his eternal condition as Urthona, Satan will not be reabsorbed into him; as the great design on plate 10 shows, Rintrah and Palamabron preserve the Boehmian categories of wrath and pity, while Satan—who represents what Boehme thought of as wrath—is "a mere negation that will go up in smoke."[52] As an inscription in mirror writing says in *Milton*, "Contraries are Positives. A Negation is not a Contrary" (*M* 30, E128/K518).

Let us be as clear as possible: we have not shown that Blake stopped

---

[49] Taylor, *Hegel*, p. 110. In the fullest elaboration of this idea, "the positive can only be the negation of the negation" (p. 523).

[50] *Faust*, I. 1338.

[51] See Fox, *Poetic Form in Blake's Milton*, esp. p. 153.

[52] Erdman, *The Illuminated Blake*, p. 226.

believing in contraries, but rather that such a belief became more and more difficult to sustain. The concept of Negation is a desperate measure intended to rescue the contraries by banishing from them whatever is irredeemably corrupt. But the act of banishment vitiates the whole meaning of contraries, either in Boehme's terms or in Hegel's. In the end we must probably conclude that Blake cannot organize the whole of his thought under the concept of contraries, and settles instead for different *kinds* of contraries, some of which are easily reconciled, others with great difficulty if at all. To put it differently, Blake's movement away from the optimistic "progression" of *The Marriage of Heaven and Hell* and toward the drastic exclusion of "negation" represents a recognition that much in our experience is radically unassimilable. Just as in his early annotations to Lavater he reserved the right to hate, so in his myth Blake remained true to the insight that prophetic wrath must treat some things as permanently unacceptable. No marriage of contraries can ultimately make all things one. Of course Blake often invokes Neoplatonic language to suggest that what he rejects never really existed at all; it is mere privation, like evil in Augustine and C. S. Lewis. But as the myth sufficiently expresses with dramatic if not logical force, the negation is all too real and its rejection is a real act of courage and imagination.

EMANATIONS

Blake's hostility to the female has come in for considerable attention lately, after a long period during which it was excused as a mere metaphor. Yet even the shrewdest critic of this issue concludes that Blake was a victim of "received attitudes."[53] I agree, of course, that Blake should not be held responsible for the prejudices of his age, although it is worth noting that a supposed reactionary like Samuel Johnson had a much more liberal view of women then Blake did. But I would argue that the status of the female in his myth is significant as betraying the same philosophical difficulties that surround the whole problem of dualism. We cannot salvage the integrity of the myth merely by imagining some alternative metaphor to take the place of the female. The metaphor is more than metaphor: it is a fundamental concept, and participates in Blake's conceptual dilemma.

My thesis will be that the female or Emanation is not a distinct entity, but instead a sort of emotional storm center, an area in which some of the most painful tensions in Blake's thought come together. To make sense of his many treatments of the subject, it will be useful

[53] Susan Fox, "The Female as Metaphor in William Blake's Poetry," *Critical Inquiry*, 3 (1977), 507-519. See also ch. 4 of Fox's *Poetic Form in Blake's Milton*.

to observe three major divisions. (a) The Emanation is the female aspect of the androgynous self, which should never exist at all in separation. (b) It is that which is desired and/or that which is created. (c) It is the body as opposed to soul, garment as opposed to body, space as opposed to time. This conception comes close to the Neoplatonic doctrine of emanations, colored by Blake's Gnostic suspicion of birth into the body; it issues in the implacable Female Will. Let us take up these categories in order. For purposes of clarity we shall postpone until the next section a still more obvious category, the female as female—actual women, suggestion for Blake of sexual delight but also of sexual entrapment.

(a) In the unfallen state the female is fully integrated into the male. The androgynous self is, in effect, a male self with a female element within it. Milton without Ololon remains Milton. In an early work Albion was conventionally female,[54] but as soon as Albion became the center of Blake's myth it was necessary to change her into him. Los says that Jerusalem is "the soft reflected Image of the Sleeping Man" and the "lovely Shadow of Sleeping Albion" (*J* 85:24, 29, E242/K730). At one point Blake even seems to suggest that marriage unites man and wife in this relationship of form and reflection: Catherine is his own "sweet Shadow of Delight" (*M* 42:28, E142/K534).

"In Eternity," as Blake puts it bluntly, "Woman is the Emanation of Man she has No Will of her own There is no such thing in Eternity as a Female Will" (*VLJ*, E552/K613). Passages like this are sufficient to show that the female is not merely a metaphor for an aspect of the human (even if it were obvious that that aspect should be called female). But in any event Blake claims that the integrated self reconciles male and female harmoniously. In a nice syntactical effect, we are told of Milton and Ololon that "they and/Himself was Human" (*M* 17:5-6, E109/K498). They (the multiple female Emanation) and himself (Milton) *was* a single human form. But of course Blake would not say "He and herself was human." The very multiplicity of Ololon suggests the greater fragmentation and lack of identity in the Emanation, which in its root meaning "emanates" from the male, as the Neoplatonic Many emanates from the One. The often noticed comparison with the Jungian *anima* fails at just this point, since Blake does not represent women as having the complementary *animus*; and whereas Jung is concerned to give both *anima* and *animus* their full value (freeing them from repression), Blake is more anxious about the domination of the female over the male. His occasional references to

---

[54] "O yet may Albion smile again, and stretch her peaceful arms, and raise her golden head, exultingly!" (*Prologue to King John*, E431/K34).

masculine Emanations, therefore, are not integrated structurally into the myth.[55]

Whatever the Emanation may be in eternity, in the world of the poems it is a symptom of the fall. To describe the relation between self and Emanation as one of contraries is to expose once again the contentiousness of contraries. "My Emanation, Alas! will become/My contrary," Los laments (*J* 17:38-39, E160/K639). As Milton made clear in *Paradise Lost*, Eve is not only subservient to Adam but was created from his body, a point that Blake develops in his illustration (see fig. 13) in which Adam lies asleep on a huge flamelike leaf while Jesus (not Jehovah) extends his hand over Eve's head as she ascends from Adam's recumbent form. It is of course true that the creation of Eve can be considered a merciful limit to the fall.[56] But Adam's slumber is all too reminiscent of Albion's, and the crescent moon above Eve's head is the emblem of Beulah, the feminized paradise which Blake regarded with deep suspicion. Moreover, Jesus' sorrowful expression hardly bespeaks the jubilation of creation. It is easy to read the picture as illustrating the inception of the fall rather than a creation that preceded it. Once the female has separated from the male she must tantalize and frustrate him, as on plate 19 of the *Book of Urizen* in which Enitharmon both leans toward and recoils from a huddled Los. Henceforth the active Emanation will be a tyrannical Female Will, the passive a "disorganized" and "evanescent shade" as Jerusalem is when severed from Albion (*J* 78:28, E232/K719).

(b) Meanwhile, the separated female can no longer represent a part of the unified self, but becomes a symbol of otherness, that which is desired or created. At the very moment when he resists sexual contact with the Daughters of Albion, Los calls Enitharmon "Piteous image of my soft desires & loves" (*J* 17:19, E160/K639). At times it may be

[55] There is a passing mention of "Shiloh the Masculine Emanation" (*J* 49:47, E197/K680), who stands allegorically for France. In Eternity, we are told, "Man cannot unite with Man but by their Emanations/Which stand both Male & Female at the Gates of each Humanity" (*J* 88:10-11, E244/K733), whereas in the fallen world "The Feminine separates from the Masculine & both from Man,/Ceasing to be His Emanations" (*J* 90:1-2, E247/K736). Apparently, then, "Man" has both a male and female Emanation, which separate at the Fall but are integrated in Eternity. And very possibly the picture on pl. 18 of *Jerusalem* shows a male Emanation emerging from a female figure and a female from a male (see John E. Grant, "Two Flowers in the Garden of Experience," in Rosenfeld, pp. 362-364). These infrequent and puzzling hints, however, only serve to emphasize how far Blake's myth is from incorporating any coherent symbolism of male Emanations.

[56] As Bindman remarks (*Blake as an Artist*, p. 188). See also Erdman's commentary on Eve emerging from Adam's body in *Jerusalem* 31 (*Illuminated Blake*, p. 310). The concept of Eve as merciful limit seems to derive from Boehme; see Raine, *Blake and Tradition*, I, 404-406.

13. *The Creation of Eve*, illustration for Milton's *Paradise Lost*.

possible to allegorize this relation as one of being and attribute, for instance interpreting Urizen as reason and Ahania as "the wise passivity
in which he must take pleasure."[57] Enitharmon would then be to Los
as Catherine Blake was to William Blake, "tincturing" his outlines
with color (*FZ* 90:36, E356/K332). At other times it makes more sense
to stress otherness rather than analogy, and to see the Emanation as the

[57] Bloom's commentary (E871). Frosch proposes similar correspondences for each of
the Zoas and Emanations (*Awakening of Albion*, p. 34). See also Weiskel, *The Romantic
Sublime*, p. 69.

object of desire. But this is strongly paradoxical. It may be that "the female portion in each of us is that which can emanate from us, our emotions and our desires and our products."[58] Emanations are then female in the sense (if it makes sense) that everything outside the self is female. But as we have seen, Blake will not concede the otherness of the object of desire, so that simply by *being* desired the female takes on a tantalizing remoteness.

Shelley's theoretical account of the epipsyche is relevant here:

> The magnificence and beauty of the external world sinks pro-foundly into the frame of [the youth's] conceptions, and affords to their modifications a variety not to be exhausted. So long as it is possible for his desires to point towards objects thus infinite and unmeasured, he is joyous, and tranquil, and self-possessed. But the period arrives when these objects cease to suffice. His mind is at length suddenly awakened and thirsts for intercourse with an intel-ligence similar to itself. He images to himself the Being whom he loves.[59]

In Blake's terms, the poet recognizes the inadequacy of Nature to the infinity of desire, and projects himself upon the external world ("im-ages to himself," Shelley says). Accordingly when Shelley's youth dreams of the desired maiden, "Her voice was like the voice of his own soul/Heard in the calm of thought."[60] She is himself. But if that is so, how can she be more than illusion?

It is usual in this connection to remark on the spousal symbolism of the Song of Songs and Revelation, and to assert that Jerusalem is united with Albion as the eternal bride. It is quite true that Blake sometimes invokes this imagery. But it is not so clear that his myth can accommodate it, for the symbolism of love is premised on the real-ity of otherness. As Shelley moved beyond *Alastor* he imagined Asia and Prometheus as genuinely complementary in a way that Enithar-mon and Urthona cannot be (or even Enitharmon and the fallen Los). And he stated very clearly in the *Defense*, "The great secret of morals is love; or a going out of our own nature, and an identification of our-selves with the beautiful which exists in thought, action, or person, not our own." There is no room in Blake's myth for that *not our own*. We need to remember Frye's observation that Jerusalem is more like the daughter of Albion than like his wife, who is the seldom men-tioned Brittannia.[61] The life of Eden is described not as a marriage but

---

[58] Fox, *Poetic Form in Blake's Milton*, p. 160.
[59] Preface to *Alastor*.
[60] *Alastor*, 11. 153-154.
[61] *Fearful Symmetry*, p. 392. In the fall "England who is Brittannia divided into

as "Universal Brotherhood" (*FZ* 3:5, E297/K264), and love is merged into this as "Brotherhood & Universal Love" (*FZ* 133:13, E386/K374). Conversely Vala claims to have been "Albions Bride & Wife in great Eternity," which cannot be right, and opposes her "Love" to the "Brotherhood" of the divine (*J* 29:39, 52, E174/K660). One comes to see that the spousal imagery is proper to Beulah, and therefore shares in all of Beulah's ambiguity.[62]

Blake in fact has little to do with the great Platonic tradition in which human love is a type of the divine. He criticizes it repeatedly in Dante. At times, as in the ninety-sixth picture, in which Saint John instructs Dante and Beatrice, the emanation seems well on the way to reunion with the self. But in others, such as *Beatrice Addressing Dante from the Car* (see fig. 14), the negative implications are inescapable.[63] Beatrice has become a crowned Vala/Rahab and her gryphon a symbol of the natural world like the leviathan and behemoth in Blake's *Job*. The wheel of the chariot is a whirling vortex containing the "Eyes of God" of fallen history—as Blake says elsewhere, "The Chariot wheels filled with Eyes rage along the howling Valley" (*J* 63:11, E212/K697)—while the Zoas float in shadowy paleness above; Urthona has the face of a sorrowing Jesus. Beatrice and the other three females dominate the scene and especially dominate the meek Dante at the far right. If they are interpreted as the fallen emanations, then the figure in white is Enitharmon, pointing to a deadening book of memory or law that emerges in smoke from the vortex. Dante believed that Beatrice was his inspiration; Blake takes over Dante's symbols and reinterprets them to show that Beatrice, clothed in seductively diaphanous robes, is actually an embodiment of the Female Will.

In Blake's clearest expression of spousal imagery, Jerusalem laments that she was Albion's "Bride & Wife" in a now-lost past, claims that Jesus gave Vala as wife to Albion, and (as Grant points out) evokes disturbing images of bondage, violation, and rape.[64] The true model for the Edenic relation between Albion and Jerusalem, as the metaphor of "Brotherhood" suggests, is not marriage but the communal activity of urban life.

Jerusalem & Vala" (*J* 32:28, E176/K663), and in the apocalypse "England who is Brittannia awoke, from Death on Albions bosom" (*J* 94:20, E252/K742).

[62] See below, pp. 220 ff.; and see Michael Ferber, "Blake's Idea of Brotherhood," *PMLA*, 93 (1978), 438–447.

[63] I follow Roe's commentary, to which the reader is referred for fuller detail (*Blake's Illustrations* . . . , pp. 164-171). See also Bindman, *Blake as an Artist*, pp. 218-219. There are color reproductions in Paley, *William Blake*, pl. 112, and Klonsky, *William Blake*, p. 111.

[64] *J* 20:39 ff., E164/K643. See Grant, "Two Flowers . . . ," in Rosenfeld, pp. 354-355.

14. *Beatrice Addressing Dante from the Car*, illustration for Dante's *Divine Comedy*.

> Thus shall the male & female live the life of Eternity
> Because the Lamb of God Creates himself a bride & wife
> That we his Children evermore may live in Jerusalem
> Which now descendeth out of heaven a City yet a Woman.
> (*FZ* 122:15-18, E376/K362)

As Erdman notes, the corresponding picture suggests the prodigal son and his father rather than a bride and her husband.[65] Spousal imagery is inappropriate to Eden because the Emanation cannot be reintegrated into the self without calling its very existence into question. The goal of infinite desire is to transform the desired object into the desiring subject, and this, as Shelley saw, is both an impossible and a self-destructive dream.

So the union of Los and Enitharmon—whose marriage is grimly celebrated in the first Night of *The Four Zoas*—is fraught with bitter ironies, not the least of which is that Urizen presides over it as a solemnization of "Moral Duty" that will cause Los to "Evaporate like smoke & be no more" (*FZ* 80:3, 6, E348/K323). One might well say that when Enitharmon is externalized from Los she becomes a projection of his self-love (and, when he tortures her and she him, of his

[65] *The Illuminated Blake*, p. 378. See fig. 27, p. 273 below; and on the theme of the Prodigal Son, see p. 272.

masochistic self-hatred). In Eden the Emanation was the medium of communication with others; in the fallen state she becomes a substitute for it, pursued in an ever-receding regress since she is not truly an "other" at all.

(c) Whatever Blake cannot reconcile himself to in the phenomenological world—bodies, matter, nature, physical space—is symbolized as female. Yet to press the analysis in these terms—to worry about whether or not the female is an appropriate metaphor—is to miss the deepest tensions of all. If we can simply grant that the female is Blake's symbol of duality, for better or worse, we may than return to the dilemma he hoped it could resolve.

Clearly Jerusalem (like Ololon) is intended as a positive figure, and whatever her relation with Albion or Jesus may finally be, that relation is supposed to be living and essential. By calling her an Emanation and sometimes an "Eon" (e.g., J 19:16, E162/K641), Blake reveals his debt to the Neoplatonic concept of emanation. And by referring to "the sports of Wisdom in the Human Imagination" (M 3:3, E96/K482) he invokes the love-play of God and the virgin Sophia ("Wisdom") in Boehme—"Thy Emanation that was wont to play before thy face" (J 4:14, E145/K622). Why is Blake drawn to this symbolic figure?

In the *Timaeus,* Plato speaks of a mysterious "third form" that mediates between the world of forms and the sensible world, calling it "the receptacle and, as it were, the nurse of all becoming and change. . . . We may indeed use the metaphor of birth and compare the receptacle to the mother, the model to the father, and what they produce between them to their offspring."[66] In the Kabbalah, whose philosophical basis is Neoplatonic, this female principle becomes the Shekhinah, literally the community of Israel (cf. Blake's Jerusalem as a city) and symbolically joined with God in "the union of the active and the passive, procreation and conception, from which all mundane life and bliss are derived."[67] The Neoplatonic theory of Emanation was conceived to explain how the perfect One could ever have distributed itself into the Many, postulating a series of intermediate stages of being that fall away from perfect Being. Such a doctrine was unacceptable to Christian theology, which saw Jesus in the incarnation as dispelling any gap between God and man that could require inferior intermediaries.[68] But the Shekhinah survives in a writer like Boehme as the virgin Sophia, the garment and outward expression of the divine spirit: "And this is called virgin Wisdom; for it is not a genetrix,

---

[66] *Timaeus,* trans. Desmond Lee (Harmondsworth, 1971), secs. 49, 50, pp. 66, 68.

[67] Scholem, *Major Trends in Jewish Mysticism,* p. 227.

[68] On this point see Chenu, *La Théologie au Douzième Siècle,* pp. 110-112. Of course in some periods Mary and the saints were used as intermediaries all the same.

neither itself reveals anything, but the Holy Spirit is the revealer of its wonders. It is his vesture and fair adornment, and has in it the wonders, colours and virtues of the divine world."[69]

Koyré's account of this figure is of the greatest relevance to Blake, since it recalls many of Jerusalem's positive aspects and in particular the crippled status of Albion apart from her. The Sophia is above all an *idea* as expressed, not in the divine reason, but in the divine imagination.

> The divine Wisdom is, so to speak, the plan, the preexisting model for creation. She does not create herself, she does not beget. She is only the ideal world, or its image. An ideal and not a fiction, which is why she possesses a certain reality; she lives in God, in a harmonious and pure life. . . . Man, the complete being, can conceive of himself as a realization of the divine Wisdom. It is above all in his soul and thought that she incarnates herself. But there too she is not a constitutive part. She is his image, his celestial spouse, with whom he must unite himself, whom he must realize in himself. But she can separate herself from him; more exactly, it is he who can separate himself from her. She then becomes the ideal that he pursues and cherishes, and she then represents what is lacking in the soul, for she is that which the soul has lost.[70]

In Blakean terms the Emanations are not that which the self creates, but rather that *through which* it creates, the feminine principle of fecundity joined with the masculine principle of fertilization. It is in this sense that Boehme develops the myth of the androgynous Adam-cum-Eve, the two principles merging in a single self.[71]

The implications of Boehme's symbol are worth exploring. The

---

[69] *Six Theosophic Points*, I.lxii, p. 19. In Eternity, Blake says, each form "Emanates/Its own peculiar Light, & the Form is the Divine Vision/And the Light is his Garment. This is Jerusalem in every Man" (*J* 54:1-3, E201/K684). The image goes back to Psalm 104:2, "Who coverest thyself with light as with a garment."

[70] Koyré, *La Philosophie de Jacob Boehme*, pp. 214-215. From man's point of view the Sophia is the essential mediator of the knowledge of God, and from the divine point of view she is essential to the self-unfolding of the primal *Ungrund*, the abyss. "His Godhead is androgynous, and without this feminine, obscure aspect . . . it cannot come in the *Ungrund* to differentiation and thereby to knowledge" (Victor Weiss, *Die Gnosis Jakob Böhmes* [Zurich, 1955], p. 69).

[71] "We know that as a complete and perfect being Adam was androgynous. He was not asexual as a pure spirit would be, but combined in himself, in his celestial body, the two *tincturae*, masculine and feminine. . . . In order to engender he had need of her aid. He had to *imagine in her*, realize her in himself, and thus unite himself to her. . . . In uniting himself to Wisdom and in seeking to realize her in himself, in reality Adam unites himself to his own ideal self (*son propre moi idéal*); he realizes *himself* in realizing *her*, and, by this act, takes on the integrity and perfection of his being" (Koyré, p. 230).

female is the mirror in which the forms of the generating Godhead are reflected; or, in another metaphor, she is the garment but not the body within it. She is female in that she represents otherness, and yet she is virgin because she is not impregnated. The role of reproducing or multiplying is, on the contrary, that of the Son, and the Father is described as generating not only *through* the Son but *in* him. The Son is the "heart," while the Sophia is "that which is uttered, which the Father utters out of the centre of the Heart by the Holy Spirit, and stands in divine forms and images . . . as a virgin without bringing forth." Or in the metaphor of the mirror, "The eternal birth of the Word in the will, in the mirror of the eternal wisdom, in the virgin, continually takes place from eternity to eternity without a genetrix or without bringing forth."[72] Boehme develops this complicated idea because the female is the principle of otherness but in his monistic universe nothing can be ultimately other. Everything turns back upon the oneness of the divine (Boehme is fond of expressions like "unto itself"). So the female is like a garment that shows the shape of the body but is not that body, or like a mirror that shows the forms but only shows them, reduplicating what is in the divine rather than giving it new existence. "For all the form of a spirit is seen in the reflection or in the mirror, and yet there is nothing which the eye or mirror sees; but its seeing is in itself, for there is nothing before it that were deeper there" (I.ix, p. 7).

Since Blake like Boehme seeks to reduce dualism to monism, he is immensely attracted to this symbolism, and it underlies many of the paradoxes of his Jerusalem and his virgin Ololon.[73] Man is God and the female principle must be fully absorbed in the divine, so that creation, with its inevitable sexual connotations, comes after the fall and has nothing to do with the fact that man exists. While Blake retains in the divine a female element, he resists the usual implications of the symbolism of the female—fecundity, maternity—and prefers a myth of eternal multiplicity instead of the primal unity of Neoplatonism.

Orthodoxy tells us that Jesus, though not made, was "begotten" of the Father (John 1:14, and the Nicene Creed). To be sure, it fails to

---

[72] *Six Theosophic Points*, I.xvii, xxii, pp. 9, 11.

[73] Ololon's role is complicated by the fact that at the very end of *Milton* "the Virgin" divides from her with a dolorous shriek and flees "into the depths of Miltons Shadow" (*M* 42:3-6, E142/K534). Frye sees a contrast with the chastity of *Comus* in this bride Ololon "purified of the stain of virginity" (*Fearful Symmetry*, p. 255), and Bloom contrasts her acceptance of sexuality with Thel's shriek as she flees back to Beulah (*Blake's Apocalypse* [Ithaca, 1970], p. 360). But not only is the sexuality of Generation filled—one might say pregnant—with ambiguity, it also seems likely that virginity here has something like the symbolic significance that it does in Boehme, suggesting a union in Eternity which is *not* implicated, as Ololon has here chosen to be, in Generation.

explain on whom or in what the begetting took place, but still it does allow for the idea of begetting. The logic of this symbolism must be that the divine is the ultimate source of everything else, so that as soon as any element of it is distinguished from the essential unity—as soon as Christ is separately imagined—the metaphor of procreation is all but irresistible. Blake, however, resists it. Moreover, Blake's historical Jesus was begotten upon Mary by an earthly lover, which explains well enough where *he* came from, but makes it hard to understand the status of the divine Savior and Lamb of God whom Blake calls upon to descend into our world and redeem it.

Another way of describing Blake's position is to say that Jerusalem continually succumbs to Vala, assimilating with the vicious Emanation of the sexual Luvah rather than with Albion or Jesus. There was a long-standing Platonizing interpretation of the two Helens, one as heavenly beauty and the other as the seductiveness of Generation.[74] Likewise in Valentinian thought the female figure of Wisdom "came to be combined . . . with the moon, mother, and love-goddess of Near Eastern religion, to form that ambiguous figure encompassing the whole scale from the highest to the lowest, from the most spiritual to the utterly sensual."[75] Blake was fascinated with the lunar goddess of the Mediterranean, and many of his pictures show Vala with her attributes. But he does more than describe Jerusalem's temptation to unite with Vala; he treats it as virtually inevitable, for two reasons. First, he is theoretically as well as temperamentally opposed to the concept of fecundity as divine. Not for him the adoration of Boehme's expositor William Law: "This loving Desire is the *generating* heavenly Parent. . . . Every Birth in Nature is a Consequence of this first prolific Love of the Deity, and generates from that which began the first Birth."[76] The second reason is that Blake wants so badly to abolish otherness. According to Hegel, another student of Boehme, "The life of God and divine intelligence can, if we like, be spoken of as love disporting with itself [*ein Spielen der Liebe mit sich selbst*]; but this idea falls into edification, and even sinks into insipidity, if it lacks the seriousness, the suf-

---

[74] Thus Spenser has the two Florimells. See Nohrnberg, *The Analogy of the Faerie Queene*, pp. 116-119, citing sources in Plato, Proclus, and other writers.

[75] Jonas, *The Gnostic Religion*, pp. 176-177. Following the prophets, Blake treats Jerusalem as at once a city, a bride, and a harlot. See the biblical references in David M. Wyatt, "The Woman Jerusalem: *Pictura* versus *Poesis*," *Blake Studies*, 7 (1975), 109-110, and Wyatt's discussion of pl. 31 (pl. 35 in Keynes) in which the body of text separates Eve emerging from Adam's side, at the bottom of the page, from the Savior at the top (p. 113).

[76] *The Spirit of Prayer*, in *Works* (London, 1762), VII, 87. For a well-known application of this symbol see Collins' *Ode on the Poetical Character*, in which the sun and the rest of the created universe are born from the union of God with Fancy.

fering, the patience, and the labour of the negative."[77] We are back to the problem of contraries: Blake wants love-play and emanation, but he does not want otherness and the negative. Hence the frustrating ambiguity of his treatment of Jerusalem.

Of the fallen female—of Vala, Rahab, and Tirzah—there is no need to say much since its status is all too obvious. The Kabbalists saw nature as the garment of God and the Shekhinah as his body, emanations of "the Divine Nature unfolding from within Itself, that it may be revealed ultimately to and within an external universe."[78] In Blake externality is always bad. At best the imagery of the garment implies that something is added to the self, even in the most clearly positive accounts:

> In Great Eternity, every particular Form gives forth or Emanates
> Its own peculiar Light, & the Form is the Divine Vision
> And the Light is his Garment. This is Jerusalem in every Man
> A Tent & Tabernacle of Mutual Forgiveness Male & Female
>   Clothings.
>
> (J 54:1-4, E201/K684)

Jerusalem is both city and woman because, as Mellor comments, they are both "the garments of the man; ideally, they are environments or vehicles that surround him, that gently follow the lines of his body and the patterns of his thought, that provide the material substance which manifests his creative will and vision."[79] But two reservations need to be added to this cheerful picture: first, that if bodies are like cities, then they are *made* rather than growing naturally (as the symbolism of Enitharmon's looms confirms); second, that if bodies are like garments, they can and should be taken off. "Truly My Satan thou art but a Dunce/And dost not know the Garment from the Man" (E266/K771). Hence the paradox of Blake's pictorial treatment of the body: whereas visible clothes are generally negative symbols (especially Vala's veil), the body itself is a form of clothing, so that although in visual terms nakedness is good, in philosophical terms the true spiritual existence is attained by taking off the garment of the body.

And whatever the female garment may be in "Great Eternity," on earth it is a manifestation of the "Female Space" that shrinks the infinite into a false Newtonian infinity (M 10:6-7, E103/K490). As always, Blake struggles to reconcile his perceptions of the "woven" body as a merciful limit and also as a material prison. The Daughters of Los labor at their looms with tears of pity to give the Spectres life, yet the

[77] *Phenomenology*, preface, p. 81.
[78] Waite, *The Holy Kabbalah*, p. 194.
[79] *Blake's Human Form Divine*, p. 296.

consequence of their work is "that Rahab & Tirzah may exist & live & breathe & love" (*J* 59:43, E207/K692), which we can hardly regard with delight. What is true of Los's daughters is true of his Emanation too: Enitharmon is often praised for weaving bodies on the looms of Cathedron (Blake's mother, sister, and wife were all named Catherine) but the dead enter Ulro and Urizen's temple "thro the Gate of Pity/ The broken heart Gate of Enitharmon" (*FZ* 99:23-24, E358/K341). Bodies are sexual and sexuality means the fallen world of Generation: "Thence to the Looms of Cathedron conveyd/The Daughters of Enitharmon weave the ovarium & the integument/In soft silk drawn from their own bowels in lascivious delight" (*FZ* 113:8-10, E362/ K346). And still more drastically: "For then the Body of Death was perfected in hypocritic holiness,/Around the Lamb, a Female Tabernacle woven in Cathedrons Looms" (*M* 13:25-26, E106/K494). No aspect of the female can remain free of physical corruption, and Jerusalem herself joins with Vala to weave the threads of "the Great Polypus of Generation" (*J* 67:34, E218/K704).

In the final plates of *Jerusalem*, Enitharmon is reluctant to lose her separate identity, but she must. She cannot go on being external to Los, and her weaving must come to an end. When Albion arises and compels each Zoa to its proper function, he restores "Luvah to his Loom" (*J* 95:17, E252/K742). Luvah's Emanation Vala had corrupted the loom by weaving the veil and net of mortality upon it; Enitharmon, the Emanation of the imaginative Zoa, was therefore *displaced* into the activity of weaving in order to put a limit to the fall. But now that Albion is awakened, Enitharmon can reintegrate with the blacksmith Urthona, and weaving can be resumed by the "sexual" Luvah/Vala. Only thus can the female in its predatory and destructive aspect be redeemed.

We need glance only briefly at the forms that dualism takes in its extreme "female" condition, for example the "Woman Old" in *The Mental Traveller* who catches the babe's shrieks and tortures him as Christ or Prometheus, later becoming a "Virgin bright" whom he impregnates with the fallen life of cyclical mortality (E475/K425). The multiple versions of Vala/Rahab/Tirzah all draw upon the classic archetypes of woman as mother and whore. When the Female Will is extended to male forms, the meaning is that the female has devoured and perverted the male:

> A Female hidden in a Male, Religion hidden in War
> Namd Moral Virtue; cruel two-fold Monster shining bright
> A Dragon red & hidden Harlot which John in Patmos saw
> (*M* 40:20-22, E140/K532)

If the united Satan and Rahab are "hermaphroditic" it is because the male aspect is subsumed in the female.

Jehovah himself can be seen as female, as when Blake says that an account of the unknowable Supreme Being implies "a Female God."[80] This God is female because it is pure illusion, a projection of the Female Will in hypocritically masculine form. By contrast with the Kabbalah's positive sense of female creativity, Blake agrees with Protestant tradition in despising the *magna mater* of Roman Catholicism: "The Pope supposes Nature and the Virgin Mary to be the same allegorical personages, but the Protestant considers Nature as incapable of bearing a child."[81] And he addresses to Tirzah the words that are supposed to be spoken by Christ to his mother, "What have I to do with thee?"[82] Consider how differently Augustine speaks: "By Jerusalem we must understand not the Jerusalem who is enslaved along with her children, but our free mother, the Jerusalem which, according to the Apostle, is eternal in the heavens. There, after the hardships of our anxieties and worries in this mortal state, we shall be comforted like little children carried on the mother's shoulders and nursed in her lap."[83] Blake's Jerusalem may represent "liberty," but only in Beulah is she a mother.

SEX

Having considered the idea of the sexual symbolically, we must now consider it sexually. We have seen that the female is the symbol of otherness, the object of desire that frustrates the self by luring it into division and materiality. It is time to face directly the emotional as well as conceptual anxiety that this theme produced in Blake, with results that call into question the common belief that he was a champion of sexual delight.

Blake's ambivalence requires neither apology nor special pleading. He simply develops two perennial themes of Western civilization, emphasizing each with his own characteristic intensity, but not inventing any paradox that was not already there. On the one hand, sex has

[80] Annotations to Thornton's *The Lord's Prayer, Newly Translated* (E658/K788).

[81] Annotations to Cellini (E659/K779. In the ninety-ninth Dante picture the visionary rose is replaced by a Blakean sunflower, with both the Virgin Mary and Beatrice depicted as emblems of female sexual enticement and domination (see Roe's commentary, *Blake's Illustrations* . . . , pp. 193-196). See also Vala/Rahab on the sunflower in pl. 53 of *Jerusalem*. Mitchell points out that pl. 4 of *Thel* seems to represent an ironic allusion to pictures of the Virgin adoring her son (*Blake's Composite Art*, p. 102).

[82] E30/K220. Stevenson traces the biblical passages conflated here: *The Poems of Blake*, p. 591n.

[83] *City of God*, XX.xxi, p. 939.

always been seen by many as liberating, even as epiphanic, a simultaneous gratification of the self and release from the prison of selfhood. On the other hand it has always been seen by many as the prison itself, compulsive, obsessive, a means of power over others and a source of unappeasable anxiety. "The burning glass of the will," Schopenhauer called it, and we have seen how suspicious Blake was of the will.

The first point to notice is that Blake's celebration of sexual enjoyment always has a negative component: it is called forth as a *reaction* against repression.

> Abstinence sows sand all over
> The ruddy limbs & flaming hair
> But Desire Gratified
> Plants fruits of life & beauty there.
> (E465/K178)

The ruddy limbs are those of Orc, the type of rebellious energy. Blake's various appeals for sexual liberation follow Eliade's description: "In human society, it is sexual life that is subject to the strictest taboos and constraints. To be free from laws, prohibitions and customs, is to rediscover primordial liberty and blessedness, the state which preceded the present human condition, in fact the paradisiacal state."[84] In Blake's early prophecies Orc was therefore symbolic of liberated energy, and all energy could be seen as sexual. "Blake envisions," as Paley says, "not revolution *and* sexual freedom, but a revolution which is libidinal in nature."[85]

Blake never relented in his hatred of repression.

> The King & the Priest must be tied in a tether
> Before two virgins can meet together.
> (E464/K177)

But he came to doubt the ideal of moving beyond repression to a sexual paradise. We cannot easily trust Tharmas' recollections of the "garden of delight," borrowed from Boehme, in which sexual seeds are sown and harvested.[86] Abstinence in the fallen world remains vicious, as in the self-denying "Aged Virgin Form," but this is also described as a "Sexual Machine" (*J* 39:25, E185/K674), for virginity is paradoxically fertile of iniquity, "Virgin Babylon Mother of Whore-

---

[84] *The Two and the One*, p. 127.

[85] *Energy and the Imagination*, p. 16.

[86] *FZ* 93:42, E397/K339. Raine quotes from Boehme's *Aurora* the description of "a Garden of Delight, into which the Master of it sows all manner of Seeds, according to his Pleasure, and then enjoys the Fruit of it" (*Blake and Tradition*, II, 173).

doms" (*M* 33:20, E132/K523). The early Blake could defy orthodoxy by declaring that "the lust of the goat is the bounty of God" (*MHH*, E36/K151), and still more defiantly could proclaim "the genitals Beauty" (E37/K152). The later Blake continues to celebrate love's temple and the human form divine, in contrast to the dark secret love of adultery (*EG*, E513–514/K755). But he appears increasingly troubled by the fact that the "places of joy & love," as the Spectre of Urthona says "in mockery & scorn," are "excrementitious" (*J* 88:34, 39, E245/K734). Blake is of course not identical with the Spectre, but it would be hard to deny that he has experienced the uneasiness that the Spectre expresses. The pictures begin to be haunted by disquieting images of winged vulvas (as on *Jerusalem* 58), and the very late sketches for the *Book of Enoch* show a degradation of sexuality into the scaly cruelty of the Female Will.[87]

Blake's view of sex is thus deeply divided, in a way that is not peculiar to him but is exacerbated by his unusual distrust of otherness. "Sex in act," Ricoeur says, "consists in making us exist as body, with no distance between us and ourself, in an experience of completeness exactly contrary to the incompleteness of perception and spoken communication."[88] Just so in Blake; insofar as he can believe that the sexual act is a completion of the self, he is glad to celebrate it. But he is also aware that mutual gratification, even if successful, requires a necessary admission of the existence of another self.

> What is it men in women do require
> The lineaments of Gratified Desire
> What is it women do in men require
> The lineaments of Gratified Desire
> (E466/K180)

As R. D. Laing has seen, this quatrain is based on the experience of *non*gratification: "When Blake suggested that what is most required is 'the lineaments of gratified desire' *in the other*, he indicated that one of the most frustrating possible experiences is full discharge of one's energy or libido, however pleasurable, without making any difference to the other."[89] And in the context of Blake's system the very existence of the other constitutes a problem. How should one gratify that which ought not to exist?

---

[87] The series cannot have been undertaken before the first English translation of Enoch in 1821. It is reproduced and discussed by Allan R. Brown in "Blake's Drawings for the Book of Enoch," in Essick, pp. 104–115, and by G. E. Bentley, Jr., "A Jewel in an Ethiop's Ear," in Essick and Pearce, pp. 213–240.

[88] *Freud and Philosophy*, pp. 382–383.

[89] *Self and Others* (Harmondsworth, 1969), p. 85.

We can trace Blake's growing gloom about sexual fulfillment even in *Visions of the Daughters of Albion*, a poem which is often regarded as a tribute to Wollstonecraft's feminism and is always treated as a celebration of free sexuality. It has not passed without notice that the ending of the poem is less than hopeful, with Oothoon wailing and the Daughters of Albion echoing back her sighs. And it is also evident that Blake chooses a female figure in order to emphasize the theme of helplessness.[90] But there seems to be general agreement that Oothoon's ideal of "happy copulation" (7:1, E49/K194) would be splendid if only the Theotormon-Bromion axis did not frustrate it, making the poem an "abortive epithalamium" instead of a successful one.[91]

Yet troubling difficulties remain. For one thing, there is the design on plate 3 (see fig. 15) in which an eagle tears at Oothoon's body, seductively displayed, in illustration of the lines in which she calls on Theotormon's eagle "to prey upon her flesh" while "incessant writhing her soft snowy limbs" (2:12-13, E45/K190). The masochism is obvious; is it obvious that Oothoon is superior to its appeal or that she later overcomes it?[92] In her last speech, having cried "Love! Love! Love! happy happy Love! free as the mountain wind!" (7:16), Oothoon utters her famous speech against jealousy:

> But silken nets and traps of adamant will Oothoon spread,
> And catch for thee girls of mild silver, or of furious gold;
> I'll lie beside thee on a bank & view their wanton play
> In lovely copulation bliss on bliss with Theotormon.
> (7:23-26, E49/K194-195)

The negative connotations of the "nets" and "traps" have gone virtually unnoticed here. Yet we have heard a little earlier of the "nets & gins & traps" of priestly oppression (5:18, E48/K193), and the imagery of the net is ubiquitous in the later poems as a symbol of female dominion.[93] Oothoon's nets are silken, her traps unbreakable ada-

[90] As Fox points out in "The Female as Metaphor," p. 513.

[91] Wagenknecht, *Blake's Night*, p. 147.

[92] The question is whether the passage about the eagle is a temporary aberration inspired by the male oppressor, or whether it reveals something about fallen sexuality which Oothoon cannot wholly overcome even though she tries. Erdman, incidentally, tries to decontaminate the image by describing it as merely "a product of Oothoon's rhetorical imagination" (*Illuminated Blake*, p. 131). One must certainly agree that it is an imaginative rather than a literal fact, especially if Oothoon is seen as a part of the psyche rather than a "real" person. But surely Blake is the one artist in whose work one can never describe an image as "just an idea" (ibid., p. 151).

[93] See especially "The Golden Net" (E474/K424). The nets and traps are noticed by D. Aers, "William Blake and the Dialectics of Sex," *ELH*, 44 (1977), p. 506. This article,

15. *Visions of the Daughters of Albion*, plate 3.

mant. Moreover, Oothoon's voyeurist fantasy—she will *watch* their play—does not sound like something Blake would recommend; we shall look presently at his picture of Satan watching Adam and Eve.

These considerations should not lead to a drastic revision of the accepted interpretation, but to a recognition that *Visions of the Daughters of Albion* is torn by the same antinomies that we find everywhere in Blake. He hates sexual repression, but he is not sure what to replace it with. Unselfish love is obviously better than selfish, but are Oothoon's fantasies, with their sadomasochism and voyeurism, really so unselfish? And if not, is that because the fallen world has perverted her pure instincts, or because the instincts themselves are impure? I am sure that Blake was not sure, and that he wrote the poem to dramatize the problem. It diminishes the poem to treat it as a simple plea for free love.

The ultimate difficulty about sex is that it is a function of the fallen world of generation, which it perpetuates by its power of reproduction. Oothoon sees with horror that the female is compelled

> . . . all the night
> To turn the wheel of false desire: and longings that wake her womb
> To the abhorred birth of cherubs in the human form
> That live a pestilence & die a meteor & are no more.

---

however, with its Marxist (or Marcusean) bias, assumes that Blake is preoccupied with the role of actual men and women in "the total socio-political structures within which life has to be led" (p. 501). I argue that sex itself is one of those structures, and that Blake is far from convinced that we should approve of it.

Till the child dwell with one he hates, and do the deed he loaths
And the impure scourge force his seed into its unripe birth
E'er yet his eyelids can behold the arrows of the day.
(5:26-32, E48/K193)

Happy copulation may be the alternative to the autoeroticism of the youth who "shall forget to generate" (7:6, E49/K194), but it looks as if remembering to generate is nearly as bad. Children born of fallen sexuality are "a pestilence" and are condemned in their turn to equally joyless procreation.

Of course one can argue that the problem lies in their attitude toward sex rather than in sex itself, but I think that Blake wants us to consider both possibilities. As he wrote in his notebook at about the same time,

> Thou hast a lap full of seed
> And this is a fine country
> Why dost thou not cast thy seed
> And live in it merrily
>
> Shall I cast it on the sand
> And turn it into fruitful land
> For on no other ground
> Can I sow my seed
> Without tearing up
> Some stinking weed
>
> (E461/K168)

Abstinence may sow sand all over the ruddy limbs, but in some moods at least Blake sees sand as the only place where seed can be sown. If it is thrown anywhere else, it is thwarted by the weeds of jealousy and diseased sexuality. Will the sand really turn into fruitful land? In Beulah it may, as in Ahania's poignant nostalgia for a Song of Songs harmony in which her spouse Urizen had a "lap full of seed" and sowed "the seed of eternal science" in human souls (*Ahania* 5:29–34, E88/K255). But that is precisely what is at issue: the gap between sex as experienced and sex as a wished-for ideal.

Read in this way, the ending of *Visions* becomes doubly equivocal. It is not only that Oothoon and the Daughters of Albion are helpless and static, but also that they gaze into the sea "conversing with shadows dire" (8:12, E50/K195). As Raine points out in a brilliant identification, the phrase about conversing with shadows recalls Plotinus on the myth of Narcissus: "Hence as Narcissus, by catching at the shadow, merged himself in the stream and disappeared, so he who is captivated by beautiful bodies, and does not depart from their embrace, is precipitated, not with his body but with his soul, into a darkness profound and horrid to intellect, through which, becoming blind both here and in Hades, he converses with nothing but shadows."[94] Raine concludes that the soul cannot be defiled by contact with the body; but since Blake holds that body is an expression of soul, it is hard to imagine that both are not involved, even if the body is a garment that will eventually be discarded. And in this light the poem's refrain takes on a new significance: the Daughters "eccho back her sighs" (8:13). Echo was the nymph who loved Narcissus, could only repeat his words, and was rejected by him. A number of critics have noticed that in the later poems Blake uses the Narcissus theme to symbolize man's futile worship of his own image.[95] And early in the *Visions*, immediately after calling for Theotormon's eagle, Oothoon has expressed the wish to reflect "The image of Theotormon on my pure transparent breast" (2:16, E45/K190).

The imagery of Narcissus perfectly expresses Blake's uncertainty about the relation of lover to beloved. Sometimes he seems to suggest that their mutual reflection is a heavenly ideal, "that Love calld Friendship which Looks for no other heaven than their Beloved & in him sees all reflected as in a Glass of Eternal Diamond" (*VLJ*, E549/K610). And Tharmas describes his lost emanation, in similar terms, as "my Crystal form that lived in my bosom" (*FZ* 97:11, E393/K334). Yet as "The Crystal Cabinet" suggests, this is finally a hopeless dream. When the maiden locks up the poem's speaker in her cabinet— borrowed apparently from Thomas Vaughan's symbolism of the body—he is trapped in a Beulah world of "Moony Night," and his sexual response leads only to the world of generation:

> I strove to seize the inmost Form
> With ardor fierce & hands of flame
> But burst the Crystal Cabinet
> And like a Weeping Babe became.[96]

The stanza that begins "Another England there I saw" is sometimes quoted as a vision of plenitude, but it turns out instead to be a swindle: it is a narcissistic image of the present self, not of a richer world, and it therefore duplicates what one already sees (London, Thames, hills,

[94] *Enneads*, I.vi.8, as translated by Thomas Taylor, quoted by Raine, *Blake and Tradition*, I, 176.

[95] See Robert E. Simmons, "*Urizen:* The Symmetry of Fear," in Erdman and Grant, pp. 150-151; J. H. Hagstrum, "Babylon Revisited, or the Story of Luvah and Vala," in Curran and Wittreich, pp. 107-108; and Wagenknecht, *Blake's Night*, p. 201, with a useful reference to Eve admiring herself in *Paradise Lost* IV. 453-465.

[96] E480/K429. Vaughan describes the body (or matter) as a crystal "palace" and "cabinet" into which the soul is lured by Venus (Raine, *Blake and Tradition*, I, 274ff.).

Surrey bower) instead of being imaginatively transformed. Like *Visions*, the lyric ends with "woes."

Theotormon and Oothoon are both prisoners. Theotormon rightly sees that fallen nature is inadequate but wrongly seeks truth in "times & spaces far remote" (4:6, E47/K192). Oothoon rightly looks to this world rather than a Urizenic heaven, but wrongly seeks delight in its physical manifestations rather than in the spiritual truth that underlies them. So she and Bromion remain bound back to back in the design which is usually the frontispiece, once the tailpiece (see fig. 16). The Urizen figure Bromion stares off to the left in horror while Theotormon and Oothoon gaze downward; Theotormon sees his own Narcissus image in the water and in her. The composition is a Laocoön, but instead of being entangled by the serpent of materiality, the three figures form the serpent with their own limbs. Fallen sex *is* the Laocoön.

It is possible to see Bromion and Theotormon as two aspects of the self, the one desiring sex (but brutally, with his slavedriver imagery) and the other rigidly repressing it. Oothoon, the emanation, is inevitably drawn into the sadomasochistic dilemma, which suggests that sex as we know it is incapable of being transformed, bound as it is to the Narcissus fixation of crystal forms. And Oothoon watching Theotormon's copulation implies a painful inner distancing: the female principle welcomes sexual enjoyment but finds that the male is gratified only if a kind of dissociation occurs. In Blake's later myth Oothoon returns briefly as a daughter of Los, again as a victim of the fallen sexual imagination.[97] "Oothoon?/Where hides my child?" cries Los in a context of building "beautiful labyrinths" (*J* 83:26–27) and shortly after confessing his sexual entrapment:

> I know I am Urthona keeper of the Gates of Heaven,
> And that I can at will expatiate in the Gardens of bliss;
> But pangs of love draw me down to my loins which are
> Become a fountain of veiny pipes: O Albion! my brother!
> Corruptability appears upon thy limbs. . . .
> (J 82:81–83:1, E238–239/K727)

The loins are frequently a place of fascinated fear, as when Gwendolen "wove two vessels of seed" for Albion and "hid them in his loins" (*J* 80:74–76, E235/K723).

Orthodox religion approved of sex only because it was necessary

---

[97] At the end of *Milton* "soft Oothoon" is described as "weeping oer her Human Harvest" while Los hears in anger "the Cry of the Poor Man" (*M* 42:32–35); see the illustration, in which her tears fall as rain from the sky, and Erdman's commentary (*Illuminated Blake*, p. 265).

16. *Visions of the Daughters of Albion*, frontispiece.

for generation (Augustine says in the *City of God* that before the fall Adam and Eve felt no sexual desire but activated their organs rationally). Blake, on the contrary, dreads its power *because* it leads to generation.

> Eternity shudder'd when they saw,
> Man begetting his likeness
> On his own divided image.
> (*Urizen* 19:14–16, E78/K232)

From this narcissistic union Orc is born, and with him the "natural" cycle of jealousy and revenge. Orc is possessed by "ceaseless rage" for "the thrilling joys of sense" (*FZ* 61:17, E334/K308), and Urizen, with bitter Blakean irony, speaks of the "breeding womb/Of Enitharmon" dominating Los "By gratified desire by strong devouring appetite" (*FZ* 80:22–25, E348–349/K323). Gratified desire becomes a tool of the Female Will.

Insofar as the male contributes to reproduction he becomes, in Blake's system, female. Vala, who has Earthquake "in her Loins," tells Albion "Thou art/Thyself Female, a Male: a breeder of Seed" (*J* 64:10–13, E213/K698). We cannot be surprised if at times Blake suggests that the proper response is to withhold the desired seed:

> But Los himself against Albions Sons his fury bends, for he
> Dare not approach the Daughters openly lest he be consumed
> In the fires of their beauty & perfection & be Vegetated beneath
> Their Looms, in a Generation of death & resurrection to
>   forgetfulness
> They wooe Los continually to subdue his strength. . . .
>   (*J* 17:6–10, E160/K638)

When he thinks of religious and political repression, as for example at the end of *America*, Blake sees sex as the symbol of freedom. When he thinks of sex itself, he is drawn into an ancient symbolism of defilement. For as Ricoeur has said,

> An indissoluble complicity between sexuality and defilement seems to have been formed from time immemorial. . . . At the limit, the infant would be regarded as born impure, contaminated from the beginning by the paternal seed, by the impurity of the maternal genital region, and by the additional impurity of childbirth. It is not certain that such beliefs do not continue to prowl in the consciousness of modern man and that they have not played a decisive role in speculation on original sin.[98]

[98] *Symbolism of Evil*, pp. 28–29.

Enitharmon is wrenched out of Los when his "loins begin to break forth into veiny pipes & writhe" until the "bloody mass" is animate, "Dividing & dividing from my loins" (*FZ* 10:11-15, E327/K300). Once separated from Los, Enitharmon and her daughters weave bodies in the "ovarium" with "lascivious delight" (*FZ* 113:9-10, E362/K346). And in a horrible image in *Jerusalem* the growing fetus is likened to a spreading malignancy:

> Then all the Males combined into One Male & every one
> Became a ravening eating Cancer growing in the Female
> A Polypus of Roots of Reasoning Doubt Despair & Death.
> (J 69:1-3, E220/K707)

The full complexity of Blake's attitude is apparent in an extraordinary lyric:

> I saw a chapel all of gold
> That none did dare to enter in
> And many weeping stood without
> Weeping mourning worshipping
>
> I saw a serpent rise between
> The white pillars of the door
> And he forcd & forcd & forcd
> Down the golden hinges tore
>
> And along the pavement sweet
> Set with pearls & rubies bright
> All his slimy length he drew
> Till upon the altar white
>
> Vomiting his poison out
> On the bread & on the wine
> So I turnd into a sty
> And laid me down among the swine
> (E458/K163)

In the usual kind of interpretation this is "the temple of innocent love, defiled by . . . repression."[99] One may well think of the chapel in "The Garden of Love" with "Thou shalt not, writ over the door" (E26/K215). E. P. Thompson notes the connection of chapels with Methodism, and comments sardonically on "a cult of 'Love' which feared love's effective expression, either as sexual love or in any social

---

[99] Stevenson, *The Poems of Blake*, p. 146n. Similarly Hazard Adams argues that the speaker's disgust is inspired by debased sexuality rather than by sexuality itself (*William Blake*, pp. 240-242).

form which might irritate relations with Authority."[100] But surely the imagery carries the argument a step further: if the phallic serpent is right to violate the chapel, the result is nevertheless horror and disgust rather than joyful consummation. Yet if the chapel symbolizes sexual represssion, how else can one fight it except by breaking down its doors?

Let us start again. The chapel doors suggest a symbol that occurs frequently in Blake's prophetic poems, the vagina as the tabernacle of the Pentateuch.[101] The female hides "The Divine Vision with Curtain & Veil & fleshly Tabernacle" (*J* 56:40, E204/K688), a "Secret place" filled with the "whisperd hymn & mumbling prayer" of lust (*FZ* 96:2-6, E393/K333). In contrast with the perfect "Cominglings" of the Eternals, fallen sex is "a pompous High Priest entering by a Secret Place" (*J* 69:43-44, E221/K708). And there is a sketch in the *Vala* manuscript (see fig. 17) in which a chapel appears literally as the vagina.

This tempting yet vicious holy of holies seems to invite a phallic assault, and it is interesting to note that such indeed was the conclusion of the ancient Ophitic ("serpent worshipping") heretics. As a scandalized St. Epiphanius described their ritual, loaves of bread were placed on an altar, a serpent was put on them, and each of the faithful ate of the loaves after kissing the serpent on the mouth. Sexual orgies followed.[102] Whether or not Blake knew of this heresy, he offers a striking parallel in his sketch *Eve Tempted by the Serpent* (see fig. 18), which can be glossed by the poem "To Nobodaddy," "None dare eat the fruit but from/The wily serpents jaws" (E462/K171). Eve's act of eating the apple is also one of kissing the serpent on the mouth.[103] To the Ophites the serpent symbolized the forbidden knowledge of the Garden of Eden, and more specifically sexual initiation. To Blake, however, it connotes sexual degradation; ejaculation is imaged horribly as the serpent "Vomiting his poison out/On the bread & on the wine." And the serpent that defiles the bread and wine is loathsome

---

[100] *The Making of the English Working Class* (Harmondsworth, 1968), p. 44. Thompson adds, "Its authentic language of devotion was that of sexual sublimation streaked through with masochism."

[101] See Paul Miner, "William Blake's 'Divine Analogy,' " *Criticism*, 3 (1961), 46-61. Not all Blakeans have been willing to admit the implications of such images as "the dreadful winged pudendum which appears like some kind of Rorschach monster in *Jerusalem*" (p. 49, referring to pl. 58).

[102] See Lacarrière, *Les Gnostiques*, pp. 99-100.

[103] The apple is not visible in this sketch, but is clearly depicted in the finished *Paradise Lost* illustration of the Temptation and Fall (reproduced in color in Klonsky, *William Blake*, p. 83).

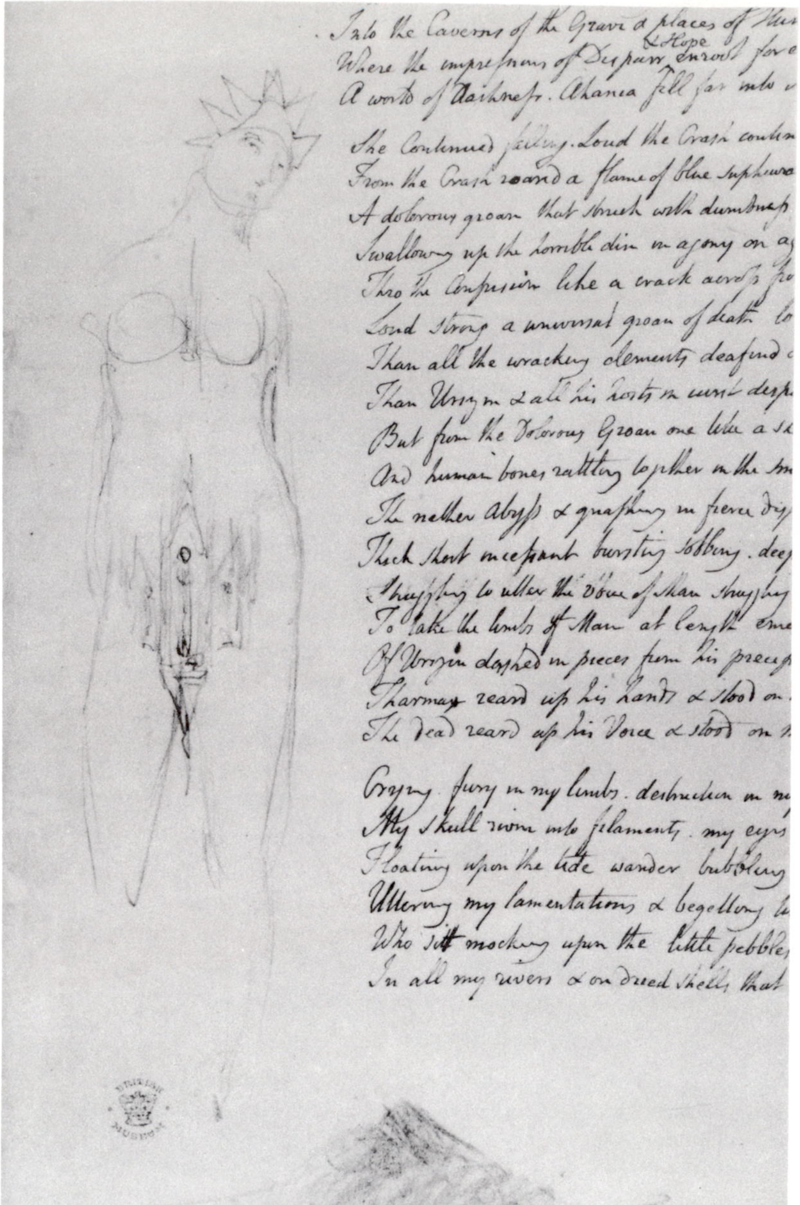

17. *Vala, or The Four Zoas*, manuscript sketch.

18. *Eve Tempted by the Serpent.*

both in his slime and in the brutal doggedness with which "he forcd &
forcd & forcd" until the vomit comes.

The poem ends with the speaker lying down among the swine, an
act which is described as having happened in the past. Sex has produced powerful imagery of fascinated attraction mingled with revul-
sion, and has driven the speaker into exile among the swine—surely an
allusion to the Prodigal Son, as well as a confession of bestial condition. What he has learned is that the phallic violation was *intended*: the
chapel was placed there precisely in order to tempt the serpent into
that response. After the horror of the response, he has fled to lie
among pigs, for he is one of them. If he is indeed the Prodigal he will
return at length to his father's house, but there is no suggestion that he
will return to the chapel all of gold, which has turned out to be a mask
for the seductive but bestializing bower of bliss.

> To whom the Palmer thus, The donghill kind
> Delights in filth and foule incontinence:
> Let Grill be Grill, and have his hoggish mind,
> But let us hence depart, whilest wether serves and wind.
> (*Faerie Queene* II.xii.87)

Both of Blake's ambivalent attitudes toward sex were anticipated in
Gnosticism. In the view of the Carpocratians and other sects, the way
to fight nature on its own terms was to recognize "a positive duty to
perform every kind of action, to leave no deed undone, no possibility
of freedom unrealized," while on the contrary the Marcionites and
others were strict ascetics in order to refrain from reproduction, which
could only serve to replenish the world of the demiurge. Both extremes sprang from a single motive, and that motive is Blake's: "Asceticism is thus a matter less of ethics than of metaphysical alignment,
and its common ground with libertinism is the determination not to
play the Creator's [cf. Urizen's and Vala's] game. The one repudiates
allegiance to nature through abstention; the other, through excess."[104]
The road of excess may lead to the palace of wisdom, but it may also
lead to the chapel all of gold.

Blake's answer to the dilemma is given in another poem, the unfin-
ished stanzas about the Spectre:

> Let us agree to give up Love
> And root up the infernal grove
> Then shall we return & see
> The worlds of happy Eternity

[104] Hans Jonas, "Gnosticism," in *The Encyclopedia of Philosophy*, ed. Edwards, III, 340,
341.

> & Throughout all Eternity
> I forgive you you forgive me
> As our Dear Redeemer said
> This the Wine & this the Bread
> (E468/K417)

In Jesus the bread and wine of forgiveness are liberated from the body of death, and the infernal grove of love can be uprooted. "If you dare rend their Veil with your Spear, you are healed of Love!" the deluded warriors cry before rushing off to war when the "Virgin has frownd & refusd" (*J* 68:42, 63, E220/K706–707). From Blake's ironic perspective they will indeed be healed of love, for the sexual initiation of the rending spear is an epiphany of disgust, and the next step is to flee to the swine, after which the Redeemer can reveal the true bread and wine.[105]

No one would claim that Blake always felt this way.

> When a Man has Married a Wife
> he finds out whether
> Her knees & elbows are only
> glued together.
> (E508/K418)

It is apparent that he was deeply divided on the subject, and, as the Notebook poems and prophecies show, his treatment of it has an obsessive quality. Without question the poems must reflect difficulties in Blake's emotional life which we have no way of knowing much about.[106] He offers a number of possible solutions. Often, of course, everything is simply blamed on repression:

---

[105] The same imagery appears early in *The Four Zoas* at the dire marriage feast of the fallen Los and Enitharmon, who partake of the sexual bread and wine of the body: "They eat the fleshly bread, they drank the nervous wine" (*FZ* 12:44, E303/K274). Unseen by them, the image is once again transformed by an epiphany of Jesus: "Eternity appeard above them as One Man infolded In Luvahs robes of blood & bearing all his afflictions" (13:8–9). And in its fallen form the imagery recurs in the eighth Night when Jerusalem mistakenly thinks that Jesus has really died and calls for the worship of death in a sepulchre embossed with "jewels & gold" (106:13, E365/K349).

[106] It seems clear that Blake was tormented by his wife's possessive jealousy, with what justification we cannot know, and increasingly saw sexuality as an instrument of the implacable Female Will. See John Sutherland, "Blake: A Crisis of Love and Jealousy," *PMLA*, 87 (1972), 424–431. Elsewhere Sutherland suggests very plausibly that the "ruddy fruit" offered to Los by Enitharmon is "on the physical level Enitharmon/Catherine Blake's breasts, which she presents in very erotic, tempting fashion" in one of the *Vala* sketches. "Thereafter Blake/Los apparently achieves the sexual consummation which had for some time been withheld; however, it is in good part spoiled for him by the sense of guilt and degradation which Enitharmon now seems to

And many of the Eternal Ones laughed after their manner:
Have you known the Judgment that is arisen among the
Zoas of Albion? where a Man dare hardly to embrace
His own Wife, for the terrors of Chastity that they call
By the name of Morality. their Daughters govern all
In hidden deceit! they are Vegetable only fit for burning:
Art & Science cannot exist but by Naked Beauty displayd
(J 32:43–49, E177/K663)

But if the vegetable body is fit only for burning, what is the "Naked Beauty" that transcends repressive chastity?

It is possible to suspect sometimes that Blake's fulminations against repression are an excuse rather than an explanation: his anxieties are not his own fault because someone else is reponsible for them. Kazin dryly remarks, "There is little doubt that he was the ideal husband; and apparently he could not stand it."[107] The golden net and myrtle tree and crystal cabinet are broodings on the same theme; whether or not Blake was ever involved with another woman, he understood that adultery would carry with it the same secrecy and guilt that evidently poisoned his experience of marriage. He told Robinson that he had learned from the Bible that wives should be in common (*Blake Records*, p. 548), and this seems to have been his fantasy ideal: men and women so free that they no longer had particular claims on each other. Yet his theory of self and Emanation implies a particular relationship.

The brief account of Blake's courtship that survives (from Tatham, who knew Catherine Blake well at the end of her life) is immensely revealing. Having sought in vain to win the "implacable" Polly Wood, he went to Kew for a change of scene and told his tale to his landlord's daughter, "upon which Catherine expressed her deep sympathy, it is supposed in such a tender & affectionate manner, that it quite won him, he immediately said with the suddenness peculiar to him 'Do you pity me?' 'Yes indeed I do' answered she. 'Then I love you' said he again. . . . After this interview, Blake left the House having recruited his health & spirits, & having determined to take Catherine Boutcher to Wife" (*Blake Records*, pp. 517–518). So Desdemona listened to Othello's tale of dangers passed, and he "lov'd her that she did pity them." Here are two familiar Blakean themes: his

---

connect with sexuality" ("Blake and Urizen," in Erdman and Grant, p. 253). A direct recollection of Catherine's behavior at Felpham is surely apparent in *Jerusalem* when Enitharmon sits "on Sussex shore singing lulling cadences," exciting pleasures in "the aching fibres of Los" while at the same time "contending against him/In pride sending his Fibres over to her objects of jealousy" (J 88:22ff., E244/K733).

[107] *Portable Blake*, p. 35.

hatred of the woman who plays hard to get (the cold Polly Wood) and his need for maternal pity as well as sexual love. In his subsequent relations with Catherine, Tatham remarks, "Blake was at once lover, husband, child." At the same time Tatham speaks of "the obedient, unassuming devotion of her dear soul to him" (*Blake Records*, p. 526n).

Blake thus acted both roles, of master and dependent, that recur throughout his poems. As master he could be stern. There is a notable story of an argument after which he forced Catherine to kneel and beg the pardon of his favorite brother Robert, his alter-ego in the *Milton* illustrations (*Blake Records*, p. 30). And he seems to have imposed on her the role of emanation; Tatham, who had only the vaguest understanding of Blake's myth, says strikingly that Catherine "brought with the spirit of a Willing mind the materials with which he was to build up the fabric of his Immortal Thoughts" (*Blake Records*, p. 534). Yet Blake remained keenly impatient of the demands of affection, both maternal and spousal.

> Grown old in Love from Seven till Seven times Seven
> I oft have wishd for Hell for Ease from Heaven.
>
> (E508/K552)

It is hardly surprising that there were bitter quarrels. And even at the end, when Blake's young disciples described the good old couple in domestic bliss, might there not be irony in Catherine's remark to a visitor, "I have very little of Mr. Blake's company; he is always in Paradise"? The writer (Seymour Kirkup) adds ingenuously, "She prepared his colours, and was as good as a servant" (*Blake Records*, p. 221).

As he did with everything else, Blake turned psychosexual experience into philosophical structure. As with many of his other preoccupations, it is possible—though of course not the whole story—to see the structure as a compensation for frustration as well as an attempt to explain it. That is why his lyrics on love and his treatment of it in the prophecies exhibit a depth of insight that had not been seen in English poetry since the early seventeenth century. "How glowing guilt exalts the keen delight!" cries Pope's Eloisa,[108] but she does not know why and neither does Pope, as the poem oscillates between honest lust and a sexualized religiosity that ends in mid-air. When Blake makes a fairy sing "stolen joys are sweet, & bread eaten in secret pleasant,"[109] the idea is gathered into a philosophical analysis of the entire human con-

---

[108] *Eloisa to Abelard*, line 230.

[109] *Europe* iii:6, E59/K237. The source is Proverbs 9:17, "Stolen waters are sweet, and bread eaten in secret is pleasant." Blake perhaps expected the reader to recall the following verse, "But he knoweth not that the dead are there; and that her guests are in the depths of hell."

dition. But so far as fallen love is concerned, Blake never really abandons the Elizabethan pessimism of his earliest lyrics. In the fallen state the classical *odi et amo* is inescapable: "And now I hate & now I love & Intellect is no more" (*J* 68:67, E220/K707).

Blake of course holds that this need not be the case, that man (and woman?) can rise above this prison. But we should understand clearly that there is no longer any place for gratified desire and sensual enjoyment in the terms of *The Marriage of Heaven and Hell*. As Shakespeare's Troilus learns, "This is the monstruosity in love, lady, that the will is infinite and the execution confined; that the desire is boundless and the act a slave to limit."[110] From the time of the Elizabethan imitations in *Poetical Sketches* Blake knew that love could be a snare and a prison. In *The Four Zoas* the subtitle is "The Torments of Love & Jealousy in the Death and Judgment of Albion the Ancient Man," and fallen sex in that poem is described as a kind of enraged rutting that indeed exposes the bestial in man:

> Opening his rifted rocks mingling together they join in burning
> anguish
> Mingling his horrible darkness with her tender limbs then high she
> soard
> Shrieking above the ocean: a bright wonder that nature shudderd at
> Half Woman & half beast. . . .
>
> (*FZ* 7:1-4, E299/K269)

The "Love & Jealousy" of Albion are those of self-love and (if the term exists) self-jealousy. "Envying stood the enormous Form at variance with Itself/In all its Members: in eternal torment of love & jealousy" (*J* 69:6-7, E221/K707).

The explanation is not the misuse of desire only, as Blake at first believed, but its essential nature. "If desire were not located within an interhuman situation," Ricoeur says, "there would be no such thing as repression, censorship, or wish-fulfillment through fantasies; that the other and others are primarily bearers of prohibitions is simply another way of saying that desire encounters another desire—an opposed desire."[111] Blake fully understands this idea. Repression is not a detachable excrescence upon human behavior, but its inevitable concomitant. So his solution is to project humanity beyond the world we know into another where desire can be infinite yet gratified, and where the other can lose its otherness. Moreover, that will be a state which will dispense not only with marriage but also with reproduc-

---

[110] *Troilus and Cressida*, III.ii.
[111] *Freud and Philosophy*, p. 387.

tion. Quid (usually identified as Blake himself) sings sarcastically in
the early *Island in the Moon,*

> Hail fingerfooted lovely Creatures
> The females of our human Natures
> Formed to suckle all Mankind
> Tis you that come in time of need
> Without you we should never Breed
> Or any Comfort find.
>
> (E450/K56)

Fingerfooted! Women pretend to be so ethereal that they possess nothing so indelicate as feet (but are therefore bizarrely prehensile, like
apes). "We" need them for breeding and suckling purposes, Quid
coarsely observes, and the consequence is imprisonment "In Mat-
rimony's Golden cage" (E451/K56). The rest of the company protest
indignantly that Quid "always spoils good company in this manner";
there is no reason to suppose that Blake's disquietude about marriage
and reproduction was eased when, later on, he himself married.

According to Mary Douglas, the millennial temperament sees society as a system that does not work, and the human body as "the most
readily available image of a system." Such a person seeks visionary
experiences that may appear to be physical but are intended as an af-
front to the body and an escape from it. "The millennialist goes in for
frenzies; he welcomes the letting-go experience, and incorporates it
into his procedure for bringing in the millennium. He seeks bodily
ecstasy which, by expressing for him the explosive advent of the new
age, reaffirms the value of the doctrine. Philosophically his bias is towards distinguishing spirit from flesh, mind from matter."[112] At the
time of the French Revolution Blake was clearly inspired by similar
ideas, and even while proclaiming the improvement of sensual enjoyment he was strongly attracted to ascetic notions of liberating the
body by shocking its usual impulses: "I then asked Ezekiel, why he eat
dung, & lay so long on his right & left side? he answerd. the desire of
raising other men into a perception of the infinite."[113]

By the time of the late prophecies Blake explicitly endorsed a
Christian—indeed a Puritan—ideal of self-denial.

> We are told to abstain from fleshly desires that we may lose no time
> from the Work of the Lord. Every moment lost, is a moment that

[112] *Natural Symbols*, p. 17.

[113] *MHH*, E38/K154. Randel Helms points out that as Blake would have known,
Ezekiel's unusual diet is a direct violation of the Mosaic law ("Why Ezekiel Ate Dung,"
English Language Notes, 15 [1978], 279-281).

cannot be redeemed. Every pleasure that intermingles with the duty of our station is a folly unredeemable & is planted like the seed of a wild flower among our wheat. . . . What are the Pains of Hell but Ignorance, Bodily Lust, Idleness & devastation of the things of the Spirit?

(*J* 77, E229-230/K716-717)

It is a measure of Blake's return to the Bible that the visionary, whether or not he can see heaven in a wild flower, is now committed to "duty" and must allow no wild flowers to grow up among his wheat. If sex remains redemptive at all, it must be, as Hirsch says, "not because it gratifies natural desire, but because it restores the fallen unity and removes desire."[114]

Here a psychoanalytic explanation is interesting, in light of Blake's pervasive distrust of otherness and of the love that seeks to gratify the other. Freud speaks of certain temperaments for whom the love of mankind represents an inhibition of libido: "These people make themselves independent of their object's acquiescence by displacing what they mainly value from being loved on to loving; they protect themselves against the loss of the object by directing their love, not to single objects but to all men alike; and they avoid the uncertainties and disappointments of genital love by turning away from its sexual aims and transforming the instinct into an impulse with an inhibited aim." There is much here that is relevant to Blake, yet his ideal is far from the state of "evenly suspended, steadfast, affectionate feeling" that Freud goes on to describe in figures like St. Francis of Assisi.[115] We are reminded once again that however much Blake might have been an attractive subject for psychoanalysis, he is also a competing theorist of human nature. And his ideal of an active Eden, as we shall see presently, constitutes his most original contribution to the attempt to get beyond jealous love without sacrificing life-giving energy.

Blake deals with the same symptoms of sexual disorder that Freud does, depicting them symbolically whereas Freud describes them clinically, and arrives at a notably similar conclusion about the status of sexuality in civilized life. Freud's celebrated essay of 1912, "The Most Prevalent Form of Degradation in Erotic Life," undertakes to explain the disjunction in many people between the sensual and the tender elements of sexual feeling. According to Freud the tender feelings are first aroused by the mother, then blocked by the incest taboo, and finally restricted in adult life to women whose maternal role forbids full sensual enjoyment, which is achieved only with women who can

[114] *Innocence and Experience*, p. 112.
[115] *Civilization and Its Discontents*, p. 49.

be perceived as degraded. Freud maintains that this division is endemic in civilized life, being present to some extent in everyone, not just in the exaggerated forms which it takes in neurosis. In men, therefore, sensual gratification is involved with degradation; in women, cut off by cultural pressures (in Freud's time at least) from even that kind of gratification, it requires the element of forbiddenness, secret intrigue as opposed to marital relations.

It will be apparent that Blake does not analyze the problem in the same way that Freud does. He has no developed theory of infantile sexuality and the Oedipal relation, although there are plenty of hints that he is aware of the latter.[116] The point is important: even if there are intimations of the Oedipal theme, it is not structural and explanatory as in Freud. Blake vividly describes what Freud calls "degradation" but explains it through a cosmic myth of self-division rather than through the individual's relationships and experiences.

Hence we find Blake profoundly divided within himself on the subject of sex. Without question he despises secrecy and perversion. Without question he seeks, in Freud's terms, to unite sensuality and tenderness in the marital relation, in contrast with the very conventional tendency to displace sensuality on to women of a lower class (both Boswell and Rousseau could have been invented by Freud). But he is aware of the persistent problem:

> In a wife I would desire
> What in whores is always found
> The lineaments of Gratified desire.
> (E465/K178)

Whores exhibit gratified desire because they are paid to do so. And still more ironically, its marital equivalent, even when achieved, is po-

---

[116] More specifically, he is keenly aware of the hostility between father and son, as in the "My Son! My Son!" emblem in *For the Sexes* (E261/K766), and in the Orc cycle throughout the longer poems. Whether he fully imagines the sexual attachment to the mother is less clear. The picture of Los, Enitharmon and Orc on pl. 21 of *Urizen* suggests that the conflict only arises in adolescence, as do the lines in *The Four Zoas* about Orc embracing his mother and plotting his father's death after "fourteen summers & winters" have passed (*FZ* 60:6ff., E334/K307). David Bindman notes that this theme resembles the classical "Venus and Cupid at Vulcan's forge" ("Blake's Theory and Practice of Imitation," in Essick & Pearce, p. 95), and it is suggestive that in "Why was Cupid a Boy" Blake says that the Greeks made love a boy because "a boy can't interpret the thing/Till he is become a man" (E470/K552)—in other words, he only learns at puberty what it is all about. Of infantile sexuality there is little hint in Blake. Heroic attempts have been made to detect it in the pictures in *Innocence*, for instance in the symbolism of girls plucking ripe bunches of grapes, but these appear to be adolescents (just as they do on pl. 2 of *MHH*) and the significance is present in the mind of the adult reader rather than in the thoughts or behavior of the children themselves.

tentially a tool of Urizen; he says grimly of Enitharmon, "By gratified desire by strong devouring appetite she fills/Los with ambitious fury that his race shall all devour" (*FZ* 80:25-26, E349/K323). The degradation of woman is extensively depicted in Vala and Rahab, with the added suggestion, of course, that the Female Will lures men on to their fate. And this theme is combined with female desire for forbiddenness and secrecy in "The Sick Rose."

The solution is constantly announced by Blakeans: abolish secrecy, improve sensual enjoyment, dispense with jealousy and indulge in Oothoon's "lovely copulation." But Blake's closest affinity with Freud lies in his deep appreciation of the difficulty of doing this. Freud concludes that sexual pleasure always requires some obstacle, and more darkly still that "Something in the nature of the sexual instinct itself is unfavourable to the achievement of absolute gratification."[117] It is the conclusion of Troilus; Blake would agree. And whereas Freud accepts this condition as inherent in the nature of things, arguing that there are compensations at least in the sublimation that produces civilized achievement, Blake has little sympathy with civilization and none at all with a sexual condition which he regards as fallen rather than inevitable. His solution therefore is to dismiss sex as we know it as an unhappy result of the division that occurred in the fall. Plato's myth of the androgyne in the *Symposium* undoubtedly interested Blake. But whereas Plato proposes an ascent, by means of sexual love, to participation in the divine, Blake portrays Luvah "bound in the bonds/Of spiritual Hate, from which springs Sexual Love as iron chains" (*J* 54:11-12, E201/K685). In the final line of the *Divine Comedy* Dante celebrates "the love that moves the sun and the other stars"; Blake more darkly places this Platonic theme in the context of the lamentations of Ololon, "When Luvahs bulls each morning drag the sulphur Sun out of the Deep" (*M* 21:20, E114/K503). Love does not move the sun and stars, it drags them.

As always, it is the otherness of love that Blake resists, for in Plato, as Iris Murdoch has said, "the centre of significance is suddenly ripped out of the self, and the dreamy ego is shocked into awareness of an entirely separate reality."[118] There is no room in Blake's myth for the immortal spirits whom Auden imagines weeping at the death of Freud—

> Sad is Eros, builder of cities,
> And weeping anarchic Aphrodite.[119]

[117] "The Most Prevalent Form . . . ," in Freud, *Sexuality and the Psychology of Love*, ed. Philip Rieff (New York, 1963), p. 68.
[118] *The Fire and the Sun: Why Plato Banished the Artists* (Oxford, 1977), p. 36.
[119] "In Memory of Sigmund Freud."

Eros builds no cities in Blake, and the anarchy of Aphrodite, just because it leads to weeping, has to be rejected. One can see why Blake feels this way, but there is no avoiding the realization that his ideal for human existence does away with human nature as the poets have always described it. Whatever the improvement of sensual enjoyment may mean, is it really continuous with sensual enjoyment as we know it? For all his hatred of asceticism, Blake often comes uncomfortably close to that primitive Christianity that longed to soar away from the vile body.

Yet even if we grant Blake his ideology, his endless depictions of the Female Will are weakened, ironically enough, by their failure to be sufficiently sexual. This is particularly apparent in the engraved pictures, where females who are supposed to be seductive seldom seem so; one has only to contrast with them the sketches for *Vala* (see figs. 19, 20) in which a noble but skeletal Albion draws the veil from a seductive Vala, and in which the bound Los looks on helplessly while Enitharmon and a massive Orc kiss with legs entwined. In the poems, a notable exception is Leutha, adapted from Sin in *Paradise Lost*, who is "heart-piercing and lovely" (*M* 11:32-33, E104/K492). In *Visions of the Daughters of Albion* Leutha's vale had been the place of sexual initiation. But Blake is not interested, finally, in developing the theme of sexual temptation, and Leutha is immediately allegorized into the female aspect of Satan that leads him astray by tempting him to try to be like Palamabron. He then drives her out, not realizing that he is even worse (Puritanical "selfish holiness demanding purity," 12:46, E105/K493) when his female element is gone. In other words, an aspect of the self has misdefined itself because it has become separate. The part of the self of which it *is* a part is negative or illusory, namely Satan. In fact Albion has collapsed into separate Zoas, of which Los is one; Los in turn has produced separate elements of which Rintrah, Palamabron, and Satan are members (his "sons"); and these in turn have split into Emanations. So when Leutha speaks, a part of a part of a part of the self is speaking!

Now, this in turn means that for healing to take place, the self has to understand the nature of its own rationalizations. Leutha is a rationalized way of representing a destructive form of psychic activity. Considered as a part of a part of a part of the self, she becomes almost impossibly complicated. But considered as an aspect of the internal disharmony within the imagination (Los), she is much more easily understood. "Sin" is not an external phenomenon, but a deluded rationalization that comes from within, a misdiagnosis of inner turmoil. Leutha's proposed remedy is consequently mistaken. She offers herself as a ransom for Satan, but throughout *Milton* ransoms are shown to be

19. *Vala*, manuscript sketch.

20. *Vala*, manuscript sketch.

ineffectual and to perpetuate disaster. What is needed is a new under-standing of Jesus (working, in this poem, through Milton) who can enter the self and rescue it—not by a ransom that appeases an angry Jehovah (whom Leutha invokes at 12:24, E105/K493) but by a recon-struction of the personality that learns to recognize the delusive nature of "sin." It is a false category, framed by a penitent but deluded ele-ment of the self. Now Milton can descend into Albion and Blake, and the process is set in motion by which he will be identified with Jesus the Divine Humanity. We understand the lesson, but Leutha does not; she goes on to copulate with Palamabron and give birth to Rahab and Tirzah. These are incestuous—perhaps even homosexual, if Leutha's attraction to Palamabron reflects something of Hayley's "feminine" feelings toward Blake—manifestations of the imagination. Leutha is delusion, not a woman.[120]

In the *Laocoön* aphorisms Blake inscribes the Hebrew letters for "Lilith" and calls her "Satan's Wife the Goddess Nature" (E270/K777). I believe that his representations of the Female Will would have been less tendentious if he had made more of the symbolism of Lilith. His Vala really belongs in a universe of sin, not of "error," despite all his claims that sin is only an invention of Satan. And she ought there-fore to have more in her of Lilith, embodying Milton's insight that "beauty, though injurious, hath strange power,"[121] and less of Rahab, the scarlet whore of the Apocalypse. Perhaps Blake's Vala could have resembled Munch's great lithograph "Sin," with her long tresses, piercing gaze, and allure that is all the more intense for not being overtly seductive. Instead, Blake's symbolism becomes excessively al-legorical. If Vala were a woman as Milton's Dalila is a woman, she would be a powerful figure even for readers who disliked the ideology involved. But to make her Nature as well, the whole world of mortal-ity and the senses—and not only that, but to make her responsible for institutional religion—is to render her abstract, precisely the kind of menacing fiction that Blake denounces in traditional morality. Lilith is seductive because she represents sexuality as sin; Vala is merely hor-rific because—in an inversion of the values of *Visions of the Daughters of Albion*—she represents the female as sadistic. As the fallen Enitharmon sings to Los,

> The joy of woman is the Death of her most best beloved
> Who dies for Love of her

[120] Notice that Sin emerges from Satan's head, as in *Paradise Lost*, but that death is the product of Leutha and Palamabron (*M* 13:38-40, E106/K494) rather than of Leutha and Satan. The change is no doubt intended to emphasize that death is "a Hell of our own making" (12:23, E105/K493) and that it is generated by the deluded imagination.

[121] *Samson Agonistes*, line 1003.

In torments of fierce jealousy & pangs of adoration.
                    (*FZ* 34:63–65, E317/K289)

Not only does she seduce man into desire, but she frustrates him with "a dead cold corse" (34:48). This is the bitter insight of Shakespeare's expense of spirit in a waste of shame, and a far from hopeful augury for sexuality even in its renegerated form.

BEULAH

In trying to explain the fallen contraries and their equivalent in the wars of Eternity, Blake developed the complementary categories of Beulah and Eden. Beulah absorbs the usual connotations of the Eden of Genesis and of the Christian heaven, and is therefore easily accessible to the imagination. Eden, since it represents a state of which we have no present knowledge, is inevitably mysterious, and is best understood by contrast with what it is not.

The immediate source of Blake's Beulah seems to have been a beautiful passage in Bunyan, inspired in turn by Isaiah and the Song of Songs. "Now I saw in my dream that by this time the pilgrims were got over the Enchanted Ground, and entering into the country of Beulah, whose air was very sweet and pleasant; the way lying directly through it, they solaced themselves there for a season. . . . In this land also the contract between the bride and the bridegroom was renewed: Yea here, *as the bridegroom rejoiceth over the bride, so did their God rejoice over them.*"[122] Blake's Beulah is very different, for two reasons: Bunyan has only positive feelings about the "married land" (Isa. 62:4) in which the pilgrim has a foretaste of heaven before death brings him there; and a person passes through Bunyan's Beulah only once. Blake's Beulah stands in a reciprocal relation with Eden: you move back and forth between them, and the fall from Eden is potentially renewable at all times.

Blake sometimes describes sexuality as the entrance to a Beulah that hides man from Satan.

There is a Grain of Sand in Lambeth that Satan cannot find
Nor can his Watch Fiends find it: tis translucent & has many Angles
But he who finds it will find Oothoons palace, for within
Opening into Beulah every angle is a lovely heaven. . . .
                    (*J* 37:15–18, E181/K668)

Lambeth, where Blake lived, is the site of the palace of the Archbishop of Canterbury, and it amused Blake to think of Oothoon's palace hid-

---

[122] *Pilgrim's Progress*, pp. 195–196.

den in the same place. But to say that Beulah is superior to Generation is not to deny that it is inferior to Eden, and in its dreamy stasis it all too closely resembles the Ulro into which it can collapse. From the point of view of Eden, accordingly, the sleep of Beulah is a lovely but dangerous temptation, like the enchantments of a fairy tale. Thus Jerusalem laments,

> O Vala! Humanity is far above
> Sexual organization; & the Visions of the Night of Beulah
> Where Sexes wander in dreams of bliss among the Emanations
> Where the Masculine & Feminine are nurs'd into Youth & Maiden
> By the tears & smiles of Beulahs Daughters till the time of Sleep is
>   past.
>
> *(J* 79:73-77, E233/K721)

In this perspective Beulah is a fall into mortality rather than a respite from intellectual war, and sex is stigmatized as selfish.

> One of the Eternals spoke All was silent at the feast
> Man is a Worm wearied with joy he seeks the caves of sleep
> Among the Flowers of Beulah in his Selfish cold repose
> Forsaking Brotherhood & Universal love in selfish clay. . . .
>
> *(FZ* 133:10-13, E386/K374)

In the fullest context of Blake's myth, Beulah can only function positively if it does resemble Bunyan's Beulah, a pause in Innocence on the way to Eden. As the Shadow of Enitharmon remembers the original Innocence, "many daughters flourished round the holy Tent of Man" in the pastures of Beulah, but the sexual urgency of Luvah caused the collapse of that pastoral state.

> But Luvah close conferrd with Urizen in darksom night
> To bind the father & enslave the brethren Nought he knew
> Of sweet Eternity the blood flowd round the holy tent & rivn
> From its hinges uttering its final groan all Beulah fell. . . .
>
> *(FZ* 83:20-26, E351/K326)

The error was in mistaking Beulah for Eden; Urizen was vulnerable to Luvah because "he forgot Eternity" (83:21). Beulah contains the seed (literally) of its own destruction; what must be achieved is the Edenic "sweet Eternity" that Luvah knew not.

The ambiguities of Beulah are essential to its conception, and they account for its fascinating richness in the myth. Its positive aspects are obvious. As in Innocence, it is a maternal and protective place, "As the beloved infant in his mothers bosom round incircled/With arms of love & pity & sweet compassion" (*M* 30:11-12, E128/K518). It is a place of repose for "the sleepers who rested from their harvest work" (*FZ* 131:20, E385/K372). It guards the sleeping Albion in his tormented slumber, and when he awakens "two winged immortal shapes" hover over him, "a Vision of All Beulah," in the Gothic-arch pattern that Blake often used in his pictures.[123] The Daughters of Beulah are Blake's muses, inspirers of the art of Los, and protectors of man in the spaces between the active moments forged by the Sons of Los: "Between every two Moments stands a Daughter of Beulah/To feed the Sleepers on their Couches with maternal care" (*M* 28:48-49, E125/K516).

Yet by the very nature of the maternal and of sleep in Blake's symbolism, these positive values must be balanced by negative ones. Maternity implies "storgous" love, which is sexual and jealous as well as protective.[124] Beulah may be "a place where Contrarieties are equally True" (*M* 30:1, E128/K518), but in the obscure account of a fourfold Beulah Blake tries to explain how it can degenerate until "the Contraries of Beulah War beneath Negations Banner" (*M* 34:23, E133/K524). In this fallen form it closes itself to imagination. In a telling revision in *The Four Zoas* Blake removed the suggestion that Enitharmon's "inward parts" could lead to Eternity and demoted them to Beulah:

> Three gates within Glorious & bright open into Beulah
> From Enitharmons inward parts but the bright female terror
> Refusd to open the bright gates she closd and barrd them fast
> Lest Los should enter into Beulah thro her beautiful gates
> (*FZ* 20:4-7, E308/K279)

Los must continually bend his force against the east, the region of the sexual Luvah, "Lest those Three Heavens of Beulah should the Creation destroy" (*M* 26:20, E122/K512). These are the three sexual heavens of mutual (or narcissistic) reflection that Tirzah made when she tied "the knot of milky seed" (*M* 19:60-20:2, E112-113/K501). This could scarcely be called the fault of Beulah, which meets its fall with bitter lamentation; but it is inevitable, given its sexual and passive characteristics.

Once it has taken place, the Daughters of Beulah are implicated in the fall. To forestall eternal death they create a "space," but with far

---

[123] *FZ* VIII, E357/K341. Mellor points out the relevance of the painting *Christ in the Sepulchre* (*Blake's Human Form Divine*, p. 209; also reproduced in Blunt, *The Art of William Blake*, pl. 37b).

[124] See the account of the "Five Females & the nameless Shadowy Mother" luring the sleepers of Beulah down to the River Storge (*M* 34:27-30, E133/K524). The problem of "storge" is further discussed below, pp. 268 ff., in connection with paternity.

from happy results, since they "namd the Space Ulro & brooded over it in care & love" (*FZ* 5:37, E299/K267). Far from being the muses of inspiration, they are now the sexual temptation that Los must overcome:

> For All Things Exist in the Human Imagination
> And thence in Beulah they are stolen by secret amorous theft,
> Till they have had Punishment enough to make them commit Crimes.
> Hence rose the Tabernacle in the Wilderness & all its Offerings,
> From Male & Female Loves in Beulah & their Jealousies
> But no one can consummate Female bliss in Los's World without
> Becoming a Generated Mortal, a Vegetating Death.
>
> (*J* 69:25-31, E221/K707-708)

In the "sweet moony night" of this sexual realm, Jerusalem "assimilated" with Vala in the sorrowful imagery of the Lily of Havilah.[125]

The symbolism of Beulah is consistently that of the Psalms and of the Christian Paradise, as is apparent in the series of pictures for *Paradise Lost* that depict a lushly vegetated Garden of Eden.[126] According to Crabb Robinson, Milton appeared to Blake in a vision and apologized for teaching in *Paradise Lost* "that Sexual intercourse arose out of the Fall." Frye—referring to Robinson's alternative version "the pleasures of sex"—objects that "Milton, of course, said nothing of the kind, as Blake, who made at least four illustrations of Satan watching the love-play of the unfallen Adam and Eve, knew very well."[127] But Blake's point was evidently that the Fall and the fact of sexual division are synonymous, so that Milton's affectionate picture of prelapsarian sexuality makes no sense. Blake's illustrations are in fact highly equivocal, for example *Satan Watching Adam and Eve* (see fig. 21). Possibly Adam and Eve might have "commingled" before the Fall, if indeed Blake would grant them separate existence in that state. What we see in the picture, at any rate, is the post-lapsarian sexuality which is a result of Man's division rather than of the serpent's temptation. Satan is a product or consequence of the Fall rather than its motivator. If he is visible, then by definition the Fall has already oc-

---

[125] *J* 19:41-43, E163/K642. See the ambiguous embrace on pl. 28 of *Jerusalem*, altered from the copulatory pose of the proof version (p. 399 of *The Illuminated Blake*); and see also Paley's discussion of the picture of Titania and Oberon seated upon lilies, repeated on the fifth plate of the *Song of Los* (*William Blake*, p. 34 and pls. 20, 21).

[126] See Bindman, *Blake as an Artist*, pp. 138, 190-191.

[127] Crabb Robinson in *Blake Records*, pp. 544, 317. Frye, "Notes for a Commentary on *Milton*," in *The Divine Vision: Studies in the Poetry and Art of William Blake*, ed. Vivian de Sola Pinto (London, 1957), pp. 101-102*n*.

21. *Satan Watching Adam and Eve*, illustration for Milton's
Paradise Lost.

curred. Adam and Eve are shown kissing in a Beulah bower, gazing
raptly into each other's eyes; the effect, with their stretched bodies and
hands behind each other's heads, is more suggestive of Donne's
Ecstasie than of warm gratification. A crescent moon hangs above Eve,
and Satan is entwined, as Paley comments, in an autoerotic embrace
with his serpent.[128]

[128] *William Blake*, p. 63.

The sexual jealousy of Satan is thus implicit in the Fall. And since Satan is but a "state" of man, this is as much as to say that the sexuality of Adam and Eve is already diseased, already contains elements of the sinful penitence of Leutha. The Fall is not a historical event but an imaginative condition inherent in Beulah, which is committed to a sexuality in which Satan is present even when he has not yet entered the scene as an actor but floats overhead as a corrupting spectator. He may even be a kind of parodic creator: the gesture of his left hand is reminiscent of the right hand with which God imparts life to Adam in Michelangelo's great fresco, and Eve may be gazing at that hand rather than into Adam's eyes as one would at first assume. In *Paradise Lost* Satan watches the healthy sexuality of Adam and Eve "with jealous leer malign" (IV.503); in Blake's picture he looks more melancholy than jealous, and the frustration seems to attach equally to Adam and Eve.

As *Milton* shows, Blake's response to Milton on this theme is exceptionally complicated. On the one hand, he rebukes Milton for authoritarian treatment of the women in his life and makes him descend to earth for a long-delayed reunion with his emanation Ololon. But on the other hand, the account of prelapsarian sex in *Paradise Lost* is much happier and more satisfying than anything Blake will permit. In Blake's Eden, as we shall see presently, sex exists only in a very peculiar way. Milton's Paradise is Blake's Beulah, not Blake's Eden, and the illustrations show Adam and Eve with marmoreal bodies and inert expressions, as if tranced and sleepwalking. The Fall has already occurred.

Beulah is feminine. The Fall is female. In Ricoeur's words, "The myth of evil choice is the myth of temptation, of intoxication, of imperceptible slipping into evil. The woman, figure of fragility, is the polar counterpart of the man, figure of evil decision."[129] "Frailty, thy name is woman!" exclaims Hamlet; she is both the victim of temptation and its agent. We remember Eve taking the apple from the serpent's mouth. In another picture (see fig. 22) Eve strikes a birth-of-Venus pose within the coils of an enormous serpent beneath the cavelike form of the arching tree, gazing raptly forward into the fallen state which her very existence both initiates and symbolizes. Adam lies in helpless slumber, a crescent moon rides above, and the water of materiality pours over a falls in the background.[130]

Blake may sometimes represent his Eden as a higher Innocence, but these reflections on the garden in Milton and Genesis should help us to

[129] *Conflict of Interpretations*, p. 295.
[130] Raine notes a passage in Porphyry in which Psyche enters material existence "near the fall of a river" (*Blake and Tradition*, I, 82).

22. *Eve, Adam, and the Serpent.*

see that Innocence and Experience are frustrating contraries and that a successful escape from their strife must go beyond both. D. G. James has perceptively said that Innocence is religious and Experience moral.[131] Behind the Urizenic complacencies of some of the speakers of the Experience lyrics we hear the titanic indignation of a poet who knows what is wrong but is not sure what is right, just as Enion bitterly laments the cruelty of the fallen world:

> What is the price of Experience do men buy it for a song
> Or wisdom for a dance in the street? No it is bought with the price
> Of all that a man hath his house his wife his children
> Wisdom is sold in the desolate market where none come to buy
> And in the witherd fields where the farmer plows for bread in vain.
> (FZ 35:11-15, E318/K290)

The answer ultimately is not to "marry" the contraries in any easy sense; that would be merely to establish the mutual exploitation of the clod and pebble.[132] It is, rather, to forge a larger vision that can go

---

[131] *The Romantic Comedy*, pp. 4-5.

[132] "The Clod and the Pebble," E19/K211. Raine cites a striking discussion in Swedenborg of love that feels "delight in another" but not in itself (*Blake and Tradition*, I, 27). But whereas Swedenborg presents a simple alternative between good and bad forms of love, Blake projects a disturbing mirror relation between masochism and sadism. Existentialist discussions of the problem are extremely interesting here; as Mary

beyond Experience. Blake scholars commonly refer to this vision as "organized Innocence," but the phrase, though convenient, leaves much to be explained. In what sense was the faith of the original Innocence unorganized? In what sense can an organized Innocence embrace, without resisting or denouncing, the facts of Experience? The answer to the first question, I believe, is that prelapsarian Innocence *was* organized; if it is now found wanting, that is because the concept of Innocence itself is inadequate to an Edenic vision. The answer to the second question is that an Edenic vision can make no compromise with the facts of Experience, which it neutralizes instead by denying that they are facts.

The implied sequence of Innocence-Experience-higher Innocence (or Beulah-Generation-Eden) is given visible form in the *Job* designs: the pastoral harmony of the opening plates, then the sexual "sins" of the sons as condemned by Urizenic morality, and only after great suffering the restitution of a new and durable fourfold Eden. Luvah can never be quelled or eliminated, but the fallen Luvah is a grotesquely Lawrentian figure, "Reasoning from the loins in the unreal forms of Ulros night" (*FZ* 28:2, E311/K283). Jesus must enter Luvah and Vala to rescue them from the "gnawing Grave" (*J* 62:21, E211/K696), and both Luvah and Vala must "resume the image of the human/ Cooperating in the bliss of Man obeying his Will" (*FZ* 126:15-16, E380/K366).

Blake's state of Innocence thus implicitly contains the fall into Experience, not because the *Songs of Innocence* are filled with overt ironies but because innocence cannot survive for long in a world that is not innocent. Specifically, it cannot survive puberty, a fact frequently hinted at in the illustrations. The very etymology of *innocence* is significant: it derives from the Latin *in-nocere* and implies a negative concept, the innocent seen as that which is not harmful.[133] In this concep-

---

Warnock interprets Sartre, "there are only three possible patterns of behavior. A lover may either become a sadist, and seek to appropriate the other completely and by violence. Or he may become a masochist, and consent to be nothing but a thing: simply an object for the consciousness of the other. Or he may adopt the attitude of indifference, which amounts to evading the conflict altogether" (*Existentialism* [Oxford, 1970], p. 118). The first two possibilities are those respectively of the pebble and clod; the third is unacceptable to Blake, and he postulates a fourth possibility (Edenic brotherhood) that can bypass all three. In Blake's lyric the apparent polarity is ironically undermined by the fact that *both* pebble and clod are trodden by the cattle's feet in the brook. They are equally imprisoned in the fallen world of Experience, and that is why their relationship embodies mutual torment.

[133] The idea is still clearer in German, *Unschuld* or "un-guilt" being the word for innocence; the idea is not so much that we are always guilty except in special cases (though Kafka would hold that) as that the "unguilty" is free of stain, as in the systems

tion a child is innocent in so far as he has not yet had the opportunity to become guilty or polluted. But any theology that regards man as polluted must impute pollution to the child even at birth. "It is not the infant's will that is harmless," Augustine says darkly, "but the weakness of infant limbs. I myself have seen and have had experience with a jealous little one; it was not yet able to speak, but it was pale and bitter in face as it looked at another child nursing at the same breast."[134]

Blake's position is more complex. In the *Songs of Innocence*—despite their echoes of Isaac Watts and other Christian writers—he goes back to Platonic rather than Christian tradition in order to emphasize the positive connotations of Innocence.[135] In his later myth he attacks the Augustinian position on its own grounds. According to Augustine the baby is guilty but does not yet know it; loss of innocence will come with the knowledge of good and evil, as in Augustine's famous boyhood raid on the pear orchard, an event that recapitulates the Genesis story of the Fall. Blake, confronting the doctrine head-on, maintains that the tree of knowledge is itself the evil, the "poison tree" that is projected like an obsessive nightmare by the human mind.

> The Gods of the earth and sea,
> Sought thro' Nature to find this Tree
> But their search was all in vain:
> There grows one in the Human Brain.[136]

Puberty brings sexuality, and sexuality, in the present state of consciousness, brings guilt.

What Blake wants to do is not to freeze life at the infantile stage but to break *through* Experience to a spiritual realm in which guilt—the knowledge of the taint of evil—does not exist because it has been exposed as mere illusion. This is not a higher Innocence that has absorbed the lessons of Experience, but a prelapsarian (or nonlapsarian) Innocence that bypasses Experience altogether. To return to Eden is to advance beyond Beulah the married land, to integrate male and female

---

of pollution and taboo common to most forms of primitive religion. A German idiom says "Ich wasche meine Hände in Unschuld" (see Psalm 73:13).

[134] *Confessions*, I.vii, p. 49.

[135] For a survey of the Platonic tradition see L. C. Martin, "Henry Vaughan and the Theme of Infancy," in *Seventeenth Century Studies Presented to Sir Herbert Grierson* (Oxford, 1938), pp. 243-255. The disparity between what children and adults understand, as in the clear ironies of the first "Chimney Sweeper" (E10/K117-118), is best understood as a reflection of what Wagenknecht calls "pastoral ignorance": innocence permits an imaginative release from experience even though it cannot be described except in language contaminated by experience (*Blake's Night*, pp. 76-77).

[136] "The Human Abstract," E27/K217.

principles in a single self, no longer exploitative as in "The Clod and the Pebble," no longer passive and externalized as in Beulah. Unlike Rousseau or Diderot, Blake countenances no primitivist alternative to guilty pleasure, which he sees as the fault not of civilization but of man. To free himself from it man must aspire not to innocent sex—nothing after puberty can be innocent in that sense—but to a higher state that transcends sex. Blake thus solves the problem by dismissing it. Reintegrated or regenerated man is post-sexual man.

The answer to Enion's lament, as Jerome McGann has seen, is that "all that a man hath" must be given to Jesus, so that "imaginative growth entails, in Blake's characteristically Pauline way of expressing it, a self-annihilation, a voluntary death to the old man and a waking to the new."[137] The Daughters of Beulah therefore pray constantly to the Divine Vision: "We perish & shall not be found unless thou grant a place/In which we may be hidden under the Shadow of wings" (FZ 56:7-8, E331/K304). In a design on the fourth plate of *Jerusalem* a female figure points to Greek words in the waning moon, *Monos o Iesous*, which have been traced to the account in John's gospel of the woman taken in adultery, in which the shamed Pharisees go away "and *Jesus was left alone*, and the woman standing in the midst."[138] This may imply, on the one hand, that Jesus will rescue the Emanations and restore them to wholeness. "I am not a God afar off," he says in the accompanying text, and promises to forgive all evil (*J* 4:18, E145/K622). On the other hand the emphasis may be placed differently, on Jesus rather than on the woman. That is, *Jesus* was left alone, and in him alone does the Female Will cease to be hostile, because in him it ceases to be female.

Without Jesus, at any rate, Beulah is both equivocal and dangerous, the world of Virgilian pastoral which Blake illustrated in some deceptively lovely woodcuts.[139] Jerusalem's nostalgic recollections of her

[137] "The Aim of Blake's Prophecies," in Curran and Wittreich, p. 18.

[138] John 8:9. Mellor shows that Blake's Greek quotation must refer to this passage rather than to one in Luke as has usually been supposed (*Blake's Human Form Divine*, pp. 292-293).

[139] These pictures, which Blake made to illustrate Thornton's edition of Virgil's *Pastorals* (1821), provide an interesting test for the interpretation of his symbolism. They are certainly very beautiful, and Blake's disciple Samuel Palmer called them "visions of little dells, and nooks, and corners of Paradise," adding that "they are like all that wonderful artist's works the drawing aside of the fleshly curtain" (*Blake Records*, p. 271). Another disciple, Edward Calvert, said that "there is a spirit in them, humble enough and of force enough to move simple souls to tears" (quoted by Raymond Lister, *Infernal Methods: A Study of William Blake's Art Techniques* [London, 1975], p. 32). Yet as a number of Blake scholars have argued, this optimistic interpretation is almost certainly wrong (see Hagstrum, *William Blake*, pp. 52-53, and Bindman, *Blake as an Artist*, pp. 204-205). Quite apart from the familiar images of Blakean negative pastoral (the blasted

amorous time with the Lamb of God are badly skewed by the element of sexual secrecy that she invokes: "There we walked as in our secret chamber among our little ones/They looked upon our loves with joy: they beheld our secret joys" (*J* 79:42-43, E233/K720). Several plates later, Los explicitly counters this vision with the plea, "When Souls mingle & join thro all the Fibres of Brotherhood/Can there be any secret joy on Earth greater than this?" (*J* 88:14-15, E244/K733). He is answered by Enitharmon's taunting reply that "This is Womans World" and her promise to "Create secret places" (88:16-17).

Just as the maternal imagery of Beulah, even when positive, is expressive of the perils of Generation,[140] so also the spousal imagery reflects Christ's descent into Beulah from the true "Brotherhood" of Eden. Jerusalem as mother is the Church, which is to say the total family of humanity: "I have seen when at a distance Multitudes of Men in Harmony appear like a single Infant sometimes in the Arms of a Female this represented the Church" (*VLJ*, E546/K607). And this maternal Jerusalem is the bride of Christ:

> She walks upon our meadows green:
> The Lamb of God walks by her side:
> And every English Child is seen,
> Children of Jesus & his Bride.
> (*J* 27:17-20, E170/K650)

The spousal imagery here has nothing to do with marriage between Zoas and Emanations. Just as in Bunyan, the "married land" Beulah symbolizes a union not between male and female but between mankind and the Savior.[141]

The wedding feast of the Lamb and his bride is a harbinger of "the

---

oak, the crescent moon) nearly all the texts from Virgil that Blake chooses to illustrate are expressive of grief and ill fate (see the pictures and texts in Klonsky, *William Blake*, pp. 126-127). One picture shows a characteristically Blakean traveler passing a milestone that says London is 62 miles behind him; this would be about the right distance by road for arrival at Felpham, the scene of Blake's pastoral interlude that failed.

[140] The Daughters of Albion tell Los that woman has power over man from cradle to grave, "He who is an Infant, and whose Cradle is a Manger"—an obvious allusion to Christ's incarnation—and they say that the Daughters of Beulah "feed the Human Vegetable" (*J* 56:3-10, E203/K688). Throughout the poem Jerusalem is heard weeping; she is drawn down into the void "in anguish of maternal love" (*J* 5:47, E147/K624), and in the same long speech in which she remembers her secret joys with the Lamb of God, she says "I walk weeping in pangs of a Mothers torment for her Children" (*J* 80:2, E234/K721).

[141] "Then the Heavenly Host gave a great shout, saying, '*Blessed are they that are called to the marriage supper of the Lamb*'" (*Pilgrim's Progress*, p. 202, quoting Rev. 19:9). Christian has left his wife behind; in Part II she undertakes the journey for herself.

glorious spiritual Vegetation" (*M* 25:60–61, E121/K511), an ambiguous condition that partakes both of spirit and of the vegetative state of materiality. In another place the Eternal Man tells Urizen that after a wintry sleep Ahania will return in a springtime rebirth:

> Thus shall the male & female live the life of Eternity
> Because the Lamb of God Creates himself a bride & wife
> That we his Children evermore may live in Jerusalem
> Which now descendeth out of heaven a City yet a Woman
> Mother of myriads redeemd & born in her spiritual palaces
> By a New Spiritual birth Regenerated from Death.
> (*FZ* 122:15–20, E376/K362–363)

This is very much a vision of Beulah: Christ *creates* a woman— whereas in Blake's Eden there is no creation, only eternal life—and the Emanation Ahania is reborn through union with Jerusalem, the bride of Christ and maternal Church. As Stevenson notes, Ahania's rebirth after winter echoes the Persephone myth.[142] This is the "natural" cycle which, even if spiritualized, remains within the realm of Generation.

In the fullest treatment of the marriage of Christ and Jerusalem, Los cries, "I see the River of Life & Tree of Life/I see the New Jerusalem descending out of Heaven" (*J* 86:18–19, E242/K731, probably alluding to Jerusalem descending as a bride in Rev. 21:2). The River of Life is the subject of one of Blake's most remarkable biblical pictures (see fig. 23), illustrating the text from Revelation, "And he showed me a pure river of water of life, clear as crystal, proceeding out of the throne of God and of the Lamb. In the midst of the street of it, and on either side of the river, was there the tree of life, which bare twelve manner of fruits, and yielded her fruit every month: and the leaves of the tree were for the healing of the nations."[143] "The Throne of God and of the Lamb" is mentioned in *Jerusalem* when the Sons of Albion set up their mother Vala in opposition to it (*J* 78:18–19, E231/K719), and again in *A Vision of the Last Judgment* when the four living creatures remove the old heaven and earth to make way for it (E550/K612). A little later Blake describes a scene very like that of his picture: "The Temple stands on the Mount of God from it flows on each side the River of Life on whose banks Grows the tree of Life among whose branches temples & Pinnacles tents & pavilions Gardens & Groves display Paradise with its Inhabitants walking up & down in Conversations concerning Mental Delights" (E552/K613). But a closer inspec-

---

[142] *The Poems of Blake*, p. 437n.
[143] Rev. 22:1–2. There is a color reproduction in Klonsky, *William Blake*, p. 106.

23. *The River of Life.*

tion of the picture shows that most of these features are present only equivocally. What we are looking at is a scene in Beulah *on the way to* the throne of God and of the Lamb in the distant setting sun, crowned by singing angels. It is usual to interpret the stooping woman as Jerusalem cutting the thread of mortal existence, but I see no evidence for this; she is moving downstream on the surface of the water, away from the heavenly throne, and like other women with shears in Blake's works she is surely a grim Fate.

Meanwhile Christ with the two children (man become as a child again, as in the "vision of light" poem) swims upstream against the current, half in the water and half out to symbolize his incarnation in materiality. "War & Hunting: the Two Fountains of the River of Life/Are become Fountains of bitter Death & of corroding Hell."[144] To resist this hideous inversion of values it is necessary to reverse the "natural" flow of the river, and to make it a detour through Beulah that will lead back to its source:

[144] *M* 35:2-3, E134/K525; see also *J* 38:31-32, E183/K672.

232

And first from the Wild Thyme, stands a Fountain in a rock
Of crystal flowing into two Streams, one flows thro Golgonooza
And thro Beulah to Eden beneath Los's western Wall
The other flows thro the Aerial Void & all the Churches
Meeting again in Golgonooza beyond Satans Seat.

(M 35:49-53, E135/K526)

Blake smells the wild thyme (and hears the lark's song) in an epiphanic
moment at Felpham; Golgonooza is the city of prophetic art, and its
representative in the watercolor is the flying figure of John of Patmos
with the sun behind him.[145] I assume that the sun is setting since travel
from west to east is regularly a negative symbol in Blake. To travel
from east to west, toward death's door, is to return to the source of
life, and the travelers glide upstream, with Christ's help, through a
landscape of Beulah innocence. They pass classical doorways (these
are not the true temple of the divine throne, which in Blake's iconography would be Gothic); the musicians try to lure them with the
seductions of Beulah, but they swim on toward the beckoning
prophet. On the left bank a young woman plucks the sexual fruit from
the tree; on the right, an aged man reads from a book, very possibly
one of Urizenic law. The travelers will pause on neither bank but will
pass *through* Beulah, guided by Jesus and inspired by prophetic art, in
order to attain their goal.

EDEN

Beyond all the tensions in Blake's myth lies the dream of Eden, a state
in which warfare will become spiritually productive and in which
infinite desire will achieve infinite gratification. Much in Blake's Eden
remains inpenetrable, and it is tempting to conclude that in his longing
for a suprahuman harmony he indulged in a fantasy of the inconceivable. As one of his most sensitive critics says of the closing lines of
Jerusalem, "He asks for too much, and perhaps at last we will be condemned to judge him as he judged Milton, a true poet when he wrote
of visual torment, but a fettered bard of the absolute when he asked us
to go beyond the abyss of the eye."[146] Even if Blake's Eden remains
ineffable, however, the fact that he imagined it at all is one of his most
remarkable achievements. By relegating the conventional attributes of
paradise to an inferior Beulah, he made a brilliant if finally unsuccessful attempt to image a more than human state that would not have to

---

[145] The identification is supported by the very similar figure of St. John in the
ninety-sixth picture in the Dante series.

[146] Bloom, *The Ringers in the Tower*, p. 45.

give up what matters most to human beings. Blake's real mistake, if I may bluntly call it that, was to give in to the dualist impulse and to dismiss sexuality to Beulah.

It is essential to stress that Blake's Eden differs decisively from the traditional heaven by reason of its continuous activity. Cromwell's soldiers went off to battle in expectation of fighting the good fight as enjoined by their religion:

> The Lord begins to honour us,
> The Saints are marching on;
> The Sword is sharp, the arrows swift
> To destroy Babylon.[147]

But at the end they looked not for eternal war but for the peace that passes all understanding, as in the title of Richard Baxter's immensely popular tract *The Saints' Everlasting Rest*. Blake, however, turns their martial rhetoric into "Mental Fight"—

> Bring me my Bow of burning gold:
> Bring me my Arrows of desire:
> Bring me my Spear: O clouds unfold!
> Bring me my Chariot of fire![148]

As Blake's conception of Eden develops it becomes less and less identified with reforming England's green and pleasant land, but the metaphor of "the great Wars of Eternity" (*M* 30:19, E128/K519) always remains.

> Our wars are wars of life, & wounds of love,
> With intellectual spears, & long winged arrows of thought:
> Mutual in one anothers love and wrath all renewing
> We live as One Man . . .
>> (*J* 34:14–17, E178/K664)

We have seen that in contrast with their fallen counterparts, war and hunting in Eden are "the Two Fountains of the River of Life" (*M* 35:2,

---

[147] A song of the New Model Army, quoted by A. L. Morton, *The Everlasting Gospel* (London, 1958), p. 59.

[148] *M* 1, E95/K481. Blake's "chariot of fire" is probably drawn from the "chariot of fire and horses of fire" that transported Elijah into heaven (2 Kings 2:11), and is echoed in his challenge to the viewer of his pictures to enter "the Fiery Chariot of his Contemplative Thought" (*VLJ*, E550/K611). In view of Milton's involvement with corporeal warfare, it is highly likely that in these stanzas Blake intends a criticism of Milton's political theology. See Nancy M. Goslee, "In Englands green & pleasant Land: The Building of Vision in Blake's Stanzas from *Milton*," *Studies in Romanticism*, 13 (1974), 105–125.

E134/K525), but it is essential to Blake's conception that the energies in both are the same.

It is not often remarked how different this is from most conceptions of heaven or eternity. Any thinker with Platonic inclinations was bound to emphasize the vitality of God's universe; as Thomas Vaughan says, "The Peripatetics look on God as they do on carpenters, who build with stone and timber, without any infusion of life. But the world—which is God's building—is full of spirit, quick and living."[149] But the dominant quality of eternity or heaven remains peace, as in the famous poem of Thomas Vaughan's brother Henry:

> I saw Eternity the other night,
> Like a great ring of pure and endless light,
> All calm as it was bright. . . .

Boehme, to be sure, speaks as Blake does of God disporting himself in love-play.[150] But in Boehme "all things stand in a wrestling and a fighting" in the lower or fallen world, while in Eden, as the alchemist Sendivogius expresses it, the contraries of male and female are united in "an incorruptible one, in which are exhibited the four elements [cf. Blake's Zoas] in a highly purified and digested condition, and with their mutual strife hushed in unending peace and good will."[151]

Blake, like theologians in the Augustinian tradition, begins from the premise that man is alienated and torn by internal conflict. But unlike the theologians he is determined to retain a version of conflict even in his Eden, the clash of contraries without which there is no life. "In that ultimate peace," Augustine says very differently, ". . . our nature will be healed by immortality and incorruption and will have no perverted elements, and nothing at all, in ourselves or any other, will be in conflict with any one of us." In that state we will be "perfectly at rest, and in stillness see perfectly that he is God."[152] Most thinkers saw man's infinite desire as a proof of his need for eternal rest; Blake insists that man would not have infinite desire if he were not capable of infinite enjoyment. "Men are admitted into Heaven not because they have

[149] *Anthroposophia Theomagica*, in *Works of Thomas Vaughan*, ed. A. E. Waite (London, 1919), p. 8. Vaughan goes on to describe relations between macrocosm and microcosm—water as blood, air as the breath of "this vast creature"—in terms that resemble Blake's various versions of the creation myth.

[150] The resemblance to Blake's "sports of Wisdom" (see above, p. 188) is noted by John Adlard, "A 'Triumphing Joyfulness': Blake, Boehme and the Tradition," *Blake Studies*, 1 (1969), 109-122.

[151] Boehme, *Aurora*; Sendivogius, *Hermetic Museum*; both quoted by Percival, *William Blake's Circle of Destiny*, pp. 150, 202.

[152] *City of God*, XIX.xxvii, p. 893, and XXII.xxx, p. 1091.

curbed & governd their Passions or have No Passions but because they
have Cultivated their Understandings. The Treasures of Heaven are
not Negations of Passion but Realities of Intellect from which All the
Passions emanate Uncurbed in their Eternal Glory" (*VLJ*, E553-554/
K615).

The crux is simply this: in what sense can desire exist unless it remains unslaked? "Not to have is the beginning of desire," Stevens
says.[153] And if it remains unslaked, must it not be perpetually frustrating? Is the myth of Tantalus an image of heaven? Hobbes thought not,
but in his sardonic way he thought that the Christian alternative was
equally unimaginable. "For there is no such thing as perpetual tran-
quillity of mind, while we live here; because life itself is but motion,
and can never be without desire, nor without fear, no more than without sense. What kind of felicity God hath ordained to them that de-
voutly honour Him, a man shall no sooner know, than enjoy; being
joys, that now are as incomprehensible, as the word of the Schoolmen
beatifical vision is unintelligible."[154] Blake agrees that the orthodox
heaven is incomprehensible: a state without energy and desire is not
superhuman but subhuman, and he wants no part of it. But he finds
himself in an awkward dilemma, for his entire philosophy of sexuality
forbids him to admit it into Eden, and yet it is precisely in it that we
ordinarily locate energy and desire. If the polarity that we know most
intimately is banished from Eden, what will the other polarities be
like?

The passage that speaks of "wars of life, & wounds of love" goes on
to present an unexpectedly pastoral vision of Eden:

> . . . we behold as one,
> As One Man all the Universal Family; and that One Man
> We call Jesus the Christ: and he in us, and we in him,
> Live in perfect harmony in Eden the land of life,
> Giving, receiving, and forgiving each others trespasses.
> He is the Good shepherd, he is the Lord and master:
> He is the Shepherd of Albion, he is all in all,
> In Eden: in the garden of God: and in heavenly Jerusalem.
> (*J* 34:18-25, E178/K664-665)

In Frye's system Eden ought to be a city, not a garden. What has become of the warring contraries here? Are we to imagine a garden full
of combative sheep? And how is it that Jesus now acts as "Lord and
master" over all?

The answer, I believe, is that Beulah imagery is always equivocal in

[153] *Notes Toward a Supreme Fiction, Collected Poems* (New York, 1961), p. 382.
[154] *Leviathan*, ed. Michael Oakeshott (Oxford, 1946), I.vi, p. 39.

Blake's poems, even when one speaker or another imputes it to Eden. The speaker here is the fallen Los attempting to express the mutual contentment of the Universal Family; to do so he chooses traditional images of innocence, of gardens and protective shepherds. Once again we are compelled to reflect upon the nature of symbols, which suggest the truth but are not themselves the truth. And if we look closely we will see that when the prelapsarian state is described in the symbols of pastoral love, the vision is usually nostalgic.

> Thou wast lovely as the summer cloud upon my hills
> When Jerusalem was thy hearts desire in times of youth & love.
> (J 24:36-37, E168/K647)

The speaker is a bewildered and desperate Albion, who exclaims a few lines later,

> Yet why these smitings of Luvah, the gentlest mildest Zoa?
> If God was Merciful this could not be: O Lamb of God
> Thou art a delusion and Jerusalem is my Sin!
> (24:52-54)

The smitings of Luvah are destructive (was he ever really the mildest Zoa?) and the wished-for pastoral love of Beulah, if not actually a delusion, is a hopeless dream.

In similar terms the Spectre of Urthona laments the loss of a "garden of delight" (FZ 84:6, E352/K327), but his longings, although we may pity them, are no guide to truth. And we have seen that Jerusalem's memory of "secret joys" (J 79:43) is permeated with the symbolism of Beulah.

The truth of the matter is expressed by Ololon:

> Altho' our Human Power can sustain the severe contentions
> Of Friendship, our Sexual cannot: but flies into the Ulro.
> Hence arose all our terrors in Eternity! & now remembrance
> Returns upon us! are we Contraries O Milton, Thou & I
> O Immortal! how were we led to War the Wars of Death?
> (M 41:32-36, E142/K533-534)

Somehow the wars of Eternity differ both from the strife of hateful contraries in Generation and the passive marriage of contraries in Beulah. "For the Soldier who fights for Truth, calls his enemy his brother:/They fight & contend for life, & not for eternal death" (J 38:41-42, E183/K672). It is important to recognize that contraries function differently at each level of Blake's mythic structure. As Edward Rose comments, they are negations in Ulro, dialectical in the "progression" of Generation, synthesized in Beulah, and merged into unity in Eden.[155] But to state it in this way is simply to reiterate that the contraries in Eden no longer function like contraries as we know them.

The essential paradox is apparent: Beulah, the place of sexuality, is passive and moony, yet as Blake's poems abundantly testify, human sex is activity itself. Energy is sexual—Orc, Vala—and an Eden without sex would be an Eden which, like the traditional heaven, would lack energy in the Blakean sense of interacting contraries. That is why Boehme placed the Sophia, and the Kabbalists placed the Shekhinah, in their heaven. Blake has demoted the green-pastures aspects of paradise to Beulah, in order to preserve the vitality of his Eden; but he has damaged the power of his insight by demoting sexuality too. In Blake's Eden they make war, not love.

Needless to say these were difficulties of which Blake was well aware. His theory of the spiritual body and of regenerated sexuality represents his attempt to deal with them. In some mysterious way the sexual act must be the entrance to an apocalypse in which fallen sexuality will be burned up and replaced by something else. In his long though doomed campaign against the pressures of dualism, Blake did his best to establish that the bodily senses will be transformed rather than annihilated in Eternity.

> But I thy Magdalen behold thy Spiritual Risen Body
> Shall Albion arise? I know he shall arise at the Last Day!
> I know that in my flesh I shall see God.
> (J 62:14-16, E211/K696)

Critics therefore argue with apparent justice that the Blakean apocalypse is "a reorganization, rather than a transcendence, of the world."[156] But the regenerated body is so different from the fallen one that they might as well be altogether distinct. "The senses as we conceive them," Frosch says, "drop out to be replaced by faculties, which, as separate entities, themselves drop out to be replaced by a fourfold organ of imagination, the body of Albion" (p. 142). Clearly this is not the body that we are equipped with. Who can say what that mysterious "commingling" would be in which Blakean man escapes what Frosch calls the "tyranny" of genital sexuality (p. 162)? For non-Blakeans, nongenital sexuality is nonhuman sexuality.

I do not deny that analogues to Blake's position may be found in Boehme and elsewhere; I deny that they make sense. "In Boehme's concept of life," Norman O. Brown proclaims, "the concept of play,

---

[155] "Blake's Fourfold Art," *Philological Quarterly*, 49 (1970), 406.
[156] Frosch, *Awakening of Albion*, p. 29.

or love-play, is as central as it is in Freud's; and his concept of the spiritual or paradisical body of Adam before the Fall recognizes the potent demand in our unconscious both for an androgynous mode of being and for a narcissistic mode of self-expression, as well as the corruption in our current use of the oral, anal, and genital functions."[157] Apart from the purely hypothetical status of alternatives to "our current use" of sexuality, this celebration of narcissism may seem futile if seductive. To postulate an androgynous satisfaction of libido is to propose an ideal which, as Blake so bitterly found, is constantly frustrated by reality. Libido, ordinarily defined by sexual desire and appeased by sexual pleasure, is transposed in this theory into a realm where no human being has ever experienced it. As a model for the operations of the unconscious the theory has its value, but if taken literally, as Boehme and Blake seem to take it, it can only give rise to acute dissatisfaction with human nature as it is. Formerly the champion of gratified desire, Blake now endorses a conception of regenerated man in which desire and satisfaction would operate in an internal economy of perpetual stability, like an electrical circuit plugged in to itself.

It is no surprise to find that Boehme, so touchingly optimistic in Brown's depiction, regarded sex with abhorrence and saw circumcision as emblematic of shame: "We here see by the circumcision the types that the bestial copulation of man and woman is an abomination before the holiness of God, which yet is borne withal, by divine patience and permission, seeing now it cannot be otherwise with man, he having lost the magical birth of Paradise."[158] How different is the prelapsarian sexuality of Adam and Eve according to Milton the Puritan and "misogynist"! Frye remarks pityingly that "the upper limit of Beulah is the limit of orthodox vision."[159] Milton, had he had the opportunity to write a poem called *Blake*, would have held that Blake was deluded in believing that it was either necessary or possible to go beyond Beulah.

As human beings if not as literary critics, we surely owe Blake the obligation of testing his myth against our experience of truth, which is no more than doing what he constantly begs us to do. As he once wrote—admittedly, with subsequent deletions that devastate the sense—"Therefore Dear Reader, forgive what you do not approve, & love me for this energetic exertion of my talent" (*J* 3, E144/K621). But as critics we must go further and try to understand why Blake's myth takes the unsatisfying form that it does. To do so will reveal his final

---

[157] *Life Against Death: The Psychoanalytical Meaning of History* (New York, 1959), p. 310.

[158] *Mysterium Magnum*, ch. 41, p. 371.

[159] *Fearful Symmetry*, p. 389.

ambivalence about the value of contraries, but will emphasize as well the special power of his dream of eternal activity.

"Many beliefs implying the *coincidentia oppositorum*," Eliade says, "reveal a nostalgia for a lost Paradise, a nostalgia for a paradoxical state in which the contraries exist side by side without conflict, and the multiplications form aspects of a mysterious Unity. Ultimately, it is the wish to recover this lost unity that has caused man to think of the opposites as complementary aspects of a single reality."[160] This is, I believe, a precise description of the driving impulse behind Blake's myth. Profoundly aware of contradictions within himself and society, he seeks to define them as contraries and to imagine a realm of existence in which their activity can produce unity instead of division. He may claim to eschew mysticism and mystery, yet in the end he cannot avoid them. If he maintains that human individuality will survive in the restored unity, it is no more than other mystics in the Western (though not the Eastern) tradition have maintained.

We have seen that Nicholas Cusanus, whose theory of symbolism so resembles Blake's, rests at last in a mysticism that transcends the intelligible in the "learned ignorance" of negative theology. "Your intellect," Cusanus says, "which is aided so much by the ignorance that is learning, then sees the impossibility of comprehending the world, its movement and form, for it will appear as a wheel in a wheel, a sphere in a sphere without a centre or circumference anywhere."[161] Despising the limitations of "reason" as much as Cusanus does, Blake would urge that the apprehension of wheels within wheels—Ezekiel's vision, the *Merkabah* and prototype of the Zoas—is positive rather than negative, the shadow of Eternity in the world of time. But to decide between the two formulations is perhaps only a matter of taste. According to either, the vision of truth transcends ordinary experience and sees beyond our familiar symbols to a deeper and richer truth.

The role of the Emanations in Eden—of the female in a realm where sex is not—must similarly be understood as a mystical attempt to keep what we have and yet transform it utterly. We can be moved by this vision without having to pretend that we believe it possible, or even that we are sure what it means. "Sexual separation," Frosch remarks, "is portrayed as a consequence of solipsism and self-will."[162] Most people believe exactly the opposite, and would consider that Blake's androgynous ideal, with the female absorbed into the male, is itself solipsistic. But once we have said that, it is interesting to ponder

---

[160] *The Two and the One*, p. 122.
[161] *Of Learned Ignorance*, II.xi, p. 110.
[162] *Awakening of Albion*, p. 164.

Blake's need for such an ideal and to compare it with similar formulations in a writer like Lawrence:

> In the new, superfine bliss, a peace superseding knowledge, there was no I and you, there was only the third, unrealised wonder, the wonder of existing not as oneself, but in a consummation of my being and of her being in a new one, a new, paradisal unit regained from duality. How can I say "I love you" when I have ceased to be, and you have ceased to be: we are both caught up and transcended into a new oneness where everything is silent, because there is nothing to answer, all is perfect and one. Speech travels between the separate parts. But in the perfect One there is perfect silence of bliss.[163]

Lawrence's impulse to escape from dualism is exactly like Blake's, but his aims are more modest. He is willing to imagine the disappearance of the "I" as well as the "you," whereas Blake apparently demands that the "I" should survive although the "you" should not. He recognizes that his vision presupposes peace and silence, while Blake's manifestly does not. And he places this passage in a mimetic (even if also symbolic) fiction that ends with a victory of the reality principle over the Edenic ideal.

Lawrence's point about speech passing between the parts is particularly suggestive, for it indicates what Blake too wants most from Eden, an immediacy of communication that will transcend the blunted and thwarted exchanges of people in this life, just as the reunion of Emanation with self will put an end to the "stone walls of separation" (*J* 90:12, E247/K736) of fallen sexuality.

> When in Eternity Man converses with Man they enter
> Into each others Bosom (which are Universes of delight)
> In mutual interchange. and first their Emanations meet. . . .
> For Man cannot unite with Man but by their Emanations
> Which stand both Male & Female at the Gates of each Humanity.
> (*J* 88:3-11, E244/K733)

In this formulation the Emanations are not females with whom males unite, but forms of expression through which any individual reaches out to any other. As Grimes puts it very well, "The feminine is the how, not the what of unity."[164] In other words, Blake envisions a state in which the female will no longer be the other, but will become the means of communication with an other that is fully oneself. It is in this

---

[163] D. H. Lawrence, *Women in Love* (New York, 1960), pp. 361-362.
[164] Ronald L. Grimes, *The Divine Imagination* (Metuchen, N.J., 1972), p. 40.

context that we must understand the famous conversations "in Visionary forms dramatic" at the end of *Jerusalem* (98:28, E255/K746): they represent an immediacy of expression that transcends art and art's symbols.[165]

In the end Blake cannot truly reconcile contraries because, like the Puritans whose moral intensity he shares, he can only solve the problem of alienation by exclusion or casting out: sheep and goats. A true acceptance of opposites demands a skeptical temperament and a commitment finally to things as they are.

> Two things of opposite natures seem to depend
> On one another, as a man depends
> On a woman, day on night, the imagined
>
> On the real. This is the origin of change.
> Winter and spring, cold copulars, embrace
> And forth the particulars of rapture come.[166]

But given his distrust of contraries, it is all the more wonderful that Blake was willing to imagine an imperfect Eden. I have said that his profoundest insight was that there can be no heaven without energy and life, intensified and purified perhaps but certainly not bleached away in endless repose. Like Hegel he perceived that conflict and opposition are fundamental to our reality, and although he continually sought an Eden in which they would compose into unity, he saw also that such an Eden could never be permanent. Hence, as every critic of *Milton* has noticed, the Eternals are confused, capable of gross error, and liable to fall just as Albion fell.[167]

At the very end of *Jerusalem* Blake describes the eternal Human Forms "living going forth & returning wearied/Into the Planetary lives of Years Months Days & Hours reposing" (99:2-3, E256/K747). Beulah and the world of time may be inferior to Eden, but they are its necessary complement, for we can imagine no human activity without weariness, while the traditional heaven of perpetual rest is an implicit repudiation of activity. Blake's fallible Eternals lead us directly to the central themes of his theology, to which we shall turn in the next chapter. The Christian myth postulates a perfect God and an imperfect world: we fell through disobedience. Why did he make us "sufficient

---

[165] See below, pp. 345-348.

[166] Stevens, *Notes Toward a Supreme Fiction, Collected Poems*, p. 392. Elsewhere Stevens speaks of poetry's response to "this contact with reality as it impinges upon us from outside, the sense that we can touch and feel a solid reality which does not dissolve itself into the conceptions of our own minds" (*The Necessary Angel* [New York, 1951], p. 96).

[167] See esp. Fox, *Poetic Form in Blake's Milton*, pp. 196-199.

to have stood, though free to fall?"[168] Blake holds that whatever God (or "Man" in Eden) is, he must be recognizably some form of what we are now. And if he (or it, or they) must be that, then the potential for repeated falls can never be dispelled. Why *that* should be, Blake does not pretend to know, but he would argue that his myth is more satisfying than those that invent a static and perfect heaven and then allege a fall from it. Blake's monism wars with his dualism because he strives unceasingly to reconcile the desires of the heart with the facts of experience, and his myth is permanently fascinating because as often as the monist dream seems to win out, the dualist realism reasserts itself and forces yet another effort to reinvent the whole.

[168] *Paradise Lost*, III.99.

[SIX]

God and Man

> You own your instincts—why, what else do I,
> Who want, am made for, and must have a God
> Ere I can be aught, do aught?—No mere name
> Want, but the true thing with what proves its truth,
> To wit, a relation from that thing to me.
>
> Browning, *Bishop Blougram's Apology*

> You're not a believer, are you? Haines asked. I mean, a believer
> in the narrow sense of the word. Creation from nothing and mira-
> cles and a personal God.
> There's only one sense of the word, it seems to me, Stephen said.
>
> Joyce, *Ulysses*

THE PROBLEM OF BLAKE'S THEOLOGY

As we have seen, the problem of the divine is ubiquitous in Blake.
Jesus is the Divine Body who sustains the life of symbols, the
savior who restores the lost unity of the Zoas, and (as in Christian theology in general) the force that binds together the otherwise
disjoined elements of a dualistic universe. With these contexts established we can now consider the symbolic and philosophical significance of Blake's God.

It is obvious that Blake hated Puritan morality while retaining, as
Frye remarks, the "Nonconformist conscience"; it is apparent also
that he shared in the Romantic tendency to produce theories of the
imagination which, in Harold Bloom's words, "are all displaced, radical Protestant accounts of the nakedness of the soul before God."[1]
What is less often noticed is that Blake went back to the central issues
of Christian tradition rather than away from them toward some "nat-
uralized" substitute. He sought to renew Christianity, not replace it.
As Perry Miller sums up Puritan theology, "The ultimate reason of all
things they called God, the dream of a possible harmony between man
and his environment they named Eden, the actual fact of disharmony
they denominated sin, the moment of illumination was to them divine

---

[1] Frye, *Fearful Symmetry*, p. 413; Bloom, "Ruskin as Literary Critic," *The Ringers in
the Tower*, p. 179. The evidence for Blake's dissenting background is at best circumstan-
tial, and one cannot even prove that he was not brought up an Anglican; see Nancy
Bogen, "The Problem of William Blake's Early Religion," *Personalist*, 49 (1968), 509-
522. His father may possibly have become a Baptist (*Blake Records*, p. 8).

grace, the effort to live in the strength of that illumination was faith, and the failure to abide by it was reprobation."[2] Every one of these tenets, restated in appropriate ways, could serve to describe Blake's system. The Puritans fought the good fight against that triple enemy the world, the flesh, and the devil; Blake redefined them drastically, but they remained his enemies too—the fallen world of Newton and Locke, the flesh of Generation's endless cycle, the Satan who is god of this world. H. Richard Niebuhr has said, "In the West the most sensitive, if not yet most, men are living in a great religious void; their half-gods have gone and the gods have not arrived." Niebuhr called for a "resymbolization" of religion.[3] Blake was one of the first to understand this crisis, and he set out with extraordinary dedication to achieve that resymbolization. But the result, both because it is symbolic and because it tries to breathe new life into old symbols, is extremely ambiguous.

There is no doubt that Blake underwent a serious spiritual crisis in the late 1790s and early 1800s, the outcome of which was a passionate if idiosyncratic return to Christianity. In a famous letter in 1804 he wrote to Hayley that he had experienced a special enlightenment after visiting an exhibition of paintings and was now "free from fetters" to pursue his art without impediment.[4] This sounds like an apology for the strange spiritual quarrel with Hayley that lies behind *Milton*, but according to Blake it goes much deeper than that: "For now! O Glory! and O Delight! I have entirely reduced that spectrous Fiend to his station, whose annoyance has been the ruin of my labours for the last passed twenty years of my life." Gone is the "Deep pit of Melancholy" of which Blake wrote to Cumberland four years before; he is now able, as he told Butts hopefully in 1802, to "Embrace Christianity and Adore him who is the Express image of God." And in another letter to Hayley he likens himself to Bunyan's Christian and speaks of having attained reintegration: "I have indeed fought thro a Hell of terrors & horrors (which none could know but myself) in a Divided Existence; now no longer Divided, nor at war with myself I shall travel on in the Strength of the Lord God as Poor Pilgrim says."[5]

[2] *The New England Mind: The Seventeenth Century* (Cambridge, Mass., 1939), p. 8.

[3] "Reformation: Continuing Imperative," *The Christian Century*, 77 (1960), 250-251.

[4] Since religion embraced the whole of experience for Blake, his conversion extended into, or was reflected in, the aesthetic realm. His contact with hundreds of European paintings at the Truchsessian Gallery seems to have crystallized his commitment to "outline" and his hatred of Flemish chiaroscuro; see Morton D. Paley, "The Truchsessian Gallery Revisited," *Studies in Romanticism*, 16 (1977), 165-177.

[5] Letters of 23 Oct. 1804 (E702-703/K851-852), 2 July 1800 (E679/K798), 22 Nov. 1802 (E691/K815), 4 Dec. 1804 (E704/K935). One notices that each of these letters an-

What the precise nature of those "terrors & horrors" was, it is now idle to speculate. Taken together, these passages are striking not for what they consign to the past but for what they declare in the present: allegiance to Christianity that is felt as a return from apostasy. Blake's religion was never that of the orthodox, and to the end of his life he continued to assert the humanity of Jesus the only God. "GOD is JESUS," he proclaimed in the late *Laocoön* aphorisms, and set up a kind of equation between the Imagination, "God himself" or "The Divine Body," and Jesus of whom we are all "Members" (E271/K776). I have no intention of ignoring the many passages like these, but I do not believe that they are self-explanatory. On the contrary, their status as aphorisms allows them to make gnomic claims that are not easily sustained in the myth as a whole. And the passages from Blake's letters suggest that he wants something more from God than a projection or confirmation of his own imagination.

"GOD is JESUS" not because God is confined to the *merely* human, but because he does not exist in the superhuman or inhuman fictions of conventional religion. If Blake had wanted to say only that the human imagination is our sole experience of the divine, it would not have cost him so many years of brooding and such tortuous formulations to say so. As Frye reminds us, "Though God is the perfection of man, man is not wholly God; otherwise there would be no point in bringing in the idea of God at all."[6] Among Blakeans, however, it is customary to deny the existence of a transcendent realm and to assert that God or Jesus is wholly human. Against the prevailing tendency to demythologize all references to transcendence and the divine, I shall argue that Blake found that he needed them and had to conceive of a Divine Humanity that was divine as well as human. Other writers, and perhaps our age in general, have found that they can do without the transcendent. I myself (to speak frankly) have no religious belief, and no ulterior reason to establish Blake as a religious poet. But I shall try to show that we cannot describe his poetry fairly or do justice to its peculiar emphases if we suppose that he simply grounds in man all the values that used to be grounded in God.

Blake's thought is so consistently religious that even the early, polemical aphorisms about the divinity of man are not so thoroughly humanist as they may seem. In *The Marriage of Heaven and Hell* Blake

---

nounces a breakthrough that evidently turns out to be temporary; and a bleak notebook jotting survives from 1807, "Between Two & Seven in the Evening—Despair" (E672/K440).

[6] *Fearful Symmetry*, p. 31.

offers what looks like an Enlightenment theory of the origin of religion. Ezekiel says that all gods will be proved to originate in the Hebrew faith, and Blake ironically adds, "All nations believe the jews code and worship the jews god, and what greater subjection can be?" (E38/K154). The nations have taken literally Jehovah and his moral code, evolving from these a grotesque natural religion in which "the Father is Destiny, the Son, a Ratio of the five senses, & the Holyghost, Vacuum" (E35/K150). But an imaginative interpretation of Ezekiel's speech can easily be assimilated to Blake's analysis in the preceding plate: religion began by a poetic *animation* of the natural world, and went wrong only when it reified the gods as external beings.[7] "Thus men forgot that All deities reside in the human breast" (E37/K153). To say that there is no God outside the human breast—no vengeful Nobodaddy on high—is not to say that there is no God. "Reside in" suggests real existence, not subjective projection. And the same is true of the much-quoted statement, "The worship of God is Honouring his gifts in other men each according to his genius, and loving the greatest men best. Those who envy or calumniate great men hate God, for there is no other God" (E42/K158). This implies that God does exist and does bestow gifts, even though the gifts have no existence apart from human beings.

As in Cusanus' theology of Jesus as the universal Form, Blake asserts an immanent God who is nonetheless divine. "All deities reside in the human breast" is a formulation intended to emphasize the divine element in man rather than to demote God to a metaphor of individual human imaginations; it is in God that the individual is freed from isolation and solipsism. Blake's position may be paradoxical, but it responds to the same problem that all the deepest thinkers of his time had to face, confronted as they were with the demolition job of the Enlightenment that Blake surveys in "Mock on." As Hegel put it, in terms that are exactly congruent with Blake's, "God is God only in so far as he knows himself; his self-knowledge of himself is moreover his self-consciousness in man, it is man's knowledge *of* God that goes

[7] Plate 11 of *MHH*, which begins "The ancient Poets animated all sensible objects with Gods or Geniuses . . . ," runs closely parallel to Hume's skeptical analysis: "Nor is a river-god or hamadryad always taken for a mere poetical or imaginary personage; but may sometimes enter into the real creed of the ignorant vulgar; while each grove or field is represented as possessed of a particular *genius* or invisible power, which inhabits and protects it" (*The Natural History of Religion*, ed. H. E. Root [Stanford, 1957], ch. III, p. 29). Hume sees this as a mental projection of human forms on to inanimate nature; Blake sees it as "whatever their enlarged & numerous senses could perceive" (E37/K153). See Hazard Adams' excellent discussion of this passage in *MHH* in "Blake and the Philosophy of Literary Symbolism," *New Literary History*, 5 (1973), 136–138.

on to become self-knowledge of man *in* God."[8] Both Hegel and Blake would regard a reductive humanism as disastrous.

If all reality is mental, then God, who is the supreme reality, must be supremely mental. Berkeley denied that anything would exist if no one were thinking it, and postulated a God who always thinks everything. Blake simply makes the relationship reciprocal: God thinks us and we think him. For we can only think at all, according to Blake, if we participate in the divine imagination; and if we do that, then the divine imagination dwells in the human breast—not in the brain, which is wrongly localized by Urizen as "the uppermost innermost recesses/Of my Eternal Mind" (*M* 9:27-28, E102/K490). It would make no sense to postulate a God who could exist outside of our thoughts, for "Where is the Existence Out of Mind or Thought?" (*VLJ*, E555/K617). Blake is more Berkeleyan than Berkeley, no doubt believing that Berkeley needs to be rescued from the errors of his orthodox theology.

Blake needs this conception of the divine because, unlike ordinary humanists, he is unwilling to give up its saving role.

> Then Los grew furious raging: Why stand we here trembling around
> Calling on God for help; and not ourselves in whom God dwells
> Stretching a hand to save the falling Man. . . .
>
> (*J* 38:12-14, E182/K672)

God dwells in us, but he must *stretch out his hand*, and a few pages later we hear that while Los stood before his furnaces "the Divine hand was upon him, strengthening him mightily."[9] Los's speech is not a cocky assertion of his own divinity; everywhere in Blake's myth the divine is invoked because it is the only agent that can reverse the Fall.

ERROR, SIN, AND FORGIVENESS

Like his myth as a whole, Blake's theology is conceived as a response to the conviction of alienation and guilt. Guilt is fairly easily explained as deluded homage to a false deity, but alienation is accepted as a fundamental fact of experience, and the difficulty of overcoming it is fully

---

[8] *Encyclopedia*, Third Part (*Die Philosophie des Geistes*), par. 564, quoted by Taylor, *Hegel*, p. 481.

[9] *J* 42:56, E188/K671. (In Keynes's edition these plates occur in reversed order.) Erdman notes the impotence of this rallying cry of Los, which reflects the frustration of revolutionary action and the necessity of waiting until "the day of Divine Power" is at hand (*J* 39:18-19, E184/K674; Erdman, *Blake: Prophet Against Empire*, p. 479).

faced. It is essential, therefore, to recognize what it is in the human condition that the divine is called upon to repair.

> Babel mocks saying, there is no God nor Son of God
> That thou O Human Imagination, O Divine Body art all
> A delusion. but I know thee O Lord when thou arisest upon
> My weary eyes even in this dungeon & this iron mill.
>
> (J 60:56-59, E209/K693)

The divine in Blake is not an a priori principle from which the rest of reality is deduced, but the *terminus ad quem*. Faithful to this imaginative insight, Blake dramatizes his ongoing struggle to find and incorporate the divine, rather than presenting a deductive system in which the divine might play a merely logical or a merely metaphorical role.

We must begin by trying to see what is wrong with man, as a preliminary to understanding the savior who is invoked to put it right. "Sin," in the ordinary sense, is rejected as a Urizenic hoax, the repressive moral law of "The Human Abstract" and the chapel with "Thou shalt not" written over the door. Instead of "sin" Blake prefers the Platonic conception of "error." But he is increasingly driven back upon a conception which comes close to the traditional idea of sin.

Following the long history of interpretations of evil as privation—a falling away from the good—Blake was at first prepared to state that evil actions are not actions at all.

> There is a strong objection to Lavaters principles (as I understand them) & that is: He makes every thing originate in its accident. he makes the vicious propensity not only a leading feature of the man but the Stamina on which all his virtues grow. But as I understand Vice it is a Negative—It does not signify what the laws of Kings & Priests have calld Vice. we who are philosophers ought not to call the Staminal Virtues of Humanity by the same name that we call the omissions of intellect springing from poverty.
> . . . To hinder another is not an act, it is the contrary: it is a restraint on action both in ourselves & in the person hinderd. for he who hinders another omits his own duty, at the time
> Murder is Hindering Another
> Theft is Hindering Another. . . .
>
> (E590/K88)

The conception of hindrance is closely related to that of restraint of desire: "Those who restrain desire, do so because theirs is weak enough to be restrained; and the restrainer or reason usurps its place & governs the unwilling" (*MHH*, E34/K149).

249

The provocative aphorism "Sooner murder an infant in its cradle than nurse unacted desires" (*MHH*, E37/K152) might seem superficially to resemble the ethic of the Sophists whom Plato opposed: "I tell you frankly," says Gorgias, "that natural good and right consist in this, that the man who is going to live as a man ought, should encourage his appetites to be as strong as possible instead of repressing them, and be able by means of his courage and intelligence to satisfy them in all their intensity by providing them with whatever they happen to desire."[10] Blake avoids this position because according to his doctrine of infinite desire, the Sophist will continually seek "More! More!" with the hopelessness of Tantalus, while the visionary will desire the "All" that his comprehension of the unity of things permits him to understand. Blake's affinities here are with Godwin (in the earnest moral Platonism of *Political Justice*, not the Dostoevskian torments of *Caleb Williams*) or with Shelley who exclaimed, when he found his friend involved with his wife, "Hogg is a mistaken man,—vilely, dreadfully mistaken."[11] Evil can be eradicated from Blake's world because it is not the central "stamina" of human nature but only a colossal *mistake*.

All sin is error, and the imaginative mind can free itself from error. "Genius has no Error. it is Ignorance that is Error."[12] Los therefore proclaims,

> I care not whether a Man is Good or Evil; all that I care
> Is whether he is a Wise Man or a Fool. Go! put off Holiness
> And put on Intellect.
>
> (*J* 91:54-56, E249/K739)

In a pregnant passage Blake says, "The Combats of Good & Evil is Eating of the Tree of Knowledge. The Combats of Truth & Error is Eating of the Tree of Life" (*VLJ*, E553/K615). The spurious tree of knowledge grows "in the Human Brain."[13] But true knowledge is not repudiated: "To Labour in Knowledge is to Build up Jerusalem" (*J* 77, E230/K717). To live *is* to know; there can be no separate and forbidden knowledge of good and evil.

Even the vicious characters in Blake, as Frosch remarks, express

---

[10] *Gorgias* 491-492, trans. Walter Hamilton (Harmondsworth, 1960), p. 90.

[11] Quoted by A. R. Humphreys, "The Eternal Fitness of Things," *Modern Language Review*, 12 (1947), 195*n*. Godwin—who was Shelley's immediate inspiration—says that "Error contains in it the principle of its own mortality" and that "The chains fall off of themselves when the magic of opinion is dissolved" (*Enquiry Concerning Political Justice*, ed. Isaac Kramnick [Harmondsworth, 1976], pp. 142, 149).

[12] Annotations to Reynolds, E641/K465.

[13] "The Human Abstract," E27/K217.

their desires through parodies of good. And this is not, as in Milton, because they hate the good and mock it, but because they retain the longing for Eden although they have forgotten the way and are "utterly singleminded in their quest to produce new worlds and new bodies, every one an image of paradise."[14] Error must be cast out, but sin is a state that can be exposed and then left behind. "Error can never be redeemd in all Eternity/But Sin Even Rahab is redeemd in blood & fury & jealousy" (*FZ* 120:48–49, E375/K361). That Blake is willing to use the term "sin" at all, however, suggests his distance from the central Platonic tradition. Though he may have denied that an evil act *was* an act, he came to see clearly that sin, even if defined as error rather than as disobedience, was ubiquitous and potent.

We thus see that Blake has involved himself in two separate issues. On the one hand, he denies that God has prohibited anything and that we sin by disobeying him. On the other hand, he perceives in man's dividedness a condition very similar to what has always been called sin, and the means he invokes to relieve it are very similar to traditional Christian ones. Confusion arises because the privation theory of evil is a department of theodicy, an attempt to explain the presence of evil in a universe created by an omnipotent God. Blake rejects any such God, and does not really need the privation theory at all in the Christian sense. He uses it instead as the Neoplatonists did to indicate the illusory status of error or nonbeing, and to explain thereby how man can regain the realm of truth.

But if the Neoplatonic account of the Fall was immensely attractive to Blake, when he moved beyond the rather simple doctrine of contraries in *The Marriage of Heaven and Hell* he must have realized its conceptual dilemma. Boehme, genius though he was, was a less daring philosophical thinker than Blake, and was content to treat in metaphor the self-expression of the One in the world of multiplicity and *Angst*. But as Augustine pointed out, commenting on the Neoplatonism which he himself had embraced and then abandoned, the metaphor fails to explain why the self-expression of a perfect One must take the form—even if interpreted as "contraries"—of disorder and suffering.[15] The Neoplatonists set out to defend an abstract conception of

---

[14] *Awakening of Albion*, p. 83.

[15] "There are some who admit that the world is created by God, but refuse to allow it a beginning in time, only allowing it a beginning in the sense of its being created, so that creation becomes an eternal process. There is force in this contention, in that such people conceive themselves to be defending God against the notion of a kind of random, fortuitous act; to prevent the supposition that the idea of creating the world suddenly came into his mind, as an idea which had never before occurred to him, that he happened to take a new decision, whereas in fact he is utterly incapable of change. But I

the immutable One and ended by denying obvious facts of human experience. To explain these one needs a concept of evil, not merely of change. Augustine never pretends to have solved every mystery, but in his opinion the mystery of evil in a world created *ex nihilo* is preferable to that of change in a world of changelessness.

The Augustinian doctrine takes for granted the gulf between man and God. Boehme's prelapsarian Adam was *like* God in his unity and happiness, but he was not God. Hence Boehme could retain the Christian conception of sin as rebellion, even though he defined it by its consequences rather than by a prior divine prohibition.[16] The guilty conscience, which Blake set out to exorcise, is for Boehme the essential means of reunion with God: "Then comes the poor conscience, in need, and with trembling, before God, and hath not many confessions or words, for it accounteth itself too unworthy to speak one word before God, but setteth itself before his face, and boweth down to the ground."[17]

Boehme's dilemma is also Blake's. If evil is merely privation, why are its effects so monstrous? Why do we inhabit a world "of pain and misery and despair and ever brooding melancholy" (*J* 13:31, E155/K633)? Cruelty is ubiquitous even though it violates the integrity of the entire universe:

> A Robin Red breast in a Cage
> Puts all Heaven in a Rage.
>
> . . .
>
> Kill not the Moth nor Butterfly
> For the Last Judgment draweth nigh.[18]

Boehme's solution, as Koyré shows, was to regard evil as privation

---

cannot see how their reasoning will stand up in application to other things, and especially if applied to the soul. If they maintain that the soul is co-eternal with God, how can it experience a change to unhappiness, to a condition from which it has been exempt for all eternity? This is something they will never be able to explain" (*City of God*, XI.iv, pp. 432-433).

[16] Sin arose because Adam hungered to "live in his own will" and was persuaded by the Serpent to enter into the outward creation rather than remaining at one with God, "which also happened to them [Adam and Eve] in the Fall, that they knew, tasted, saw and felt evil and good: whence arose unto them sickness, disease, pains and corruption (or the dissolution of this carcass)" (*Mysterium Magnum*, ch. 17, p. 101). Boehme argues (rather tortuously) that the tree of knowledge was not prohibited until, by willfully tasting its fruit, Adam and Eve made it so; but at any rate he accepts the theology of guilt and punishment.

[17] *Mysterium Magnum*, ch. 70, pp. 702-703.

[18] *Auguries of Innocence* (E481-482/K431-432). No doubt the moth and butterfly refer emblematically to the escape of the soul from the fallen body.

and to describe it as necessary with respect to *essence* (it is a positive force, just as shadow is the complement of light) but as accidental with respect to *existence*. If evil were defined negatively, as the absence of good, then its existence (or its paradoxical nonexistence) might threaten to be permanent, as indeed it is in Neoplatonism. But if it can be defined positively, then the combat against it may have an end: "It is precisely in consequence of the real and positive character of evil that Boehme can hope that one day its defeat will be definitive."[19] In Blake's language, "To be an Error & to be Cast out is a part of Gods Design" (*VLJ*, E551/K613).

Despite his moral passion, Blake feels obliged to deny the validity of morality, in order to separate himself from its psychology of guilt and punishment. The seven virtues are "the seven Diseases of Man" (*FZ* 98:27, E395/K336). As the "aged Mother" Eno says at the beginning of the *Book of Los*, the various sins arose after the Fall, when they could no longer be satisfied as before, when "Covet was poured full:/Envy fed with fat of lambs," and so forth (3:14–15, E89/K256). The notion is sufficiently delphic, since it is hard to imagine what envy would occupy itself with if it were purged of envying. But Blake's meaning is that each of these "sins" is the deformation of a valid impulse rather than its opposite or negation. He does not, however, propose that they are admirable in their fallen form, and indeed seems to subsume all of the sins together under the heading of Despair, the most dreadful condition that can befall Albion or any of his members.[20]

What is needed, then, is a divine principle that can forgive sins not by excusing affronts to itself but by unmasking the false Accuser who has perverted action. "Forgiveness of Sin is only at the Judgment Seat of Jesus the Saviour where the Accuser is cast out, not because he Sins but because he torments the Just & makes them do what he condemns as Sin & what he knows is opposite to their own Identity" (*VLJ*, E555/K616). Reliance on the natural world can only lead to disillusionment: "Rousseau thought Men Good by Nature; he found them Evil & found no Friend. Friendship cannot exist without Forgiveness of Sins continually" (*J* 52, E199–K682). But this does not entail loving one's enemies; it is one thing to say that Leigh Hunt or Cromek is in the state of Satan, and quite another to love him in that state. Lavater piously declares, "Know that the great art to love your enemy consists in never losing sight of MAN in him." Blake grimly retorts, "I cannot love my enemy for my enemy is not man but beast & devil, if I have any. I can love him as a beast & wish to beat him" (E578/K72). To lack

---

[19] Koyré, *La Philosophie de Jacob Boehme*, pp. 72–73.

[20] See Janet Warner, "Blake's Figures of Despair: Man in his Spectre's Power," Paley and Phillips, pp. 208–224.

enemies would be evidence of blindness to bestiality; as Blake wrote a few pages earlier, "I fear I have not many enemies" (E576/K70). If the forgiveness of enemies be taken as a universal ethical prescription, then Blake would agree with Freud that it is an impossible demand.[21] This is not to say that enemies should not forgive each other through the mediation of Jesus: "O point of mutual forgiveness between Enemies!/Birthplace of the Lamb of God incomprehensible!" (*J* 7:66–67, E149/K626). But it means that the enemies must first cease to be enemies by expelling the Satanic part of themselves. So long as they persist in it there can be no forgiveness, which requires the annihilation of selfhood in "the Perpetual Mutual Sacrifice in Great Eternity" (*J* 61:23, E210/K694). And if this is understood then Blake is perfectly willing to use the term "sin" instead of "error": "There is none that liveth & Sinneth not!" (61:24).

We began with the premise that forgiveness is important to Blake because of his awareness of alienation. Biographically speaking, this seems to reflect an obsessive need; as Kazin says, "It is impossible to read Blake's vehement and repeated cries against the 'Accuser' without being moved by the tremendous burden of guilt he carried despite his revolt and independence. . . . What was it that made him long at the end, above everything else, for 'forgiveness'? What was it he had to be 'forgiven' for?"[22] One of the chief functions of the myth is to neutralize the Accuser, to relieve guilt by explaining its origins and translating it into less self-lacerating terms. Error or sin is a result of man's dividedness, but it can be cured, just as in Hegel's system it is cured, by "the renunciation of self, of its *unreal* essence."[23] And that, as we have seen, is the driving motive behind Blake's theory of the selfhood: to displace on to a repudiated part of the self everything which the self does not wish to acknowledge as its own. If a fundamental distinction between Plato and Christianity is that error is an offense against the truth whereas sin is disobedience of the Father, then Blake's position does finally look Platonic. He calls for something like *gnosis*, a recognition of things as they really are, instead of moral purity or righteousness or holiness or goodness. But he recognizes also that man cannot lift himself out of the alienated condition by his own bootstraps; there must be a divine principle in which the individual is at once ratified and liberated from the isolation of selfhood. Blake diagnoses the cause of alienation as sin or error that is perpetrated by the selfhood in the state of Satan. Diagnosis is not cure; for that he must have Jesus.

---

[21] *Civilization and Its Discontents*, pp. 89-90.
[22] *Portable Blake*, pp. 53-54.
[23] *Phenomenology*, p. 677.

J E H O V A H ,   E L O H I M ,   S A T A N

In the Lambeth books and in the original version of *Vala*, the role of the Judaeo-Christian God is essentially taken by Urizen, which is as much as to say that it is a projection of fallen reason. But as Blake reflected upon his myth in the 1800s he must have become aware that this was too simple, particularly if the false God were reduced (as he is in so many popular accounts of Blake) to the satiric caricature of old Nobodaddy aloft.[24] For if Jehovah is really a product of the human mind, then he cannot be altogether empty; he must embody real human attributes, even if distorted. Moreover, as Blake pondered the Bible he evidently saw that there are *many* imaginative versions of divine activity, and the symbolism of the Seven Eyes of God was accordingly conceived as a way of suggesting them. The Seven Eyes figure mainly in a historical sequence that issues in Jesus. Without denying the importance of that sequence, I propose to study three of the most significant figures—Jehovah, the Elohim, and Satan—as interrelated aspects of the fallen or perverted divinity. I am more interested in their symbolic function than in the rather abstract, and never fully dramatized, succession of the Seven Eyes.[25]

It is important to recognize what Blake gains by dividing up God in this way. The Christian Trinity indicates the multiple activity of a single divinity, but has always had to struggle with the literalism of dogma; hence the endless theological explanations of how three can be one. Blake, as usual, operates symbolically rather than dogmatically. The various names of God are alternative ways of *interpreting* the idea of the divine. Some symbols are more adequate than others, and Blake settles for Jesus (or the Lamb, or the Divine Humanity, etc.) as the best symbol. But something of positive value survives in Jehovah and the Elohim, who are given different names in order to help us interpret their meaning. By proceeding in this way Blake can be seen as striving to undermine the long-standing conflation of the God of Judaeo-Christian theology with the Absolute of Greek philosophy. In one sense the attack fails, since Blake's thought is sufficiently metaphysical to presuppose the absolute, even if he refuses to call it that. But in

[24] See "To Nobodaddy" (E462/K171) and "When Klopstock England Defied" (E491/K186).

[25] Damon, in his edition of Blake's *Job*, presents a particularly baroque diagram of the Seven Eyes. For a simpler and more usable version see Ben F. Nelms, "Text and Design in *Illustrations of the Book of Job*," in Erdman and Grant, pp. 356-357, showing how both Jehovah and Elohim are stages in the progressive humanization of God. The final state is of course Jesus, which means that God becomes Jesus and also that Jesus becomes, or assimilates, all that was valid in the previous versions of God.

another sense it succeeds, for by insisting on the symbolic character of all thinking—by following Plato the mythmaker rather than Plato the mathematician—Blake intimates that a concept like "the absolute" has no meaning until it is given human form. Whereas Neoplatonism saw its emanations as successively degraded expressions of the unchanging One, Blake regards the unchanging One as a philosophical fiction.

To work out the negative part of his antitheology Blake joins to the positive emanations of Neoplatonism (equally apparent in the Kabbalah as in Plotinus) the negative myth of the fallen demiurge that had been developed by the Gnostics. When Crabb Robinson tried to refute Blake's description of Nature as diabolical by quoting the beginning of Genesis, "I was triumphantly told that this God was not Jehovah, but the Elohim, and the doctrine of the Gnostics repeated with sufficient consistency to silence one so unlearned as myself" (*Blake Records*, p. 545). Just where Blake picked up his knowledge of Gnosticism is hard to determine; he could have learned a good deal from standard histories of religion.[26] The crucial point is the corruption of the created universe, a heresy against which orthodox Christianity has always stood firm, holding that "every creature of God is good" (1 Tim. 4:4). The Gnostics liked to represent the demiurge as a parody of the God of Genesis; it is interesting that Blake at least once spoke of the Old Testament "as if it were the evil element" (*Blake Records*, p. 548). However offensive this may have appeared to orthodox minds, it reflects a coherent attempt to confront the conditions of experience. The Gnostics refused to believe that a creator who could make a good world would allow it to deteriorate, and unlike the Neoplatonists they denied that a theory of emanation was sufficient to explain the existence of evil. Our world must therefore be the work of an inferior demiurge, either misguided or actively vicious, who was himself already fallen when he made it.

Within the subdivisions of Gnosticism, which was always a way of regarding reality rather than an organized school, Blake's affinities lie with the Valentinians (even if Robinson mistook him for a Manichaean) who located "the origin of darkness, and thereby of the dualistic rift of being, *within* the godhead itself."[27] The demiurge vainly attempts to imitate the perfect order, and uses the fallen world as a power system with which to enslave man, but he is "more misguided than evil, thus open to correction and remorse, even to final

---

[26] See Stuart Curran, "Blake and the Gnostic Hyle: A Double Negative," *Blake Studies*, 4 (1972), 117-133. Modern discoveries of Gnostic texts have refined but not significantly altered the interpretations that were available to Blake.

[27] Jonas, *The Gnostic Religion*, p. 174.

redemption."[28] This is true likewise of Blake's Urizen, but unlike the Gnostics Blake distinguishes between the symbolic status of the demiurge and the regenerated Zoa who rises above that status.

Blake's fundamental point of difference from the Gnostics is highly instructive: they held that the true God was an "alien God" in a far-off heaven, and that the Gnostic elect ("pneumatics," filled with spirit) were likewise as alien to our world as beings from outer space, which indeed they literally were, having fallen from the remote heavens. In the expressive French translation of the term, man is *l'étranger*. Blake never believed that. He always longed for the renovation of the world we know, whose natural appearances could furnish him with viable symbols because they participated in the unfallen reality that lay within them. The Gnostics found their favorite symbols in the remote constellations; Blake preferred more immediate phenomena like larks and grains of sand, and was suspicious of the stars unless he could perceive them as human. The Gnostic demiurge is the enemy of man, creator of a malign universe in which man is an impotent victim. Urizen, on the other hand, is within us. Blake thus unites the Christian myth of the Fall with the Gnostic myth. He may reject the orthodox account of the Fall as disobedience toward an omnipotent lawgiver, but he accepts its ultimate premise of human responsibility.

> I went not forth. I hid myself in black clouds of my wrath
> I calld the stars around my feet in the night of councils dark
> The stars threw down their spears & fled naked away
> We fell.
>
> (FZ 64:25-28, E337/K311)

So speaks Urizen. If the Gnostics brooded upon "the evil forces that ceaselessly broke loose upon our heads,"[29] Blake locates them instead *inside* our heads.

For all its mythography, Gnosticism represented the creation, just as Christianity did, as a historical fact, though regarding it as a disastrous fall into historical change rather than as the providential inception of history. Blake treats creation as a metaphor: we have not fallen from eternity, we are *in* eternity, but because we see through delusive Urizenic structures we do not know it. Properly understood, nature is not our enemy but the sandal of the "Vegetable World" with which we can walk through Eternity (*M* 21:12, E114/K503). With these crucial distinctions in mind Blake joins the Gnostic demiurge to the Elohim of Genesis: "Elohim planted a garden eastward in Eden"

---

[28] Jonas, "The Gnostic Syndrome," *Philosophical Essays*, p. 269. See also *The Gnostic Religion*, pp. 192-193.

[29] Lacarrière, *Les Gnostiques*, p. 27.

(Gen. 2:8). Commentators normally took Elohim and Jehovah to be two names for the one God, and some of the later texts in the Old Testament use both names at once, as did the Kabbalists.[30] Some Gnostic writers, on the other hand, puzzling over the two names, concluded that Elohim was a benevolent angel and Yahweh, whom they identified with Satan, a hostile adversary.[31] Blake sometimes speaks of "the Elohim" (the noun is plural) and sometimes of "Jehovah Elohim," with the suggestion that each name points in its own way to the fallen divinity.[32]

As epigraph to *The Four Zoas* Blake quotes (in Greek) Ephesians 6:12, "For we wrestle not against flesh and blood, but against principalities, against powers, against the rulers of the darkness of this world, against spiritual wickedness in high places" (E296/K263). Modern scholars regard this text as a clear allusion to the Gnostic *archons*, the planetary angels who rule the fallen cosmos.[33] Whether Blake knew of this context or not, he certainly interprets "the rulers of the darkness of this world" very much as the Gnostics did. This is the God of the extraordinary picture *Elohim Creating Adam* (see fig. 24), who touches the forehead of a staring Adam while the serpent of materiality winds around Adam's body.[34] This God is deluded, even deranged, but hardly despicable; Hagstrum rightly calls him a "haunted and haunting old man."[35] He has eagle wings, not Satanic bat wings. And we may remember that in the schema of the Seven Eyes, he fell from weariness rather than like Jehovah from hypocritic holiness (*M* 13:22, E106/K494). This creator resembles the fallen but redeemable demiurge of the Valentinians. Blake often says that Adam was created as a limit of contraction, and Raine notes that Robert Fludd associated the Elohim with contraction.[36] His work will have to be remade by Los, but it is not therefore in vain.

A particularly striking comment on the Elohim occurs in *A Vision of the Last Judgment*: "The Aged Figure with Wings having a writing tablet & taking account of the numbers who arise is That Angel of the

---

[30] "Jehovah Elohim, Spouse and Bride, Father and Mother, God and His Shekinah are in Kether [primal unity] in a state of oneness, without separation and without distinction" (A. E. Waite, *The Holy Kabbalah*, p. 362).

[31] See Grant, *Gnosticism and Early Christianity*, p. 59.

[32] Blake may have followed rabbinical tradition in interpreting the "Jehovah Elohim" as the union of mercy with justice (see Damon, *A Blake Dictionary* [Providence, 1965], p. 206). But I shall argue that these names are not used so restrictively.

[33] Grant, *Gnosticism and Early Christianity*, p. 161.

[34] There are color reproductions in Bindman, *Blake as an Artist*, pl. I, and Paley, *William Blake*, pl. 28.

[35] *William Blake: Poet and Painter*, p. 127.

[36] *Blake and Tradition*, II, 79-80.

24. *Elohim Creating Adam.*

Divine Presence mentioned in Exodus XIVc 19v & in other Places. this Angel is frequently calld by the Name of Jehovah Elohim The I Am of the Oaks of Albion" (E549/K610). The text in Exodus in fact speaks of "the angel of Jehovah," which is however often equated with God (Michael, the usual identification, being a manifestation of God). The mention of the oaks, often druidic and associated with the crucifixion by Blake, suggests that this figure is to be regarded with suspicion. And the Angel of the Divine Presence consistently signifies the Satanic creator of the fallen body: "Thou Angel of the Presence Divine/That didst create this Body of Mine" (*EG*, E513/K754). He is the creator in the *Job* series and the demiurge in the *Laocoön*; and in a far from cheerful picture he is *The Angel of the Divine Presence Clothing Adam and Eve with Skins* after their fall into sexuality.[37] But why is this

[37] Illustrated in color in Raine, *William Blake*, pl. 94 (p. 129). See pl. 2 of the *Job* series, a symbiosis of the feeble Urizenic creator and the fiery Satanic Accuser. At the top Blake has inscribed "The Angel of the Divine Presence," together with Hebrew characters meaning "Jehovah is King." The same figure is pretty clearly involved in pls. 13–15, though Damon insists on regarding this as the true God. The central figure in the *Laocoön* group is identified as "The Angel of the Divine Presence," with a Hebrew text meaning "Angel of Jehovah" and a Greek one meaning "Serpent-holder" (E270/K775); the demiurge is trapped in the serpent coils of materiality together with his "sons" Satan

aberrant demiurge identified with the aged figure writing down the numbers?

The answer is probably iconographic, and serves to remind us of the rich complexity of Blake's symbolism. Blake illustrated the same figure in the Dante series as the Recording Angel, a clearly Urizenic figure with arched wings but scaly legs.[38] The traditional source for this figure (see fig. 25) was Claudian's description of the Cave of Eternity, with Nature at the door and an old man, the Demiurge or Demogorgon, writing down the number of stars in the constellations that determine the life and death of all things.[39] Blake is evidently making the ironic comment that this figure is not God or his agent at all, but far below the Divine Humanity that presides at the top of his picture. In Blake's interpretation he is powerless to write eternal laws of fate, but can only note the numbers of those who pass by him on their way to salvation.

Moreover, the traditional iconography includes the female figure of Nature (see the many-breasted woman on the right in fig. 25, a lunar goddess faced on the left by Apollo); it is she who sends babies into the world. Blake, again in ironic contrast, has "the Church Universal represented by a Woman Surrounded by Infants. There is such a State in Eternity it is composed of the Innocent civilized Heathen & the Uncivilized Savage who having not the Law do by Nature the things containd in the Law [cf. Rom. 2:14]. This State appears like a Female crownd with Stars driven into the Wilderness She has the Moon under her feet" (E548–549/K609–610). As Nature she is lunar and fallen, in fact an accomplice of the Urizenic demiurge. But symbolically she can be transformed into the eternal Church, spiritual mother of those who are above the repressive Law. Vala can become Jerusalem. And in exactly the same way the fatalistic Angel of the Divine Presence, surrogate for the miscreating Elohim, can be restored to spiritual life.

The Seven Angels, led by "Hillel who is Lucifer," tell Milton on the couch of death,

---

and Adam. As Morton Paley comments, Blake thought that his engraving corresponded to a visionary "original" which the Greeks presumably misinterpreted when they called it *Laocoön* (" 'Wonderful Originals'—Blake and Ancient Sculpture," in Essick and Pearce, p. 191).

[38] Reproduced in Roe, *Blake's Illustrations* . . . , pl. 92, and in Raine, *William Blake*, p. 205.

[39] Claudian, *De Consulatu Stilichonis*, II. 424–476. The topic was developed by Boccaccio and illustrated, among other places, in Cartari's *Imagini degli Dei de gli antichi* (1615), from which my illustration is taken. I owe this identification, and much helpful elucidation, to my colleagues David Burchmore and James Nohrnberg.

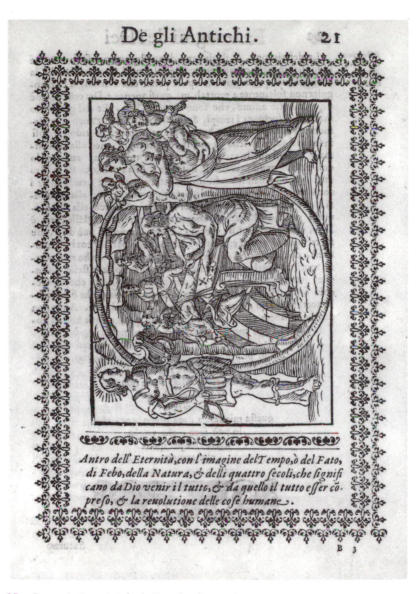

De gli Antichi. 21

Antro dell' Eternità, con l' imagine del Tempo, ò del Fato, di Febo, della Natura, & delli quattro secoli, che signifi cano da Dio venir il tutto, & da quello il tutto esser cō- preso, & la reuolutione delle cose humane .

B 3

25. Cartari, *Imagini degli Dei de gli antichi* (1615), p. 21.

> We are not Individuals but States: Combinations of Individuals
> We were Angels of the Divine Presence: & were Druids in
>   Annandale
> Compelld to combine into Form by Satan, the Spectre of Albion,
> Who made himself a God, & destroyed the Human Form Divine,
> But the Divine Humanity & Mercy gave us a Human Form
> Because we were combined in Freedom & holy Brotherhood. . . .
>   (*M* 32:10-15, E130/K521)

Lucifer is Hillel the Day-Star (Isa. 14:12) and can resume his place in the light, just as Urizen can recover his Apollonian glory. In their Satanic form the Angels of the Presence were druidical (cf. the "Oaks of Albion" in the description in *A Vision of the Last Judgment*). But the Divine Humanity can rescue them from the fallen state and restore them to human form. As Urizen or Satan or Elohim or Angel of the Presence, this is not a permanent god or archon but a spiritual state that can be purged of error and left behind. And ultimately the idea of creation must be integrated with that of imagination, so that Los must take on the labor of the Elohim: "Such is the World of Los the labour of six thousand years./Thus Nature is a Vision of the Science of the Elohim" (*M* 29:64-65, E127/K518).

The Elohim is (or are) God in the relatively simple role of creator. The other half of the "Jehovah Elohim" pairing is more complex by far, since Blake invests Jehovah with all the ambiguities of father, law-giver, and judge, and consistently identifies his fallen or negative aspects with the state of Satan. The orthodox Jehovah, trapped in the coils of nature with his sons Satan and Adam, is the "god of this world" (2 Cor. 4:4) whom the Bible ordinarily mistakes for his chief enemy. As Blake says to "My Satan" in the epilogue to *For the Sexes*, "To the Accuser who is The God of This World,"

> Tho thou are Worshipd by the Names Divine
> Of Jesus & Jehovah: thou art still
> The Son of Morn in weary Nights decline
> The lost Travellers Dream under the Hill.
>   (E266/K771)

In the picture,[40] a bat-winged Satan leaves a sleeper, evidently an awakening pilgrim or Albion, at sunrise. The lost traveler (alluding to various folk tales of the True Thomas and Rip Van Winkle variety, and to Bunyan's Christian asleep in the arbor on the Hill Difficulty) is a type of the sleeping Albion; he dreams of the spiritual realm in which Lucifer ("the Son of Morn") properly belongs, but men blindly wor-

---

[40] See *The Illuminated Blake*, ed. Erdman, p. 279.

ship him as the accusing God of this world. In Christian doctrine the
Law is exploited by Satan, since it defines the impossible standards of
moral perfection that would confront fallen man without divine grace.
As Ricoeur comments, "This hell of guilt, engendered by the law and
its curse, finds its supreme symbol in the Satanic figure itself. We
know that the Devil was understood not only as the Tempter but as
the Accuser of man at the last judgment (while Christ becomes the
Advocate, the Paraclete). Thus the demon stands not only behind aggression but behind the law itself, inasmuch as it is a law of death."[41]

Blake is profoundly Pauline (and Protestant) in his rejection of the
stony tablets of Moses, the letter that killeth, "the ministration of
death, written and engraven in stones" (2 Cor. 3:7). And the final and
most bitter irony of Blake's Accuser is that he is also Jehovah in his
fallen or Urizenic form, forever reinscribing the stony law of death
(with the "iron pen" of Job 19:24 and Jer. 17:1) in a heroic but hopeless
attempt to satisfy a morality of guilt.

> But still his books he bore in his strong hands & his iron pen
> For when he died they lay beside his grave & when he rose
> He seizd them with a gloomy smile for wrapd in his death clothes
> He hid them when he slept in death. when he revivd the clothes
> Were rotted by the winds the books remaind still unconsumd
> Still to be written & interleaved with brass & iron & gold
> Time after time for such a journey none but iron pens
> Can write And adamantine leaves receive nor can the man who goes
> The journey obstinate refuse to write time after time. . . .
> (FZ 71:35-72:1, E342/K316)

Thus Urizen in the *Book of Urizen*

> . . . curs'd
> Both sons & daughters; for he saw
> That no flesh nor spirit could keep
> His iron laws one moment.
> (23:23-26, E80/K235)

The thought is the same as Paul's: "For as many as are of the works of
the law are under the curse: for it is written, Cursed is every one that
continueth not in all things which are written in the book of the law to
do them" (Gal. 3:10). In Blake's opinion this state of affairs is
Jehovah's fault, not man's, but he would fully agree with Paul's conclusion, "Christ hath redeemed us from the curse of the law" (Gal.
3:13). Paul cries out for deliverance from "the body of this death"

[41] *Symbolism of Evil*, p. 146n.

(Rom. 7:24); Blake says that "the Body of Death was perfected in hypocritic holiness" by Jehovah himself (*M* 13:25, E106/K494). In the *Interpreter's Parlour* picture for *Pilgrim's Progress*, Blake explicitly illustrates the Law as a devil.[42]

Such a God as this is immensely complex, especially as Blake constantly exploits the rich associations that have gathered round it in Western culture. Considered imaginatively it is a powerful conception, built upon feelings about fatherhood and kingship that Blake criticizes but has no intention of ignoring. Considered ontologically it is a fiction, a nonentity, and can be dismissed with derision. But to collapse every reference to Jehovah into Old Nobodaddy is to mistake gravely its symbolic power. In Blake's myth every symbol must be founded in reality. The problem with the Jehovah Elohim is to purge the symbol of false meanings and get back to the true.

This is very clearly the case in the famous frontispiece to *Europe* (also issued as a separate print) known as *The Ancient of Days* (see fig. 26).[43] Blake may have known that the title "Ancient of Days" was sometimes associated with the demiurge rather than with the supreme God.[44] Uninstructed viewers are always astonished to learn that Blake invested this figure with negative implications, and, as we have already remarked, their feelings are not irrelevant.[45] Of all of Blake's eidetic visions, the Ancient of Days was the one he saw most often and was most impressed by, and a copy of this print was the last thing he ever worked on (*Blake Records*, pp. 470-471n, 527). The compasses held in the left hand certainly symbolize mathematical constriction, as does the figure's cramped posture in the orb that blocks out the sun. But the windblown hair and beard and the light shining out of darkness combine to suggest powerful energy, and the geometries of the composition (circle and triangle within a rectangle) convey the clear impression that mathematical form is much better than no form at all. The figure is reminiscent of Gray's lines in *The Bard*, "Loose his beard and hoary hair/Streamed, like a meteor, to the troubled air," which Gray said had been inspired by a painting of God the Father by Raphael.[46] At the moment when Milton announces his decision to

[42] Reproduced in Klonsky, *William Blake*, p. 121; Paley, *William Blake*, pl. 92; Raine, *William Blake*, p. 206.
[43] Reproduced in color in Klonsky, *William Blake*, p. 40.
[44] See Lindberg, *William Blake's Illustrations . . .* , p. 157n.
[45] See above, p. 120.
[46] The painting is Raphael's *Vision of Ezekiel*, which Gray had seen in Florence (note to lines 19-20 of *The Bard*); the painting itself, which literalizes Ezekiel's symbolic beasts with zoological accuracy, is much less Blakean than Gray's lines. Many other sources are of course possible; Blake may for instance intend a sarcastic reference to a frontispiece to the *Principia* that showed Newton as an old man in the heavens with a pair of

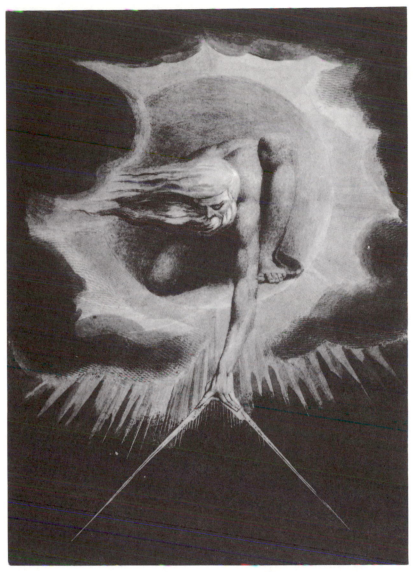

26. *Europe*, frontispiece (called *The Ancient of Days*).

enter Eternal Death, Blake associates clouds with Jehovah and winds with the Elohim (*M* 14:26, E107/K495).

Blake thus confronts the imaginative meaning of the idea of the holy. It is a product of the fallen imagination, but it is imaginative all the same. As defined by Rudolf Otto, the holy might seem to represent everything Blake hates: the "wholly other," the *mysterium tremendum*, the god before whom one prostrates oneself in fear and trembling and bizarre physical reactions. In the ninth picture of *Job* Blake rejects as nightmarish delusion the dream of Eliphaz, which Burke had praised as an example of mysterious sublimity: "Then a spirit passed before my face; the hair of my flesh stood up" (Job 4:15).[47] Above all Blake rejects what Otto calls creature-consciousness, "the emotion of a creature, submerged and overwhelmed by its own nothingness in contrast to that which is supreme above all creatures."[48]

Yet a thoughtful reading of Otto must provoke second thoughts about Blake. For the holy represents the supra-rational side of religious experience, whereas dogmatic theology represents the rational. Blake is obviously no rational theologian. Yet he will not admit mystery, postulating imagination or vision as a middle term between mystery and reason. He splits the idea of God into two parts, the remote Urizenic fiction of hypocritic holiness and the immanent Jesus in whom everything that lives is holy. And perversely he goes on to claim that rational logic is the instrument of mystery religion, allying Newton and Locke with Satan and Rahab. The special function of "mystery" in this context should not blind us to the fact that Blake's Jesus is also mysterious, though Blake may not choose to admit it. If visionary insight is immediate and perfect, then of course the vision of Jesus—which takes place *in* Jesus—can entail no mystery. But a reader who cannot share in the Blakean epiphany will find a good deal of mystery in his account of Jesus, and will feel that although this divine

---

compasses (see Martin K. Nurmi, "Blake's 'Ancient of Days' and Motte's Frontispiece to Newton's *Principia*," in *The Divine Vision*, ed. V. de S. Pinto, pp. 207-216).

[47] See Nelms's commentary in "Text and Design . . . ," pp. 343-344. Burke quotes this text and says, in terms that must have infuriated Blake, "Is it not, wrapt up in the shades of its own incomprehensible darkness, more aweful, more striking, more terrible, than the liveliest description, than the clearest painting could possibly represent it?" (*A Philosophical Inquiry into the Origin of Our Ideas of the Sublime and Beautiful*, ed. J. T. Boulton [Notre Dame, 1968], II.iv, p. 63). In light of Blake's sweeping reinterpretation of Job, it is of some interest that it does not appear among the biblical books accepted as canonical in the Swedenborgian document which Blake signed in 1789 (*Blake Records*, p. 36*n*). As Bentley notes, the same list, also lacking Job, is created by "the Divine Lord" in pl. 48 of *Jerusalem*.

[48] *The Idea of the Holy*, p. 10. Otto discusses the Book of Job at some length to illustrate the mysteriousness of the numinous.

principle is humanized as Otto's *mysterium* is not, it still retains the emotional charge of the holy. Los appears as "a terrible flaming Sun" before taking on human form (*M* 22:6, E116/K505), and Blake would not have chosen Ezekiel's chariot of the "Zoas" for his central symbol if numinous dread had meant nothing to him. "Such is the Mighty difference between Allegoric Fable & Spiritual Mystery. Let it here be Noted that the Greek Fables originated in Spiritual Mystery & Real Vision" (*VLJ*, E545/K605).

Underlying Blake's symbols of the true and false divine is a searching critique of the basis of religious feeling. Reinhold Niebuhr defines three essential aspects in the Christian view of man: spiritual self-transcendence as the image of God; man's finiteness and creatureliness; and the origin of evil in man's refusal to admit dependence upon God.[49] In Blake's opinion only the first category is justified. Evil originates in exactly the opposite way from the orthodox explanation, in man's assumption of creatureliness and his projection of an omnipotent creator and judge. But the human condition remains what the theologians said it was—alienated, guilt-ridden—and Blake retains the belief that a divine principle is needed to heal it.

How did man get from the true to the false divine? In a brilliant aphorism Blake says, "God is only an Allegory of Kings & nothing Else."[50] Freud would say that kings are fathers, and Blake would agree. The whole idea of fatherhood is contaminated by Generation, in Blake's opinion, and has to be rethought. He goes on to say, "Thus we see that the Real God is the Goddess Nature"; mothers as well as fathers are responsible for the imaginative wreckage of our fallen state. Here Blake seems to have intuited the deepest weakness of the Gnostic myth, its projection of a father far away. As E. R. Dodds suggests, "The splitting of God into two persons, on the one hand a remote but merciful Father, on the other a stupid and cruel Creator, seems to reflect a splitting of the individual father-image into its corresponding emotional components: the conflict of love and hate in the unconscious mind is thus symbolically resolved, and the gnawing sense of guilt is appeased."[51] Blake refuses to split God like this, not only because Nobodaddy is nobody's father, but also because he regards a solution that banishes the divine to a distant heaven as no solution at all. Guilt would be appeased, in such a doctrine, by rejecting the sum total of human experience, stranding man on an alien shore where he could only wait for uncertain rescue. "Seek not thy heavenly father then beyond the skies" (*M* 20:32, E113/K502).

[49] *The Nature and Destiny of Man* (New York, 1943), I, 150.
[50] Blake's parody of Thornton's translation of the Lord's Prayer (E659/K789).
[51] *Pagan and Christian in an Age of Anxiety* (Cambridge, 1965), p. 20.

"I am not a God afar off," the divine voice tells Albion at the very beginning of *Jerusalem*; "I am a brother and friend; / Within your bosoms I reside, and you reside in me" (4:18-19, E145/K622). Blake ironically alludes to Jeremiah 23:23, where God declares that he is both more immediately present and also more universal than the local gods of the idolaters: "Am I a God at hand, saith the Lord, and not a God afar off?" The deluded Albion may echo the Psalms in protesting his emptiness in the face of the Almighty, but he is then "Idolatrous to his own Shadow."[52] So also in the *Job* series, Job learns not to adore an implacable God above the heavens but to welcome a humanized God, who is associated on plate 17 with texts from Saint John that emphasize the identity of the Son with the Father.

It was a basic Gnostic point that Christ was not the son of the biblical Jehovah, and Blake sometimes echoes it: "Thinking as I do that the Creator of this World is a very Cruel Being, & being a Worshipper of Christ, I cannot help saying the Son O how unlike the Father. First God Almighty comes with a Thump on the Head. Then Jesus Christ comes with a balm to heal it" (*VLJ*, E555/K617). Very similarly the Christian heretic Marcion denied that the Jesus of the New Testament could be the son of the exterminating Jehovah of the Old. But Blake carries the idea much further and attempts to rethink the whole issue of the emotional and symbolic content of fatherhood.

The protective father is appropriate to childlike seeing, as Blake illustrates throughout the *Songs of Innocence* and as he states explicitly in his annotations to Berkeley: "Little Children always behold the Face of the Heavenly Father" (E653/K774). At its best, the father image belongs in the family love of Beulah where "Each shall behold the Eternal Father & love & joy abound" (*FZ* 133:26, E387/K374). But family love is "storgous" (from the Greek word for parental affection) and possessive, and in an adult perspective it must be severely criticized if not rejected.

> Is this thy soft Family-Love
> Thy cruel Patriarchal pride
> Planting thy Family alone,
> Destroying all the World beside.[53]

Blake's ideal of family is one of brotherhood, and excludes submission to parents.

---

[52] *FZ* 40:12, E321/K293, repeated at *J* 43:46, E190/K654. The texts from the Psalms echoed in this passage had a particular appeal, as Weiskel shows, for the Kantian "negative sublime" (*The Romantic Sublime*, p. 73).

[53] *J* 27:77-80, E172/K651. On Blake's hatred of patriarchy see Mitchell, *Blake's Composite Art*, pp. 186–187.

Once you have reached puberty you enter into inevitable conflict with parents, and this only brings into the open a resistance to domination that has been present from the very beginning. In the light of Experience the son realizes that he was born "Struggling in my fathers hands" and that he took a sulking refuge—with equal futility—on his mother's breast; the image is repeated in *The Four Zoas* when the twins Los and Enitharmon sulk upon Enion's breast.[54] The tormented conflict of the Orc cycle is epitomized in the picture in *For the Sexes* entitled "My Son! My Son!" (alluding to David's lament for Absalom) in which a young man points a spear at his aged father. But Blake knows also that "Aged Ignorance" clips the wings of the young (E261-262/ K766-767), and his apparent solution is to do away with paternity altogether. Whether this makes sense in human terms in doubtful but perhaps irrelevant, since the myth treats family relationships metaphorically rather than literally. In religious terms, it means that we must outgrow Innocence and resist the impulse to project an idealized image of parents as God the Father and Mother Nature.[55]

In finding a symbolic equivalent for the Oedipal relation, Blake very subtly attributes the Chain of Jealousy to Los rather than to his son Orc (who is, of course, the fallen form of the sexual Luvah). When Orc is fourteen Los nails him down upon a Promethean rock.[56] But it is Los whom the chain constricts. As is shown in a manuscript sketch for *Vala*, Los gazes in bitter jealousy while Orc and Enitharmon twine their limbs in amorous embrace (see fig. 20, p. 218). At this point in the narrative we are told that Los consigns Orc to the Spectre "Concenterd into Love of Parent Storgous Appetite Craving" (*FZ* 61:10, E334/K308). In Freud's Oedipal myth the small child punishes himself for jealousy of the father; in Blake's myth the child is adolescent and his jealousy is both preceded and determined by that of the father. The family relation is hopelessly contaminated by fallen sexuality. The point is perhaps made in another way on the fourth plate of *Europe*, in which a gorgeously physical Enitharmon draws a curtain aside from the sleeping Orc in a composition that alludes to pictures of Psyche gazing at Cupid.[57]

We may well be reminded that Blake was a son but never a father. Any psychoanalyst would take it for granted, after considering Blake's

[54] "Infant Sorrow," E28/K217; *FZ* 8:8, E300/K270.

[55] Baudouin comments, "Not only does the image of a personal God form part of the symbolic system 'father,' but the images of the Church, the interior life, and the Abyss or Nature-God with a pantheistic coloration, arrange themselves in the symbolic system 'maternal bosom' " (*Psychanalyse du Symbole Religieux*, pp. 28-29).

[56] See Damon, *Blake Dictionary*, p. 76, for a narrative summary of the theme from various places in the poems.

[57] As Bindman notes (*Blake as an Artist*, p. 81).

myth of paternity and his lifelong hatred of authority, that his relations with his own father must have been troubled. What little we
know does not suggest unusual cruelty: the elder Blake took pains to
place his son in a suitable apprenticeship and respected his wish not to
be sent to school because of the punishment he would have met there
(*Blake Records*, p. 510). But the son's guilt at hostility toward his father
might well have been intensified by the recognition that his father was
well-meaning and kind, for it is precisely the loving father, according
to Blake, who imposes guilt:

> To her father white
> Came the maiden bright:
> But his loving look,
> Like the holy book,
> All her tender limbs with terror shook.[58]

The father is oppressive because his role is not limited to specific in-
junctions that are either obeyed or disobeyed; as W. J. Verdenius has
said of the theology of God as father, "The child, refusing to submit to
the father's will, struggles not so much against the content of his instructions as against the father's entire personality."[59]

In the poem to Butts that ends with the "fourfold vision," Blake
describes an extraordinary apparition of his father and two brothers,
which abruptly shatters a mood of happiness:

> With my Father hovering upon the wind
> And my Brother Robert just behind
> And my Brother John the evil one
> In a black cloud making his mone
> Tho dead they appear upon my path
> Notwithstanding my terrible wrath. . . .
>
> (E692/K817)

Robert was Blake's alter ego, John his anti-ego. What little we know
of John suggests intense competition and, on William's part, the prob-
ability of subsequent guilt when John failed and disappeared.[60]

---

[58] "A Little Girl Lost," E29/K219.

[59] "Plato and Christianity," *Ratio*, 5 (1963), p. 25. Verdenius quotes T. Steinbüchel's
remark that sin is "more than a transgression of the divine law, it is the hardening of the
self's I against God's Thou, the individual's contradiction against God's personal demand." Blake rejects God's personal demand, but his many invocations of Jesus respond
to the problem of the hardening selfhood.

[60] John seems to have been the parents' favorite, and William when young was often
told that one day he would beg his bread at John's door. But according to Tatham, John

Next, a thistle blocks Blake's path in the guise of an old gray man, and predicts what Blake certainly reproached himself with during the difficult time at Felpham:

> Poverty Envy old age & fear
> Shall bring thy Wife upon a bier.

Blake then kicks the old man aside in wrath, whereupon Los appears in glory—"Twas outward a Sun: inward Los in his might." Blake defies the earthly sun and commits his "Arrows of Thought" to the flames of the imaginative sun, but not without another vision of family that turns into the blood of retribution:

> My brothers & father march before
> The heavens drop with human gore.

It is striking that in the manuscript continuation of "Infant Sorrow" Blake put "father" in place of "priest" and then wrote,

> So I smote him & his gore
> Staind the roots my mirtle bore
> But the time of youth is fled
> And grey hairs are on my head
> (E720/K890)

The Oedipal conflict poisons the son's marriage (the myrtle) as well as his filial relationship, and ends once again in murder and gore. The son in his turn will grow old, and if he should have sons of his own the cycle will be repeated.

Blake was aware, then, that the theme of paternity was obsessive, and he well knew that an obsession cannot be banished simply by denying it. The retaliation of Absalom's spear and the resulting nightmare of dripping gore can provide no answer.[61] What is needed is a version of the doctrine of forgiveness, which will transform the paternal relation without neglecting its emotional power. The myth must somehow get from the protective father of Innocence to a relationship that is free from both repression and dependence. The bond with the

---

failed in his apprenticeship, "became abandoned & miserable & literally, contrary to his parents' presage, sought bread at the Door of William. He lived a few reckless days, Enlisted as a Soldier & died" (*Blake Records*, p. 509).

[61] John Beer suggests that the picture in *For the Sexes* alludes to *Paradise Lost* II.729-730, where Sin rebukes Death for aiming "that mortal dart/Against thy father's head" (*Blake's Humanism* [Manchester, 1968], p. 236). Patricide is the revenge, literally, of death.

father, Thomas Mann says, resides in the child's identification with "a father-image elected out of a profound affinity."[62] That is exactly what Blake seeks: to develop a symbol of the father that can be *elected* rather than imposed, to attain a love that is mutual and brotherly rather than "storgous" and possessive.

Such a symbol was suggested to Blake by the parable of the Prodigal Son, which moved him with unusual force. Samuel Palmer told Gilchrist some three decades after Blake's death, "I can yet recall it when, on one occasion, dwelling upon the exquisite beauty of the parable of the Prodigal, he began to repeat a part of it; but at the words, 'When he was yet a great way off, his father saw him,' could go no further; his voice faltered, and he was in tears" (*Blake Records*, p. 283). At the end of *Jerusalem* Blake gives the motif his own interpretation (see fig. 27): in the same pose that appears in pictures of the Prodigal, he shows an androgynous child or youth, arms outstretched in the cruciform pose of Jesus, embraced by a haloed father.[63] The son (or son/daughter) becomes the Jesus who, as we suggested earlier, is needed to rescue the sexual initiate of the "Chapel All of Gold" from the swine.[64] In the context of *Jerusalem*, man has here achieved mutual forgiveness, and the patriarch is forgiven just as much as the younger figure is.[65]

In exploiting this traditional symbol Blake indicates that symbols build upon human experience and also reinterpret it. For as Ricoeur says, "If symbols are fantasies that have been denied and overcome, they are never fantasies that have been abolished. That is why one is never certain that a given symbol of the sacred is not simply a 'return of the repressed'; or rather, it is always certain that each symbol of the sacred is also and at the same time a revival of an infantile and archaic symbol."[66] Having reconstructed the symbol, Blake hopes to free it from repression. If he succeeds, he can hope to recover the language of Innocence and to refer once more to the divine as "the Universal Father" (*J* 97:6, E254/K744). And he can say in a letter, without in the least abandoning his critique of Urizen as Nobodaddy, "I see the face of my Heavenly Father he lays his Hand upon my Head & gives a blessing to all my works" (E697/K823).

[62] "Freud and the Future," in *Essays of Three Decades*, trans. H. T. Lowe-Porter (New York, 1947), p. 426.

[63] On the iconographic tradition, see Blunt, *The Art of William Blake*, p. 81 and pl. 49.

[64] See above, p. 209. The picture can even be interpreted (like pl. 96) as an "ecstatic union of male and female" (Mellor, *Blake's Human Form Divine*, p. 328), although that would exaggerate the value of a mode of sexuality that Blake claims we should rise above.

[65] As Mitchell observes, *Blake's Composite Art*, p. 214.

[66] *Freud and Philosophy*, p. 543.

27. *Jerusalem*, plate 99.

In much the same way Blake labors in *Jerusalem* to rehabilitate the idea of man's covenant with God. In its Old Testament form he can hardly approve of it, since it implies a legalistic agreement between creature and creator. "The blood of their Covenant" is a phrase of Moses applied to the ghastly sacrifices of the Daughters of Albion.[67] Addressing the Satanic Angel of the Divine Presence, Blake exclaims, "Thy Covenant built Hells Jail" (*EG*, E513/K754). In the picture *God Writing upon the Tables of the Covenant* Jehovah is clothed in white and has his back to us, writing the Law on the stones while angels in flames sound their trumpets and a tiny Moses huddles beneath. Jehovah's hair is blown to the left by the wind, exactly as in *The Ancient of Days*.[68] But the covenant must be transformed rather than renounced. "Mutual Sacrifice" is the new "Covenant/Of Jehovah: If you Forgive one-another, so shall Jehovah Forgive you" (*J* 61:23-25, E210/K694-695). These words of the angel to Mary the adulteress are generalized at the end of the poem when "the Mutual Covenant Divine" is established as "Forgiveness of Sins" (98:41, 45, E255/K746). Similarly in the late *Ghost of Abel* Jehovah opposes the unforgiving Elohim and then unites with him as the Elohim Jehovah "In Thy Covenant of the Forgiveness of Sins."[69]

In exploring the meaning of the divine as Elohim and Jehovah, Blake draws upon all the resources of symbols as available for manipulation by the artist who knows them to be symbols (as contrasted with the naïve believer who takes them for facts). Locke inveighed against the "absurdities" that arise from imagining God in human form: "How many even amongst us [Christians] will be found upon inquiry to fancy him in the shape of a man sitting in heaven?"[70] Blake says very differently in annotating Swedenborg, "Think of a white cloud

---

[67] *J* 67:1, E217/K704, echoing Exodus 24:8, and no doubt recalling the Christian reinterpretation of Hebrews 13:20 (see Stevenson, *Poems of Blake*, p. 770n). Moses is generally villainous in Blake's myth, and Blake would doubtless have been delighted by Freud's hypothesis in *Moses and Monotheism* that he was an Egyptian who "chose" the Chosen People, endowing them with a punitive Yahweh and with ritual circumcision.

[68] See the color reproduction in Paley, *William Blake*, pl. 32. Paley notes that in *The Woman Taken in Adultery* Christ bows before the woman and writes with his finger on the ground (as in John 8:3-9), "the New Dispensation's counterpart to the finger of God writing on the Tables of the Covenant" (p. 56; see pl. 81).

[69] E270/K781. In this work Blake contrasts a vengeful and Satanic Elohim with a forgiving Jehovah, drawing brilliantly on the Epistle to the Hebrews to suggest that mutual (rather than unilateral) forgiveness is the attribute of Christ. Elsewhere he identifies Cain iconographically with the Prodigal Son. See two essays by Leslie Tannenbaum: "Lord Byron in the Wilderness: Biblical Tradition in Byron's *Cain* and Blake's *The Ghost of Abel*," *Modern Philology*, 72 (1975), 350-364; and "Blake and the Iconography of Cain," in Essick and Pearce, pp. 23-34.

[70] *Essay*, II.xxxiii.17.

as being holy you cannot love it but think of a holy man within the cloud love springs up in your thought. for to think of holiness distinct from man is impossible to the affections. Thought alone can make monsters, but the affections cannot" (E593/K90). Urizen may concoct the hypothesis of a disembodied God, but Urizen himself is human, like the Son of Man on a "white cloud" in Revelation 14:14. In the *Book of Urizen* he is depicted in a full range of embodied forms, from the potent heavenly tyrant to the collapsed, fetal skeleton of the eighth plate. In Eternity he is the farmer who sows "the seed of eternal science" and who represents "Faith & certainty" rather than reasoning doubt.[71] Even at his fallen worst Urizen cannot be wholly dead, and gives "life & sense by his immortal power" to his engines of deceit (*FZ* 102:14, E360/K344). He does so in hope that "perhaps he might avert/His own despair" (102:21-22). What he must learn, instead of trying to dominate other elements of the self, is that he shares in its sickness.

> He could not take their fetters off for they grew from the soul
> Nor could he quench the fires for they flamd out from the heart
> Nor could he calm the Elements because himself was Subject.
> (*FZ* 71:1-3, E341/K315)

Every image of God is thus a symbolic expression of the human imagination, in which God resides. As Shelley put it in a remarkable passage,

> Prometheus
> Gave wisdom, which is strength, to Jupiter,
> And with this law alone, "Let man be free,"
> Clothed him with the dominion of wide Heaven.[72]

In classical lore the demiurge (or Angel of the Divine Presence, as Blake adapts the idea) imposes rigid fate upon men. In Shelley and Blake, bondage to Urizen/Jupiter is a consequence of *freedom*, of our freedom to invent him and willfully abase ourselves before him as Job does before his vengeful deity. It follows then that Urizen is a part of ourselves, an essential Zoa. This is why Blake agrees with the *philosophes*' attack on priestcraft while despising their attack on superstition. Even at its most repressive, religious faith expresses deep human impulses. Voltaire's confident manifesto, *Écrasez l'infâme*, is suicidal unless properly qualified; as it stands, it is a call to erase ourselves.

In just this way we must interpret the symbolism of Satan. When

---

[71] *Book of Ahania* 5:34, E88/K255; *FZ* 27:15, E311/K282.
[72] *Prometheus Unbound*, II.iv.43–46.

Blake calls him "The God of This World" in the poem "To the Accuser," he invokes a Gnostic conception.[73] He is the Accuser because
he is the self-created guilt which we can never hope to placate. In a
striking phrase Blake speaks of him as "the Mind of the Natural
Frame,"[74] or in other words the form that the fallen mind gives to itself. "Every Religion that Preaches Vengeance for Sin is the Religion
of the Enemy & Avenger, and not of the Forgiver of Sin, and their
God is Satan, Named by the Divine Name" (*J* 52, E199/K682). Similarly Blake says of the *Divine Comedy* that any book that preaches
vengeance is "of Satan the Accuser & Father of Hell" (E669/K785).

As in our examination of evil as privation, we have to recognize that
this Satan both is and is not real. Robinson reports, "We spoke of the
Devil And I observed that when a child I thought the Manichaean doctrine or that of two principles a rational one. He assented to this—and
in confirmation asserted that he did not believe in the *omnipotence* of
God—The language of the Bible on that subject is only poetical or allegorical. Yet soon after he denied that the natural world is any thing.
It is all nothing and Satan's empire is the empire of nothing" (*Blake
Records*, p. 316). The Emperor of Nothing is a superb conception; just
making a word of it turns it into *something*. It is nothing because "Error or Creation will be Burned Up . . . the Moment Men cease to behold it" (*VLJ*, E555/K617). Until they cease to behold it, it survives
because it is an illusion built upon reality, an imaginative perversion of
the true divine.

This idea was clear to Blake as early as *The Marriage of Heaven and
Hell*, in his often misunderstood pronouncement about Satan in
Paradise Lost. Since Satan is not heroic, the heroic figure depicted in
Paradise Lost cannot be the real Satan. Milton has displaced on to Satan
heroic qualities that actually belong to Christ, and has thereby emptied
Christ of meaning. Blake adds that "the Jehovah of the Bible [is] no
other than he [*deleted:* the Devil] who dwells in flaming fire. Know
that after Christs death, he became Jehovah" (E35/K150). In other
words, the true God, as in Boehme, dwells in fire as well as light,
whereas the Miltonic God dwells in blinding light while fire is reserved for the misnamed Satan. But a Jehovah who was *only* fiery
would be a disaster, and Blake writes in his notes for an allegorical

[73] In apocalyptic Christianity Satan was often described as the god of this *age*, but the
Almighty remained God of this *world*. Paul speaks of Satan as "the god of this age" (2
Cor. 4:4) and of "the archons of this age" (1 Cor. 2: 6-8). But only the Gnostics referred
to a Satanic god of this world (see Grant, *Gnosticism and Early Christianity*, pp. 175-176;
on p. 57 Grant observes that John calls Satan "the archon of this world" in several
places: 12:31, 14:30, 16:11).

[74] Annotations to Bacon (E615/K403).

painting, "God out of Christ is a Consuming Fire" (E669), implicitly correcting the Biblical text, "Our God is a consuming fire" (Heb. 12:29; see Deut. 4:24). The word "WRATH" appears in the upper right corner of Blake's picture and "MERCY" in the left.[75] These are Boehme's wrath and meekness, equivalent to Blake's wrath and pity, Rintrah and Palamabron. But Boehme held that God is to the Son as the speaker is to the word and as fire is to light.[76] Blake will not allow any such separation of functions: Jesus must *be* Jehovah. When they grow disjunct Jehovah becomes Satan and both wrath and mercy (Boehme's "meekness") become tools of the Female Will, as when the Shadow embraces Orc's fire "that he might lose his rage/And with it lose himself in meekness" (*FZ* 91:4–5, E395/K336). Blake calls instead upon "Jesus our Lord, who is the God of Fire and Lord of Love" (*J* 3, E144/K621). Meekness without wrath is only a cloak for exploitation—"Now the man Moses was very meek, above all the men which were upon the face of the earth" (Num. 12:3). The "Creeping Jesus" of traditional piety, Blake says roundly, is none other than the Antichrist (*EG*, E511/K750). That is why the mild and kindly Hayley can be allegorized as Satan in the opening section of *Milton*. The solution is not to cast him headlong from heaven as in *Paradise Lost* but to teach him, through forgiveness, to relinquish his accusatory role. "The Accusation shall be Forgiveness that he may be consumd in his own Shame."[77]

Blake's characteristic practice is thus to transform rather than to reject the traditional symbols. An orthodox reader would find nothing objectionable in the statement that "Satan & Adam & the whole World was Created by the Elohim" (*J* 27, E170/K649). The informed reader understands the statement in a radically different way: Adam is Man and God is Man, so that a separate creation of Satan and Adam (the limits of "opacity" and "contraction," as Blake frequently puts it) reflects a badly mistaken conception of what is real. The words remain the same but their symbolic value alters.

The same is true of the picture *The Fall of Man* (see fig. 7, p. 92). Satan appears twice, as the serpent entwined around the spiky Tree of Knowledge and as the youthful Lucifer at the bottom who is described in Blake's note: "SATAN now awakes Sin, Death, & Hell, to celebrate with him the birth of War & Misery" (E662/K441). And the Urizen-

---

[75] See the reproductions in Damon, *Blake Dictionary*, pl. 11, and Paley, *William Blake*, pl. 88. The picture illustrates Hervey's *Meditations Among the Tombs*.

[76] See Stoudt, *Sunrise to Eternity*, pp. 205–206.

[77] Annotations to Thornton, E658 (Keynes, K788, gives instead the deleted text "Let his Judgment be Forgiveness . . . "). Satan is "consumed" in the consuming fire of the false God; pl. 10 of *Milton* shows him in that fire.

God appears at both top and bottom: as "the Father indignant at the Fall" on his throne on high—in Urizen's pose on *America* 8—and as a bat-winged Death below who faces in the opposite direction, in a mirror image of the Father's gesture. The two figures are one. When Blake wrote *America* he thought that Orcian energy could vanquish Urizenic repression, and the pose of fiery Orc on plate 10 of that work echoes that of Urizen on plate 8. When he painted *The Fall of Man* he had thought more deeply about the meaning of the crucifixion, and his Jesus is now contrasted more subtly with the paternal God. "The SAVIOUR, while the Evil Angels are driven, gently conducts our first Parents out of Eden through a guard of Weeping Angels" (E662/ K441). The "INRI" of the cross appears above the Father's right hand, since it is really he who has crucified the Son, while angels with spear and sword hold up the bread and wine out of reach of two falling angels, Tantalus-like. Both the top and bottom of the picture are Urizenic caves, the former a cloudy cavern on high, the latter within the earth (and at the brink of the sea of time and space, in which an army with spears subsides—"When the stars threw down their spears"). In the middle is a pastoral scene in which the apple-hung Tree of Life awaits the return of Man when he shall be strong enough to recover what is his own.

When Jehovah is transformed into the true Divine Body, purged of Satanic distortions, his unreal form will disappear like the bat-winged shape in the picture for "To the Accuser," and in his regenerated form he can resume his role as Lucifer the son of the morning.

> Tho thou art Worshipd by the Names Divine
> Of Jesus & Jehovah: thou art still
> The Son of Morn in weary Nights decline
> The lost Travellers Dream under the Hill.
>
> (E266/K771)

In the cave of selfhood it does not matter which name is wrongly applied to Satan. Either as Jehovah or as Jesus he remains what he was. But when the traveler awakens, the state of Satan is dissipated into nothingness, and the positive elements of the symbol reorganize themselves around the true Christ.

Everything depends, therefore, on knowing how to interpret and use symbols. The point is made again on the eleventh plate of *Job* (see fig. 28). The terrifying God of Job's nightmare betrays his diabolical nature with his cloven hoof. An orthodox viewer, noticing this clue, would conclude that the picture shows Satan instead of God; Blake's meaning is more complex and interesting, that the orthodox God *is* Satan. The hovering posture reminds one of *Elohim Creating Adam*,

The triumphing of the wicked
is short, the joy of the hypocrite is
but for a moment
Satan himself is transformed into an Angel of Light & his Ministers into Ministers of Righteousness

My bones are pierced in me in the
night season & my sinews
take no rest

My skin is black upon me
& my bones are burned
with heat

11

With Dreams upon my bed thou scarest me & affrightest me
with Visions

Why do you persecute me as God & are not satisfied with my flesh. Oh that my words
were printed in a Book that they were graven with an iron pen & lead in the rock for ever
For I know that my Redeemer liveth & that he shall stand in the latter days upon
the Earth & after my skin destroy thou This body yet in my flesh shall I see God
whom I shall see for Myself and mine eyes shall behold & not Another tho consumed be my wrought Image
Who opposeth & exalteth himself above all that is called God or is Worshipped

W Blake invent & sculp

London Published as the Act directs March 8. 1825 by Will Blake N 3 Fountain Court Strand

Proof

28. *The Book of Job*, plate 11.

but here the serpent winds around Satan/God instead of Adam (just as
it did in *Satan Watching Adam and Eve*). Above the picture is the text
"Satan himself is transformed into an Angel of Light" (2 Cor. 11:14).
This Satan, the consolidation of error, is the agent by whom Job is
awakened to illumination, and the true Lucifer or "morning star" will
later be revealed as Jesus, as anticipated by the quotation of Job 19:25,
"For I know that my Redeemer liveth."[78] Job is trapped like Albion in

[78] On Satan and illumination, see Lindberg, *William Blake's Illustrations* . . . , p. 61; on

nightmare, but the symbols of truth shine through the symbols of error, and presage the union with Jesus that will bring the new dawn.

The main outlines of Blake's Jesus have been repeatedly touched upon in this book: he is the universal Form in whom all particulars are unified, the universal Imagination in whom we perceive, and the divine principle that is at once present in our deepest selves and able to enter us in order to save us. As the paternal God is associated with Urizen, so the imaginative Jesus is, for obvious reasons, associated with Los. But this leaves unexplained his incarnation and crucifixion in Luvah, an idea upon which Blake places special emphasis, since he repeatedly describes it as the action that frees man from bondage and makes apocalypse possible.

In dramatizing the activity of God-as-Jesus in the Incarnation and Crucifixion, Blake returns to the subject of the first great Christian controversies, which focused on the nature of the Trinity. The issues can seem sterile or hyperintellectual only to an age that has forgotten their philosophical significance: the attempt to explain the connection between a good God and the world of sin and suffering. In Jesus—in the mystery of God made man—Christian doctrine sought to bridge the gap between the immanent and the transcendent. And Blake too must seek his solution there, for otherwise he is left without the answers his system was supposed to provide: on the one hand a wholly immanent God and therefore no explanation for the fact of alienation, or on the other hand a wholly transcendent God and the concomitant burden of sin and guilt.

Blake thus cannot do without the concepts to which the names of God and Jesus were traditionally attached. As Tillich comments, "If one finds that a green light is not so expedient as perhaps a blue light (this is not true, but it could be true) then we simply put on a blue light, and nothing is changed. But a symbolic word (such as the word 'God') cannot be replaced. No symbol can be replaced when used in its special function."[79] Of course Blake holds that orthodox Christianity has grossly misconceived the meaning of its own symbols, worshipping Satan under the divine names of Jehovah and Jesus. But he continues to need the *concepts* of God and Jesus. In the Enlightenment confrontation with existential isolation, skeptics like Hume and Diderot surveyed the threat of meaninglessness, but in their own lives con-

---

Jesus as the morning star, see Nelms, "Text and Design in . . . *Job*," p. 338.

[79] Paul Tillich, *Theology of Culture* (New York, 1964), p. 58.

tinued to manifest a conviction that the self was stable and reliable. Blake is concerned as they never were with the total breakdown of the self and the threat of annihilation. To put the self together again he needs an agency which is in a real sense transcendent, because without "the Saviour Even Jesus" (*FZ* 100:10, E358/K342) the fall into formlessness would have no end.

Since Blake is interested in Jesus as a saving symbol and as the imaginative basis of symbolism, his attention to the historical Jesus is intermittent and not really central to his myth. There is no question but that he deeply admired Jesus' energy: "Jesus was all virtue, and acted from impulse, not from rules."[80] Admiration of a Jesus who preached spontaneity and love was a not uncommon reaction to orthodoxy in Blake's era; it is found, for instance, in the young Hegel and Hölderlin. But if Blake were pressed to state *who* the historical Jesus was, I believe he would have called him a prophet like Ezekiel or Milton, not the unique Son of God. The Jehovah Elohim comforts Jerusalem with a vision of Mary being forgiven for adultery: the historical Jesus was the product of a sexual union, not of virgin birth. But as he came to understand the symbolic meaning of his role, he repudiated sonship:

> No Earthly Parents I confess
> I am doing my Fathers business.[81]

Physically, Jesus had human parents, Mary (mother of his mortal part) and her unnamed lover. Spiritually, he had no earthly parents at all. This Jesus was distinct from God just as any embodied mortal is, "Humble to God Haughty to Man" (E511/K750). The "Jesus" of Blake's myth is the spiritual principle in which the historical Jesus participated, not a literally resurrected version of him. Blake often refers to the empty tomb as an emblem of the irrelevance of the physical body, but he never says anything about Christ's reappearance to his followers (described in the Gospels as inviting the disciples to touch his limbs, eating a fish, and so on).

The Jesus whom Blake venerates is not the carpenter's son of Nazareth but a vision of the imagination, which each person must see as an embodiment of his own best qualities.

> The Vision of Christ that thou dost see
> Is my Visions Greatest Enemy

[80] *MHH*, E42/K158. See Frye's eloquent discussion of this point, *Fearful Symmetry*, pp. 78–84.

[81] *EG*, E510/K750. Blake alters his source, "Wist ye not that I must be about my Father's business?" (Luke 2:49). Cf. "What have I to do with thee?" in "To Tirzah" (E30/K220).

Thine has a great hook nose like thine
Mine has a snub nose like to mine.[82]

And the historical Jesus, as distinct from the universal Form, was perfectly capable of error, indeed of an Orcian energy that got out of hand. In 1825 Blake told Robinson that Christ "was wrong in suffering himself to be crucified. He should not have attacked the government; he had no business with such matters." And when Robinson protested that since Christ was God he ought not to be criticized, Blake retorted, "He was not then become the father" (*Blake Records*, p. 311). Only by undergoing some sort of purification, perhaps of the kind that Milton experiences in his turn when Christ enters him in *Milton*, could the historical Jesus become fully divine. "We are all coexistent with God," Blake told Robinson, "Members of the Divine Body"; and when asked about the divinity of Jesus he replied, "He is the only God," and added, "And so am I and so are you" (*Blake Records*, p. 310).

These pronouncements, and others like them, bear an evident similarity to the beliefs of the left-wing Protestants known as antinomians, who held that man is fully identified with Christ who has washed away all sin. The insistence that God really became and becomes man is common to various forms of Christian Platonism.[83] The antinomians asserted it so literally that they made themselves a joke as well as a nuisance. Sometimes their formulations sound very Blakean indeed, like the Ranter claim that "man cannot either know God, or believe in God, or pray to God, but it is God in man that knoweth himself, believeth in himself, and prayeth to himself," or Henry Nicholas' assertion that "he is godded with God and co-deified with him, and that God is hominified with him."[84] But statements like these refer to the saving power of grace, not to man's literal and complete identity with God, which was asserted only by fringe fanatics like the unhappy James Naylor.[85] Despite their claims of direct experience of God, most

[82] *EG*, E516/K748. Cf. the remark in the notebook, "I always thought that Jesus Christ was a Snubby or I should not have worshipd him if I had thought he had been one of those long spindle nosed rascals" (E673/K555).

[83] "The deification of man is one of the most thoroughly Greek ideas espoused by the Cambridge Platonists. Its infrequent appearances in the West never managed to overcome the opposition of St. Augustine, and it was in time stamped to death by Calvin" (C. A. Patrides, *The Cambridge Platonists*, p. 19).

[84] John Holland Porter, *The Smoke of the Bottomless Pit* (1651), p. 4; Nicholas (leader of the Continental Familists) as described by Ephraim Pagitt in *Heresiography* (1645), p. 77; both quoted by A. L. Morton, *The Everlasting Gospel*, in the course of pointing out various parallels with Blake.

[85] As Hume took some glee in recounting in his *History of England*, Naylor thought himself Christ and carried out the role in detail, for instance by raising a person from the

antinomians continued to hold that God was very different from man. "I am a spirit though a low one," a typical statement runs, "and God is a spirit, even the highest one, and God is the fountain of this spirit."[86]

Blake too calls the Holy Ghost an "intellectual fountain," but are we sure what he means by it?

> Go, tell them that the Worship of God, is honouring his gifts
> In other men: & loving the greatest men best, each according
> To his Genius: which is the Holy Ghost in Man; there is no other
> God, than that God who is the intellectual fountain of Humanity.
> (J 91:7-10, E248/K738)

The final statement, though usually interpreted as meaning "There is no God but man," might well mean "there is no God other than the one who inspires imagination"—that is, no Nobodaddy, no insane tyrant on high, but nevertheless a God who remains more than man. Such a concept is wholly consistent with the Swedenborgian manifesto that Blake and his wife signed in 1789:

> VIII. That it is the opinion of this Conference, that all Faith and Worship directed to any other, than to the one God Jesus Christ in his Divine Humanity, being directed to a God invisible and incomprehensible, have a direct tendency to overturn the Holy Word, and to destroy everything spiritual in the Church. . . .
> X. That it is the opinion of this Conference, that the Lord and Saviour Jesus Christ is the only God of Heaven and Earth, and that his Humanity is Divine. . . .[87]

Such a "Divine Humanity" must be genuinely divine as well as human.

There need be nothing unorthodox in all of this; Hopkins writes, "I

---

dead and by being ministered unto by women. George Fox, like Naylor a Quaker, scandalized the orthodox by insisting that man was without sin in Christ, but was careful to repudiate Naylor.

[86] Francis Rous, *Mysticall Marriage* (1653), p. 2, quoted by Gertrude Huehns, *Antinomianism in English History* (London, 1951), p. 51. Similarly Eckhart could say that "the eye by which I see God is the same as the eye by which God sees me," but when charged with heresy on a similar point could fall back on the metaphor of Christ and his members: "If this should be taken to mean that I am God, this is false; but if it should be taken to mean that I am God, as being a member of him, it is true, as Augustine frequently says" (*Meister Eckhart: A Modern Translation*, trans. Raymond B. Blakney [New York, 1941], Sermon 23 and the *Defense*, pp. 206, 303).

[87] Quoted by J. G. Davies, *The Theology of William Blake* (Oxford, 1948), pp. 34-35. The complete list of resolutions is summarized in *Blake Records*, pp. 35-37. See also Bindman, *Blake as an Artist*, pp. 49-50, on Robert Hindmarsh's doctrine of God as Christ.

am all at once what Christ is, since he was what I am.''[88] Unor-
thodoxy enters rather in the denial of the distinct persons of the Trinity, and in the peculiar impersonality that seems to characterize Blake's
Jesus. The orthodox maintain that the man who died on the cross *was*
the Christ who reigns at the right hand of God. Blake holds only that
he participated, as we all do, in the divine, and his concept of the divine is thus humanized but not personified. All the same, the appeals
to Jesus in Blake's writings reflect religious urgency as well as
mythopoeic inventiveness. ''And now let me finish with assuring you
that Tho I have been very unhappy I am so no longer I am again
Emergd into the light of Day I still & shall to Eternity Embrace Christianity and Adore him who is the Express image of God'' (E691/
K815). This faith is not confined to private letters; Blake states plainly
at the beginning of *Jerusalem* that he is ''perhaps the most sinful of
men'' but that ''the Spirit of Jesus is continual forgiveness of Sin,'' so
that one must not wait to be righteous in order to enter ''the Saviours
kingdom, the Divine Body'' (E144/K621). The Divine Body is what
we enter when Jesus descends to us; it is not what we merely are.
Swinburne put it very well: ''As God is the unfallen part of man, man
the fallen part of God, God must needs be (not more than man, but
assuredly) more than the qualities of man.''[89]

In order to explain how this God enters into man and saves him,
Blake decided to reconstruct the central Christian symbols of Incarnation and Crucifixion. It may be that these symbols are inseparable
from Bethlehem and Calvary and that the reconstruction finally fails.
But Blake thought it essential to try, and his treatment of these two
themes is highly original because it implies, to put it simply, that *the
incarnation is the crucifixion*.

At the beginning of *Milton* Blake asks the Daughters of Beulah to
tell how Jesus, ''the image of the Invisible God,'' became the prey of
the False Tongue and its world of error, ''a curse, an offering, and an
atonement,/For Death Eternal in the heavens of Albion'' (2:12-14,
E95/K481). This is very far from the orthodox atonement that
Boehme (for instance) accepts, in which ''Christ, with his great love
and humility in our assumed humanity in our fiery burning angry
soul, changed his Father's anger into such great mercy and compassion, that the divine righteousness in the anger ceased and departed
from our souls.''[90] According to orthodox theology we suffer by our

[88] ''That Nature is a Heraclitean Fire.'' ''I live,'' says Paul, ''yet not I, but Christ liveth
in me'' (Gal. 2:20).
[89] *William Blake*, p. 155.
[90] *Mysterium Magnum*, ch. 61, p. 576. On Blake's rejection of the Atonement, see Flor-

own fault for the sin of Adam, both collectively as his descendants and individually as sinners in bondage to Satan. Election and grace represent the mercy of God, not a cruel rejection of those who are not elected; as Pascal says, we should be surprised that any are elected, not that many are reprobate.[91] Christ is then the only possible agent of our salvation. By becoming man he takes our guilt upon himself, with all the implications that Christians deduced from the Suffering Servant of Isaiah 53.

But one is then confronted with the difficulties that Milton gets entangled in, the incongruity and unpleasantness of a colloquy in heaven in which the Father asks for volunteers to save man and the Son, although guiltless, offers to incur guilt by incarnation into the race of Adam. Blake avoids this theology both by defining sin as error and by rejecting the orthodox Trinity. The Reverend Jacob Duché, a clergyman and Swedenborgian sympathizer whom Blake may well have known, wrote to Thomas Paine in 1767, "I never could understand the doctrine of the Trinity, & had an irreconciliable aversion to the Systematical Notion of atonement & satisfaction. A wrathfull God whose anger could only be appeased by the blood of His own Son pour'd out in behalf of Sinners allways appear'd to me next to blasphemous."[92] Blake told Robinson, "It is a horrible doctrine—If another man pay your debt I do not forgive it" (*Blake Records*, p. 337).

In the later prophecies, accordingly, the Atonement is repudiated, but the theology that exacts it is grimly recognized. Let us look again at the passage about the False Tongue:

Tell also of the False Tongue! vegetated
Beneath your land of shadows: of its sacrifices, and
Its offerings; even till Jesus, the image of the Invisible God
Became its prey; a curse, an offering, and an atonement,
For Death Eternal in the heavens of Albion, & before the Gates
Of Jerusalem his Emanation, in the heavens beneath Beulah.
(*M* 2:10-15, E95/K481)

---

ence Sandler, "The Iconoclastic Enterprise: Blake's Critique of 'Milton's Religion'," *Blake Studies*, 5 (1972), 13-57.

[91] "La justice envers les réprouvés est moins énorme et doit moins choquer que la miséricorde envers les élus" (*Pensées*, no. 343 [Lafuma], 233 [Brunschvicg]). For a highly ironic Blakean allusion to election, see the passage in which the Elect say, "We behold it is of Divine/Mercy alone! of Free Gift and Election that we live" (*M* 13:32-33, E106/K494).

[92] Letter of 18 Dec. 1767, quoted by Désirée Hirst, *Hidden Riches: Traditional Symbolism from the Renaissance to Blake* (London, 1964), p. 11. Duché was active in radical

The False Tongue is the emblem of the fallen Tharmas in the vegetative realm "beneath Beulah." Jesus as ransom or atonement is the "prey" of this corrupted world, a grisly sacrifice like those of the Aztecs or Druids. But Jesus is "the image of the Invisible God" only in a fallen world that refuses to see the ever-visible God. This is the temporary condition ironically described as "Death Eternal." In fact there is no death in Blake's myth, only sleep, and eternal death is therefore an illusory state into which Jesus descends. This speech begins by invoking the Daughters of Beulah, well-meaning but handicapped muses; one purpose of the poem *Milton* will be to correct their mistaken vision. Los in *Jerusalem* has the true perspective when Albion asks, "Will none accompany me in my death? or be a Ransom for me/In that dark Valley?"

> Los answerd, troubled: and his soul was rent in twain:
> Must the Wise die for an Atonement? does Mercy endure
>   Atonement?
> No! It is Moral Severity, & destroys Mercy in its Victim.
>   (*J* 35:19-26, E179/K666)

Only those languishing in error will appeal, as the deluded Sons of Albion do, to the "Sacrifice of the Lamb/And of his children, before sinful Jerusalem" (*J* 18:27-28, E162/K640).

The orthodox doctrine, Blake clearly says, is an appalling and futile form of revenge, a suicide on the cross followed by punitive retribution in a literal rather than imaginative Last Judgment. So a spectral voice suggests:

> . . . Thy Revenge abroad display
> In terrors at the Last Judgment day
> Gods Mercy & Long Suffering
> Is but the Sinner to Judgment to bring
> Thou on the Cross for them shalt pray
> And take Revenge at the Last Day.
>   (*EG*, E512/K750-751)

The indignant answer is that the fallen world does not deserve to be prayed for:

---

circles and in 1776 was chaplain to the American Congress. It is very possible that Blake attended meetings of the Theosophical Society that became the Swedenborgian New Church, as his friends Sharp and Flaxman are known to have done. If so, he had direct contact with Duché (see John Howard, "An Audience for *The Marriage of Heaven and Hell*," *Blake Studies*, 3 [1970], 21-23).

> Jesus replied & thunders hurld
> I never will Pray for the World.

The fallen body is a veil or husk which can be thrown off at will, and the Crucifixion thereby loses its ultimate significance.

> Nail his neck to the Cross nail it with a nail
> Nail his neck to the Cross ye all have power over his tail
>
> (E509/K557)

The neck and tail of Jesus as Orc-serpent may be injured with the horrible tools of "Cross & Nails & Thorns & Spear" (*J* 89:1, E245/K734), but the Crucifixion in this sense is only significant for provoking the malice of the fallen world. It has no power over Christ, and it certainly cannot implicate him in a suicidal sacrifice that substitutes revenge for mercy and mutual forgiveness.

The Crucifixion is therefore the blasphemous symbol of a Satanic world that makes a murdered God the symbol of moral repression.

> Jehovahs Finger Wrote the Law
> Then Wept! then rose in Zeal & Awe
> And the Dead Corpse from Sinais heat
> Buried beneath his Mercy Seat
> O Christians Christians! tell me Why
> You rear it on your Altars high[93]

But like all Satanic symbols in Blake, this one parodies something divine; it is not made up out of the whole cloth. For if that were the case, then Blake would have no need of the Christian myth at all, and would not insist on calling himself a Christian. As Duché goes on to say, Christ's death is a symbolic death in which all men must participate:

> I see plainly that there is no other Road to Heaven, but that which was trod by Jesus Christ himself, the same process must every Individual of our fallen race pass thro' before we can ascend with him to the Heaven of Heavens—A painfull process 'tis True,—self denial, mortification, total contempt of the World, and death of the outward Life, are the only method by which we are to be divested of our fallen, and clothed with our redeemed Life. The purifying fire, light & spirit of Heaven, must consume the Animal Nature and change it into a cloud of Glory, a white robe & a house not built with hands. This new body can only be imparted to us, by an ema-

[93] *For the Sexes*, E256/K761.

287

nation from the heavenly flesh and blood of Jesus and thus alone it is
he that atones & satisfies & appeases a wrath in us and not in the
Everblessed God of Love.[94]

Every word of this could have been written as commentary on Blake.
Even the appeal for self-denial, which might seem incompatible with
The Marriage of Heaven and Hell, is fully confirmed by the later Blake
in his campaign against Nature and the selfhood: "Jesus is the bright
Preacher of Life/Creating Nature from this fiery Law,/By self-denial &
forgiveness of Sin" (*J* 77:21-23, E230/K718).

The "veil" of Moses of which Paul speaks (2 Cor. 3:13 ff.) is the veil
of Vala, fallen nature and natural religion, to be replaced by the garment of Jerusalem.

> In Great Eternity, every particular Form gives forth or Emanates
> Its own peculiar Light, & the Form is the Divine Vision
> And the Light is his Garment. This is Jerusalem in every Man. . . .
>
> (*J* 54:1-3, E201/K684)

It is for this reason that incarnation is crucifixion: by entering the
fallen body Jesus becomes the prey of the Satanic Law and is nailed
upon the cross. But since he is Jesus—the imaginative principle, the
universal Form—he gives to all men, participating in his action, the
power to shed the material body and reenter Great Eternity. Thus
while Blake retains the story of the historical Jesus, he turns Jesus into
a function or principle rather than the unique God-Man.

> With one accord the Starry Eight became
> One Man Jesus the Saviour, wonderful! round his limbs
> The Clouds of Ololon folded as a Garment dipped in blood
> Written within & without in woven letters: & the Writing
> Is the Divine Revelation in the Litteral expression:
> A Garment of War, I heard it namd the Woof of Six Thousand
>   Years.
>
> (*M* 42:10-15, E142/K534)

Blake's Jesus resembles the saved savior, the *salvator salvandus* of Gnosticism, who enters the fallen world to rescue the lost parts of his disintegrated self.[95] And in joining with Milton to complete the Eight he
fulfills a function similar to that of the Gnostic Ogdoad, the principle
that joins and completes the fallen Heptad.[96] To do so he must de-

---

[94] Quoted by Hirst, *Hidden Riches*, pp. 11-12.

[95] See Jonas, *The Gnostic Religion*, pp. 78-79, 127-128.

[96] The relations between Albion, Jesus, and the Eternals are among the most mysterious in Blake's myth. At one point the Eternals say, "The Eternal Man/Walketh among

scend into the body, or, in Blake's terms here, accept a garment that is woven by the female, covered with writing, and dipped in blood. We have here a complex symbol of incarnation and crucifixion at once, and the reference to revelation "in the Litteral expression" points further to the symbolic meaning of religious myth.

The Crucifixion is implicit in the Incarnation, in Christ's entry into the world of matter, born to the virgin mother of a mystery religion.

> A Vegetated Christ & a Virgin Eve, are the Hermaphroditic
> Blasphemy, by his Maternal Birth he is that Evil-One
> And his Maternal Humanity must be put off Eternally
> Lest the Sexual Generation swallow up Regeneration
> Come Lord Jesus take on thee the Satanic Body of Holiness.
> (J 90:34-38, E247/K736-737)

The hermaphrodite is the appalling union of Satan and Rahab, a hideous parody of the Edenic androgyny, doubling its sexual organs instead of casting them away. In Milton's epics Satan and Jesus are the great antagonists, and Jesus becomes man without ever sinning. Blake denies that such a doctrine has any meaning. If Jesus becomes man he must become what man is, which includes sinfulness, whatever that may mean. And if the fallen world is Satanic then he must enter into the state of Satan.

The implications of the myth are developed with great conciseness in the eighth Night of *The Four Zoas*. Rahab kills the Lamb of God with her knife of flint and the Daughters of Beulah wipe his feet with their hair, like Mary the sister of Lazarus (*FZ* 113:32-37, E362/K347). The Daughters then implore the Lamb of God to "come quickly" (104:17, echoing Rev. 22:20). The irony is that his coming is already ensured by the fact that the females have woven human bodies: there is no Second Coming as contrasted with the first, and incarnation means crucifixion. This is a symbolic act that must be repeated "time after time," as Los goes on to tell Enitharmon, so that the vegetative body may be left behind.

> Los said to Enitharmon, Pitying I saw

---

us, calling us his Brothers & his Friends" (J 55:9-10, E202/K686). In *Milton* the Family Divine appear "as One Man even Jesus" (21:58, E115/K505). Perhaps the metaphor of brotherhood implies that Albion is, as a repentant Urizen calls him, the "brother of Jesus" (*FZ* 123:25, E378/K364). At all events he needs Jesus to save him, for in the lines that follow, echoing Luke 21:27, the Son of Man descends in a cloud "with power and great Glory" (123:28). Perhaps the best way to summarize Jesus' role would be to say that he is both *primus inter pares* among the Eternals and also present in all of them at once.

Pitying the Lamb of God Descended thro Jerusalems gates
To put off Mystery time after time & as a Man
Is born on Earth so was he born of Fair Jerusalem
In mysterys woven mantle & in the Robes of Luvah.
He stood in fair Jerusalem to awake up into Eden
The fallen Man but first to Give his vegetated body
To be cut off & separated that the Spiritual body may be Reveald.

(104:31-38, E363/K348)

From another point of view the Savior has himself formed woman from the body of Adam, the limit of contraction, so that he may "be born Man to redeem" (*J* 42:32-34, E187/K670). Birth is crucifixion; the female is both the "fair Jerusalem" who gives birth and the cruel Rahab who kills her son, and Jesus is the saving principle that transforms generation into regeneration, eternally putting off "his Maternal Humanity" (*J* 90:36, E247/K737).

The Crucifixion has a dual significance, like every Blakean symbol. To fallen vision it represents victory over the divine, while to spiritual vision it is the transformation of nature by the divine.

And thus with wrath he did subdue
The Serpent Bulk of Natures dross
Till he had naild it to the Cross
He took on Sin in the Virgins Womb
And put it off on the Cross & Tomb
To be Worshipd by the Church of Rome

(*EG*, E515/K749)

The Roman church—the Whore of Babylon of Reformation polemic—mistakes the death of Orc for that of Jesus-in-Luvah, and worships a Jesus subdued by the triple whore Rahab/Vala/Tirzah (with the Virgin Mary as their special avatar) instead of perceiving that it is he who has subdued them. Having put on the serpent body of materiality, he now removes it, and it is he who nails it to the cross.

Lucifer, the first Eye of God, "refusd to die for Satan & in pride he forsook his charge," whereas Jesus, the seventh Eye, "Came & Died willing beneath Tirzah & Rahab" (*FZ* 115:43, 50, E366/K351). The Incarnation is a state through which Jesus passes in order to redeem fallen nature:

Jesus replied, I am the Resurrection and the Life.
I Die & pass the limits of possibility, as it appears
To individual perception. Luvah must be Created
And Vala; for I cannot leave them in the gnawing Grave.

(*J* 62:18-21, E211/K696)

The Jesus who redeems nature raises "Lazarus who is the Vehicular Body of Albion the Redeemd" (*M* 24:27, E119/K508). And Lazarus or Man participates in Jesus through visionary belief: "The Saviour mild & gentle bent over the corse of Death/Saying If ye will Believe your Brother shall rise again" (*FZ* 56:17-18, E331/K304, echoing John 11:25, 40). The opposite of belief is error and doubt, and the consequence of error is the fallen world. When man believes he will arise from the Fall; thus Blake's Jesus both calls for and embodies the eternal life of vision. Very much as in the heretical Christology of Origen, Blake's Jesus can be seen as a function or principle that "becomes" other individuals in order to save them.[97] Such a theology is unacceptable to orthodox Christianity, and Origen was roundly condemned in the Fifteen Anathemas of the Second Council of Constantinople. Yet he must have felt that he was rescuing Christianity, not subverting it; so also with Blake.

Such is the theory. As always, Blake's persistent dualism makes it hard to make complete sense of the theory, to accept the Incarnation into the body of death as more than metaphor. In contrast with Gnostic and other ancient systems, Christianity was remarkable for insisting on incarnation rather than embodiment: Christ was born a man, rather than temporarily inhabiting a human body as the deities of other faiths were said to do. The Fourth Gospel is often said to exhibit Platonic and Gnostic influence, but it is unequivocal on this point: "The Word was made flesh, and dwelt among us" (John 1:14). But in Blake the "Body of Death" is woven by the dissociated Emanation, so that it is hard to avoid the conclusion that it is something external that is draped, like Luvah's robes, around Christ: "For then the Body of Death was perfected in hypocritic holiness,/Around the Lamb, a Female Tabernacle woven in Cathedrons Looms" (*M* 13:25-26, E106/K494). Nonetheless, the orthodox often betray the same tendency, responding to an instinctive Platonism that refuses to imagine God as really being physical. The faithful sing in Wesley's Christmas hymn,

Veiled in flesh the Godhead see;

---

[97] According to Origen Christ is equal, not superior, to the other rational beings created by God, but after the Fall is the only one to preserve unimpaired the ontological status of *Nous*, mind (what Blake calls "vision" or "imagination" or sometimes "intellect"). He then enters into the various forms—Blake would say "states"—of fallen existence in order to restore the lost unity. In this theology, as Jonas comments, Christ "is a function rather than a unique event," and his death is an instance of "divine pedagogy" that inspires the individual to act rather than an expiatory atonement ("Origen's Metaphysics of Free Will, Fall, and Salvation: A 'Divine Comedy' of the Universe," *Philosophical Essays*, pp. 321-323).

Hail the incarnate Deity.[98]

There is no need to pursue the point, since the ambiguity of the body in Blake has been treated already. At any rate, his Jesus fully enters that body, whatever its status may be, and he does so not once but "time after time" (*FZ* 104:33, E363/K347).

A remarkable poem in the preface to the second chapter of *Jerusalem* opens with an invocation of the rural scenes of Blake's boyhood, moves to a lament for victims of legal tyranny and war, and then invokes the Satanic body into which Jesus descends:

> He [Satan] witherd up the Human Form,
> By laws of sacrifice for sin:
>   Till it became a Mortal Worm:
> But O! translucent all within.
>
>   The Divine Vision still was seen
> Still was the Human Form, Divine
>   Weeping in weak & mortal clay
> O Jesus still the Form was thine.
>
>   And thine the Human Face & thine
> The Human Hands & Feet & Breath
>   Entering thro' the Gates of Birth
> And passing thro' the Gates of Death
>
>   And O thou Lamb of God, whom I
> Slew in my dark self-righteous pride:
>   Art thou return'd to Albions Land!
> And is Jerusalem thy Bride?
>
>   Come to my arms & never more
> Depart; but dwell for ever here:
>   Create my Spirit to thy Love:
> Subdue my Spectre to thy Fear.
>
>   (E171/K651)

In this moving lyric Blake confesses, just as any orthodox homilist might, that *he himself* in his pride is one of the crucifiers. That is to say, Blake is not identified with Jesus but with the Satanic Accuser who has murdered him in the name of morality. Jesus must come to Blake, must dwell in his arms, must create religious love and fear. And in numerous places Blake states clearly that Jesus is distinct from any individual person.[99]

[98] "Hark! the herald angels sing."
[99] This is evidently true in Blake's own experience, as he testifies in the "vision of

Jesus is the divine principle that reconstructs and liberates Lucifer, the Elohim, Jehovah, and the other Eyes of God. The Gospel is the imaginative expression of the true Jesus, while the Moral Law is the weapon wrenched from it by the Accuser, who employs it in a futile attempt to overcome the body of clay:

> When Satan first the black bow bent
> And the Moral Law from the Gospel rent
> He forgd the Law into a Sword
> And spilld the blood of mercys Lord.
> (*J* 52:17-20, E200/K683)

The Crucifixion is therefore not the great goal of the divine plan, the purpose for which the Incarnation took place, the fulfillment that makes the fall itself a *felix culpa*. Rather, it is the inescapable result of incarnation in the mortal worm—"Ye all have power over his tail"— and it is horrible and Satanic, not positive. The mingled imagery of Tyburn and Calvary reminds us that crucifixions recur as often as there are public executions.[100] Blake invests the cross with its original meaning: instead of accepting it as a pious sign, he returns it to its full status as a symbol. A modern equivalent would be the gas chamber or electric chair; for Blake it is Tyburn's "Fatal Tree" (*J* 27:29, E170/K650).

The Crucifixion has for Blake an even richer sense of paradox than it does in conventional theology, in which Christ has died so that all men may live. In Blake's myth Christ enters the Satanic body of death so that Satan may kill him and Satan (who is the real serpent) may thereby die. The Crucifixion is an aspect of the Last Judgment, not a historical prelude to it. "Satan is seen falling headlong wound round by the tail of the serpent whose bulk naild to the Cross round which he wreathes is falling into the Abyss. Sin is also represented as a female bound in one of the Serpents folds surrounded by her fiends. Death is

---

light" poem (see above, pp. 45 ff.), in which Jesus receives him as a little child even while Blake's sacrificial attributes (the ram horned with gold) assimilate him to the Savior. Jesus says in *Jerusalem* that he "passes the limits of possibility, as it appears/To individual perception" (*J* 62:19-20, E211/K696). The picture on Pl. 62 shows a gigantic suffering Luvah (compare the very different but analogous picture of Christ the Vine, fig. 1, p. 32). As Erdman remarks, the tiny Blake figure at the bottom can only see the feet of this giant form (*The Illuminated Blake*, p. 341). Later on Los declares that "No Individual ought to appropriate to Himself" the universal characteristics of Jesus, or indeed of any other symbolic figure (*J* 90:28, E247/K736).

[100] See *M* 4:21-22, E97/K484. Howard comments on the relation of Tyburn's cruelty to a series of "atonements" by Charles I and Cromwell: "The historical sequence suggests that atonement or retribution becomes an endless process of sacrifice" (*Blake's Milton*, p. 266).

Chaind to the Cross & Time falls together with death" (*VLJ*, E546/
K606). The same idea is apparent in *Michael Foretells the Crucifixion* (see
fig. 8, p. 108) in which the serpent's head is nailed through, together
with Jesus's feet, while Eve lies asleep in a sort of hollow in the earth,
and Michael—in *Paradise Lost* a prophet of truth—looks suspiciously
like the Roman soldier who pierced Christ's side with his spear.[101]

Just as incarnation means taking on a body in the womb of the
female, so it means entering into Orc, the fallen form of Luvah, in the
world of phallic sexuality.

> The State namd Satan never can be redeemd in all Eternity
> But when Luvah in Orc became a Serpent he descended into
> That State calld Satan. . . .
> (FZ 115:25-27, E366/K351)

Ordinarily Satan is a manifestation of the fallen Urizen, but since he
presides over the material world it is equally true to say that "Satan is
the Spectre of Orc & Orc is the generate Luvah" (*M* 29:34, E126/
K517). Nietzsche said sarcastically, "We are most dishonourable towards our God: he is not *permitted* to sin (*er darf nicht sündigen*)."[102] But
in Blake "Christ took on Sin in the Virgins Womb, & put it off on the
Cross" (*M* 5:3, E97/K484). Mary was not free from sin and neither
was her son, but he "put it off" on the cross in the symbolic death that
proved the insubstantiality of the body. Sin, like Satan, is a state to be
transcended.

> Satan is the State of Death, & not a Human existence:
> But Luvah is named Satan, because he has enterd that State.
> A World where Man is by Nature the enemy of Man
> Because the Evil is Created into a State, that Men
> May be deliverd time after time evermore. Amen.
> (J 49:67-71, E197/K680)

If "the state calld Luvah should cease" then man would indeed be consigned to eternal death. Jesus becomes Luvah so that man may live.

> For the Divine Lamb Even Jesus who is the Divine Vision
> Permitted all lest Man should fall into Eternal Death
> For when Luvah sunk down himself put on the robes of blood

---

[101] As Wagenknecht suggests, *Blake's Night*, p. 179.

[102] *Beyond Good and Evil*, IV.65a, in *The Philosophy of Nietzsche*, p. 451. Pauline theology is much troubled by this problem and struggles in various ways to resolve it, for
instance in the assertion that God has made Christ "to be sin for us, who knew no sin"
(2 Cor. 5:21; in the New English Bible, "Christ was innocent of sin, and yet for our sake
God made him one with the sinfulness of man").

> Lest the state calld Luvah should cease. & the Divine Vision
> Walked in robes of blood till he who slept should awake.
> (FZ 33:11-15, E315/K287)

In developing the image of Luvah's robes of blood, which he inserted at numerous places in the manuscript of *The Four Zoas*, Blake sought to convey a complex sense of incarnation as both crucifixion and apocalypse. The most obvious source is Isaiah 63:3, "I will tread them in mine anger, and trample them in my fury; and their blood shall be sprinkled upon my garments, and I will stain all my raiment." The Crucifixion is further suggested by the "scarlet robe" in which Christ was mocked (Matt. 27:28). The blood is symbolic at once of life and death:

> The arrows flew from cloudy bow all day, till blood
> From east to west flowd like the human veins in rivers
> Of life upon the plains of death & valleys of despair.
> (FZ 92:6-8, E396/K337)

Fallen life is a landscape of death. Immediately after this passage comes the crucifixion of Luvah.

In his condition as the fallen and ruddy Orc, Luvah is bloody because he is the sexual energy that drives the life that is eternal death. In the apocalyptic wine-presses the "Human grapes" endure

> The cruel joys of Luvahs Daughters lacerating with knives
> And whips their Victims & the deadly sport of Luvahs Sons.
> They dance around the dying, & they drink the howl & groan
> They catch the shrieks in cups of gold, they hand them to one
>   another,
> These are the sports of love, & these the sweet delights of amorous
>   play
> Tears of the grape, the death sweat of the cluster the last sigh
> Of the mild youth who listens to the lureing songs of Luvah.
> (M 27:35-41, E123-124/K514)

The orthodox believed that Jesus was asexual; Blake answers tauntingly, "Was Jesus Chaste or did he/Give any Lessons of Chastity" (*EG*, E512/K753). But it does not follow that this is a celebration of gratified desire. On the contrary, Jesus' unchastity is a feature of his implication in the fallen Luvah, in the seductive romance suggested by the alliteration in "listens to the lureing songs of Luvah," which leads to the ghastly sports of the Female Will. In *The Mental Traveller* the boy is given to an aged woman "Who nails him down upon a rock/ Catches his shrieks in cups of gold" (E475/K425), and the image is re-

peated here. In the ninth Night of *The Four Zoas* the sexual apocalypse
is threatening but finally positive. In this passage in *Milton* (which occurs at the middle of the poem, not at the end) it is clearly negative, an
incomplete and dangerous vision. Jesus enters this fallen state in order
to expose and end its cruelties, not in order to condone them.

Incarnation is crucifixion. "I gave thee liberty and life O lovely
Jerusalem/And thou hast bound me down upon the Stems of Vegetation" (*J* 60:10-11, E208/K692). In the apocalypse of the ninth Night,
"Luvah was put for dung on the ground by the Sons of Tharmas &
Urthona" (*FZ* 137:24, E390/K378): he is restored to his proper sexual
role. But in the later writings Blake seems far more dubious that there
is a proper sexual role, and the dung on the ground is symbolic of disastrous sexual union with its attendant curse of reproduction:

> O how sick & weary I
> Underneath my mirtle lie
> Like to dung upon the ground
> Underneath my mirtle bound.[103]

Blake has in mind two grim texts in Jeremiah (8:2, 25:33) in which the
Lord deals with the bodies of his enemies by forbidding them burial
and commanding that they be put as dung upon the ground. But Jesus,
by accepting Luvah's robes, is able to free man from the prison of sexual generation.

> These are the Sexual Garments, the Abomination of Desolation
> Hiding the Human Lineaments as with an Ark & Curtains
> Which Jesus rent: & now shall wholly purge away with Fire
> Till Generation is swallowed up in Regeneration.
> (*M* 41:25-28, E141/K533)

The Resurrection is the symbol of the rejection of the body of death.
From the time of *The Marriage of Heaven and Hell* Blake was fascinated
by the empty tomb and the linen clothes folded up (E34/K149). After
describing the lark's song and the wild thyme he adds, "Luvah slept
here in death & here is Luvahs empty Tomb" (*M* 35:59, E135/K526).
After the imaginative epiphany, Luvah's body is no more. In one of
the engravings for *Night Thoughts* (see fig. 29) a youthful, muscular
Christ springs into the air, thrusting aside clouds with his hands, while
the linen clothes are held by an angel below. The arms retain the
cruciform pose, but the legs are liberated in an athletic leap. The ascen-
sion is the consequence of man's recognition of the divine in himself.

In the third chapter of *Jerusalem* the sleeping Albion is in such

---

[103] "In a mirtle shade," E460/K169.

29. *The Christian Triumph*, frontispiece to Night IV of Edward Young's *Night Thoughts*.

danger that Los is afraid to wake him, for fear that he will slip forever into the void: "But he spoke not to Albion: fearing lest Albion should turn his Back/Against the Divine Vision: & fall over the Precipice of Eternal Death" (*J* 71:58–59, E224/K711). But soon afterwards, in the picture on plate 76, we see Albion turn his back on *us* while he adores the crucified Christ from whose head pours a radiance brighter than that of the "natural" sun on the far horizon. Albion's outstretched arms mirror those of Jesus, while his arms and legs together recall his posture in the engraving *Albion Rose*.[104] The next step will be for the vegetative world to be blown away and the suffering of the Crucifixion transformed (in contrast with the churches that institutionalize it by displaying its effigy on their altars).

By redefining the meaning of the Crucifixion in this way, Blake gives up a good deal of its symbolic power. Since there is no Atonement, there is no vindictive God who demands a ransom; but then there cannot be, either, the God who "so loved the world, that he gave his only begotten Son, that whosoever believeth in him should not perish, but have everlasting life" (John 3:16). And since the Crucifixion is a submission to error in order to banish error, it cannot be a willing acceptance of real suffering on behalf of those who would otherwise suffer in vain. Blake's crucified Christ is incapable of uttering the profound cry, echoing the twenty-second Psalm, "My God, my God, why hast thou forsaken me?" (Mark 15:34). Blake's dualism is in the end more radical than Paul's. He is indifferent to the potent oxymoron of an immanent transcendence in which the death of a god can be the real death of a man.

Yet, as in so many other instances, Blake's practice cannot altogether stand up to his theory. God ought to be fully expressed by Christ, but the deepest symbolism of Christ is a response to man's sense that he is *not* at one with God, that a mediator is needed to reestablish contact. As an anthropologist has put it, "Jesus as God symbolizes anthropomorphically the love, compassion and mercy which man feels to be necessary to save him from his baser self; he also symbolizes the protection against divine judgment—which in turn symbolizes the verdict of man's own inner logic in reflecting on his shortcomings."[105] Blake is aware of man's shortcomings and knows that he needs protection; in a number of pictures Jesus supports the fainting Albion.[106] Beulah may be defective, but the Jesus of Innocence is still needed in the spirit of those lovely lines in "Night" in which the lion watches the fold,

> Saying: wrath by his meekness
> And by his health, sickness,

---

[104] As Mitchell notes (*Blake's Composite Art*, p. 210). The text for that picture suggests obvious affinities between Albion and Christ: "Albion rose from where he labourd at the Mill with Slaves/Giving himself for the Nations he danc'd the dance of Eternal Death" (E660/K160). Samson—Milton's "at the mill with slaves"—was a traditional type of Christ.

[105] Raymond Firth, *Symbols Public and Private* (Ithaca, 1973), p. 406.

[106] See *Jerusalem*, pls. 33, 37, 99.

Is driven away
From our immortal day.
                (E14/K119)

And this is so because, as the speaker of "On Another's Sorrow" knows, incarnation and crucifixion imply a real experience of the bitterness of suffering.

He doth give his joy to all.
He becomes an infant small.
He becomes a man of woe
He doth feel the sorrow too.
                (E17/K122)

In psychoanalytic terms, the sacrifice of the Son liberates man from guilt toward the father, for the son *is* God. On the one hand, the desired death of the father is covertly accomplished, but on the other, Christ rises from the dead and is reunited with the now-placated Father.[107] For all his interest in the Oedipal theme, Blake denies himself this classic Christian means of resolving it. And although scholars are fond of ascribing a "kenotic" Christ to his myth, there can be no kenosis because there is no question of the divine emptying itself of divine attributes in order to enter the limitations of mortal life.

However much he may try to abolish the Trinity, Blake retains so much of the biblical Jesus that he cannot really do without it. Just as Jehovah and the Elohim take on active roles even though we are supposed to see them as mistaken versions of the true Jesus, so Christ frequently plays the role of a mediator in the traditional sense. In Augustine's words, he "is not the Mediator in that he is the Word; for the Word, being preeminently immortal and blessed, is far removed from wretched mortals. He is the Mediator in that he is man."[108] This bridge seems so shaky to Blake that he constantly tries to get rid of it by denying the existence of the gulf. But the gulf remains, for it is inherent in the nature of religion. In the formulation of a psychoanalyst of religion, two different kinds of anxiety are involved, the feeling of inner division and the feeling of separation from one's fellows. "Is not religion that which joins together (*celle qui relie*)? . . . On the one hand, to the being that feels itself *mutilated*, separated from itself, and suffering from its incompletion, religion gives the feeling of unity and *plenitude;* on the other hand, to the being that feels itself *separated from the other*, abandoned in the consciousness of its isolation, it gives the

---

[107] See Rosolato, *Essais sur le Symbolique*, p. 78.
[108] *City of God*, IX.xvi, p. 361.

feeling of *communion*."[109] Blake gives ample evidence of both impulses: Albion scattered upon the void; Blake lamenting that he was born with a different face. In his myth the two are complementary, since to be internally divided is the same thing as to be cut off from others. Jesus is the principle that reunites. Is he not then a mediator between man and those forces (whether internal projections or otherwise) that man perceives as blocking and judging him?

I believe that Blake might have accepted such a conclusion, since it is quite explicit in his painting of 1799 entitled *Christ the Mediator*, illustrating 1 Timothy 2:5, "For there is One God, and one mediator between God and men, the man Jesus Christ." In a scene probably inspired by a treatise by Bunyan on Christ as advocate, God is seated on the throne of judgment, gazing sternly at Mary Magdalen, who is surrounded, as Bunyan says, by blushing angels. Around the throne swirls a flame; again in Bunyan's words, "The Law broken, is the holy and perfect Rule of God, in itself a consuming fire." We remember Blake's pronouncement that God out of Jesus is a consuming fire.[110] Here Jesus stands between the Magdalen and God, his arms outstretched in the familiar cruciform pose. As usual Blake implicitly criticizes the received doctrine: sexual sin is nothing to blush about, as is made clear in the passage about Mary Magdalen in *The Everlasting Gospel*, and the consuming fire is that of the punitive Jehovah who must be reintegrated with Christ. It is easy to interpret Christ's gaze as sadly reproachful. Yet the fact remains that a mediator is necessary between man and Jehovah, just because Jehovah *is* what he is. As the Accuser who is god of this world, he must be confronted by a Christ who enters into the state of Satan and Eternal Death.

Just as in Boehme's writings, some version of the Trinity is needed if God is to be as dialectically active as man; and he could hardly be less. Koyré asks, "Is not the metaphysical significance of the trinitarian doctrine to introduce 'life and movement' into the divine absolute, or, if one prefers, to introduce a multiplicity and interior structure into the too-rigid unity of a God who is solely *one*?"[111] Having rejected the Trinity, Blake has to reinvent it. It is easy to banish Nobodaddy, but Jehovah returns; it is easy to deride the Holy Ghost as "vacuum," but the creative spirit returns. "Teach me O Holy Spirit the Testimony of Jesus!" (*J* 74:14, E227/K714; see Rev. 19:10).

God and Jesus are identical, yet Blake can echo Revelation on "God

[109] Baudouin, *Psychanalyse du Symbole Religieux*, p. 87.

[110] See above, p. 277. Bunyan is quoted by Geoffrey Keynes, *William Blake's Illustrations to the Bible* (London, 1957), p. xiii; the picture is reproduced in color as pl. VIII and may also be seen in Blunt, *The Art of William Blake*, pl. 34b.

[111] *La Philosophie de Jacob Boehme*, p. 341.

and the Lamb" as if they were the separate persons of the Trinity.[112] Where he differs from orthodoxy is in his insistence that Jehovah must be reformed; but in the end he comes close to Hegel's position, which is that the Trinity reflects the dialectical movement of consciousness itself. "The first unchangeable is taken to be merely the alien, external Being, which passes sentence on particular existence [cf. Blake's Jehovah]; since the second unchangeable is a form or mode of particularity like itself [Christ], it, i.e. the consciousness, becomes in the third place spirit (Geist), has the joy of finding itself therein, and becomes aware within itself that its particularity has been reconciled with the universal."[113] The dialectic moves forward, but no part of it can be permanently rejected. So also with the multiple aspects of the divine in Blake.

[112] See above, p. 231.
[113] Phenomenology, p. 253.

[S E V E N]

Blake and Los

And I took the little book out of the angel's hand, and ate it up; and
it was in my mouth sweet as honey: and as soon as I had eaten it,
my belly was bitter.

Revelation 10:10

For in my nature I quested for beauty, but God, God hath sent me
to sea for pearls.

Christopher Smart, Jubilate Agno

The secret of Romanticism, from Blake and Wordsworth down to
the age of Yeats and Stevens, increasingly looks like a therapy in
which consciousness heals itself by a complex act of invention.

Harold Bloom, The Ringers in the Tower

PROPHETIC INSPIRATION

We have seen that Blake's myth is founded in vision, by which he means a mode of perception that sees through symbols rather than with them.

> Now I a fourfold vision see
> And a fourfold vision is given to me.
> (E693/K818)

To ask in what sense it is "given" is to approach the final complex of problems that will occupy us, those surrounding the work of the prophetic poet who labors to mediate his vision to other human beings. Ultimately the pictures and poems are intended to lead us to the brink of an inner apocalypse which each must experience in his own way. But they do so only with extraordinary difficulty and pain, and Blake's exploration of the dilemmas of the artist, rooted in his own sense of psychic struggle, is both moving and profound.

To begin with, it is essential to recognize Blake's conviction of inspiration. This is what sustains him even in moments of near despair. In a letter to Butts he says that his poems are composed "from immediate Dictation," and in another letter that in effect they are not his at all and can therefore be discussed by him as objectively as by anyone else. "I may praise it, since I dare not pretend to be any other than the Secretary; the Authors are in Eternity. I consider it as the Grandest

Poem that this World Contains."[1] This is not automatic writing, for the poet is free to choose his metrical mode (*J* 3, E144/K621), but it is nevertheless written under direct inspiration with "the Saviour over me/Spreading his beams of love, & dictating the words of this mild song" (4:4-5, E145/K622). Milton explored the same paradox: the prophetic poet is charged with the execution of the vision in mortal images but must remain faithful to his heavenly guide.[2]

Tatham left a remarkable account of Blake's nocturnal composition: Catherine "would get up in the night, when he was under his very fierce inspirations, which were as if they would tear him asunder, while he was yielding himself to the Muse, or whatever else it could be called, sketching and writing. And so terrible a task did this seem to be, that she had to sit motionless and silent; only to stay him mentally, without moving hand or foot: this for hours, and night after night" (*Blake Records*, p. 526*n*). Blake was interested in the image of Saint John writing under angelic inspiration.[3] And in the strange drawing (see fig. 30) on which Tatham noted, "I suppose it to be a Vision," a tiny figure follows angelic dictation, under a lamp or sun of inspiration, in a little room at the end of a much larger room or hall. Very likely Blake intended the disconcerting perspectives, which have been likened to those of Cubism,[4] to suggest that the artist's vision is a refuge from the imprisoning geometry and receding perspective of the Newtonian universe. The poet seems far away, but it is we who are cut off, peering down that corridor from our "real" but in fact illusory world outside the picture. We see through a vortex. The strangeness of vision is even more strikingly suggested by the drawing known as *Blake's Instructor* or as *The Man Who Taught Blake Painting* (see fig. 31). It is an eerie face: eyes far apart and wide open, arched eyebrows,

---

[1] Letters to Butts, 25 Apr. 1803 (E697/K823) and 6 July 1803 (K825; not in E). Milton also refers to himself as God's "Secretary," which, according to his modern editor, means simply that he is privy to God's secrets (*The Reason of Church-Government*, in *Complete Prose Works of John Milton*, ed. Don M. Wolfe [New Haven, 1953], I, 822). Wittreich calls attention to this passage (*Angel of Apocalypse*, pp. 172-173). I think Blake understood "secretary" quite literally.

[2] See William Kerrigan, *The Prophetic Milton* (Charlottesville, Va., 1974).

[3] See the watercolor *The Angel of Revelation* (reproduced in Mitchell, *Blake's Composite Art*, pl. 110) in which a small John of Patmos, pen poised over his scroll, looks up at the towering angel of Revelation 10 while the "seven thunders" ride on horseback through the clouds. Lindberg identifies the winged female figure of *Job* pl. 17, writing with a quill on a scroll, as the angel who inspired the evangelist John, texts from whom fill the bottom of the page (*William Blake's Illustrations . . .*, p. 64). Wittreich suggests that the picture in *MHH* 10 shows a deluded Milton who listens to a Daughter of Memory instead of a Daughter of Inspiration (*Angel of Apocalypse*, p. 270).

[4] Rosenblum, *Transformations . . .*, p. 190.

30. *A Vision.*

pursed mouth, forehead divided into phrenologically significant lobes, and (according to Keynes's recent identification) a seven-branched menorah or Tree of Life at the center hairline.[5] The effect is of an unwavering gaze filled with calm expectation, like that of a being from another universe.

But although Blake's inspiration may have come from Eternity, all the work was yet to do. The message had to be incorporated in words and pictorial forms. And this task was peculiarly demanding because

[5] Keynes, letter in *TLS*, 7 Apr. 1978, p. 393. Anne K. Mellor has shown that the lobes are phrenological clues to imaginative abilities, and also that the face is an idealized or abstracted version of Blake's own ("Physiognomy, Phrenology, and Blake's Visionary Heads," in Essick and Pearce, pp. 63-67).

31. *Blake's Instructor.*

Blake, unlike Milton, rejected the idea of an omnipotent deity of whom he should be the trembling and obedient servant. Of whom is Blake the prophet? Certainly not the Jehovah who promised fearful retribution for anyone who should tamper with the inspired text: "For I testify unto every man that heareth the words of the prophecy of this book, if any man shall add unto these things, God shall add unto him the plagues that are written in this book" (Rev. 22:18). Certainly not the God upon whom it is impious to look, and who must cleanse the mouth of the prophet before words may be spoken: "Then flew one of the seraphim unto me, having a live coal in his hand, . . . and he laid it upon my mouth, and said, Lo, this hath touched thy lips; and thine iniquity is taken away, and thy sin purged" (Isa. 6:6–7). Blake has no need of asking with Milton, "May I express thee unblam'd?"[6] There is no sin to purge and no temerity to blame. In Blake's myth Milton addresses this sort of prayer to his own creation, inadvertently revealing his need for regeneration from the fallen state in which such a prayer could be made at all (*M* 20:15–19, E113/K502).

These considerations suggest that we have not fully appreciated the difference between Blake's myth of the Zoas and the chariot or *Merkabah* that Ezekiel beheld. Ezekiel's spectacular vision—the flames, the mysterious living creatures, the incandescent holiness of the enthroned deity—is repeated in his tenth chapter when God withdraws protection from the Temple at Jerusalem, and it then signifies the departure of the Almighty after a brief epiphany to a distant realm where he rules on high. His involvement in Jewish history in no way minimizes this absolute transcendence, a point still further emphasized in the Merkabah mysticism that took Ezekiel's vision as its starting point: "The true and spontaneous feeling of the Merkabah mystic knows nothing of divine immanence. . . . Throughout there remained an almost exaggerated consciousness of God's *otherness*."[7]

Christian typology interpreted the Merkabah as a Christophany: the living creatures are the cherubim who bear Christ aloft, and are associated with the four evangelists. But Blake is always on the watch for the perverted doctrine of cherubs who guard the inaccessible deity, identifying them with the "Covering Cherub" of Ezekiel 28:14 and with the cherubim who protect the holy of holies in the Temple Moreover, in the sixth book of *Paradise Lost* Jesus rides the *Merkabah* chariot in trimuph over the bodies of the fallen angels, a use of the symbol which Blake must have regarded as a ghastly blasphemy. So he seizes upon the symbol in order to reconstruct it; the four Zoas are both God and Man, neither guarding nor concealing any further manifestation of deity. Separated, they fragment into blocking or "covering" figures. United, they are the unified self, and the godhead they bear aloft is the same self in visionary form, not a transcendent deity who for that moment only has descended to mortal view.

Not surprisingly, Blake experienced the same turbulent relationship with his guides in Eternity as he did with ordinary mortals. At times he seems to have regarded writing from "dictation" as an end in itself,

[6] *Paradise Lost*, III.3.
[7] Scholem, *Major Trends in Jewish Mysticism*, p. 55.

for as he told Robinson, "When I am commanded by the Spirits then I write, and the moment I have written, I see the Words fly about the room in all directions. It is then published.—The Spirits can read and my MS. is of no further use. I have been tempted to burn my MS, but my wife won't let me" (*Blake Records*, p. 547). Yet at other times he indicated that he could resist these impulses and even that it might be right to do so. "The oddest thing he said was that he had been commanded to do certain things, that is to write about Milton, and that he was applauded for refusing; he struggled with the Angels and was victor" (*Blake Records*, p. 320).

Blake's inspiration thus operated in complex ways. For the most part it allowed him to speak with a confidence of ultimate authority, making possible the forceful impersonality of his poems that contrasts strikingly with the personal voice of the other Romantic poets. But it also meant that he could not always be sure of the meaning of what he wrote, needing to interpret his symbols just as the reader must:

> Before Ololon Milton stood & perceivd the Eternal Form
> Of that mild Vision; wondrous were their acts by me unknown
> Except remotely. . . .
>
> (*M* 40:1-3, E140/K532)

And it imposed in addition the constant burden of determining whether the symbols were valid or not. Los's creation is both commanded and made possible by a power greater than himself, yet it is Los who must create.

BLAKE AND THE SPECTRE

An approach to the role of the artist–prophet must begin by facing the implications of Blake's extraordinary isolation as poet and thinker. He always had friends who admired his engravings and paintings, but if there was a single human being who really understood what his poems were about, we have no evidence of it, and at best there can have been only a few. On the whole his isolation seems to have been creatively fruitful, since it freed him to pursue his ideas with a special purity of commitment, and to launch a more penetrating critique of the whole structure of Western philosophy and psychology than anyone working comfortably within the tradition could have achieved. It is hard to imagine a public of any size that would have been prepared to think its way into Blake's symbols, and impossible to imagine him altering his symbolism to suit the public. "Fit audience find tho' few," he quotes from Milton in the advertisement of his one public exhibition (E518/K560), and Milton was a popular poet compared to Blake.

What is sadder, even infuriating, is that even the greatest poets mingled condescension with their approval of those of Blake's lyrics that met their attention. Both Coleridge and Wordsworth praised the *Songs of Innocence and of Experience*, but they did not, as we could wish, conclude that a great poet was living in their midst and hasten to seek him out.[8] What if Blake had gone to Grasmere in 1800 instead of to Felpham?

No great English poet has ever been isolated to anything like the extent that Blake was, and the fact cannot be irrelevant to his art. There is surely a strong element of compensatory fantasy in the myth. The visions which began in Blake's childhood and persisted so strongly were clearly necessary to his psychic life, as well as expressions of psychic conflict.[9] The compulsively complicated myth was a continuing assertion of power: "I have traveld thro Perils & Darkness not unlike a Champion I have Conquerd and shall still Go on Conquering Nothing can withstand the fury of my Course among the Stars of God & in the Abysses of the Accuser."[10] When we read of Los swinging his loud hammer and using the Thames as his blacksmith's trough, it is easy to think of the obscure and powerless William Blake summoning the entire British landscape to feed his rage and embody his ideas. The zeal to domesticate him for English Literature should not obscure what Swinburne called "the incredible fever of spirit under the sting and stress of which he thought and laboured all his life through."[11] If the soldier Schofield is generalized into a larger symbol, it is also true that Blake's poems contain his revenge against his actual and historical accuser: "Go thou to Skofield. . . . Tell him: I will dash him to shivers, where & at what time/I please" (*J* 17:59-62, E161/ K640).

To notice this is not in the least to diminish Blake's imaginative achievement. On the contrary, it is to celebrate it, for Blake succeeds in channeling his personal preoccupations—relations with his father and wife, feelings about authority—into a brilliant investigation of the human condition. As with the Gnostic heresiarchs whom Jonas describes, his thought has a "revolutionary and angry" aspect, and the anger gives birth to potent symbols. The Gnostics' "rejection of the

[8] There is a tantalizing remark in a letter from Robinson to Dorothy Wordsworth: "Coleridge has visited B[lake] & I am told talks finely about him" (*Blake Records*, p. 325).

[9] Blake told Robinson that he had visions "from early infancy," and some of them indicate serious emotional disturbance; his wife remarked in conversation, "You know, dear, the first time you saw God was when You were four years old And he put his head to the window and set you ascreaming" (*Blake Records*, pp. 317, 543).

[10] Letter to Butts, 22 Nov. 1802 (E691/K815-816).

[11] *William Blake*, p. 276.

world, far from the serenity or resignation of other nonworldly creeds, is of peculiar, sometimes vituperative violence, and we generally note a tendency to extremism, to excess in fantasy and feeling." And Jonas goes on to suggest, "We suspect that the dislocated metaphysical situation of which gnostic myth tells had its counterpart in a dislocated real situation: that the crisis-form of its symbolism reflects a historical crisis of man himself."[12] Are not Blake's Gnostic tendencies the metaphysical expression of the historical and social dislocations that Erdman describes in *Prophet Against Empire?*

But the prophetic stance carries its penalties. While the prophet may glory in a sense of righteousness or special vocation that sets him apart from the corrupt herd, he is also likely to feel deep anxiety as a result of his separateness. "O why was I born with a different face?" Blake participates in Jeremiah's suffering as well as Ezekiel's vision: "The word of the Lord was made a reproach unto me, and a derision, daily. Then I said, I will not make mention of him, nor speak any more in his name. But his word was in mine heart as a burning fire shut up in my bones, and I was weary with forbearing, and I could not stay" (Jer. 20:8-9). Such a prophet is impelled to attack with special urgency the culture that he both wants and fears to rejoin. Or to put it the other way round, to continue to assert a private system of values and ideas requires a constant effort of will. As Mary Douglas comments, "To remain free of the public system of classification, the person needs above all not to covet its rewards. Every glance he cocks towards the prize-giving juries makes him vulnerable to their criticisms and liable to be sucked into the general grid."[13] And if Douglas is right in asserting that anthropomorphic symbolism mirrors the perceived social order, then Blake's myth of universal Man is cut off from the normal source of validation.

These tensions, which are human before they are aesthetic, have much to do with the peculiarities in Blake's poems. They were no doubt psychologically unresolvable, as is suggested by Flaxman's rather grim comment when Blake was embroiled in the Schofield fiasco, "Blake's irritability as well as the Association & arrangement of his ideas do not seem likely to be Soothed or more advantageously disposed by any power inferior to That by which man is originally

[12] "The Gnostic Syndrome," *Philosophical Essays*, p. 272. Jonas adds that Gnosticism differs from other radical and hyperbolic faiths in the "peculiar *impietas*" with which it criticized and remade traditions.

[13] *Natural Symbols*, p. 85. "Grid" is Douglas's term for a continuum that extends from culturally shared ideas at one extreme to wholly private ones at the other. Blake's incessant attacks on Reynolds and the Royal Academy are obviously relevant here, and his quarrel with Hayley reflects a still deeper contact with temptation—Hayley the Satan who would lure Blake back by kindness into the group.

endowed with his faculties" (*Blake Records*, p. 138). But the tensions were also philosophically unresolvable, and Blake's willingness to keep reshaping his myth is expressive of a real heroism. In the face of worldly failure and a general incomprehension of his ideas, he might easily have made his thought rigid and have protected himself with defense mechanisms. Instead, sustained by the example of the prophets and Milton, he worked continually to revitalize the myth and to make it responsive to the complexity of psychic and social experience.

That experience is reflected in the increasing importance of Los in the later works. *Milton* begins with the long and involved Bard's Song, recounting a complex struggle among the Sons of Los that alludes obliquely to Blake's troubles at Felpham. In *The Four Zoas* the fall had originated in the competition of Urizen and Luvah; in *Milton* Blake wants to explore the role of Urthona/Los, and in *Jerusalem* he carries still further his analysis of the negative figure called the Spectre of Urthona.

Blake scholars, anxious not to be identified with those who "dare to mock with the aspersion of Madness" (*M* 41:8, E141/K533), have been hesitant to speculate about the terrible psychic pressure which Blake evidently experienced in the late 1790s and which came to a head at Felpham in the early 1800s.[14] In elaborating his account of the Spectre, Blake confronted with deep insight the possibility that his visionary experience might be—as the fallen Albion charges—a "Phantom of the over heated brain" (*J* 4:24, E145/K622). Of course he could reassure himself with the reflection that "There are States in which all Visionary Men are accounted Mad Men" (*Laocoön*, E271/K777), a statement whose implied obverse is perfectly true: some cultures would have hailed Blake as a prophet or shaman instead of condescending to him as a crank. But his letters to Butts from Felpham are filled with indications that the burden of prophecy imposed deep anxiety. "I am under the direction of Messengers from Heaven Daily & Nightly but the nature of such things is not as some suppose, without trouble or care. Temptations are on the right hand & left; behind the sea of time & space roars & follows swiftly. He who keeps not right onward is lost & if our footsteps slide in clay how can we do otherwise than fear & tremble" (10 Jan. 1802, E688/K812-813).

The same anxiety appears in *Jerusalem*, with an explicit recognition that Blake's friends are worried about him: "Trembling I sit day and night, my friends are astonish'd at me./Yet they forgive my wander-

---

[14] For a suggestive though brief comparison of Blake's prophetic claims with those of paranoid schizophrenics, see Randel Helms, "Blake at Felpham: A Study in the Psychology of Vision," *Literature and Psychology*, 22 (1972), 57-66.

ings, I rest not from my great task!" (5:16-17, E146/K623). And the "fourfold vision" poem begins with a pastoral harmony which is abruptly shattered by a confrontation with Blake's father and brothers; he kicks the thistle-father aside and Los then appears in glory.[15] It is easy to imagine that this experience projects on to the landscape Blake's frustrations at Felpham, where Hayley and an unhappy Catherine reproached him for not doing his "duty" as a commercial artist. Fourfold vision is a refuge from that torment and at the same time an affirmation of prophetic vocation.

The evidence of Blake's troubles at Felpham, together with many features of the myth that was elaborated during that period, point to something very like the schizoid experience that R. D. Laing documents in *The Divided Self*.[16] The sufferer feels himself to be paralyzed or dead, very much like Albion on the Rock of Ages, and images of caves and petrifaction abound.

> And Los was roofd in from Eternity in Albions Cliffs
> Which stand upon the ends of Beulah, and withoutside, all
> Appear'd a rocky form against the Divine Humanity.
> $\qquad$ (*J* 19:33-35, E163/K642)

The body is perceived as allied with the inimical other instead of being united with the self, and the true self therefore feels itself trapped within this stony prison. Meanwhile, in Laing's words, "one finds a second duality developing whereby the inner self splits to have a sado-masochistic relationship with itself."[17] The Zoas rage. So the self is at once passive and active, and what the outside world regards as the "real" self is precisely what the sufferer perceives as a false screen or mask. Sometimes this mask is deliberately manipulated, in which case the person enjoys a feeling of power in deluding those who mistake it for the true self. But at other times it is felt to have a life of its own and to threaten the true self with cruel hostility; and this is precisely the

---

[15] See above, pp. 270-271.

[16] I must emphasize once again that the poems are not insane, but that they deal profoundly with the threat of insanity. It appears that Blake went through a particularly grave disturbance at Felpham, exacerbated by the unexpected disaster of Schofield's accusation and the treason trial. I do not claim, however, that he was ever clinically schizophrenic; his behavior at Felpham perhaps corresponded to what psychoanalysts call the borderline type of person in whom the tendency to paranoia or schizophrenia is controlled, so that they possess "a fair degree of normal functioning which enables them to live in reality to a sufficient degree" (Melitta Schmideberg, "The Borderline Patient," in *American Handbook of Psychiatry*, ed. Silvano Arieti [New York, 1959], I, 398). As I shall argue shortly, Blake's art was not so much a symptom of his distress as an effective therapy for it.

[17] *The Divided Self*, p. 83.

role of the Spectre of Urthona. "While Los spoke, the terrible Spectre fell shuddring before him/Watching his time with glowing eyes to leap upon his prey" (*J* 8:21-22, E150/K627). It is common, Laing says, for people in this condition to say that they do not "really" have intercourse with their sexual partners, since the body is under the control of the false self (p. 87). We remember that when the Daughters of Albion woo Los to subdue his strength he withholds himself and "continually/Shews them his Spectre" (*J* 17:10-11, E160/K638).

Morton Paley has demonstrated that Blake's Spectre has much in common with William Cowper, victim of religious despair.[18] Insofar as the Spectre resembles Cowper, Blake (as Hayley accurately noticed) resembles Cowper too. The relationship between despair and the false self is very clearly diagnosed by Kierkegaard: "As according to the report of superstition the troll disappears through a crack which no one can perceive, so it is for the despairer all the more important to dwell in an exterior semblance behind which it ordinarily would never occur to anyone to look for it. This hiddenness is precisely something spiritual and is one of the safety-devices for assuring oneself of having as it were behind reality an enclosure, a world for itself locking all else out, a world where the despairing self is employed as tirelessly as Tantalus in willing to be itself."[19] But this unremitting effort may break down, and Laing describes such a breakdown in terms that conform closely to what happened to Blake at Felpham:

> The observable behavior that is the expression of the false self is often perfectly normal. We see a model child, an ideal husband, an industrious clerk. . . . Hatred is also necessarily present, for what else is the adequate object of hatred except that which endangers one's self? However, the anxiety to which the self is subject precludes the possibility of a direct revelation of its hatred. . . . Indeed, what is called psychosis is sometimes simply the sudden removal of the veil of the false self, which had been serving to maintain an outer behavioural normality that may, long ago, have failed to be any reflection of the state of affairs in the secret self. Then the self will pour out accusations of persecution at the hands of that person with whom the false self has been complying for years.[20]

One remembers Kazin's remark that Blake was an ideal husband and could not stand it. Hayley worked hard to ensure Blake's acquittal in the sedition trial, but with part of his mind at least Blake saw him as

[18] "Cowper as Blake's Spectre," *Eighteenth-Century Studies*, 1 (1968), 236-252.
[19] *The Sickness unto Death*, in *Fear and Trembling and The Sickness unto Death*, trans. Walter Lowrie (Princeton, 1954), pp. 206-207.
[20] *The Divided Self*, pp. 99-100.

alienating Catherine and suborning Schofield to destroy him; and this in turn was perceived as inseparable from Hayley's suggestions for Blake's art.

> When H[ayley] finds out what you cannot do
> That is the very thing he'll set you to. . . .
> And when he could not act upon my wife
> Hired a Villain to bereave my Life.
>
> (E497/K544)

Curiously, that last line swims up from the distant *Poetical Sketches*,[21] as if during all those years it had been waiting to describe the Schofield incident.

One measure of Blake's greatness is the power of genius with which he mastered these obsessions and gave them universal significance in art. As Laing says, "Deterioration and disintegration are only one outcome of the initial schizoid organization. Quite clearly, authentic versions of freedom, power, and creativity can be achieved and lived out" (p. 89). The Bard's Song in *Milton* does not mention William Hayley because it is a searching examination of the meaning of Blake's feelings about Hayley and about himself, not a simple allegory of what Hayley did or failed to do. When Blake tells Hayley in 1804 (after leaving Felpham) that he has been "in a Divided Existence" but is now "no longer Divided, nor at war with myself" (E704/K935), he testifies to liberation from paranoid hatred; Hayley may never have suspected the extent of Blake's resentment against him, but he was certainly aware of Blake's divided existence. And if in one sense the mythic poems allow Blake to unleash revenge against Schofield and his other enemies, in another sense they allow a working out of hostility that releases forgiveness instead of revenge, with Los's recognition that "he who takes vengeance alone is the criminal of Providence" and his warning to Albion, "If thou revengest thy wrongs/Thou art for ever lost" (*J* 45:32–37, E192/K657). This is, as Bloom says, "the great moral admonition of the poem,"[22] and it has been earned by personal experience of the bitterest kind.

In some moods Blake explicitly states that the real Spectres are the visionary forms that withdraw him from reality, and that the imaginary world rather than the physical one is "abstract."

> I labour incessantly & accomplish not one half of what I intend, because my Abstract folly hurries me often away while I am at work, carrying me over Mountains & Valleys which are not Real in a Land

---

[21] "Fair Elenor," line 68 (E404/K6).

[22] *Blake's Apocalypse*, p. 401.

of Abstraction where Spectres of the Dead wander. This I endeavour to prevent & with my whole might Chain my feet to the world of Duty & Reality, but in vain! the faster I bind the better is the Ballast, for I so far from being bound down take the world with me in my flights & often it seems lighter than a ball of wool rolled by the wind. . . . [23]

Here speaks the Spectre of Urthona. Butts wrote tactfully that he hoped life at Felpham would help Blake to get over "certain opinions imbibed from reading, nourished by indulgence, and rivitted by a confined Conversation" (*Blake Records*, p. 75). And on some occasions, evidently, Blake was willing to agree with his friends that his visionary works, far from exposing the deceptions of Abstraction, were themselves abstractions, and that the work Hayley and Butts wanted him to do was worth doing. [24]

Los's answer must be that the Spectres take living form only in his creative art. As Enitharmon appeals to him,

> . . . if thou my Los
> Wilt in sweet moderated fury, fabricate forms sublime
> Such as the piteous spectres may assimilate themselves into
> They shall be ransoms for our Souls that we may live.
> (*FZ* 90:21-24, E356/K331)

Los responds with "his hands divine inspired." Invariably we are brought back to the necessity of the divine, for Los suffers from the same alienation that Albion does—he is divided just as Albion is divided—and the separate existence of the Spectre is a sign of his disorganization.

If Blake had wanted to assert that art was totally opaque to rational thought, he could have dismissed the Spectre as irrelevant. But to abandon reason would have been to ratify, however ironically, Urizen's claim to a status apart from the rest. Just as Urizen must be rehabilitated before Albion can rise again, so also he must cooperate with Urthona in the development and interpretation of artistic symbols. The Spectre of Urthona is Blake's way of expressing this insight:

[23] Letter to Butts, 11 Sept. 1801 (E685/K809).

[24] See also the passage in a letter (E679/K798) on Blake's fear when young that art was a mere indulgence, even a sin, since he ought to be making a proper living. This old sense of guilt in his vocation cannot have been easy to overcome, since the vocation did indeed lead to poverty. As Hagstrum says, "He must have been a greatly tempted man. . . . Blake's friends and collaborators were often successful conformists, who pointed the way to quick achievement in several accepted modes" (*William Blake: Poet and Painter*, pp. 58-59).

314

with all the tensions and hostilities that are involved, the Spectre nonetheless plays the essential role of Urizen-in–Urthona.

By definition the Spectre is confined to a negative role. "The Almighty hath made me his Contrary/To be all evil," he cries, and Los wipes his tears in vain, for "Comfort none could give! or beam of hope" (*J* 10:56-61, E152/K630). But his negativity is a function of a mistaken theology, not of inveterate malice, and his despair is not to be despised.

> I said: now is my grief at worst: incapable of being
> Surpassed: but every moment it accumulates more & more
> It continues accumulating to eternity!
>
> (10:44-46)

This is the tone of Hopkins' great sonnet that begins "No worst, there is none." The speaker is imprisoned within a destructive Augustinian-Calvinist theology, but Blake pities him and labors to rescue that part of himself that the Spectre represents. And at other times, in other circumstances, it is the Spectre who comforts Los (*FZ* 87:26, E355/K330).

To Blake's friends who trembled at his divided state, the Spectre must have appeared to be his true self while the inner visionary self, which Blake himself regarded as the true self, looked like a dangerous tendency to madness like Cowper's. Like Laing's schizoids Blake thus inverts the evaluation of the outside world. One of the Eternals calls the Spectre "insane, and most deform'd" (*J* 33:4, E177/K664), and in another place the Spectre himself laments to Enitharmon,

> Thou knowest that the Spectre is in Every Man insane brutish
> Deformd that I am thus a ravening devouring lust continually
> Craving and devouring. . . .
>
> (*FZ* 84:36-38, E352/K327)

To have rejected this "insane" Spectre altogether—to have denied that it had any relationship at all with the true self—would have meant acceptance of psychosis. Instead Blake strives superbly to reintegrate the divided self and to make the Spectre's labors, so acceptable to the outside world but so inimical to the true self, a part of his visionary creation.

In itself the Spectre is despair and therefore hell, in the traditional metaphors (as in Mark 9:44) of eternal fire and the worm that dies not.

> Thou shalt be a Non Entity for ever
> And if any enter into thee, thou shalt be an Unquenchable Fire

And he shall be a never dying Worm, mutually tormented by
Those that thou tormentest, a Hell & Despair for ever & ever.
(*J* 17:44–47, E160–161/K639)

The answer is neither to reject the Spectre nor to compromise with it, but to compel it to labor as a servant at Los's forge, Caliban to his Prospero.

Thou art my Pride & Self-righteousness. . . .
Now I am living; unless
Thou abstain ravening I will create an eternal Hell for thee.
Take thou this Hammer & in patience heave the thundering Bellows
Take thou these Tongs: strike thou alternate with me: labour
obedient.

(*J* 8:30–40, E150/K627)

"Everyone carries a shadow," Jung says, "and the less it is embodied in the individual's conscious life, the blacker and denser it is. . . . If it comes to a neurosis, we have invariably to deal with a considerably intensified shadow. And if such a case wants to be cured it is necessary to find a way in which man's conscious personality and his shadow can live together."[25] Since Blake rejects the unconscious, he inverts Jung's categories: in Blake's myth the "shadow" is the excessively rational part of the self rather than—as the metaphor would normally suggest—the hidden and more "primitive" part. But he agrees with Jung that the Spectre cannot simply be repudiated, in the way that the state of Satan was dismissed into Nonentity; it must be reintegrated with the self. "This is the Spectre of Man: the Holy Reasoning Power," without whose aid the city of art cannot be built. "Los stands in London building Golgonooza/Compelling his Spectre to labours mighty" (*J* 10:15–18, E151/K629).

Hegel says in his famous chapter on lordship and bondage that labor is a negative agency, differing from desire by entering into the object instead of assimilating it to the self. "The negative relation to the object passes into the *form* of the object, into something that is permanent and remains."[26] Blake's grandiose claims for the infinity of desire are finally not irresponsible because he recognizes, with pain and sorrow to be sure, that the permanent forms of art cannot be achieved without the labor of the Spectre of Urthona. And similarly his notorious obscurity, though perhaps sometimes a refuge from those whose

[25] C. G. Jung, *Psychology and Religion* (New Haven, 1938), p. 93. Jung was writing under the shadow of Hitler and the oncoming war.
[26] *Phenomenology*, p. 238.

316

comprehension he does not wish to invite, is in the end an obstacle which the outward-facing Spectre must help him to overcome. Los commands the Spectre, "As far as my Hammer & Anvil permit/Go, tell them that the Worship of God, is honouring his gifts/In other men" (*J* 91:6–8, E248/K738). "After my three years slumber on the banks of the Ocean," Blake says at the beginning of *Jerusalem*, "I again display my Giant forms to the Public" (E143/K620). The three years' slumber is the spiritual "death" of those tormented years, and the public—not just the private self—is the beneficiary of the art which the suffering at Felpham has produced. Scholars like to debate which of Blake's poems were begun at that time, and to what extent they were executed there, but he is telling us in effect that all of them were, no matter how extensively they may have been augmented in later years. The experience at Felpham, where Blake came to terms with his Spectre and recovered his prophetic role, was the seed-bed of all three of the great prophecies.

In the end Blake's self-therapy seems to have succeeded. Surrounded in old age by artistic disciples—the spiritual sons to whom at last he could act as a loved and admired father—he overcame, so far as one can tell, the spiritual torment of the prophetic books. As Palmer sums up, "He was a man without a mask; his aim single, his path straightforwards, and his wants few; so he was free, noble, and happy. . . . He was one of the few to be met with in our passage through life, who are not, in some way or other, 'double minded' and inconsistent with themselves."[27] The warring Zoas were at peace. And as George Richmond reported to Palmer, Blake's death was attended by joyful hope of the kind that the myth strenuously sought for so long. "He said He was going to that Country he had all His life wished to see & expressed Himself Happy hoping for Salvation through Jesus Christ—Just before he died His countenance became fair—His eyes brighten'd and He burst out in Singing of the things he Saw in Heaven. In truth He Died like a Saint" (*Blake Records*, p. 347).

THE STUBBORN STRUCTURE

As the struggle with the Spectre suggests, Los's creative activity is significant for its fallenness. He is man's best hope of recovery from the fall, and Jesus, after submitting to crucifixion in Luvah, appears in "the likeness & similitude of Los" (*J* 96:22, E253/K743). Even at his nadir Los is the principle of prophetic imagination that makes possible the eventual reunion with Jesus, and therefore the Divine Family

[27] To Gilchrist, in *William Blake: The Critical Heritage*, ed. Bentley, pp. 31, 34.

> ... with one accord delegated Los
> Conjuring him by the Highest that he should Watch over them
> Till Jesus shall appear: & they gave their power to Los
> Naming him the Spirit of Prophecy, calling him Elijah.
> (*J* 39:28-31, E185/K674)

But if it would be wrong to minimize the importance of Los's creative work, it would also be wrong to romanticize it and to equate his city of art, Golgonooza, with the Edenic state that is to replace it. Golgonooza is the new Golgotha, the new place of the skull, the setting for an incarnation and crucifixion whose ambiguities we have already noticed.[28] In his struggle with the Spectre Los testifies to inspiration but also to a condition of horror:

> I am inspired: I act not for myself: for Albions sake
> I now am what I am: a horror and an astonishment
> Shuddring the heavens to look upon me.
> (*J* 8:17-19, E150/K627)

And many of the designs emphasize his suffering in ways that monochrome reproduction cannot show.[29]

Los's work is sacrificial, like that of Jesus who appears in his likeness. To perform it he must enter "the Door of Death," as illustrated on the frontispiece of *Jerusalem*, and he looks forward to the apocalypse that will bring his work to an end: "The long sufferings of God are not for ever there is a Judgment" (*J* 1:10, E143/K620). We have seen that the Elohim are manifestations of the divine spirit, however distorted and limited, and it follows that Los's creation too must share in their work: "Such is the World of Los the labour of six thousand years./Thus Nature is a Vision of the Science of the Elohim" (*M* 29:64-65, E127/K518). But this really means that nature, never good in itself, is being hammered into a stable form preparatory to regeneration. In themselves the Elohim can create only the fallen, sexual body of death.

> ... here Los who is of the Elohim
> Opens the Furnaces of affliction in the Emanation
> Fixing the Sexual into an ever-prolific Generation

---

[28] Frosch is especially good on Los's limitations and the stopgap status of Golgonooza (*Awakening of Albion*, pp. 152-159). See also Mitchell on the significance of Los's quarrel with his Sons ("Blake's Radical Comedy," in Curran and Wittreich, pp. 298-300).

[29] For instance, on *Urizen* 11 an exhausted Los slumps beside a skeletal Urizen in vivid flames, and on *Urizen* 17 a gory sun streams from his head (see the color reproductions in Paley, *William Blake*, pls. 22, 23).

Naming the Limit of Opakeness Satan & the Limit of Contraction
Adam. . . .
(J 73:24–28, E226/K713)

Los's furnaces are the fiery forge at which nature is hammered into
shape, but they are also the "Furnaces of affliction" in which the sexual
is generated in anticipation of being burned up. "Behold, I have refined thee, but not with silver; I have chosen thee in the furnace of
affliction" (Isaiah 48:10).

In a passage in *Milton* that describes the creative work of the Sons of
Los, their function is described as follows:

> Some Sons of Los surround the Passions with porches of iron &
>   silver,
> Creating form & beauty around the dark regions of sorrow,
> Giving to airy nothing a name and a habitation
> Delightful! with bounds to the Infinite putting off the Indefinite
> Into most holy forms of Thought: (such is the power of inspiration)
> They labour incessant; with many tears and afflictions:
> Creating the beautiful House for the piteous sufferer.
(M 28:1–7, E124/K514–515)

This passage is invested with more ambiguity than is commonly recognized. The indefinite is certainly intolerable; we are told elsewhere
that it characterizes Rahab, who hates and defaces "every definite
form" (*J* 80:53, E235/K723). Thought is good; inspiration is good.
Yet to achieve this saving limit, there must *be* a limit, a fact which had
troubled Blake ever since *The Marriage of Heaven and Hell*: "Reason is
the bound or outward circumference of Energy" (E34/K149). The
wiry bounding outline is good, but desire should be infinite. Is Reason
here the inevitable but thwarting contrary to Energy, or the agent that
shapes and fulfills it? Clearly man must be saved from the indefinite,
but do not "bounds to the Infinite" represent a considerable price? The
passions (uncontrolled, Orcian energy?) need to be surrounded by
organized entrances, "porches of iron & silver;" but is not that to fab-
ricate a "beautiful House" that is an external shell, like the garment-
body?

> The soft hands of Antamon draw the indelible line:
> Form immortal with golden pen; such as the Spectre admiring
> Puts on the sweet form; then smiles Antamon bright thro his
>   windows

The Daughters of beauty look up from their Loom & prepare
The integument soft for its clothing with joy & delight.
                              (*M* 28:16-20, E124-125/K515)

There is plenty of delight here, but irony too. These are the sexual
garments whose form, though far better than no form at all ("airy
nothing," with a sardonic glance at Shakespeare) can only give a shape
to that which is and remains fallen. We have seen the intimate relationship between Cathedron's looms and Vala's nets.[30]

We hear of Antamon again when Los declares himself to be Urthona and says that Oothoon hides with Antamon

In graceful hidings of error: in merciful deceit
Lest Hand the terrible destroy his Affection, thou hidest her:
In chaste appearances for sweet deceits of love & modesty
Immingled, interwoven, glistening to the sickening sight.
                              (*J* 83:29-32, E239/K727)

Damon calls Antamon "the male seed."[31] He is, in effect, a sexualized
expression of the imagination, a conflation of Los and Luvah. To draw
outlines at all, in a symbolic system in which outline is male and body
or matter female, is to be a progenitor. The limit that rescues the
female from Hand (the reasoning Spectre) does so at the cost of "sweet
deceits of love & modesty," and the sight grows sick watching it. It is
no wonder that the Sons of Los labor with tears and afflictions.

None of this calls into question the saving purpose of Golgonooza
and its various symbolic manifestations. Whereas Babylon is built of
groans and miseries (*J* 24:31-32, E168/K647), Golgonooza is built of
virtues. Yet the imagery remains deeply troubling:

What are those golden builders doing? where was the burying-place
Of soft Ethinthus? near Tyburn's fatal Tree? is that
Mild Zions hills most ancient promontory; near mournful
Ever weeping Paddington? is that Calvary and Golgotha?
Becoming a building of pity and compassion? Lo!
The stones are pity, and the bricks, well wrought affections:
Enameld with love & kindness, & the tiles graven gold
Labour of merciful hands: the beams & rafters are forgiveness:
The mortar & cement of the work, tears of honesty: the nails,
And the screws & iron braces, are well wrought blandishments. . . .
                              (*J* 12:25-34, E154/K632)

Erdman has shown that the builders in Paddington were renovating

---

[30] See above, p. 193.
[31] *Blake Dictionary*, p. 24.

London after years of war, putting to humane use an area which had been a slum for poor laborers, and from which the bones of Tyburn victims had been dug up.[32] But the symbol of the crucifixion is far from joyful in Blake, and we may suspect that Golgonooza, the new Golgotha, is contaminated by the Tyburn-Calvary associations. It rises above them in the double sense that it transcends them but also has them permanently in its foundations. Ethinthus is "the mortal flesh, . . . love reduced to the physical act."[33] She too is buried here, at the roots of a city that cannot escape its basis in Generation. Compassion and pity are virtues, but always equivocal ones in Blake; here they are well intended, but good intentions often go awry. And the nails and screws and braces, even if positive in implication—which they may not entirely be: we often hear of the nails of the cross and the screws of Urizen—are instruments of rigidity, of a structure that cannot move and change.

Moreover, the whole passage is a systematic point-for-point allegory of a kind that Blake usually denounces. It a later place, when Enitharmon and the Spectre have separated from Los, Albion shrinks away in pain "Rending the fibres of Brotherhood & in Feminine Allegories/Inclosing Los" (*J* 44:18-19, E191/K656). Allegory is implicated in Blake's conception of the female, for although other symbolic systems might represent abstract thought as male and physicality as female, Blake reasons that the female is physical, the physical abstract (unreal), and the female therefore abstract. Golgonooza is a city of art in the fallen world and cannot escape the confinement of the female. In artistic terms, this means that Golgonooza is put together with allegorical rigidity (no doubt Blake has in mind the Jerusalem Temple in this passage). The energies of Golgonooza come from the physical Bowlahoola and Allamanda, and its very form is a sexual propagation by Antamon. Golgonooza represents the best that can be done with physical materials—with *material* materials—but in using them at all it confesses its distance from Eden.

Thus we should not exaggerate the power of art in Blake's system. As a mode of vision art is unquestionably his permanent ideal. "Art is the Tree of LIFE GOD is JESUS." But in the same set of aphorisms Blake describes art as an activity rather than as an achieved product:

> Prayer is the Study of Art
> Praise is the Practise of Art
> Fasting &c. all relate to Art[34]

---

[32] *Blake: Prophet Against Empire*, pp. 472-475. The same images appear in the lyric at the beginning of *Jerusalem* II (E170/K650).

[33] Damon, *Blake Dictionary*, p. 130.

[34] *Laocoön*, E271/K777, E272/K776.

Anything that Los can make is a temporary structure, hammered and bent into rigid form, that serves as a stay against chaos until the apocalypse arrives and man can "converse" in visionary forms instead of having to beat them into shape on the anvil. Meanwhile his labors bear a troubling resemblance to those of Mulciber, the fallen Vulcan and architect of Hell (see Appendix below).

Paradoxically, then, Blake gave his life to art but considered art to be more limited than many of his modern interpreters assume. We are urged to value it highly today for existential reasons that do not properly apply to Blake, though we are often told that they do: "Blake understands his work as a human affirmation of meaning in the face of a cosmos from which all transcendent, objective guarantees of meaning have vanished."[35] Blake is not Camus. The transcendent has not in the least vanished from his cosmos; it has been assimilated (whether or not we can agree that the assimilation is convincing) to the immanent. Art and the divine imagination are equivalent: "ART is the Tree of LIFE GOD is JESUS." And the *work* of art, as opposed to the artistic activity of vision, need not survive the apocalypse in which art will become a mode of being instead of a collection of wrought objects.

The artist must work with what he has, and Blake audaciously turns the Thames itself into the trough that quenches his hot metal:

> The Hammer loud rages in Rintrahs strong grasp swinging loud
> Round from heaven to earth down falling with heavy blow
> Dead on the Anvil, where the red hot wedge groans in pain
> He quenches it in the black trough of his Forge: Londons River
> Feeds the dread Forge, trembling & shuddering along the Valleys
> (*J* 16:11-15, E158/K636)

But in the apocalypse the images will suddenly merge and the fiery forge will flow with the water of life:

> So Albion spoke & threw himself into the Furnaces of affliction
> All was a Vision, all a Dream: the Furnaces became
> Fountains of Living Waters flowing from the Humanity Divine.
> (*J* 96:35-37, E253/K744)

Until then Los is imprisoned in the world of Generation, in which the female must weave the bodies on which he imposes form with his loud hammer. Wagenknecht makes the essential point: "Without the Female Los is powerless in Generation, for he can desire nothing, his spectre can will nothing, without the female space which provides body and form, the realization of will and desire. Henceforth, the

---

[35] Mitchell, *Blake's Composite Art*, p. 216.

problem of Generation is for Blake the problem of the female: the conundrum of *Jerusalem* is the apparently insoluble bond between two females, Vala and Jerusalem."[36]

The sexual element in Los's art is clearly indicated on plate 6 of *Jerusalem* (see fig. 32), the text of which describes Los's division from his Spectre and Emanation. He pauses perplexed in his work while the Spectre hovers with bat wings above his head—covering its ears, as Erdman says, against his voice.[37] But it also looks disturbingly like the flying vulvas that recur in the *Jerusalem* pictures, and is positioned appropriately enough above Los's phallic hammer. We are reminded once again of the ambiguous and difficult status of Los's art, a status symbolized in the psychic myth by his birth with Enitharmon from the fallen Enion. The unfallen Urthona is a Zoa equal among the others. The fallen Los is not simply that Zoa, but instead is a product of the disintegration of the instinctual or unifying aspect of the self (Tharmas and Enion). So from the very outset the fallen imagination is *displaced*. Moreover, the siblings Los and Enitharmon have in turn a son, Orc, and Orc is not simply the fallen Luvah; fallen sexuality is a product of the fallen imagination, and fallen imagination in turn is a product of the divided self. The Spectre of Urthona is indigenous to this fallen existence: he claims to have been born, a kind of parodic afflatus, as an obscure cloud from Enion's nostrils (*FZ* 50:22, E327/K300). And when Los binds down his son Orc it is the Spectre who holds him in place (60:27-28, E334/K307).

In Blake's symbolism Los is time as Enitharmon is space. It is a commonplace that poetic creation does away with ordinary temporality, and Blake of course claims as much with his "eternal Now" (E581/K77). But since Los *is* time—defining it by his spiralling fall through the void, or forging it with the blows of his hammer—he can no longer be Los in the world of Eternity. If time is the mercy of Eternity, that is because it supports us until we need it no longer, not because it is an end in itself.

> Los is by mortals nam'd Time Enitharmon is nam'd Space. . . .
> He is the Spirit of Prophecy the ever apparent Elias.
> Time is the mercy of Eternity; without Times swiftness
> Which is the swiftest of all things: all were eternal torment.
> (*M* 24:68-73, E120/K509-510)

As Bloom comments, Elias (or Elijah) is a type of John the Baptist, a prophet who builds up a temporal refuge against chaos but will give

[36] *Blake's Night*, p. 244.
[37] *Illuminated Blake*, p. 285.

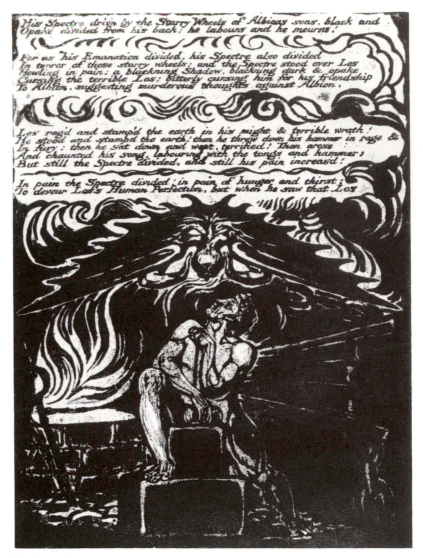

His Spectre driven by the Starry Wheels of Albions sons. black and
Opake divided from his back: he labours and he mourns!

For as his Emanation divided, his Spectre also divided
In terror of those starry wheels; and the Spectre stood over Los
Howling in pain: a blackning Shadow, blackning dark & opake
Cursing the terrible Los: bitterly cursing him for his friendship
To Albion, suggesting murderous thoughts against Albion.

Los rag'd and stampd the earth in his might & terrible wrath!
He stood and stampd the earth! then he threw down his hammer in rage &
In fury; then he sat down and wept, terrified! Then arose
And chaunted his song, labouring with the tongs and hammer;
But still the Spectre divided, and still his pain increas'd!

In pain the Spectre divided: in pain of hunger and thirst:
To devour Los's Human Perfection, but when he saw that Los

32. *Jerusalem*, plate 6.

324

way later to a greater successor: "Los is therefore an artificer, and everything he builds is only an artifice of Eternity, a sculpture that the fire of fresher vision will burn down."[38] And is it not, in the end, an artifice of Generation?

If Los's works were to survive permanently they would become restrictive prisons, and so he must continually destroy and recreate them. It is the activity, not the product, that matters. To be sure, "whatever is visible to the Generated Man,/Is a Creation of mercy & love, from the Satanic Void" (J 13:44–45, E156/K634). But only the warped vision of natural religion mistakes the "limits" for anything more than temporary scaffolding.

> Voltaire insinuates that these Limits are the cruel work of God
> Mocking the Remover of Limits & the Resurrection of the Dead
> Setting up Kings in wrath: in holiness of Natural Religion
> Which Los with his mighty Hammer demolishes time on time
> In miracles & wonders in the Four-fold Desart of Albion
> Permanently Creating to be in Time Reveald & Demolishd.
> (J 73:29–34, E226/K713)

The limits temporarily define the "states" through which man must pass. As Ault has shown in detail, they have a Newtonian, mathematical connotation, and Los's relation to them is destructive as much as creative.[39] Creation must be uncreated lest it imitate the stony structures of Urizen. It is at best a "Divine Analogy" built of the female materials that form "an Allegory around the Winding Worm" (J 85:7, 1, E241/K730). An analogy is not the thing itself.

True creation is a continual birth, not from mothers but from Jesus. In the great painting of the Last Judgment, of which only preliminary sketches survive, Jesus is shown seated on the throne of judgment with the scroll open on his knees, and *at the same time* is the source of a host of infants who are created not in historical succession but in a continuous outflowing of life. "Many Infants appear in the Glory representing the Eternal Creation flowing from the Divine Humanity in Jesus who opens the Scroll of Judgment upon his knees before the Living & the Dead."[40] In contrast with this perpetual creation, Los's creations resemble those of the Elohim, and are symbolic of the Fall as

---

[38] *Blake's Apocalypse*, pp. 336–337. In *VLJ* Elijah "comprehends all the Prophetic Characters" and is seen "on his fiery Chariot bowing before the throne of the Saviour" (E550/K611).

[39] *Visionary Physics*, pp. 76–89.

[40] From a description of the painting sent to Ozias Humphry in 1808 (E543/K444). In the corresponding passage in *VLJ* the infants are described as "the Eternal Births of Intellect from the divine Humanity" (E552/K613).

well as of the impulse to reverse the Fall. After the collapse of Urizen
the world we live in was put together by Los, and its faults are his
faults, as he well knows. Critics who exalt the status of art in Blake's
myth should remember its relation to the fallen artist: "In his vast disdain he labourd beating/The Links of fate link after link an endless
chain of sorrows" (*FZ* 53:27-28, E329/K302). Urizen may be associated with Miltonic fate, but it is the blacksmith Los who forges its
links.

Both as poet and as artist Blake develops symbols to convey the
difficulty of Los's position: the stubborn structure of language, the
sculptures of Los's halls. The emanations are born

> In vegetable mould: created by the Hammer and Loom
> In Bowlahoola & Allamanda where the Dead wail night & day.
> (I call them by their English names: English, the rough basement.
> Los built the stubborn structure of the Language, acting against
> Albions melancholy, who must else have been a Dumb despair.)
> (*J* 36:56-60, E181/K668)

In the expressivist development of post-Enlightenment thought,
words were seen not as signs referring to things but as the creative
expression of the individual consciousness, which they help to shape
even as they give it voice. *Logos* gives way to *poesis*.[41] But to glory in
the flexibility of expression and the primacy of language is more Shel-
leyan than Blakean:

> Language is a perpetual Orphic song,
> Which rules with Daedal harmony a throng
> Of thoughts and forms, which else senseless and shapeless were.[42]

Albion would have been "a Dumb despair" if Los had not created language, but as Blake very acutely sees, its structure is recalcitrant and its
very existence reflects the peculiar relationship between form and substance. According to Saussure, "Language is a form and not a substance."[43] Los gives the form, but Enitharmon gives the substance;
how could the structure not be stubborn? Syntax is tyrannical, forcing
us to think along its lines, and every individual word is haunted by
associations that the user cannot escape. As Gadamer says, "When you
take a word in your mouth you must realize that you have not taken a
tool that can be thrown aside if it won't do the job, but you are fixed in

---

[41] See Charles Taylor's discussion of the significance of Herder's theory of language
(*Hegel*, pp. 18-20).

[42] *Prometheus Unbound*, IV. 415-417.

[43] *Course in General Linguistics*, p. 122.

a direction of thought which comes from afar and stretches beyond you." Blake's fascination with mythological traditions shows his recognition of this truth: every word, every thought, is built up by human usage, and any serious attempt at reconstruction calls for a thoroughgoing rethinking of tradition. In so doing the artist frees language from its unexamined rigidities and makes it live again, for as Gadamer adds, "Language is not its elaborate conventionalism, nor the burden of pre-schematization with which it loads us, but the generative and creative power unceasingly to make this whole fluid."[44]

Blake's awareness of the conventionality of language is profoundly modern, as is his rebellion against conventionality. For if language is, in Sapir's phrase, "the reduction of experience to familiar form,"[45] then Blake's conception of its stubbornness reflects his determination to defamiliarize it. "I call them by their English names," he says, but those names—Bowlahoola and Allamanda—are unlikely to spring to the lips of most speakers of English. Even as he makes this assertion, therefore, Blake is transforming the language.

Blake is unmodern, however, in his belief that the limits imposed by language are only provisional, and that a deeper reality lies behind the linguistic structures that are our normal way of pointing to it. Truth is not dependent on language, as the "vision of light" poem shows, even though the communication of truth to others—to the artist's audience—undoubtedly is. "In vain," exclaims Berkeley, "do we extend our view into the heavens, and pry into the entrails of the earth; in vain do we consult the writings of learned men, and trace the dark footsteps of antiquity; we need only draw the curtain of words, to behold the fairest tree of knowledge, whose fruit is excellent, and within the reach of our hand."[46] Blake does not think it so easy to draw the curtain of words, and he wants to gain access to the Tree of Life, not the Tree of Knowledge. That can only take place in Eternity, where words become truly creative as in the symbolism of the first chapter of John's gospel, the living breath of the Almighty rather than a stubborn structure.

Lo the Eternal Great Humanity
To whom be Glory & Dominion Evermore Amen
Walks among all his awful Family seen in every face

---

[44] *Truth and Method*, pp. 496, 498.

[45] Edward Sapir, "Language," in *Culture, Language and Personality* (Berkeley, 1949), p. 14.

[46] *Principles of Human Knowledge*, introduction, par. 24.

As the breath of the Almighty. such are the words of man to man
In the great Wars of Eternity, in the fury of Poetic Inspiration,
To build the Universe stupendous: Mental forms Creating.
                                    (*M* 30:15-20, E128/K519)

Meanwhile, we are confined to a world in which the word is woven
into the garment of the Shadowy Female:

I will have Writings written all over it in Human Words
That every Infant that is born upon the Earth shall read
And get by rote as a hard task of a life of sixty years.
                                    (*M* 18:12-14, E110/K499)

At the very end of *Milton*, Ololon descends as a moony ark "in
streams of gore," and the garment reappears upon the limbs of Jesus:

With one accord the Starry Eight became
One Man Jesus the Saviour. wonderful! round his limbs
The Clouds of Ololon folded as a Garment dipped in blood
Written within & without in woven letters: & the Writing
Is the Divine Revelation in the Litteral expression,
A Garment of War; I heard it namd the Woof of Six Thousand
    Years.
                                    (42:10-15, E142/K534)

Blake alludes to Isaiah 63:3 on the vesture dipped in blood, traditionally a prophecy of Christ, and to a passage at the end of Revelation: "And he was clothed with a vesture dipped in blood: and his
name is called The Word of God" (Rev. 19:13). That is the true Word.
But in Blake's interpretation, the garment of the revelation, although
an imaginative transformation of the Shadowy Female's garment, *is
still a garment*. It is dipped in blood, emblematic of Christ's torture in
Luvah, and since its expression is necessarily "Litteral," being adapted
to fallen consciousness, it is a garment of warfare in the world of history ("the Woof of Six Thousand Years") rather than of Eternity. The
eternal vision may be communicated in symbols, but it is not itself reducible to material form. In Eden the garment will be needed no more.
Poetic creation becomes literal as it is reduced to "expression," but in
Eden expression will be immediate and intuitive rather than mediated
and literal. Meanwhile, we have to try to look through language and
not with it, for as the Antinomian prophet Muggleton said, "The letter of the scripture is as a veil before reason's face, because reason cannot see forth in the letter of the scripture by literal and temporal expression."[47] Los as artist has to work within the world of Urizen and

[47] Ludowick Muggleton, *A True Interpretation of the Eleventh Chapter of the Revelation*

Vala, where the divine revelation is indeed temporal—Los is time—
and is mediated "in the Litteral expression."

If art produces rigid artifacts, then an appropriate symbol for visual
art is sculpture.

> All things acted on Earth are seen in the bright Sculptures of
> Los's Halls & every Age renews its powers from these Works
> With every pathetic story possible to happen from Hate or
> Wayward Love & every sorrow & distress is carved here
> Every Affinity of Parents Marriages & Friendships are here
> In all their various combinations wrought with wondrous Art
> All that can happen to Man in his pilgrimage of seventy years
> Such is the Divine Written Law of Horeb & Sinai:
> And such the Holy Gospel of Mount Olivet & Calvary.
>
> (*J* 16:61–69, E159/K638)

It is quite remarkable that this passage is commonly quoted as a celebration of art, for in fact it is richly ambiguous. It is of course true that
the imagination preserves the events of history, but history itself is
fallen and its events are filled with "Wayward Love & every sorrow &
distress" as well as with human sympathies. Blake seems to have believed that Solomon's Temple contained statues of the cherubim and
other figures that furnished the models for later art.[48] But the
cherubim and the Temple are both highly suspect in Blake's myth,
and there is no reason to think that the sculptures are a symbol of the
fully liberated imagination. On the contrary, they express its limitation in a fallen world that reduces life to rigid forms. "Lots Wife being
Changed into Pillar of Salt alludes to the Mortal Body being renderd a
Permanent Statue" (*VLJ*, E546/K607).

Putting the matter more generally, Los's sculptures or "embodied
semblances" (*FZ* 90:9, E356/K331) give fixed shape to human existence in much the same way that the classes of men do, which are also
forged by Los. In his discussion of Chaucer's pilgrims as eternal types,
Blake says, "Accident ever varies, Substance can never suffer change
or decay." But this leaves unclear the status of individual human beings who are born into the world of accidence. With evident irony
Blake says in the next paragraph, "As Newton numbered the stars,
and as Linnaeus numbered the plants, so Chaucer numbered the
classes of men" (*DC*, E523–524/K567). Fallen art is tied down to a

---

of St. John (1662), quoted by Joseph A. Wittreich, Jr., *Visionary Poetics: Milton's Tradition and His Legacy* (San Marino, Cal., 1979), p. 29.

[48] See Bindman, *Blake as an Artist*, pp. 157–158, and Morton Paley, " 'Wonderful Originals'—Blake and Ancient Sculpture," in Essick and Pearce, pp. 170–171.

world of number and of static sculptural form, and the Laocoön is a statue that perfectly symbolizes man's entrapment in the coils of materiality and fallen reason—"Reasonings like vast Serpents/Infold around my limbs, bruising my minute articulations" (*J* 15:12-13, E157/K635). The work of the artist can be a saving one, as for instance when Milton resists Urizen's baptism in the water of materiality and instead gives him human form:

> Silent Milton stood before
> The darkened Urizen; as the sculptor silent stands before
> His forming image; he walks round it patient labouring.
> (*M* 20:7-9, E113/K502)

But Urizen is still Urizen. And Los's sculptures are rich in painful stories of "sorrow & distress" and of "Hate or/Wayward Love." They are emblematic of the world of Experience, of the "Written Law of Horeb & Sinai" and the cruel though ultimately saving symbolism of the cross ("the Holy Gospel of Mount Olivet & Calvary," *J* 16:69).

The function of Los's sculptures is something more than to record history for its own sake or to provide archetypes for artistic creation. It points beyond its images to the truths which they symbolize yet petrify. Blake indicates this very clearly in the eightieth Dante picture (see fig. 33), showing a rock in Purgatory with relief sculptures of David recovering the ark and of the Annunciation.[49] David dances with his harp before the ark while Saul's daughter Michal looks down from a window in contempt because he is no longer a warrior. The Daughters of Beulah (or cherubim) hover over the ark with facing wings, while Uzzah is struck down by the lightning of the Law. The ark is a far from positive symbol, and Blake certainly does not want it to be treated as the holy of holies. In the right-hand sculpture a curiously constricted Gabriel appears to a scantily clad Mary who is writing in a book (as in traditional iconography). This may, as Roe supposes, signify the divine form of female love, but it is equally likely that it connotes all the ambiguities of birth to a mother in the fallen world, which we have already discussed in connection with the Incarnation.

And it is essential to see that these are *only* sculptures, mute images on a cliff face that demand interpretation. Dante and Virgil stand at the edge of the precipice, with the Sea of Time and Space rolling far below. It is for them to make imaginative use of these images, to respond to their imaginative element while rejecting their errors, and then to *go on* around the corner of the path to a visonary wholeness that needs no

---

[49] I follow Roe's exegesis in *Blake's Illustrations* . . . , pp. 150-153.

33. *The Rock Sculptured with the Recovery of the Ark*, illustration for
Dante's *Divine Comedy*.

didactic sculptures. The ark and the Incarnation both have good and bad aspects, good and bad modes of interpretation. Blake's fundamental message is that we should aspire to a condition in which the sacred ark becomes an irrelevant symbol and in which generation (as in the Incarnation) is transformed into regeneration.

In the penultimate plate of the *Job* series (see fig. 34), Job, arms outstretched, expounds the meaning of allegorical wall paintings to his three daughters, whom Damon identifies as representing the arts of poetry, painting, and music.[50] "Poetry as it now exists on earth, in the various remains of ancient authors, Music as it exists in old tunes or melodies, Painting and Sculpture as it exists in the remains of Antiquity and in the works of more modern genius, is Inspiration, and cannot be surpassed; it is perfect and eternal. . . . To suppose that Art can go beyond the finest specimens of Art that are now in the world, is not knowing what Art is; it is being blind to the gifts of the spirit" (*DC*, E535/K579). Existing works of art are never fully adequate as artifacts, but they perform as well as can be done the function of pointing to eternal truth. There can be no progress in art because refinements in style or technique can have no bearing on that function. So Blake goes on to say, "The Beauty proper for sublime art, is lineaments, or forms and features that are capable of being the receptacles of intellect." In themselves the forms are only containers which the imagination must fill.

The most challenging interpretation of the *Job* plate is Frye's: "Job's arms, outspread over his daughters, show that he with his daughters forms part of a larger human body, so that although the objective order from which his calamities came has been annihilated for Job, the calamities being depicted on the walls 'In the shadows of Possibility,' as Blake says in *Jerusalem*, Job's renewed state is not a subjective one."[51] Characteristically, Frye has it both ways: the story of Job is one of inner warfare, which is to say of the mind of a man, yet at the same time it is assimilated to the psychic experience of universal Man, so that it is not subjective at all. Blake's theory certainly supports this formulation. Universal Man includes everything that Newton or Locke would call "objects" within his subjectivity. Art, too, must be objective and universal on this hypothesis, since if all men share in the same experience, then art shows them what they already know and already are. But if we think of Los in his arduous struggle against inhibitions and obstacles, not least among which is his own Spectre, we

---

[50] *Blake's Job*, p. 50. Damon points out that in the watercolor version the daughters hold emblems of their arts.

[51] "Blake's Reading of the Book of Job," in Rosenfeld, p. 231. The reference is to *J* 92:18, E250/K739.

How precious are thy thoughts
unto me O God
how great is the sum of them

There were not found Women fair as the Daughters of Job
in all the Land & their Father gave them Inheritance
among their Brethren

If I ascend up into Heaven thou art there
If I make my bed in Hell behold Thou
art there

London Published as the Act directs March 8 1825 by William Blake N 3 Fountain Court Strand

34. *The Book of Job*, plate 20.

may be more skeptical about the definitive value of this kind of art. The Job series ends with an evocation of music on the final plate, an art which lives only while it is being performed, rather than with the static medium of pictorial art. Plate 21 is thus a step forward from the fallen (though inspired) art of plate 20. And of course the music of plate 21 is unheard; it is suggested by a pictorial image to which the viewer must bring the imaginative sounds, just as Blake heard a

heavenly host singing in the sun. Similarly Milton stands "silent" before Urizen while giving him form, but the picture on plate 18 of
Milton shows a sunrise with dancing musicians and a youthful bard
making music above the figures of Milton and Urizen.

Without denying that Job's daughters are emanative parts of himself, we may also see them as his pupils. As Lindberg has shown, the
role of the daughters in this plate, unmentioned in the Book of Job,
derives from the apocryphal Testament of Job of which Blake pretty
clearly knew (through pictorial rather than literary tradition). In the
Testament Job dictates the Book of Job to his daughters—Blake must
have been struck by the parallel with Milton—and gives them musical
instruments, as on Blake's plate 21, with which to praise God in continual song.[52] When we look closely at Job's pictures on plate 20, we
notice that they do not all record what has happened in the preceding
plates. The right-hand oval in particular is remarkable, showing a man
apparently fainting at the plow, which makes one think of Urizen the
plowman fainting in *Milton* and the cognate myth of Satan fainting at
the harrow.[53] In other words, Job depicts his experience by means of
symbolic equivalents which are drawn—since Blake is the artist—from
Blake's myth. Other writers or prophets might have other symbols,
for it is the truth that is eternal, not the visible images that adumbrate
it. As with all of Blake's art, we are challenged to enter these images in
the fiery chariot of our imagination and make them our own. Mitchell
has well said, "If both the senses and works of art are windows, the
implication is that Blake sees his illuminated prints as sensory open-
ings in the walls of our dark skull or body-cave."[54]

The ambiguities of art are superbly imaged on the final plate of
Jerusalem (see fig. 35), which is often described—at the cost of distort-
ing its evident symbolism—as a vision of Edenic art. On the contrary,
it presents the poem *Jerusalem* as the best that the fallen imagination
can do, and by implication invites the viewer-reader to go beyond it.
Los leans on his hammer and tongs, and the often-noticed resemblance
of the tongs to Urizen's compasses must cut both ways: if Los has redeemed the creation of the Elohim, on the other hand he has inevitably
participated in that creation by imposing form and limit. The sun,
meanwhile, is borne on the shoulder of the indispensable Spectre, and

[52] See Lindberg, *William Blake's Illustrations . . .* , p. 343.

[53] It may be significant also that this figure's posture resembles that of "William" as
the star of Milton enters his foot on *Milton* 32, and the mirror image figure of "Robert"
on pl. 37. A similar figure appears in a circle on the left-hand side of *The Fall of Man*, fig.
7, p. 92 above. Martin Butlin identifies the scene as the destruction of Job's plowmen
by Satan, rather than by the Sabeans as in Job 1:15 ("Cataloguing William Blake," in
Essick and Pearce, p. 87).

[54] *Blake's Composite Art*, p. 61, referring to *FZ* 9:10-13, E300/K270.

35. *Jerusalem*, plate 100.

the crescent moon of Beulah hangs near Enitharmon, light descending
from it like a waterfall or veil, while she weaves the bloody fibres of
the body on the loom of Cathedron, holding a spindle in her left hand.

Behind these noble but fallen figures—for the trio of Zoa, Spectre,
and Emanation have no separate existence in Eden—lies a Druid serpent temple like the ones at Stonehenge and Avebury, resembling also
the winged serpent-sun that Blake sometimes liked to imitate.[55] In earlier pictures the Druid megaliths had towered over tiny human
figures, whereas here the human forms are dominant. And the stones
are no longer dispersed at random but are arranged in perfect symmetry. Yet this too is inseparable from fallenness: it may be fearful,
but it remains symmetry. Blake saw Stonehenge as an astronomical
instrument

> . . . of Reasonings: of unhewn Demonstrations
> In labyrinthine arches. (Mighty Urizen the Architect.) thro which
> The Heavens might revolve & Eternity be bound in their chain.
> (*J* 66:3-5, E216/K702)

And we remember that Stonehenge was built when "Thought
chang'd the infinite to a serpent. . . . Then was the serpent temple
form'd, image of infinite/Shut up in finite revolutions" (*Europe* 10:16,
21-22, E62/K241). The serpent is a symbol of the Fall, fabricated by

[55] See the illustrations from Stukeley and Bryant in Raine, *Blake and Tradition*, I, 50,
289.

thought. Los in his triumph has built the city of Golgonooza and has compelled the serpent symbolism of Stonehenge, where Luvah was cruelly sacrificed, to bend to his will. But Los is still "of the Elohim."

In Eden all this must pass.

> Urthona is arisen in his strength no longer now
> Divided from Enitharmon no longer the Spectre Los
> Where is the Spectre of Prophecy where the delusive Phantom
> Departed & Urthona rises from the ruinous walls
> In all his ancient strength to form the golden armour of science
> For intellectual War. The War of swords departed now
> The dark Religions are departed & sweet Science reigns.
>
> (*FZ* 139:4-10, E392/K379)

Here is a "science," a mode of knowledge, that liberates the energy of war without its destructiveness, and has no further need of the Spectre or of a separated Enitharmon. Urthona is now a warrior of the imagination rather than a maker of artifacts; *logos* has replaced *poesis*. But William Blake is not Urthona and knows he is not. The myth cannot be sustained, with its assertion of a reality that transcends fallen art, without something like the faith that sustained the prophets. "Then the Lord put forth his hand, and touched my mouth. And the Lord said unto me, Behold, I have put my words into thy mouth" (Jer. 1:9). Critics who admire Los (and of course Los is admirable) sometimes exaggerate the prophet's self-righteousness, and underestimate the importance of the enslaved Spectre of externalized creation. What Hegel calls the "negative mediating agency" is inseparable from labor of any kind, and just as self-forgiveness is Blake's answer to man's dividedness, so forgiveness and reintegration of the Spectre are essential for the longed-for leap from art into Eternity. Only when the artist subordinates himself to the Divine Vision can he be confident that his hard-won images, clumsy and rigid though they may be, are reflections of the Savior's dictation.

> Again he speaks in thunder and in fire!
> Thunder of Thought, & flames of fierce desire.
> Even from the depths of Hell his voice I hear,
> Within the unfathomed caverns of my Ear.
>
> (*J* 3, E144/K621)

LOS AND APOCALYPSE

Los precipitates the Last Judgment, tearing the sun and moon from the heavens which are then rolled up while the last trump sounds (*FZ*

117:6ff., E390/K377). But he does not create it. The role of art is to
make apocalypse possible and then give way. By himself Los is the
crippled smith, and he cannot be whole until he reunites in Man—
"Urthona limping from his fall on Tharmas leand" (FZ 137:8, E390/
K377). Apocalypse is internal and individual, though it may also be
social and historical, since "whenever any Individual Rejects Error &
Embraces Truth a Last Judgment passes upon that Individual" (VLJ,
E551/K613). Each person must achieve for himself a communion with
Eternity like that which Blake experienced when "the Lark mounted
with a loud trill from Felphams Vale" (M 42:29, E142/K534).

Now, this individualizing of vision places a special strain on the
conception of apocalypse. If I am right about Blake's theory of symbolism, reality is not subjective; our visions differ because we build
them out of fallen materials, not because the archetypal or eternal
Forms are infinitely diverse. "The Last Judgment is one of these
Stupendous Visions. I have represented it as I saw it. To different
People it appears differently as every thing else does for tho on Earth
things seem Permanent they are less permanent than a Shadow as we
all know too well" (VLJ, E544/K605). In the fallen world, therefore,
imagination exists in the spaces *between* experience as ordinarily understood.[56]

An Eternity perpetually created by the imagination is very different
from a consummation at the end of historical time, and *Milton* and
Jerusalem are accordingly much more elliptical about the apocalypse
than *The Four Zoas*. As Grimes reminds us, Blake's theology escapes
history by locating salvation in the interstices between historical
events rather than at their culmination.[57] In writing *The Four Zoas*,
where apocalypse retains a historical basis and alludes systematically
to biblical precedent, Blake evidently came to realize that traditional
eschatology was incompatible with his myth; and it is worth considering why this should be so.

In traditional terms man awaits not himself but the king. "I saw in
the night visions, and behold, one like the Son of man came with the
clouds of heaven, and came to the Ancient of days, and they brought
him near before him. And there was given him dominion, and glory,
and a kingdom, that all people, nations, and languages, should serve

[56] See the discussion of Los creating spaces larger than a globule of blood, and of
those that are smaller than the globule of blood opening "into Eternity of which this
vegetable Earth is but a shadow" (M 29:22, E126/K516-517).

[57] "What prevents the prophecies from being eschatalogical in the strict sense of the
word is that the time of renewal is not the new aeon which succeeds the old, evil aeon.
Rather the time of renewal is the instant between aeons. The time of transition *is* the
time of imagination" (*The Divine Imagination*, p. 56).

him: his dominion is an everlasting dominion, which shall not pass away, and his kingdom that which shall not be destroyed."⁵⁸ Blake will have nothing to do with Christ the King, but he needs a divine agent of the *eschaton*, the "end," who can embody the ending in personal form instead of presiding over it from above.

In a moving passage in the eighth Night of *The Four Zoas*, Los and Jerusalem take down the body of Jesus from the cross and bear it to the sepulchre which Los had hewn for himself in the rock of the fallen world, "despairing of Life Eternal" (*FZ* 106:16, E365/K349). Rahab then cuts off "the Mantle of Luvah from/The Lamb of God," revealing "the Temple & the Synagogue of Satan & Mystery," the whole system of repression concealed in the profane misuse of Jesus in the symbolism of the Antichrist. (Only the fallen church sees Jesus as dead; the true Christ, disguised from fallen eyes by Luvah's robes of blood, is life everlasting.) At this crisis Los appeals to Rahab:

> He answerd her with tenderness & love not uninspird
> Los sat upon his anvil stock they sat beside the forge
> Los wipd the sweat from his red brow & thus began
> To the delusive female forms shining among his furnaces:
> I am that shadowy Prophet who six thousand years ago
> Fell from my station in the Eternal bosom. I divided
> To multitude & my multitudes are children of Care & Labour
> O Rahab I behold thee I was once like thee a Son
> Of Pride and I also have pierced the Lamb of God in pride & wrath.
> (*FZ* 113:44–52, E365/K350)

The Miltonic turn of "love not uninspired" is keenly ironic. Rahab refuses this plea, just as Eve betrayed Adam's love, and unites with Urizen to bring about the final consolidation of Error that precedes apocalypse. What we feel most deeply here is the hopelessness of Los's art unless aided by divine power. Far from being Jesus, he has pierced Jesus, has labored to exhaustion but in vain, and has placed the divine corpse (as he imagines it) in a tomb hewn in despair for himself.

As we noticed in the last chapter, Luvah's robes of blood recall the passage in Isaiah that lies behind the winepress image in Revelation: "I have trodden the winepress alone; and of the people there was none with me: for I will tread them in mine anger, and trample them in my fury; and their blood shall be sprinkled upon my garments, and I will stain all my raiment" (Isa. 63:3). Jesus is at once the sacrifice whose blood takes the place of that of beasts (a contrast made explicit in the Epistle to the Hebrews) and the trampler of the grapes of humanity in

⁵⁸ Dan. 7:13–14; see Mark 13:26.

the apocalypse. The traditional interpretation of wine symbolizing immortality—casting off the wineskins of mortality—should not blind us to the violence and even sadism in the Dionysiac drunkenness of Luvah's sons and daughters. Blake exploits the rhetoric of revolution, and does not minimize the anguish of the end of the world as we know it.

> The blood of life flows plentiful Odors of life arose
> All round the heavenly arches & the Odors rose singing this song
> O terrible wine presses of Luvah O caverns of the Grave
> How lovely the delights of those risen again from death
> O trembling joy excess of joy is like Excess of grief.
>   (*FZ* 135:38–136:3, E389/K376)

Here the apocalypse is still imagined as coming at the end of a narrative sequence, and the real suffering that it entails is fully acknowledged.

In displacing Luvah from the center of apocalypse, Blake considerably alters his vision of its significance. To substitute Los for Luvah is to place a very great, perhaps an intolerable, burden upon the imagination, which must now act as judge, pardoner, and victim all at once. "The blow of his Hammer is Justice, the swing of his Hammer: Mercy./The force of Los's Hammer is eternal Forgiveness" (*J* 88:49–50, E245/K734). The death of Jesus is an eternally recurring act of unselfishness, not a unique sacrifice that gives meaning to human suffering and identifies the Judge of the *eschaton* with the human beings whom he judges.

> Jesus said, Wouldest thou love one who never died
> For thee or ever die for one who had not died for thee
> And if God dieth not for Man & giveth not himself
> Eternally for Man Man could not exist! for Man is Love:
> As God is Love: every kindness to another is a little Death
> In the Divine Image nor can Man exist but by Brotherhood.
>   (*J* 96:23–28, E253/K743)

Death happens over and over again, eternally, and every act of kindness, since it involves a suppression of selfhood, is a kind of death. In such a system there is not much room left for a decisive apocalypse after which all things will be made new.

Since Los is Time, the implications of this shift in Blake's thought deserve attention. It is of course true that his view of history took on, as Frye says, a Spenglerian pessimism, and that it participates in the widespread Romantic internalization of apocalypse that Abrams has described so well.[59] But it needs to be said also that Blake's ambivalence about the meaning of history reflects a conception of time and eternity that has often surfaced in the Western tradition. From the Old Testament, Christianity inherited an idea of history as linear progression embodying the will of God, in contrast to the endless cycles of Greek and oriental thought. Buber speaks of the prophetic "turning to the future," and since in Blake it is Urizen who broods upon futurity, Bloom rightly reminds us that the prophets "refused to yield up history to the Accuser to the extent that Blake did."[60] But Christian typology drastically altered this pattern by interpreting the events of the Old Testament as symbolic units planted there by God to foreshadow the events of the New, and looked forward to an ending in which history would be gathered up into eternity. In such an eschatology, as Bultmann has said, "The end is not the completion of history but its breaking-off," and the meaning of history is not grounded in events as such, for "in every moment slumbers the possibility of being the eschatological moment."[61] Accordingly, there has always been a strong impulse in Christianity toward a conception of eternity that could liberate man from time by affording a breakthrough out of temporal succession.

It was a frequent theme in Renaissance speculation that eternity, far from being separate from or above the world of time, is fully present in every instant.[62] In phenomenological experience this eternal moment is revealed in the sudden lightning flash of the mystics, Boehme's *Blitz*: "For when the dark anguish . . . receives freedom in itself, it is transformed in the terror, in freedom, into a flash, and the flash embraces freedom or gentleness. Then the sting of death is broken."[63] We continue to inhabit the same universe as before, but for the first time we see it truly.

Blake's Los says, "I walk up and down in Six Thousand Years: their Events are present before me" (*J* 74:19, E227/K714). The cycles of fallen history, Los's handiwork, forever repeat themselves, but Jesus breaks into them and gathers them into eternity.

> But Jesus breaking thro' the Central Zones of Death & Hell
> Opens Eternity in Time & Space; triumphant in Mercy.

[59] Frye, *The Stubborn Structure*, p. 184; Abrams, *Natural Supernaturalism*, esp. ch. 6.

[60] Martin Buber, *The Prophetic Faith*, trans. Carlyle Witton-Davies (New York, 1960), ch. 7; Bloom, *Blake's Apocalypse*, p. 441.

[61] Rudolf Bultmann, *History and Eschatology: The Presence of Eternity* (New York, 1962), pp. 30, 155.

[62] See for instance G. F. Waller, "Transition in Renaissance Ideas of Time and the Place of Giordano Bruno," *Neophilologus*, 55 (1971), 3-15.

[63] Boehme, *Six Theosophic Points*, I.lvii, p. 18.

Thus are the Heavens formd by Los within the Mundane Shell
And where Luther ends Adam begins again in Eternal Circle
To awake the Prisoners of Death; to bring Albion again
With Luvah into light eternal, in his eternal day.

(J 76:21-26, E229/K716)

The effect is not so much to end time as to redeem it, freeing man from Urizenic preoccupation with past and future so that he can live each moment in the fullness of eternity. As Wittgenstein says, "If we take eternity to mean not infinite temporal duration but timelessness, then eternal life belongs to those who live in the present."[64] The final vision of the Zoas, conversing in visionary forms dramatic, represents them as "going forward irresistible from Eternity to Eternity," a phrase which we have seen in Boehme and which probably derives from biblical locutions like "from everlasting to everlasting."[65] Eternity is no static nontemporal state, but neither is it the bottomless draining away of atomistic historical moments; it is a succession of fully living moments each one of which embodies or expresses eternity.

Blake never relaxed his lifelong hatred of social injustice, as is obvious in the brilliant attack on factory labor and press-gang militarism in Jerusalem 65, or in aphorisms like "The Princes Robes & Beggars Rags/Are Toadstools on the Misers Bags" (Auguries, E482/K432). But given his philosophy of time, it is no wonder that he moved toward a political quietism that should make us qualify the usual assumption that he was a fiery radical. The seventeenth-century Antinomians whom he so much resembles were similarly ineffective in (or detached from) the political arena of their equally turbulent times. To a modern Protestant spokesman they may look like "fanatical and violently subversive elements, . . . forerunners of the French Revolution and of Marxism," since their rhetoric was certainly inflammatory enough. But as their historian dryly remarks, "Inexplicable knowledge of the true laws of all happening is not easily translated into workable rules of ordinary political intercourse."[66]

Similarly, Blake after the early 1790s was radical but not political. He was philosophically more radical than the philosophes, since he believed that society could not be changed until man himself was changed. But politically he lacked their strong commitment to reform,

---

[64] Tractatus Logico-Philosophicus, 6.4311.

[65] J 98:27, E255/K745. For Boehme, see p. 190 above; "from everlasting to everlasting" is found in Psalm 90:2.

[66] J. S. Whale, The Protestant Tradition: An Essay in Interpretation (Cambridge, 1955), p. 127; Huehns, Antinomianism in English History, p. 91.

and wrote as a spectator of history rather than as a particpant in it, much as the Old Testament prophets viewed the victories of Assyria or Babylon as expressions of God's will. There is a strong providential element in Blake's thought, and since he awaits the total renovation of man before expecting the renovation of society, he is chiliastic where the Enlightenment was utopian. And the hope of change soon alters into a private and internal form; there can be no apocalypse in the state of bondage that we are accustomed to, which can be escaped only by escaping the body of death. "Many Persons such as Paine & Voltaire with some of the Ancient Greeks say we will not converse concerning Good & Evil we will live in Paradise & Liberty. You may do so in Spirit but not in the Mortal Body. . . . While we are in the world of Mortality we Must Suffer" (*VLJ*, E554/K615-616).

In such a philosophy the relation of the artist to events grows increasingly tenuous. In the third illustration to Gray's *Bard* the bard is shown as a gigantic figure staring down at the doomed king whose fate he weaves in bloody cords, which are also the strings of a gory harp. We are reminded both of the poet's power and of his immersion in the natural world (imaged also by the enraged figures of oak, cave, and torrent in the next illustration but one). We admire the rebel against tyranny but we recognize as well his complicity in the bloodbath that rebellion brings about.

In reinterpreting the apocalypse Blake has thus to deal in a new way with the material of suffering and punishment. It might be said that he retains the imagery but not the meaning of the wrath of God, the Day of Yahweh, *dies irae*. Man is alienated, but from himself only; he dwells in error but not in sin, and the erroneous aspects of himself can be dismissed as Satanic rather than confronted and worked through in a narrative progression (which is one reason why *Jerusalem* has so much less narrative form even than *Milton*, let alone *The Four Zoas*).

> With such a horrid clang
> As on Mount Sinai rang
>   While the red fire, and smould'ring clouds out brake:
> The aged earth aghast
> With terror of that blast,
>   Shall from the surface to the centre shake;
> When at the world's last session,
> The dreadful judge in middle air shall spread his throne.[67]

Blake has the Judgment but not the omnipotent Judge, the imagery of punishment without its justification.

---

[67] Milton, *On the Morning of Christ's Nativity*, stanza xvii.

It would be still truer, however, to say that in retaining traces of the orgiastic drunkenness (see _Milton_ 27, E123-124/K513-514), Blake means to remind us of the physical and temporal nature of such a Last Judgment as this. Puritans often rejoiced in the grisly images of the Book of Revelation because they enjoyed the thought of their enemies weltering in blood. Blake's conception is much closer to Boehme's, in which Christ "treads the winepress of the fierceness and wrath, and enters into the wrath as into the center of fire, and extinguishes the fire with his heavenly blood."[68] The wrath of apocalypse is the wrath of the contraries. Christ enters the wrath as he enters the mortal body, and is not himself wrathful except insofar as he takes upon him the wrathfulness of the fallen world. In Blake the apocalypse, like the Incarnation and the Crucifixion, must be inseparable from the misery of the fallen body.

Since Blake's usage differs from the usual Christian connotations of apocalypse, some commentators prefer to use the term "eschatology" or to point out that Blake sometimes contrasts visionary rebirth during the present life with a later entrance into life everlasting, much as Paul does in Colossians.[69] This would imply a fairly traditional view of the _Parousia_, Christ's presence in the believer's soul and his ultimate coming in the apocalypse. But we must be careful not to ascribe to Blake a wholehearted acceptance of the usual interpretations of the familiar "kingdom of God is within you" (Luke 17:21). For if this text often encouraged "a process of de-eschatalogization, whereby the _Parousia_ hope was given a completely spiritual content,"[70] then Blake's suspicion of the fallen imagination must once again be emphasized.

Leslie Brisman distinguishes usefully between prophetic time, which seeks to create temporal structures against the mere confusion of chaos, and apocalyptic time, the vision of reality as instantaneous and atemporal. Since Los's task is carried out in prophetic time—since in fact he creates and _is_ prophetic time—his role is deeply problematic. Even if the time he creates is the mercy of eternity, he inevitably violates the atemporal ideal and participates in the fall.[71] The winepress of

[68] _Von der Menschwerdung Jesu Christi_, I.vii, quoted by Stoudt, _Sunrise to Eternity_, p. 282.

[69] At the great moment of vision at the end of _Milton_, "My Soul returnd into its mortal state/To Resurrection & Judgment in the Vegetable Body" (_M_ 42:26-27, E142/K534). And in one place at least, in the passage already quoted about suffering "in the world of Mortality" (_VLJ_, E554/K616), Blake seems to look forward to a new spiritual condition which cannot be attained until physical death. Cf. Colossians 3:1-4.

[70] S.G.F. Brandon, _History, Time, and Deity_ (Manchester, 1965), p. 183n.

[71] "Any extension of time," Brisman observes, "is a spinning out of a web that catches man in the net of history when he should be liberating himself from temporal-

Los is inseparable from fallen conflict, and it doubles as the printing press of fallen art:

> This Wine-press is call'd War on Earth, it is the Printing-Press
> Of Los; and here he lays his words in order above the mortal brain
> As cogs are formd in a wheel to turn the cogs of the adverse wheel.
>
> (*M* 27:8-10, E123/K513)

Much suffering must be endured before this winepress can produce the wine of eternity. The printing press is a Urizenic machine of "cogs tyrannic" that move each other "by compulsion" and must be contrasted with "those in Eden: which/Wheel within Wheel in freedom revolve in harmony & peace" (*J* 15:18-20, E157/K636).

Just as art is not apocalypse but a prelude to it, so apocalypse may be a prelude to a new fall. Eden gives way to Beulah, Beulah to Generation and then Ulro. I would interpret "whenever" as meaning "over and over again" rather than "once and for all" in the statement "Whenever any Individual Rejects Error & Embraces Truth a Last Judgment passes upon that Individual" (*VLJ*, E551/K613). No one lives in a perpetual epiphany. And in the fallen world the fearfulness of apocalypse, of the winepress of Luvah and its sadistic torments, is no mere metaphor.

> Loud the Serpent Orc ragd thro his twenty Seven
> Folds. The tree of Mystery went up in folding flames
> Blood issud out in mighty volumes pouring in whirlpools fierce
> From out the flood gates of the Sky The Gates are burst down pour
> The torrents black upon the Earth the blood pours down incessant
> Kings in their palaces lie drownd Shepherds their flocks their tents
> Roll down the mountains in black torrents Cities Villages
> High spires & Castles drownd in the black deluge Shoal on Shoal
> Float the dead carcases of Men & Beasts driven to & fro on waves
> Of foaming blood beneath the black incessant Sky till all
> Mysterys tyrants are cut off & not one left on Earth.
>
> (*FZ* 119:3-13, E373/K359)

The vision of rivers of black blood, of men and beasts and cities drowning in it, is obsessive and appalling.

When Blake reimagines the apocalypse in the later prophecies he does not reject these dreadful images but, as always in his symbolism,

---

ity" (*Milton's Poetry of Choice and Its Romantic Heirs* [Ithaca, 1973], p. 204). In Blake's terms, Los thus exhibits complicity in the weaving of the web of Enitharmon, which in turn is uncomfortably similar to the web of Vala. Brisman notes also (p. 202) that Blake strongly objected to Milton's division of eternity into temporal periods.

transvalues them. And the basis for this is present in *The Four Zoas* too, for directly after the passage just quoted we read,

> From the clotted gore & from the hollow den
> Start forth the trembling millions into flames of mental fire
> Bathing their Limbs in the bright visions of Eternity.
>
> (119:21-23)

Fire and strife in Eternity are symbols of life, not death. What changes in *Milton* and *Jerusalem* is the recognition that history is not the theater of this transformation, which comes instead in an accession of Jesus into the individual imagination. Just as Los enabled Blake to fight free of an obsessive vision of his father and brothers in which "The heavens drop with human gore" (E693/K818), so Jesus liberates man by turning the blood of apocalypse into wine: "Whence is this sound of rage of Men drinking each others blood/Drunk with the smoking gore & red but not with nourishing wine" (*FZ* 120:11-12, E374/K360). And this is the answer to the torment of the Spectre and of "Female Love"—

> Throughout all Eternity
> I forgive you you forgive me
> As our Dear Redeemer said
> This the Wine & this the Bread.
>
> (E468/K417)

If apocalypse is a matter of individual (and perhaps temporary) vision rather than of universal Last Things, the function of art must be to urge us toward our own epiphanies and to sustain us during the bleak periods between them, keeping the Divine Vision in time of trouble. The vision of Edenic harmony at the end of *Jerusalem* is just that—a vision, not a condition which the poem has made available to its readers.

> And they conversed together in Visionary forms dramatic which
>   bright
> Redounded from their Tongues in thunderous majesty, in Visions
> In new Expanses, creating exemplars of Memory and of Intellect
> Creating Space, Creating Time according to the wonders Divine
> Of Human Imagination, throughout all the Three Regions immense
> Of Childhood, Manhood & Old Age. . . .
>
> (*J* 98:28-33, E255/K746)

There are two subjects here, the Eternals' mode of activity and the particular forms which that activity creates. *As* forms, these serve as "exemplars" for the fallen world. They create time and space (Los and

345

Enitharmon); they appeal to memory as well as intellect (i.e., to a faculty which Blake consistently associates with the fallen state); and they take account of the temporal sequence of human life (childhood, manhood, old age) which has no place in Eternity but is inherent in mortal existence. As readers we overhear the conversation in visionary forms, or possibly (Blake certainly does not make it clear) we are the forms. But what they mean to us is very different from what they mean to the Eternals.

To the Eternals, what matters is the ongoing activity, not the forms that it creates. They enjoy an Edenic wholeness in which the body and its senses are renovated and infinite. As Cusanus describes the paradise that contains the harmony of opposites, "Thou art there where speech, sight, hearing, touch, reason, knowledge, and understanding are the same, and where seeing is one with being seen, and hearing with being heard, and tasting with being tasted, and touching with being touched, and speaking with hearing, and creating with speaking."[72] In such a state the *logos* would be more than an analogue of human speech; every "conversation" would be a poetic making of the most fundamental kind, a making that had no need of the static forms made by Los. The structure would no longer be stubborn because structure as such would cease to have meaning. Jerusalem would be felt rather than seen; in Frosch's eloquent expression, "Now there is no perspectival imagery of any kind, but simply the joyful crying of her name, and she surrounds the perceiver like a sound."[73] For as we saw in our discussion of the female, Blake can come to terms with the Emanation only by seeing it as a mode of activity rather than as a part of the self.

The metaphor of conversation suggests the directness of communication (between eternal beings? between parts of the self?) that Blake sought in vain to achieve in the externalized fallen world. When Albion awakens he is heard "speaking the Words of Eternity in Human Forms" (*J* 95:9, E252/K742). Words are not signs but living beings, in reminiscence of the sound as of "the voice of speech" that Ezekiel heard the moving "Zoas" make (Ezek. 1:24). And conversation must therefore be more than language as we know it, the stubborn structure of Los. Poetry, painting and music are all together the powers "of conversing with Paradise which the flood did not Sweep away" (*VLJ*, E548/K609), and just as in the final plate of *Job* or the song of the heavenly host in the sun, we may imagine that music rather than poetry is the best intimation of Edenic "conversation." The mysterious figure Sotha, who seems to be warfare on earth and music in

[72] *The Vision of God*, x, pp. 46–47.
[73] *Awakening of Albion*, p. 110.

Eden,[74] suggests that the energies that feed fallen war are translated in Eden into the dynamic interrelations of musical harmony. Contraries are equally true in Beulah; in Eden they interact in continual "strife." Listening to a Bach fugue work itself out, one would not speak of its elements as "equally true" but as developing dynamically one out of another. Even "harmony" may be the wrong word, since Blake preferred the line of melody, just as he preferred outline to coloring; and we know that he composed and sang melodies for his songs which some listeners thought "most singularly beautiful."[75]

In contrast with the rigid forms hammered out by Los, these forms are *dramatic*. They resemble the give and take of conversation or the forward movement of music, not the static shape of an artifact. An idealist philosopher of language declares almost exactly as Blake does, "The 'symbolic form' in which reality is represented or pictured by poetry is always dramatic."[76] But the dramas of the fallen world, like the tragedies that Blake despised for accepting the finality of Experience, constantly degrade this vital interaction.

> What is a Wife & what is a Harlot? What is a Church? & What
> Is a Theatre? are they Two & not One? can they Exist Separate?
> Are not Religion & Politics the Same Thing?
>
> (*J* 57:8-10, E205/K689)

A wife and a harlot are the same not only because marriage is institutionalized prostitution, but also because at best they both gratify the desires of Luvah and Vala. A church and a theater are the same not only because religion ought ideally to be communication, but also because it usually degenerates into a transaction between actors and spectators. Blake would hear the voice of Satan in Eliot's remark, "The only dramatic satisfaction that I find now is in a High Mass well performed."[77]

The visionary forms are an ideal to which we can aspire, furnishing "exemplars" for our art; they are not our art. If Aristotelian drama has a beginning, middle, and end, Blake's ideal of spontaneous dramatic speech would be a perpetual beginning with no sense of an ending, a joy that is set free even as it is possessed:

> He who binds to himself a joy
> Doth the wingèd life destroy

[74] See Frye, *Fearful Symmetry*, p. 261.

[75] *Blake Records*, p. 457; see also p. 305. Fisher points out that music, "the least naturalistic of the arts," is associated with imagination (*Valley of Vision*, p. 241).

[76] Urban, *Language and Reality*, p. 465.

[77] The speaker "E" says this in "A Dialogue on Dramatic Poetry," *Selected Essays*, p. 47.

But he who kisses the joy as it flies
Lives in Eternitys sun rise.

(E465/K179)

Reshuffle the plates of *Jerusalem* as he might, Blake was still confined to permanent sequences of words on plates of metal, and he could not altogether dispel the image of himself as Urizen writing on books of brass with an iron pen. And *Jerusalem* ends, not with the visionary forms, but with a perpetual return to the world as we know it, where we are sustained by the Beulah-comforts of Albion's Emanation Jerusalem until we can break through into Eden.

All Human Forms identified even Tree Metal Earth & Stone, all
Human Forms identified, living going forth & returning wearied
Into the Planetary lives of Years Months Days & Hours reposing
And then Awaking into his Bosom in the Life of Immortality.
And I heard the Name of their Emanations they are named
  Jerusalem.

(99:1-5, E256/K747)

If we could speak in visionary forms dramatic we would have no further need of Los and his art. But the apocalypse can never come permanently, for we will always sink in weariness into Jerusalem's bosom; and therefore, lest we fall still further into the Satanic void, Los must rouse himself again and again to keep the Divine Vision and point toward the path of release.

[C O N C L U S I O N]

Blake and the Reader

> We called upon Blake yesterday evening found him & his wife
> drinking Tea, durtyer than ever however he received us well &
> shewed his large drawing in Water Colors of the last Judgement he
> has been labouring at it till it is nearly as black as your Hat.
>
> George Cumberland, 1815 (*Blake Records*, p. 235)

> That a man who wanted to "create difficulties everywhere" and be
> an offense should be praised and buried in academic appreciations
> without offending anybody is tragic.
>
> Walter Kaufmann, *From Shakespeare to Existentialism*
> (on Kierkegaard)

FORM

I have been concerned throughout this book to understand the
shape of Blake's thought, both as a structure of ideas and as a warfare of antitheses whose tremendous energy constantly threatens
to break that structure apart. It will be obvious that I admire Blake
most deeply for the intransigence of this ever-reconstructed vision,
which defiantly rejects all of art's customary accommodations with
conventional ways of interpreting reality. But it would be idle to pretend that Blake's prophetic poems are not, in the end, very strange as
well as very difficult. In trying to come to terms with Blake's claims to
be announcing the truth, we may profitably begin by considering the
special demands he makes upon our ordinary expectations of literary
form and language.[1]

No art could be further than Blake's from the familiar maxim that
poetry should exhibit organic form, with every part where it must be
and no part alterable without damage to the whole. This conception is
usually opposed to the anti-ideal of the machine, no doubt because
modern machinery is composed of interchangeable parts. But how
well, really, does the analogy work? A specific machine, however interchangeable its parts may be with those of a similar machine, is a

---

[1] At this point I shall leave the visual art out of the discussion. As we have repeatedly
noticed, it can be profoundly challenging for interpretation, and at times is almost im-
penetrably mysterious (as in the extraordinary androgynous swan, apparently an
emblem of the fallen artist, on *J* 11). But on the whole the pictures are "read" in traditional pictorial terms, and the problems of interpretation which they raise are less radical
than those of Blake's language and form.

perfect instance of a whole where every part must be where it is. You cannot connect the distributor to the carburetor, let alone transpose them. But Blake's poems are notoriously built up of transferrable parts; *Milton* and *Jerusalem* seem to have grown progressively over the years and were issued in varying sequences of plates. Although each sequence can be defended by critical ingenuity, the very existence of the variations makes it impossible to claim that the poem embodies a single and inevitable form. Nor is this all. Owing to the technical considerations of engraving, Blake was obliged to leave each plate essentially unchanged once it was made. He could add a few lines if there happened to be space, or delete a few words or lines (often demolishing the sense in the process, so that modern editors have had to recover the lost fragments). But on the whole the plates had to remain as they were unless they were thrown away altogether—and of course we have no way of knowing how many were thrown away. This procedure leads to a kind of poetry almost entirely recalcitrant to theories of organic form. The poetic whole is made up of interpenetrating symbolic facets that can be juxtaposed with each other in an almost infinite variety of ways; the poems are kaleidoscopes.

After several generations of Blakeans have banged their heads against the brick wall of artistic form, we can safely conclude that Blake's poems do not possess form in any familiar sense. The many attempts to define the form of *Jerusalem* have failed because Blake is either indifferent or opposed to the kinds of form the critics have been looking for. As Hazard Adams acutely remarks, attempts to establish the sequence of *Auguries of Innocence* are futile, since the poem is a standing rebuke to discursive structure: "Each augury contains all the others just as each moment contains all time and each grain of sand all space."[2] But this anti-aesthetic is so destructive of poems as we usually understand them that critics have not ceased in the attempt to find some principle, organic or otherwise, that can organize the prophecies.

There is a valuable lesson in the best of these attempts, Susan Fox's analysis of the thematic parallels, verbal echoes, and other devices which Blake uses in *Milton* to suggest the simultaneity of the "eternal Now." Such an analysis must use the term "form" in a defiantly paradoxical way. "This curious pattern of temporally and spatially divergent events unified only by a network of verbal echoes reveals that all the events are a single event."[3] The problem is really philosophical rather than formal. Blake is committed to a theory of reality that subverts art as we normally know it, and puts in its place a mode of art that points toward a realm which it is by definition unable to

[2] *William Blake*, p. 168.
[3] *Poetic Form in Blake's Milton*, p. 53 (referring to Leutha's speech).

image or describe. For as Fox rightly observes, "The 'delusions' of Beulah . . . are the only means we mortal beings have of witnessing reality" (p. 27). In other words, through a glass darkly.

Blake's poetic practice follows not only from the atemporality of his ideal of Eternity, but also from his preference for interpreting existence as a system of interrelated categories rather than as an irreversible sequence of events. Lévi-Strauss says that there is a fundamental antipathy between history and classificatory systems, and he speaks of the "totemic void," the indifference to history in civilizations that explain themselves by reference to fixed features in nature, in contrast with the civilizations of Europe and Asia which "have elected to explain themselves by history."[4] While there is no question in such cultures of denying the reality of events, neither is there much interest in their historicity. In Blake's myth, very similarly, the Creation, Fall, Incarnation, and Apocalypse—the nodal points of the Christian historical myth—are detemporalized and located in the imagination in an eternally synchronous present. We fall when we see the world through Urizenic vortices, and the fallen world is simultaneously "created" through that error; as a direct corollary of it, Jesus is simultaneously incarnated and crucified; and apocalypse occurs whenever we throw off the veil of error and live again in the clear air of Eternity. The many things that happen in the historical world are expressions or symptoms of these fundamental constants, which are best understood, though of course not easily understood, when they are apprehended synchronously. "Each part of *Jerusalem*," Frye says, "presents a phase of imaginative vision simultaneously with the body of error which it clarifies."[5] In Lévi-Strauss's terms, classificatory systems "allow the incorporation of history" (p. 243); they absorb it and, as it were, neutralize its historicity.

Now, such a vision is inimical to artistic form in nearly all of its usual manifestations. Frank Kermode, who contrasts imaginative *kairos* and *aevum* with the deadly monotony of clock-time *chronos*, insists on fictive development as the precondition for humanizing time: we hear *tick-tock* instead of identical *ticks*. "The clock's *tick-tock* I take to be a model of what we call a plot, an organization that humanizes time by giving it form; and the interval between *tock* and *tick* represents purely successive, disorganized time of the sort that we need to humanize."[6] But Blake, as we have seen, holds that it is precisely those interstitial moments that contain humanized reality, for they free us from history by liberating us into eternity. "There is a Moment in

---

[4] *The Savage Mind* (Chicago, 1966), p. 232.

[5] *Fearful Symmetry*, p. 357.

[6] *The Sense of an Ending: Studies in the Theory of Fiction* (Oxford, 1967), p. 45.

each Day that Satan cannot find" (*M* 35:42, E135/K526). Kermode dislikes myth because he sees it (as anthropologists do) as allied to ritual, "which presupposes total and adequate explanations of things as they are and were; it is a sequence of radically unchangeable gestures. Fictions are for finding things out, and they change as the needs of sense-making change" (p. 39). Kermode's formulation helps us to see just how decisively Blake, who abhorred ritual, expected myth to remain open and changing. But at the same time he refused to let it surrender to the explanatory seductions of narrative, and the ending in Blake's myth must forever be sought anew, since each moment is potentially an ending but also potentially a renewal of the Fall.

Blake's synchronous vision is remarkable for the density of its symbolic life. Unlike the many mystics who have asserted a vision of eternity similar to his, Blake goes beyond aphorism to what looks like narrative, and forces us to experience the mind-twisting complexity of a truly universal simultaneity. His poems embody a form against form. The two versions of Night VII of *The Four Zoas*, for example, are recalcitrant to critical reconstruction, for as scrupulous study has made clear, they can neither be pieced together in a single sequence nor separated as preliminary and final versions.[7]

Milton's epic, like its classical models, can begin *in medias res* because it rests upon an unambiguous though tacit chronology. Milton varies chronological exposition for dramatic purposes, but at every point he makes us understand that he has the entire sequence under perfect control. But Blake denies the very notion of sequence, and in this instance he makes us feel profoundly that the turning point of *The Four Zoas* points in contradictory directions. He has not decided—perhaps he could never have decided—how to convey this artistically in a "final" version of the seventh Night. But he has thereby left us with a valuable lesson in the limitations of art, which is all too often obliged to impose one form at the expense of another, just because the mind demands coherence and insists on constructing it even when the clues are ambiguous. This would be merely the fallacy of imitative form if Blake only wanted to say that reality is incoherent. But he wants to say just the opposite: reality is supremely coherent, but its coherence embraces contradictory impulses, as in the image of wheels within wheels from Ezekiel which is, as he frankly admits, "incomprehensible" (*J* 98:24, E255/K745).

It is easy to call Blake's poetic mode modern, invoking for instance

---

[7] See John Kilgore, "The Order of Nights VIIa and VIIb in Blake's *The Four Zoas*," *Blake: An Illustrated Quarterly*, 12 (1978), 107-113. Several other articles in the same number deal with the problem, notably David Erdman's "Night the Seventh: The Editorial Problem" (pp. 135-139).

the cinema as an analogue. But the cinema has its own grammar of conventions and is ordinarily received as a coherent sequence of images (usually, indeed, as a narrative). As Bloom observes, Blake compels us to act like film directors rather than viewers.[8] It is of course true that modern art in general rejects old-fashioned notions of temporality, so that Blake may appear a useful precursor; and in the last decade or so there have been many subtle analyses of this aspect of his work. But most claims for Blake's modernity result from trying to assimilate his prophecies to a modern poetics, regardless of the jamming and backfiring that ensues. We might see them more clearly if we were to look backward rather than forward and if we considered them simply as prophecies. Blake's practice may seem remarkable in the context of conventional literary scholarship, but it is familiar in the study of myth.

As Edmund Leach points out, biblical hermeneutics is similar in many respects to structuralist interpretation of myth, relying on significant patterns and symbolic identifications rather than on narrative form. "Myth proper lacks a chronology in any strict sense, for the beginning and the end must be apprehended simultaneously; significance is to be discerned only in the relations between the component parts of the story; sequence is simply a persistent rearrangement of elements which are present from the start."[9] Or as Eliade says, "The myth is supposed to happen . . . in a non-temporal time, in an instant without duration, as certain mystics and philosophers conceived of eternity."[10] In a word, as Blake conceived of it.

Nor is this understanding of myth confined to the twentieth century. As Leach indicates, it is basic to biblical interpretation, and is implicit above all in the discontinuities of the Book of Revelation. We are not surprised therefore to find medieval exegesis of that work sounding very much like commentaries on Blake's *Jerusalem*. Here is Alcuin:

> This is the sequence of the narration. Sometimes it starts with the arrival of the Lord and carries through to the end of time. Sometimes it starts with the arrival of the Lord, and before it finishes, it returns to the beginning and by repeating in different figures both what it has left out and what it has said, it hastens to the second coming of the Lord. Sometimes it begins with the last persecution. But before it comes to the end it recapitulates and connects both [beginning and end]. Sometimes in order to narrate, it temporarily abandons its themes and introduces something totally unconnected.

[8] *The Ringers in the Tower*, p. 38.
[9] *Genesis as Myth and Other Essays* (London, 1969), p. 28.
[10] *Images and Symbols*, p. 57.

Afterward in concise order it teaches thoroughly what it had begun. Sometimes in this kind of style, a figure is changed in such a way that it is confused, as it were, with other things so that it signifies something quite other than what it began to represent. And you should note that very rarely in the revelation do the Angel or John retain their own persons.[11]

Nothing could be closer to Blake's practice, which constantly resumes and recapitulates the mythic materials, jumps away to introduce unexpected topics or commentary, and avoids anything like the reliable narrator of conventional epic. Events, if they can be called by that name, succeed each other with astonishing abruptness. The decisive crises have the unexpectedness of a thunderclap, just as they do in the Gnostic system of which Tertullian complained—"Suddenly Christ, suddenly John: everything happens like that, according to Marcion."[12] Critics sometimes suggest that events in Blake's myth have the dislocated logic or illogic of the dream. So they do, but dreaming is an analogy, not an ideal; Blake wants to understand the meaning of reality, not to imitate the phenomena of dreaming. The illogic is intended to spur us into thought and help us to break out of the natural world with its coherent narratives and mimetic fictions.

I do not claim that Blake's extraordinary project succeeds at every point. His repeated revisions, though they greatly enriched and deepened his myth, tended also to increase its obscurity, and there is a sadly emblematic ring to the report that he repainted his *Vision of the Last Judgment* until it was "nearly as black as your Hat." Kermode certainly describes fictions as we normally expect them to behave, and our normal expectations are not easily dispensed with. But at all events Blake's poems offer a salutary alternative to a critical tradition that seeks "unity" in art and encourages us to find elaborately coherent structures even in works which are supremely open, inquiring, and metamorphic in their imaginative life. The great sin of Blake scholarship is *gnosis*, a determination to find all the answers and to impose on the myth a drastically un-Blakean explanatory structure.

Edward Said summarizes five fictional conventions that were taken more or less for granted before Freud and Nietzsche: the posteriority

---

[11] *Commentariorum in Apocalypsim*, quoted by Barbara Nolan, *The Gothic Visionary Perspective*, p. 7. The hermeneutic tradition of Revelation has recently been studied by Wittreich in *Visionary Poetics;* see also his application of this tradition to Blake in "Opening the Seals: Blake's Epics and the Milton Tradition," in Curran and Wittreich, pp. 23-58. Fox notes some relations between Revelation and *Milton* (*Poetic Form in Blake's Milton*, pp. 185-187).

[12] "Subito Christus, subito Johannes: sic sunt omnia apud Marcionem" (*Adv. Marcion*. IV.xi, quoted by Puech, "Gnosis and Time," p. 83).

of the verbal text to its "material" in experience; a structural logic based on progressive movement toward a conclusion; a "convention of adequacy, according to which the text is assumed to be fully equal to the task of conveying, incarnating, containing, realizing, or fulfilling its intention, its meaning, or both together"; a mode of reading in which each unit of the text is considered as primary when encountered in its place in the sequence, instead of being considered in its interconnection with the rest; and an attempt to ground the putative unity of the text in "a series of genealogical connections: author-text, beginning-middle-end, text-meaning, reader-interpretation, and so on."[13] Blake's dream of visionary truth is fundamentally incompatible with modern theories of intertextuality, indeterminacy, and deconstructive license. The Book of Revelation is a very different model from the speculations of Jacques Derrida. Yet these problems are recognizably Blake's, and indeed to show in detail how he contradicts every one of the traditional assumptions listed by Said would be to recapitulate the argument of this book.

LANGUAGE

Poems are made of language, and Blake's language offers as many obstacles to critical response as his form does, though for different reasons. Once again, he knows exactly why he is affronting our expectations as readers of poetry. There are many passages of great beauty, to be sure, and many more of great rhetorical power, but to single these out for appreciation is to misrepresent the effect of the whole, which readers who are not committed Blakeans tend to find wearying and even monotonous. Let us first state the case against Blake's use of language and then consider his reasons for it.

In negative terms, Blake has two fatal Cleopatras, one being what has been well described as "impassioned technicality,"[14] and the other being Ossianic bombast. At his best he is Miltonic and biblical; but then, so is Ossian at its best. What is most strikingly absent is the Shakespearean style—the flexible movement and dramatic immediacy that transforms common speech into art. Blake's indifference to it (after the Shakespearean pastiches in the *Poetical Sketches*) is a mark of his great distance from the other Romantic poets, who constantly sought that special power and grace that can only be called Shakespearean:

> It is the unpastured sea hungering for calm.
> Peace, monster; I come now. Farewell.[15]

[13] *Beginnings: Intention and Method* (Baltimore, 1975), p. 162.
[14] Fox, *Poetic Form in Blake's Milton*, p. 139.
[15] *Prometheus Unbound* III.ii. 49-50.

Blake avoids the Shakespearean style because he does not want it. Putting the matter baldly, it is too human. His mythy beings cannot talk like that, and neither can the oracular prophet who presents them. The lyric poet who was capable of wonderful metrical mastery—

> The Son of Morn in weary Nights decline
> The lost Travellers Dream under the Hill
> (E266/K771)

—is capable in the epics of sustained Ossianic bumble, a fact which becomes startlingly apparent, despite anything one can say in favor of his loose "fourteeners," when an extended passage is printed as it if were prose.[16] Milton thought rhyme a troublesome bondage, and Blake adds that blank verse too is "a Monotonous Cadence" (J 3, E144/K621). "Whatever the length of the line that Blake is using," Raine comments, "we find that there is a continual pressure to make it longer."[17] That is exactly the appeal of Ossian for Blake: the liberation of the reader's mind to move freely among evocative images.

> O Carun of the streams! why do I behold thy waters rolling in
>   blood?
> Has the noise of the battle been heard; and sleeps the king of
>   Morven?
> Rise, moon, thou daughter of the sky! look from between thy
>   clouds. . . . [18]

It is an easy matter to transcribe almost any passage of Ossian as Blakean verse.

There is no Romantic particularity in such poetry, in spite of Blake's many invocations of minute particulars. As Josephine Miles summarizes his characteristic vocabulary, "All the eternal, divine, and human, dark, bright, and deep forms of Man, god, Satan, spectre, son, daughter, child, in hand, foot, head, voice, eye, tear, joy, over the earth and heaven, mountain, rock, in cloud and light, shadow and fire, come, go, rise, stand to see, behold, and hear, to know, love, and weep."[19] For all his hatred of Lockean and Johnsonian generality, Blake's universal forms resemble the classical ones in practice if not in theory, and despite his contempt for poetic artifice as cultural emollient—

---

[16] As Swinburne sometimes does, e.g. pp. 252-253 of *William Blake*.

[17] "A Note on Blake's 'Unfetterd Verse,' " in Rosenfeld, p. 389.

[18] *Comala: A Dramatic Poem*, fifth paragraph.

[19] "Blake's Frame of Language," in Paley and Phillips, p. 89. Miles has constructed this sentence out of the words that appear most frequently in a Blake concordance.

traditionalist

> Thus Hayley on his Toilette seeing the sope
> Cries Homer is very much improvd by Pope
>   (E496/K555)

—it may seem that his language too tends to neoclassical abstraction.

Once again it is essential to see that Blake meant to do exactly what he did; the style of the epics was deliberately chosen and labored with care. Some precedent for his use of language is available in eighteenth-century theory, which increasingly emphasized affective possibilities. Berkeley says, "I entreat the reader to reflect with himself and see if it does not often happen, either in hearing or reading a discourse, that the passions of fear, love, hatred, admiration, disdain, and the like, arise immediately in his mind upon the perception of certain words, without any ideas coming between."[20] From mid-century onward critics liked to praise the emotive power of descriptions that depended on disjunct images instead of discursive syntax; the taste for this was so strong that they looked for it even in Milton.[21] The prose-poems of "Ossian" are a perfect illustration of this kind of writing. But Blake is immensely subtler than Macpherson, the fabricator of Ossian; his verses may sometimes *sound* Ossianic, but in context their function is radically different. Macpherson uses emotive words to arouse stock responses; Blake uses them to shock the reader into awareness of the opacity of symbols and the potential duplicity of the language that embodies them. He takes Macpherson's language apart and rebuilds it, in exactly the same way in which he rebuilds Macpherson's themes: *Oithona* is a cloudy romance filled with Celtic twilight and exploiting a conventional fate-worse-than-death, while *Visions of the Daughters of Albion* takes *Oithona* apart to find out what it means.

If we translate Blake's practice into the terms of modern speech-act theory, he uses all three of J. L. Austin's categories in interesting ways. Locutionary acts, which are "roughly equivalent to 'meaning' in the traditional sense," are inevitably frequent, but they are often problematic in comparison with everyday speech that takes place between particular persons in a social context. The poems are also filled with illocutionary acts, which perform conventional functions like commanding or warning; nothing could be more illocutionary than a

---

[20] *Principles of Human Knowledge*, introduction, par. 20.

[21] Thus Burke quotes the description of Satan in *Paradise Lost* I.589–599 and says, "Here is a very noble picture; and in what does this poetical picture consist? in images of a tower, an archangel, the sun rising through mists, or in an eclipse, the ruin of monarchs, and the revolutions of kingdoms. The mind is hurried out of itself, by a croud of great and confused images; which affect because they are crouded and confused" (*A Philosophical Enquiry into . . . the Sublime and Beautiful*, II.iv, p. 62).

prophecy. But most of all they exemplify Austin's perlocutionary acts, "what we bring about or achieve *by* saying something, such as convincing, persuading, deterring, and even, say, surprising or misleading."[22] Blake's words will not stay on the page as objects for aesthetic contemplation; they invade the reader's mind and attempt to transform his world.

In making these aggressive demands, Blake refuses to be bound by the ordinary contract between author and reader, in which (to use Saussure's terms) the *parole* of the individual speaker operates within the framework of the larger *langue*. Of course both the reader and Blake speak English ("the rough basement") and its fundamental grammar is taken for granted. But rather like Wittgenstein he campaigns energetically against our normal tendency to be guided by language without seeing how it imposes the rules of a game. "A *picture* held us captive," Wittgenstein says of his discarded referential theory, "and we could not get outside it, for it lay in our language and language seemed to repeat it to us inexorably." In everyday life we fail to realize how much this is so, for "we remain unconscious of the prodigious diversity of all the everyday language-games because the clothing of our language makes everything alike." And therefore "Philosophy is a battle against the bewitchment of our intelligence by means of language." So is Blake's poetry. And whereas Wittgenstein seeks to expose the premises of the various language-games rather than to alter them—philosophy "leaves everything as it is"—Blake plays a language-game in which he constantly reinvents the rules.[23]

Saussure maintained that the individual could not alter the *langue* because it is a communal system of relationships that is intuited rather than spelled out, present in every act of speaking as a total system. As such it is the medium through which we apprehend existence; in Gadamer's phenomenological terms, "Language is the fundamental mode of operation of our being-in-the-world and the all-embracing form of the constitution of the world."[24] This Blake will not allow. Language is the stubborn structure hammered out by Los, an instrument which we construct and use. Hence his heavy demands on the reader: instead of participating in a language-game that reflects a common reality—as in Shakespeare, whom eighteenth-century critics admired as the poet of "nature"—we have to learn to live in Blake's imaginative world and to play his game by his rules.

The most baffling passages in Blake resemble the much-debated paradoxes of mystical writers, and it may be that his most paradoxical

---

[22] *How to Do Things with Words* (Oxford, 1962), p. 108.
[23] *Philosophical Investigations*, I.115, II.xi, I.109, I.124 (pp. 48, 224, 47, 49).
[24] *Philosophical Hermeneutics*, p. 3.

formulations are attempts to talk like them rather than to express his own intuitions in his own language.

> What is Above is Within, for every-thing in Eternity is translucent:
> The Circumference is Within: Without, is formed the Selfish Center
> And the Circumference still expands going forward to Eternity.
>
> (*J* 71:6-8, E222-223/K709)

Whether or not this statement, if that is what it is, can be translated into discursive language, it reflects a common enough mode of expression among the mystics. "The inner will," Boehme declares, "which exists within in itself, has stirred up its own nature, as the centre, which, passing out of itself, is desirous of the light which is pressing forth from the centre."[25] Or as Blake says in another place,

> There is an Outside spread Without, & an Outside spread Within
> Beyond the Outline of Identity both ways, which meet in One.
>
> (*J* 18:2-3, E161/K640)

In passages like these I believe that Blake is trying to translate his visionary experience into the conventional language of mystical writing, which is, as Peter Moore says of similar texts, a second-order mode of exposition that uses general or abstract language that is "retrospective," seeking after the fact to describe the immediacy of first-order experience, and is "incorporated," taking a shape influenced by prior expectations (in Blake's case, expectations created by writers like Boehme).[26] Blake's accounts of first-order visionary experience are nothing like this abstract dialectic of inside and outside, focusing instead on humanized symbols as in the "vision of light" poem or in the lines in *Jerusalem* that immediately follow the passage about the circumference expanding: "For all are Men in Eternity. Rivers Mountains Cities Villages,/All are Human . . ." (*J* 71:15-16, E223/K709).

Blake's purpose, I believe—though this is necessarily speculative—is not, like that of the mystics whom he sometimes imitates, to suggest that ordinary language is unequal to ineffable truth, but rather to expose the slipperiness of ordinary language in its most ordinary manifestations.

> Lo, a shadow of horror is risen
> In Eternity! Unknown, unprolific!
> Self-closd, all-repelling: what Demon
> Hath form'd this abominable void

---

[25] *Six Theosophic Points*, II.xvii, p. 27.

[26] "Mystical Experience, Mystical Doctrine, Mystical Technique," in *Mysticism and Philosophical Analysis*, ed. Katz, pp. 103, 108.

This soul-shudd'ring vacuum?—Some said
"It is Urizen," But, unknown, abstracted
Brooding secret, the dark power hid. . . .

For he strove in battles dire
In unseen conflictions with shapes
Bred from his forsaken wilderness,
Of beast, bird, fish, serpent & element
Combustion, blast, vapour and cloud.
(*Urizen* 3:1-7, 13-17, E69/K222)

This parodic creation (the four elements and their emblematic creatures) emerges from the Boehmean abyss, filled with the negative
definitions of conventional theology, the hiding place of a Urizen who
will not show his face. Its nature is defined by the relentless oxymo-
rons. "He strove . . . in unseen conflictions with shapes"—they are unseen yet they are shapes; they derive from Urizen himself, or his abyss,
yet they must be distinct from him since they oppose him in "conflictions." As in Valentinian Gnosticism, the primal unity is not an omnipotent God but a potentially fragmented condition, and the language indicates as much by constantly turning back, or inward, upon
itself. A few lines later Urizen is called "a self-contemplating shadow"
(3:21). A shadow is usually thought of as the not-self, so how can it
have a self of its own to contemplate? Blake's difficult symbolism of
the Spectre is implicit in this line.

It may help in defining Blake's use of language to contrast it with
two antithetical modes. First, here is Pope's favorite couplet out of all
of the thousands in his poems:

Lo! where Maeotis sleeps, and hardly flows
The freezing Tanais thro' a waste of snows. . . . [27]

The lines are beautiful—Tillotson says that Keats might have chosen
this couplet for Pope[28]—but their beauty is deliberately contrasted
with the thing they describe, the Asian spawning ground of the Goths
and Huns who poured forth to wreck Western civilization. As always
in Pope, imagery functions as analogy: just as the Vandals broke loose
from the fabled bog of Maeotis, so Dullness always breaks loose from
the mind when its natural vitality has been chilled.

As it happens, Pope's waste of snows turns up in *The Four Zoas*:

---

[27] *Dunciad* III.87-88. "I have been told," Johnson reports, "that the couplet by which
he declared his own ear to be most gratified was this; but the reason of this preference I
cannot discover" (*Life of Pope*, in *Lives of The English Poets*, ed. G. B. Hill [Oxford,
1905], III, 250).

[28] Geoffrey Tillotson, *On the Poetry of Pope* (Oxford, 1950), p. 160.

Anon a cloud filld with a waste of snows
Covers thee still obdurate still resolvd & writing still
Tho rocks roll oer thee tho floods pour tho winds black as the Sea
Cut thee in gashes tho the blood pours down around thy ankles
Freezing thy feet to the hard rock still thy pen obdurate
Traces the wonders of Futurity. . . .

(79:11-16, E347/K322)

Metaphor is raised immediately to the level of symbol; this is a dramatic speech addressed by one part of the self to another (Orc to Urizen), and it is filled with animated images from nature, rocks "rolling" over a body—which itself symbolizes the reason—just as the sea normally would, and winds "black as the Sea" cutting it until it bleeds. The phantasmagoria of symbolism is not so much descriptive of Urizen as expressive of the fiery Orc's impression of the snowy Urizen; the symbolism becomes more and more audacious until the "bread of Sorrow" kneaded by Urizen's three daughters is identified with the doughy clouds of winter storm (79:23, 30), much as in the emblem "Air" in *For the Sexes*, Urizen huddles brooding on a cloud that resembles a lump of dough (E259/K763). These are not universal analogies but Orcian symbols, and they are countered by Urizen's cool reply, "Read my books" (79:20), like a professor who answers a burning question with "See my article." Language bends and metamorphoses in order to convey states of feeling.

To take a different comparison, consider the theme of apocalypse in a poem like Herbert's "Decay," which begins by recalling God's ubiquity at every "oak, or bush, or cave, or well" in patriarchal days, goes on to say that he is now imprisoned "In some one corner of a feeble heart" where Sin and Satan strive to "pinch and straiten" him, and concludes with a stunning reversal:

I see the world grows old, when as the heat
Of thy great love, once spread, as in an urn
Doth closet up it self, and still retreat,
Cold Sinne still forcing it, till it return,
 And calling *Justice*, all things burn.

Herbert is wry and indirect in his paradoxes, which are of the sort that the New Critics admired so much; his God is all-powerful and all-seeing, so that it can only be through human folly that he seems imprisoned in the heart instead of manifest as in the Old Testament. The Last Judgment appears very abruptly indeed, as a deliberate shock to the mood of resignation which the poem, in its measured and ironic exposition, had seemed to countenance. By contrast with Herbert's subtlety Blake is remorselessly direct. His symbols batter the reader ceaselessly like the hammer blows of Los. Blake refuses to acknowledge a historical gulf between Old Testament immediacy of experience and modern alienation, and he refuses to accept an apocalypse that will occur at the end of time instead of here and now. Herbert explores the paradoxes and complexities of the paradise within; Blake, who celebrates the inner paradise more than any other poet in our literature, insists upon seeing its lineaments in the outer world as well. What is without is within.

The peculiarities of Blake's language derive, then, from a determination to make us break through language, a refusal to accept it as the structure in which we think and exist. It is only partly a matter of violating the reader's expectations, although that is integral to Blake's procedure.[29] More than this, Blake refuses to let language be the focus of attention, even though it is necessarily the vehicle of his thought (just as a pictorial language must convey his visual ideas). Fredric Jameson speaks of the tendency in modern poetics "of form to veer around into content, of a formalism to supply its structural absence of content by a hypostasis of its own method."[30] Both in linguistic and in structural form, Blake constantly points *beyond* his artifacts to a visionary realm that leaves them behind; to put it differently, he deconstructs symbols but continues to insist on their content. But he does this in a most peculiar way, since ordinarily we say that a symbol is a concrete or intelligible object that stands for, or participates in, something less clear than itself (either because it is too abstract or complex to hold clearly in mind, or because it occupies an ontological realm to which we do not have direct access). But in Blake's theory, owing to his suspicion of the fallen world, symbols are vitiated by their fallen status, for example in the various versions of the sun. And the symbols therefore point to, or participate in, a reality which is more vivid and immediate than they are, *so long as* we can achieve an apocalyptic breakthrough and ascend into vision on the fiery chariot of the imagination. Instead of a vivid symbol pointing to a less vivid and more mysterious object, we therefore have slippery and ambiguous symbols pointing to a more vivid and organized reality "within." No wonder Blake constantly frustrates our expectations of language.

Lacking, as most of us must, the visionary conversion experience that Blake demands, we can still appreciate the value of his implied

[29] For instance, by joining adjectives to nouns in ways that would normally seem incongruous, in order to provoke rethinking about "normal" attitudes (see Robert F. Gleckner, "Blake's Verbal Technique," in Rosenfeld, pp. 321-322).

[30] *The Prison-House of Language: A Critical Account of Structuralism and Russian Formalism* (Princeton, 1972), p. 206.

attack on a referential theory of language. Any good poem liberates language from conventional referentiality and gives it a kind of palpable presence. As Sigurd Burckhardt says, "To attain the position of creative sovereignty over matter, the poet must first of all reduce language to something resembling a material. He can never do so completely, only proximately. But he can—and that is his first task—drive a wedge between words and their meanings, lessen as much as possible their designatory force and thereby inhibit our all too ready flight from them to the things they point to. Briefly put, the function of poetic devices is dissociative, or divestive."[31] The metaphor is highly appropriate to Blake, whose entire myth is a stripping off of Vala's veils, even while it is an "ana-calyptic" imposition of new barriers that spur the reader into thought.[32] And Burckhardt's point about "creative sovereignty over matter" is profoundly Blakean, for if the ordinary poet is frustrated by the communal leveling off of linguistic possibility—"he must deal in an already current and largely defaced coinage" (p. 23)—Blake reinvigorates language by transposing it into his own special contexts and by literally inscribing it on his plates of metal. The words we read are *his* words. When he tells us that "every word and every letter is studied and put into its fit place" (J 3, E144/K621), he means not only its syntactical position but also its place on the page and its size and shape. It is crucially significant that the words are engraved (including visual oddities like the habitual "&" for "and"), so that instead of allowing them to pass into our minds as if they spoke themselves inside our heads, we are forced—or we would be if we used Blake's original texts—to see them as objects put there by a human artist. Many of the tiny curlicues and interlinear pictures, which scholars seek so earnestly to gloss, may be intended not as miniature allegories but as simple reminders that these are not printed documents but living acts.[33]

As in so many other ways, Blake's thought is profoundly modern in its critical analysis but profoundly unmodern in its assertion of a realm of truth beyond the realm of images. Wallace Stevens, surveying the

[31] *Shakespearean Meanings* (Princeton, 1968), p. 24. In a later chapter Burckhardt brilliantly shows how a short lyric by Mörike is liberated from conventional pastoral by the poet's use of "disturbing elements" that force the reader to respond on an unexpectedly deep level (pp. 306-313). Blake's lyrics do the same thing.

[32] See above, p. 74.

[33] Since the various copies of Blake's poems were individually hand-colored, they exemplify Walter Benjamin's theory of the "aura" of the handmade work of art ("The Work of Art in the Age of Mechanical Reproduction," *Illuminations*, trans. Harry Zohn [New York, 1968], p. 223). But one cannot be certain that Blake would not have welcomed modern techniques of reproduction, so long as the handmade quality of the original was conveyed.

collapse of the high claims of Romantic symbolism, strikes an attitude
that is instructively different from Blake's:

> It is an artificial world. The rose
> Of paper is of the nature of its world.
> The sea is so many written words; the sky
> Is blue, clear, cloudy, high, dark, wide and round. . . .

The catalogue of adjectives resembles Miles's summary of Blakean
diction, but words in Blake have other uses than they do in Stevens.

> And in what covert may we, naked, be
> Beyond the knowledge of nakedness, as part
> Of reality, beyond the knowledge of what
> Is real, part of a land beyond the mind?[34]

In Blake there is no nostalgia for a land beyond the mind, because he
hopes to attain the ultimate Eden, the life of visionary forms in which
words are passionate actions. And he is therefore remote from the
modern acquiescence in a provisional and never completed condition:

> The imperfect is our paradise.
> Note that, in this bitterness, delight,
> Since the imperfect is so hot in us,
> Lies in flawed words and stubborn sounds.[35]

Blake knows all there is to know about flawed words and stubborn
sounds, but he longs for a state in which they will no longer afford our
best delight, and in which paradise will be perfect once more.

TRUTH

Blake believed that his symbols, although compromised by participation in a fallen world, were ultimately guaranteed by being "comprehended" in the divine body of Jesus.[36] If we do not share that faith,
how shall we respond to the symbols? It is one thing for Blake to assert that they afford a privileged insight into truth, and another for us
to agree that they do. Critics all too easily—one might say uncritically—embrace the doctrine that symbolism is supremely suited to

[34] "Extracts from Addresses to the Academy of Fine Ideas," *Collected Poems*, p. 252.
Stevens was writing in wartime, and his poem ends with a grim evocation of the finality
of death, a theme that Blake always rejects: "Behold the men in helmets borne on
steel,/Discolored, how they are going to defeat" (p. 259).
[35] "The Poems of Our Climate," *Collected Poems*, p. 194.
[36] See above, p. 31.

penetrating the nature of reality. At the very least, they assume what they ought to demonstrate, no doubt as a result of their general campaign against positivist science and their claim to possess a special mode of understanding. But one should remember that, as an anthropologist remarks, "Assertions that symbols provide a unique way of knowing the truth seem to be often equivalent to defence-mechanisms. A powerful way of arguing that 'what I say is true' is to assert that 'I have a unique way of getting at the truth which is inaccessible to ordinary knowledge.' "[37] If Romanticism was spilt religion, then much literary criticism is spilt Romanticism.

The preeminent exponent of Blake's desire-fulfilling symbols is Northrop Frye, who asserts with truly Blakean logic, "Imagination creates reality, and as desire is a part of imagination, the world we desire is more real than the world we passively accept." This claim, as in Frye's later criticism where it is generalized to accommodate all symbolic writing, is offered in support of a rejection of science that is just as bitter and unfair as Blake's: "As long as science means knowledge organized by a commonplace mind it will be part of the penalty man pays for being stupid." And since men who are not stupid understand that desire creates reality, it follows that "the work of art is the product of this creative perception, hence it is not an escape from reality but a systematic training in comprehending it."[38] Such an approach does a disservice to Blake, exaggerating the achieved security of his visions of desire and minimizing the great theme of man's struggle against the internal obstacles that thwart desire. Blake's imaginative vision is admirable because it wrestles so honestly with the intractable facts of fallen experience. Moreover, the symbolist approach depends upon what Murray Krieger has called "the mythification of art,"[39] whereas Blake is expressly concerned to define the limits of both myth and art.

It would be more just to Blake to say that he is profoundly aware of the anguish of experience, but wants to believe that experience is finally an illusion. If we deny the conclusion we can still appreciate the brilliance of the diagnosis. The *Songs of Experience* are widely admired because they analyze the facts of experience so tellingly and protest against them with so noble a passion. And our admiration need not be any the less if we cannot follow Blake into a philosophical system that locates Experience near the bottom of a hierarchy of levels and dismisses most of it as mere "error."

[37] Firth, *Symbols Public and Private*, p. 83.
[38] *Fearful Symmetry*, pp. 27, 28, 85.
[39] *Theory of Criticism* (Baltimore, 1976), p. 189.

> For he saw that life liv'd upon death
> The Ox in the slaughter house moans
> The Dog at the wintry door
> And he wept, & he called it Pity
> And his tears flowed down on the winds.[40]

The speaker is Urizen, and his pity is futile if not downright hypocriti-cal, but Blake's myth is large enough to do justice to the depth of feel-ing here even as he criticizes Urizen's response. Enion, Emanation of Tharmas the parent power, also speaks of the dog at the wintry door and the ox in the slaughterhouse; her words haunt us because Blake means them to be haunting.

> What is the price of Experience do men buy it for a song
> Or wisdom for a dance in the street? No it is bought with the price
> Of all that a man hath his house his wife his children
> Wisdom is sold in the desolate market where none come to buy
> And in the witherd field where the farmer plows for bread in vain.
> (FZ 35:11-15, E318/K290)

Perhaps a clarified vision should sweep these images away as delusions of Satan and Vala, but they come from Blake's most bitter experience, and we respond to them truly even if we cannot accept his hopeful call for their abolition. What one carries away most of all from the prophecies is man's desperate need for reintegration, not the ease with which he can hope to gain it.

Where the poems are most disappointing, by the same token, is in their frequent refusal to be true to the experience from which they were born. Just as suffering is finally translated into other terms, so also death is so far from being real that what we call life is Blake's "Eternal Death." Of course one may say that death is omnipresent in the myth by the very urgency with which Blake denies it. Imagination itself, according to Bergson, is "a defensive reaction of nature against the representation by intelligence of the inevitability of death."[41] Blake's art is a fight to the death against death. But any Christian poet denies the ultimate reality of death. What is harder to accept is Blake's concomitant rejection of life, which is dismissed as entrapment in ma-teriality except in those epiphanic moments when it breaks free of life as we ordinarily live it. There can be no Wordsworthian solitary

---

[40] *Urizen* 23:27-24:4, E80-81/K235.

[41] Henri Bergson, *Les Deux Sources de la Morale et de la Religion* (Paris, 1932), p. 137. Bergson sees the *fonction fabulatrice* as giving expression to this campaign of imagination against the unwelcome insights of the intelligence. Los forces the Spectre of Urthona to labor at his forge.

reaper in Blake, with her mournful song that fills the heart of the way-
farer, and no Michael with the tragedy of his family and land.[42] Hegel
exalts tragedy because it mediates the destructive fury of warring
"truths"; Blake, like Plato, despises it because it encourages an emotional acceptance of destruction as a necessary consequence of the nature of things. "Drinking & eating, & pitying & weeping, as at a trajic
scene/The soul drinks murder & revenge, & applauds its own holiness" (*J* 37:29-30, E181/K669). It is not that nothing is destroyed in
Blake, but that what is destroyed is not *real*. "You cannot go to Eternal Death in that which can never Die" (*M* 32:24, E131/K521). No
wonder Blake draws so little upon the greatest of English poets;
Shakespeare is the repudiated master in the descent of the spirit from
poet to poet that culminates in Blake.[43]

It is not only tragedy that we miss in Blake; it is much of human life.
The notebook lyrics of love or anti-love are fascinating because they
deal with themes that are usually submerged or allegorized out of recognition in the prophecies. It is inconceivable that Blake could have
written the lines,

> Then, while time serves, and we are but decaying,
> Come, my Corinna, come, let's go a-Maying.

For that is merely the Beulah world of *A Sunshine Holiday*.[44] And because it is only Beulah, Blake will make no compromise with it. Herrick's speaker addresses a real woman, not an idea ("O Rose thou art
sick"), he accepts mortality and the consequent attitude to pleasure,
and his slow and thoughtful verse is remote from Blake's declarative
(often declamatory) style. Such a mood is not incompatible with religious faith:

---

[42] Underlining a passage in Wordsworth about hearing "Humanity in fields and
groves/Pipe solitary anguish," Blake comments, "Does not this Fit & is it not Fitting
most Exquisitely too, but to what? not to Mind but to the Vile Body only & to its Laws
of Good & Evil & its Enmities against Mind" (E656/K784).

[43] Blake confesses, in a letter to Flaxman in 1800, that he came late to an imaginative
appreciation of Shakespeare: "Shakespeare in riper years gave me his hand" (E680/
K799). It would be hard to prove that, apart from incidental allusions, Shakespeare
makes any significant contribution to the great myth, which of course is not surprising,
since the poet of negative capability and human drama is remote from Blake's prophetic
themes. In the preface to *Milton* Blake says that both Milton and Shakespeare were
"curbd" by the infection of classical values (E94/K480). Kermode's remark is apposite
here: "In apocalypse there are two orders of time, and the earthly runs to a stop; the cry
of woe to the inhabitants of the earth means the end of their time; henceforth 'time shall
be no more.' In tragedy the cry of woe does not end succession; the great crises and ends
of human life do not stop time" (*The Sense of an Ending*, p. 89).

[44] See above, p. 61, and fig. 5, p. 60. The quoted lines are the conclusion of Herrick's
"Corinna's Going a Maying."

> It is the blight man was born for,
> It is Margaret you mourn for.[45]

But it must be a faith like Hopkins' that accepts both the reality and the significance of mortal life. In the end, for all his awareness of the weight of experience, Blake cannot come to terms with

> . . . the very world which is the world
> Of all of us,—the place in which, in the end,
> We find our happiness, or not at all.[46]

"A roller & two harrows lie before my window," Blake wrote to Butts on reaching Felpham. "I met a plow on my first going out at my gate the first morning after my arrival & the Plowboy said to the Plowman, 'Father The Gate is Open'" (E682/K803). The plow and harrows get into *The Four Zoas* and *Milton;* the plowboy and his father do not.[47]

If Blake deliberately cuts himself off from the phenomenology of lived experience, and if the modern reader cannot join him in that exclusion, why should one read him? Among other reasons two seem particularly compelling: his exploration of the possibilities and limits of the symbol, and his passionate demand for moral commitment. Let us consider symbols first.

I have argued against the assumptions that symbols offer a privileged view of reality (unless artistic symbols be accepted as having the same status as all other symbolic forms) and that they should be welcomed for their tendency to construct reality in accordance with heart's desire. I hold rather with Cassirer that although all thought is symbolic, this represents a problem rather than a victory, and that mythical thinking needs to be criticized as well as admired for its tendency to reshape the world in conformity with desire. But I would argue also that Blake understands this very point and wants to make us understand it. For if the fallen world is the only world we have, then its symbols are the only symbols; and in that case Blake's deconstruction of symbols can be immensely valuable. At the same time, by clinging to symbols in spite of their flaws, Blake exemplifies the all but universal refusal to imagine a truly empty universe. The imagination must people it with symbols of vitality, as Stevens tells us in so many ways, even if it knows them to be untrue. Jonas says, "Gnostic man is

---

[45] Hopkins, "Spring and Fall."

[46] Wordsworth, *The Prelude*, X. 726-728 (1805), XI. 142-144 (1850).

[47] It is interesting that Butts in his reply seized on the symbolic possibilities just as Blake did: "You have the Plough & the Harrow in full view & the Gate you have been prophetically told is Open, can you then hesitate joyfully to enter into it?" (*The Letters of William Blake*, ed. Geoffrey Keynes [Cambridge, Mass., 1970], p. 44).

thrown into an antagonistic, anti-divine, and therefore anti-human nature, modern man into an indifferent one. Only the latter case represents the absolute vacuum, the really bottomless pit. In the Gnostic
conception the hostile, the demonic, is still anthropomorphic, familiar
even in its foreignness."[48] So also with Blake; he insists that the entire
universe participates in the agony of the divided mind. In this sense
Hume is a modern and Blake a late inheritor of Plotinus and Valentinus. But as the modern yearning for myths—even the most home-
built and rickety—has proved, the desire for humanized symbols is
irresistible. And here again Blake can help us to regard them critically,
just because he himself aspires to transcend them and therefore regards
them with suspicion.

Shelley suggests that symbols may represent the only reality there is
and may protect us from the abyss of unmeaning that lies beyond. For
as he says in the *Defense*, "All things exist as they are perceived; at least
in relation to the percipient. . . . But poetry defeats the curse which
binds us to be subjected to the accident of surrounding impressions.
And whether it spreads its own figured curtain, or withdraws life's
dark veil from before the scene of things, it equally creates for us a
being within our being. It makes us the inhabitants of a world to
which the familiar world is a chaos." Blake, by the very force of his
belief, compels us to recognize the provisional and wish-fulfilling nature of such a manifesto. If reality only exists as it is perceived "in relation to the percipient," then there is no guarantee that it exists at all
except as subjective construction. And if poetry spreads a figured curtain rather than drawing the veil aside, then it is only a mask to hide
the chaos of the world, and we would do well to know it. In his ab-
solutism Blake encourages us to recognize—even if we continue to
need—the groping and imperfect nature of the achievements available
to the imagination.

Finally, we come to Blake for the exhilaration of contact with a
prophetic spirit that never relents in the quest for truth.

> I will not cease from Mental Fight,
> Nor shall my Sword sleep in my hand:
> Till we have built Jerusalem,
> In Englands green & pleasant Land.
>   (*M* 1:13-16, E95/K481)

To read Blake at all is to enter, however provisionally, into the quest,
for as Auerbach says of biblical narrative, "Without believing in
Abraham's sacrifice, it is impossible to put the narrative of it to the use

---

[48] *The Gnostic Religion*, p. 338.

for which it was written."[49] And if in the end we cannot believe it, if we must put it to other uses, we are then forced to confront the meaning of our disbelief, to see plainly the empty universe which no religion of art can fill again with spilt meaning. It may be that aesthetic disinterestedness is the right response to art, but if so, it is all the more salutary to immerse oneself for a time in an art like Blake's that violently repudiates it.

Kant emphasizes the formal properties of beauty, from which intellectual content is a distraction. Blake admires beautiful forms but rejects the abstract conception of beauty, implying at every point that forms are beautiful because they embody meaning, participating in the activity of the Divine Imagination. A recent commentator on Kant says approvingly, in language which the New Criticism has made all too familiar, "Every moral judgment is in some sense propagandistic, every aesthetic judgment is neutral."[50] Blake would retort that in that case Sir Joshua Reynolds was a great artist and Michelangelo a great propagandist. Such a criticism is worth taking seriously.

We read Blake's myth to know what it would be like to believe in man's spiritual power while fully recognizing the self-deluding tendencies of the imagination and its symbols. In Blake there is no reliance on received faith, as in the later Wordsworth, or on natural piety as a mode of transposed faith, as in the earlier Wordsworth. On the contrary, he provides a searching analysis of the basis of *all* faiths, and of their inevitable corruption, in the human imagination. His extraordinary exploration of the psyche is framed in a myth that offers imaginative answers to the fact of alienation. If we cannot share Blake's faith and accept his answers, we must admire the honesty and insight with which he strives to reconcile the direst aspects of human experience with our profound longing for harmony and meaning.

Within the category of moral and religious writing—as contrasted with tragedy or elegy or the other modes that Blake dismisses—his poems retain the power of their conception in spite of all obstacles of execution, and in spite of the gaping philosophical rifts that no amount of revision could ever close. In contrast with an extinct document such as, for instance, Pope's *Essay on Man*, Blake's epics survive because their religious passion overwhelms mere ethical earnestness. In Auden's terms, the ethical writer offers knowledge which he happens to possess while others do not, whereas the religious writer is committed to the truth. For the former, truth is universal but all men do not possess it equally; for the latter, truth is absolute, and if you do not possess

[49] Erich Auerbach, *Mimesis*, trans. Willard Trask (New York, 1953), p. 12.
[50] Robert L. Zimmerman, "Kant: The Aesthetic Judgment," in *Kant: A Collection of Critical Essays*, ed. Robert Paul Wolff (New York, 1967), p. 396.

it absolutely you do not possess it at all.[51] Pope's vision of truth, in all its judiciousness and conscious incompleteness, requires readers who share its intellectual world, and is therefore admired today only by scholars, although their admiration may respond to real kinds of excellence. Blake's vision of truth, in its violence of commitment, is exciting to many a reader who has only the sketchiest idea of what he is actually talking about. As Auden observes, "In a sense, the religious hero is not related to others at all: his authority cannot command admiration, or transfer knowledge, it can only enkindle by example a similar absolute passion, not necessarily for the same god."

My book has been directed toward elucidating Blake's meanings, but I want to close by affirming that all of this would have a merely antiquarian function if Blake did not possess the power of religious vision. His meanings command our imaginative as well as scholarly respect because they are forged and reforged in the furnace of that vision; Blake does not force us to accept his answers, but he demands that we enter into his mental strife and make it ours. And if we inhabit a world that no longer believes in its symbols—if we can neither trust the products of our symbol-making imagination nor bear to live without them—then Blake speaks to us with a special poignancy. His Eden is forever closed to us by the Cherub with the flaming sword, but we are all too well acquainted with Los weeping at the silent forge, struggling to make the accusing Spectre of despair join again in creative labor. Rather than rhapsodizing about Blake's apocalyptic breakthrough as if it were easily attained, we might dwell instead on the bitter honesty with which he has dramatized the pre-apocalyptic condition, which may be the only condition we can ever know. And in that case what continues to move us in Blake's myth is not its answers but its questions, which are posed with a prophetic urgency that remains alive and life-giving.

[51] W. H. Auden, *The Enchafèd Flood* (New York, 1950), pp. 95-98. Auden's distinction here derives from Kierkegaard.

[APPENDIX]

Los, Mulciber, and the Tyger

To appreciate the ambiguity of artistic creation in Blake's myth, it may be helpful to look closely at the relation between Los and Vulcan or Mulciber. Most of Blake's allusions to smiths point to the Old Testament, where as Frye says "Isaiah associates the building of a New Jerusalem with precious stones and the work of a divine smith."[1] Los is more often a blacksmith than a goldsmith, and the text to which Frye points is suggestive of a frightening display of energy: "Behold, I have created the smith that bloweth the coals in the fire, and that bringeth forth an instrument for his work; and I have created the waster to destroy" (Isa. 54:16). In Ezekiel too this symbol has connotations of purgation and anger: "Yea, I will gather you, and blow upon you in the fire of my wrath, and ye shall be melted in the midst thereof. As silver is melted in the midst of the furnace, so shall ye be melted in the midst thereof; and ye shall know that I the Lord have poured out my fury upon you" (Ezek. 22:21-22). This smith is no fabulous artificer, but an agent of divine retribution. In alchemy, it is true, Vulcan symbolized the transmuting of evil into good through the purgation of fire, but it is also true that the wrathful fire of the prophets resembles Boehme's dark flame of fallen selfhood rather than his bright flame of visionary "meekness" and love.

What all this means is that we should not forget that Los is "loss," and that we can only guess at the role of the unfallen Urthona in Eden. Commentators point to the brilliant phrase in *The French Revolution*, "Fire delights in its form."[2] Such a fire would be the ever-changing but always vital organic form to which Blake aspires, with every particular "organized" according to its true nature, and with no need of the rigid structure that a smith could hammer out. Los's work in setting "limits" to the Fall is always in danger of imitating Urizen's crude imposition of dead form, the mechanical act of cutting chaos into slices.

The smith in Milton carries the same implications of fallen industry. The sons of Cain are smiths, with unsettling similarity to the devils in Pandemonium, in contrast with the pastoral sons of Seth.[3] And

---

[1] *Fearful Symmetry*, p. 254.
[2] See Frye, *Fearful Symmetry*, p. 196 (the reference is to line 189, E291/K142).
[3] *Paradise Lost* XI. 564-573.

Mammon, the architect of Hell, is expressly related to the Mulciber or
Vulcan whom Jove cast down from heaven:

> Nor was his name unheard or unadored
> In ancient Greece; and in Ausonian land
> Men called him Mulciber; and how he fell
> From heaven, they fabled, thrown by angry Jove
> Sheer o'er the crystal battlements; from morn
> To noon he fell, from noon to dewy eve,
> A summer's day; and with the setting sun
> Dropped from the zenith like a falling star,
> On Lemnos the Aegaean isle: thus they relate,
> Erring; for he with this rebellious rout
> Fell long before; nor aught availed him now
> To have built in heaven high towers; nor did he scape
> By all his engines, but was headlong sent
> With his industrious crew to build in hell.
>
> *(Paradise Lost* I. 738-751)

In a typical syntactic reversal Milton surprises us with "Erring"; Mulciber fell with Satan long before the Greek poets made him fall in
lovely song. The myth of Mulciber serves, in Geoffrey Hartman's
term, as a "counterplot" to the temporary triumph of the devils, reflecting the "divine imperturbability" that foreknows and controls
all.[4]

Now, we know that in Blake Milton's story of the Fall is supposed
to be inverted. "It indeed appear'd to Reason as if Desire was cast out,
but the Devils account is, that the Messiah fell, & formed a heaven of
what he stole form the Abyss" (*MHH*, E34/K150). Satan in his corrupt
form is translated into Urizen, "the Prince of Light" who tries to
tempt Los to mistake the Spectre for the Man (*FZ* 12:30, E303/K273).
Still it would be wrong to suppose that the fallen Los, however well
meaning, is free of the negative connotations of Mulciber. In the years
immediately following *The Marriage of Heaven and Hell* Blake came to
see that the energy symbolized by Orc was too simple an ideal,[5] and
he invented Los precisely in order to express the complexity of a fallen
imagination whose materials are a fallen world.

The Book of Los marks the decisive shift, and contains an extremely
interesting version of the Mulciber story.

> Falling, falling! Los fell & fell
> Sunk precipitant heavy down down

---

[4] "Milton's Counterplot," in *Beyond Formalism*, pp. 113-123.
[5] As Paley shows in detail in *Energy and the Imagination*.

Times on times, night on night, day on day.
Truth has bounds. Error none: falling, falling:
Years on years, and ages on ages
Still he fell thro' the void, still a void
Found for falling day & night without end.
For tho' day or night was not; their spaces
Were measured by his incessant whirls
In the horrid vacuity bottomless.

(E91/K258)

Milton's tightly organized syntax reflects the mastery of the divine
mind over this falling rebel; Blake's looser and more imitative style
precipitates the reader along with Los. As the world of fallen time is
defined by the regular movement of the heavenly bodies, so the time
defined by Los, even if it is the mercy of eternity, is "measured" with
Newtonian regularity as he whirls downward.

Blake has no Miltonic counterplot; there is no hint of a "summer's
day" that could suspend the Fall and assimilate it into a larger pattern.
Los's fall is an inner fall through psychological space. The fall of Milton's Satan is contained in time; the fall of Los defines time. It is true
that we hear in *Paradise Lost* of an illimitable ocean of chaos "Without
dimension, where length, breadth, and highth,/And time and place are
lost" (II. 893–894). But it is not really illimitable, for God fills everything and hence there can be no ultimate void.

Boundless the deep, because I am who fill
Infinitude, nor vacuous the space.
Though I uncircumscribed my self retire,
And put not forth my goodness, which is free
To act or not, necessity and chance
Approach not me, and what I will is fate.

(VII. 168–173)

Blake certainly understood the implications of the Miltonic doctrine
that since God informs the universe, reality is determined by his will
and what he wills is fate. Both the voluntarism (the will as primary)
and the fatalism of this theology were unacceptable to Blake.

At this point Los is isolated in chaos. He is not evil like Milton's
Satan, but he has fallen *into* evil (or "error") just as Blake's Milton falls
like a star from heaven, and just as Urizen remembers the Fall as occurring when the stars threw down their spears.[6] The act of reintegration therefore resembles the heroic activity of Milton's Satan even
while it repudiates the project of building a world out of chaos.

[6] *FZ* 64:27-28, E337/K311.

> Incessant the falling Mind labour'd
> Organizing itself: till the Vacuum
> Became element, pliant to rise,
> Or to fall, or to swim, or to fly:
> With ease searching the dire vacuity.
>
> (E92/K258)

So in *Paradise Lost* Satan "swims or sinks, or wades, or creeps, or flies" (II. 950). Satan is there setting forth to find and ruin Eden; Blake's Los, by proceeding to form the organs of the living body, hopes to re-create Eden out of chaos. But a central lesson in Blake is that chaos can produce only chaos; nothing will come of nothing. What Los in fact produces is not Eden but Urizen: "a Form/Was completed, a Human Illusion/In darkness and deep clouds involvd" (E94/K260).

Throughout Blake's myth Los continues to exhibit this ambiguous function. He is creative, yet his creations are doomed to be parodies of true life unless they can somehow attain the vitality that needs no external creator. "Whatever can be Created can be Annihilated" (*M* 32:36, E131/K522), and this is true of all of Los's creations. Urizen must be built up and then bound down, but his binding establishes the links of fate, the remorseless determinism of the fallen world that Blake hated so bitterly.

> And thus began the binding of Urizen day & night in fear
> Circling round the dark Demon with howlings dismay & sharp
>   blightings
> The Prophet of Eternity beat on his iron links & links of brass
> And as he beat round the hurtling Demon. terrified at the Shapes
> Enslavd humanity put on, he became what he beheld
> Raging against Tharmas his God & uttering
> Ambiguous words blasphemous filld with envy, firm resolvd
> On hate Eternal, in his vast disdain he labourd beating
> The Links of fate link after link an endless chain of sorrows
>
> (*FZ* 53:20-28, E329/K302)

Becoming what he beholds, the Los who is filled with envy and hate is indeed Milton's Satan. We are far from the simple inversions of *The Marriage of Heaven and Hell*.

In much the same way, Blake seems to have invested the blacksmith image of "The Tyger" with increasing subtlety, so that if one reads that great lyric from the perspective of the later myth it takes on a weight of mystery almost unbearable in a poet who hated mystery. In pondering the poem we are reminded of the primacy of the symbol in Blake's thought; the various possible interpretations all run the risk of reducing the poem to a doctrinaire "meaning," whereas its whole purpose is to ask questions rather than to furnish answers.[7] In conventional religious terms, the answers would be familiar and inevitable. As Marcus Aurelius says, "The lion's gaping jaws, and that which is poisonous, and every harmful thing, as a thorn, as mud, are after-products of the grand and beautiful." But Blake is very far from endorsing the answers of conventional religion. As in his attacks on natural religion, he starts out from the same questions that a skeptic would put, in this case the argument from Cicero that Hume quotes in the *Dialogues Concerning Natural Religion*: "How could your friend Plato in his mind's eye comprehend so vast a piece of architecture as the building of a universe, and how God laboured to create it? How did he think God went about it? What tools did he use? What levers? What machines?"[8]

The myth of the demiurge, in other words, poses questions rather than supplying answers. Answers can be obtained only by internalizing and living the myth's meaning, experiencing its imaginative truth rather than criticizing it destructively as Cicero's skeptic does. Blake's "Tyger" is not so much about the god who makes tigers—that would be Marcus Aurelius' point—as about the god who makes anything at all. Very possibly the questioner of the poem is deluded by Urizenic religion into being afraid of energy, so that in Frye's words "it shows us our accusing enemy who frightens us out of Paradise behind the menacing blaze of a tiger's eyes."[9] But to see that energy is not evil is

[7] Hirsch rightly emphasizes that the poem asks questions without giving explicit answers (*Innocence and Experience*, p. 244). Paley usefully summarizes the three prevailing kinds of interpretations: critics disagree as to whether the Tyger is "good," created by the Lamb's creator; ambiguous, its creator unknown and the poem's questions unanswerable; or "evil," created by a maleficent force (*Energy and the Imagination*, p. 39). Ambiguity is integral to nearly all of the poems of Experience, since it is a condition of the fragmented self. In any case "The Tyger" is a symbolic structure that invites interpretation rather than a dogmatic statement.

[8] Marcus Aurelius, *Meditations*, trans. George Long (Chicago, 1956), VI.xxxvi, p. 71; Cicero, *The Nature of the Gods*, trans. Horace McGregor (Harmondsworth, 1972), I.viii, p. 77. Hume quotes this passage (in Latin) at the beginning of the *Dialogues Concerning Natural Religion*. See also Raine's quotation from the Hermetic *Pymander* (*Blake and Tradition*, II, 16-17).

[9] *Fearful Symmetry*, p. 237. As Frosch expands the point, "The forests of the night are Enion-Benython, the forests of illusion, the depths of the caverned mind in which energy appears demonic and Urizen frightens us to his altars by showing us monsters. . . . The tiger visualized by the poem's dramatic speaker is a product of incomplete perception; it is a phantasy, a delusion" (*Awakening of Albion*, p. 114). Many variations on this theme are possible. For an interesting account of the poem's speaker as deluded but also as a Los figure who invents a necessitarian God in order to endure the agony of Experience, see Wagenknecht, *Blake's Night*, pp. 84-99. I would add that if this sort of interpre-

only the beginning of insight. One has still to answer the real question of the poem—not why tigers exist, but how and why the god or demiurge creates.

To that larger question Blake's myth supplies two kinds of answers. In the fallen world the tiger is rightly dreaded, for its creator is at worst Urizen as Satan and at best Los as Mulciber. In the world of imagination there is no need for dread, since the blacksmith is Los who shapes the living forms that express the harmony of the universe. In the poem itself the work of Mulciber is most in evidence:

> What the hammer? what the chain,
> In what furnace was thy brain?
> (E25/K214)

Why a chain in a poem about a tiger? It is probably the backbone, as in *The Book of Los* (E93/K260). Chains are always ambiguous and usually repressive in Blake, though they are necessary as the containing links of the limits forged by Los. The stars represent, among other things, the structure that Los makes to arrest the fall into nonentity:

> Thus were the stars of heaven created like a golden chain
> To bind the Body of Man to heaven from falling into the Abyss
> Each took his station, & his course began with sorrow & care. . . .
> (*FZ* 33:16-18, E315/K287)

As Percival observes, "In its descent the chain loses its golden and benignant character, and becomes iron and oppressive."[10] Similarly the image can suggest the world of time:

> The Eternal Prophet heavd the dark bellows,
> And turn'd restless the tongs; and the hammer
> Incessant beat; forging chains new & new
> Numb'ring with links, hours, days & years.[11]

Since time, however merciful, represents a falling away from Eternity, the "chains of the mind" (E74/K228) are suggestive of Newtonian forces.[12]

But in apocalypse the chain becomes the one with which God binds "Old Satan" (*EG*, E515/K749), as in Revelation 20:2, "And he laid hold on the dragon, that old serpent, which is the Devil, and Satan,

---

tation is accepted, then Los must be both subject and object, so that the speaker becomes the object that he addresses and must be Los/Mulciber himself.

[10] *William Blake's Circle of Destiny*, p. 61. Percival identifies the chain as the moral law. Blake evidently alludes to the "golden chain" of *Paradise Lost* II. 1051.

[11] *Book of Urizen*, E74/K227.

[12] See Ault, *Visionary Physics*, p. 151.

and bound him a thousand years." Likewise the tiger plays various roles in various contexts. Perverted by Urizen in the building of Ulro, the "tygers of wrath" harness the horses of instruction in human forms, "Petrifying all the Human Imagination into rock & sand" (*FZ* 25:3-6, E310/K281). Elsewhere they are created by the merciful Sons of Los "in compassionate thunderings" in the organization of Experience that precedes the recovery of imagination (*M* 28:27, E125/K515). And in the final lines of *Milton* they rejoice, liberated:

> terrific Lions & Tygers sport & play
> All Animals upon the Earth, are prepard in all their strength
> To go forth to the Great Harvest & Vintage of the Nations
> (E143/K535)

These associations do not dispose of the questions of "The Tyger," which of course can be read independently rather than as part of the myth. They enrich the questions, making us see more clearly why they should be asked at all. If we must have a literal answer to the question "Did he who made the Lamb make thee?" then we can find one in *Jerusalem*, where Los creates both the tiger and the woolly lamb (*J* 73:17-18, E226/K713). The answer is yes. Similarly "Did he smile his work to see?" is answered in *The Book of Los*, where Los "smild with joy" after creating the sun (E93/K260).[13] But the questions are intended as questions. Prometheus is both thief of fire and type of Christ, and Mulciber/Los is both liberator and repressor. The furnace is at once purgative, tormenting, and creative; the artist strives to achieve living form but always risks imposing constraint. As the developing myth of the Zoas confirms, the speaker of "The Tyger" is right to fear the fires of energy, though it would be wrong to draw the conclusion (which in the poem he does not, though critics sometimes claim he does) that energy is therefore evil. Surely "The Tyger" conveys excitement and awe rather than neurotic fear, and although its questions may betray a Urizenic concept of dread, it is the Urizen of *The Ancient of Days*. "Is not my word like as a fire? saith the Lord; and like a hammer that breaketh the rock in pieces?" (Jer. 23:29).

Denis Donoghue, surveying "Promethean" artists whose charisma is more powerful than their individual works and who force thought beyond the limits of language, recommends Adrian Stokes's distinction between sculpture as carving (seeking to liberate the implicit form) and as modeling (imposing the artist's form upon the medium). "I have more concern," Stokes says, "with restoration, reparation, than with the versatile interior giants that seem to infect the artist's

---

[13] These parallels are noted by Paley, *Energy and the Imagination*, p. 59.

material with shadowy or stark power."[14] In Blake's powerful myth this distinction breaks down: the thrust of the whole is toward restoration and reparation, but it is the poet himself, like his Los, who strives to bring it about by imposing the fiction of interior giants, just as the artist Blake liberates forms from metal plates by cutting them with a graver or burning them with acid. The myth is dictated by spirits in Eternity, it embodies what has always existed, yet the poet hammers it out with profound anguish on the anvil of the word. And always he labors in the fear that his work will grow rigid and his forge become an instrument of imprisonment in the fallen world:

> The Human Dress, is forged Iron
> The Human Form, a fiery Forge.
> The Human Face, a Furnace seal'd
> The Human Heart, its hungry Gorge.[15]

Los's creation is suspect not only because it works with fallen materials, but also because creation is a *consequence* of the Fall and in Eden would not occur at all. In orthodox thought, human creation imitates the divine; in modern skepticism, at the other extreme, artistic creation gives an illusion of order and meaning to materials which have none in themselves. But in Blake's myth the beings in Eden *converse* in visionary forms dramatic; they do not create forms, they live them. Los's creation is thus deeply ambiguous, and we are brought back to the equivocal status of art and its symbols. They are useless unless we can look through them to the truth which, once apprehended, needs them no more.

One further Miltonic allusion in "The Tyger" deserves notice here. The lines "When the stars threw down their spears/And water'd heaven with their tears" are suggestive, as various critics have noted, of the passage in *Paradise Lost* in which the Messiah, mounted upon the Merkabah chariot, overwhelms the fallen angels who drop their weapons and are left "Exhausted, spiritless, afflicted, fallen" (VI. 826ff.). The implacable advance of Milton's syntax, his editorial judgments ("his impious foes"), and the darkness of a wrathful God ("dreadful shade," "gloomy as night") all convey the inexorability of a punishment in which the Son need not even summon his full might ("Yet half his strength he put not forth"). To Blake this account must be altogether impious, perverting Ezekiel's vision into a war chariot and then claiming to overwhelm the foe with absurd ease. If God is really as powerful as this, one might well ask with Defoe's Friday,

---

[14] Quoted by Donoghue in *Thieves of Fire* (London, 1973), p. 28.
[15] "A Divine Image," E32/K221.

"Why God no kill the Devil?" We remember that Blake told Robinson that he did not believe in God's omnipotence.

Milton's answer is the elaborate hypothesis of the *felix culpa*, the Fortunate Fall that God has orchestrated (or at least permitted) so that greater good may come. Blake, rather like Boehme, holds that Satan or Urizen chose to reject the light and fell from a status of equality (being a member of the divine unity) rather than of subservience. "The mild & holy voice" told Urizen to shine forth as light, but he hid himself in dark council of wrath, the stars threw down their spears, and "We fell" (*FZ* 64:21-28, E337/K311). If Urizen had heeded the divine voice he would have played his proper role as Lucifer the Light-giver, not Satan the Accuser, and the Zoas would have continued to interact in harmonious strife, which is Blake's symbolic interpretation of Ezekiel's Merkabah. The dark clouds of wrath in which he hid himself were the selfhood that defines the Fall. "I seized thee dark Urthona In my left hand falling/I seizd thee beauteous Luvah" (64:28-29). The other Zoas inevitably fall as soon as any one of them does, but this means that the Merkabah has disintegrated, not that it rides in triumph over their bodies as in *Paradise Lost*. And if Urizen is now both Jehovah Elohim and Satan the Accuser, Urthona/Los is his Mulciber.

[INDEX]

Abraham, 46n, 102, 369-370

Abrams, M. H., 29n, 146, 339-340

Absalom, 269, 271

"Abstinence sows sand . . . ," 195

abstraction, 27, 74, 313-314

abyss, 178-179, 293, 360, 374

Accuser, the, 253-254, 263, 276, 292, 308

Acts, Book of, 78n, 85

Adam, 26, 27, 107-109, 124n, 174n, 183, 189, 223-225, 239, 252, 258, 259-260n, 277, 285, 319, 338

Adam Naming the Beasts, 90-91

Adams, Hazard, 33n, 52, 103, 204n, 247n, 350

Addison, Joseph, 88n

Adlard, John, 235n

Aers, D., 197-198n

Ahania, 184, 199, 231

Ahania, Book of, 199, 275

Albertus Magnus, 48n

Albion, 138-152, 157, 161, 173, 182-183, 185-186, 189, 201, 203, 212, 217, 237, 242, 253, 268, 279-280, 291, 296-298, 300, 310, 311, 322, 346

Albion Rose, 119, 297-298, 298n

alchemy, 46, 74-75,106, 235, 373

Alcuin, 353-354

Alexander, Archibald, 142

All Religions Are One, 26, 81

Allamanda, 173, 321, 326, 327

Alleau, René, 67-69, 116n

allegory, 41, 63, 70, 93-97, 267, 321, 325

Alston, William P., 50n

Altizer, Thomas J. J., 93, 144n

America, 109-111, 203, 278

"anacalyptic," 74, 363

Ancient of Days, The, 120, 264-266, 379

androgyny, 238-241, 272

Angel of the Divine Presence, 258-260, 274-275

Angel of the Revelation, The, 53n, 303n

animism, 247

annotations (by Blake). *See* individual authors

Antamon, 319-321

Antinomians, 282-283, 328, 341

Antony, 158

Aphrodite. *See* Venus

apocalypse, 25, 29, 51, 72, 74, 131, 138, 149, 238, 276, 286, 295, 318, 322, 325-326, 336-348, 361-362, 367n

Apocalypse, Book of. *See* Revelation

Apollo, 54, 57, 125, 131, 260

Aquinas, St. Thomas, 134

archons, 258, 276n

Aristotle, 18, 21, 347

Arlington Court Picture, 119

Arnold, Matthew, 162

asceticism, 217

astrology, 74-75

Atlantis, 41

atomism, 98-100

Atonement (ransom), 217-219, 285-286

Auden, W. H., 216-217, 371

Auerbach, Erich, 369-370

Auguries of Innocence, 35, 53, 102, 252, 341, 350

Augustine, St., 6, 23n, 69, 70, 77, 95, 134, 136, 161, 162, 171-172, 181, 194, 203, 228, 235, 251-252, 282n, 283n, 299, 315

Ault, Donald, 33n, 34n, 44n, 99n, 136n, 325, 378n

Austin, J. L., 357-358

Aztecs, 286

Babylon, 195, 320, 342

Bachelard, Gaston, 71

Bacon, Francis, 20, 35, 101, 136

Bard's Song (in *Milton*), 310, 313

Barrett, William, 156n

Baudelaire, Charles, 70

Baudouin, Charles, 159, 269n

Baumgardt, David, 48n

Beatrice Addressing Dante from the Car, 186-187

Beer, John, 271n

belief, 34-36, 66

Benjamin, Walter, 363n

Bennett, Jonathan, 26n

Bentley, G. E., Jr., xiii-xiv, 124n, 196n, 266n

Benz, Ernst, 50

Bergson, Henri, 366

Berkeley, George, 15-20, 24, 26, 34, 39, 41, 58, 76, 140-141, 157, 169, 248, 327,

Library of Congress Cataloging in Publication Data

Damrosch, Leopold.
   Symbol and truth in Blake's myth.
   Includes bibliographical references and index.
   1.   Blake, William, 1757-1827—Criticism and inter-
pretation.   2.   Myth in literature.   3.   Symbolism in
literature.   I.   Title.
PR4148.M82D3   821'.7   80-7515
ISBN 0-691-06433-4
ISBN 0-691-10095-0 (LPE)